PERFORMANCE RESEARCH METHODS

Performance Research Methods

Interdisciplinary Methods for Theatre, Dance and Performance Studies

Edited by
Liesbeth Groot Nibbelink and Laura Karreman

https://www.openbookpublishers.com

©2025 Liesbeth Groot Nibbelink and Laura Karreman

Copyright of individual chapters is maintained by the chapter authors

This work is licensed under a Creative Commons Attribution-NonCommercial 4.0 International (CC BY-NC 4.0). This license allows you to share, copy, distribute and transmit the text; to adapt the text for non-commercial purposes of the text providing attribution is made to the authors (but not in any way that suggests that they endorse you or your use of the work). Attribution should include the following information:

Liesbeth Groot Nibbelink and Laura Karreman (eds), *Performance Research Methods: Interdisciplinary Methods for Theatre, Dance and Performance Studies*. Cambridge, UK: Open Book Publishers, 2025, https://doi.org/10.11647/OBP.0469

Further details about CC BY-NC licenses are available at
https://creativecommons.org/licenses/by-nc/4.0/

Copyright and permissions for the reuse of many of the images included in this publication differ from the above. This information is provided in the captions and in the list of illustrations. Every effort has been made to identify and contact copyright holders and any omission or error will be corrected if notification is made to the publisher.

All external links were active at the time of publication unless otherwise stated and have been archived via the Internet Archive Wayback Machine at https://archive.org/web

Digital material and resources associated with this volume are available at
https://doi.org/10.11647/OBP.0469#resources

Information about any revised edition of this work will be provided at
https://doi.org/10.11647/OBP.0469

ISBN Paperback 978-1-80511-607-3
ISBN Hardback 978-1-80511-608-0
ISBN PDF 978-1-80511-609-7
ISBN HTML 978-1-80511-611-0
ISBN EPUB 978-1-80511-610-3
DOI: 10.11647/OBP.0469

Cover image by Lone Twin, *Spiral* (2007), courtesy of Gregg Whelan
Cover design by Jeevanjot Kaur Nagpal

Table of Contents

List of Illustrations	vii
List of Audio/Video files	ix
About the Contributors	xi
Acknowledgments	xxi

Introduction   1
Liesbeth Groot Nibbelink and Laura Karreman

PART I: OBJECT-ORIENTED DRAMATURGIES AND CULTURAL ANALYSIS   **19**

1. Concept-Based Analysis   21
Laura Karreman

2. Dramaturgical Analysis: A Relational Approach   43
Liesbeth Groot Nibbelink and Sigrid Merx

3. Spectatorship Analysis   67
Maaike Bleeker

4. Movement Analysis   85
Andrew Fuhrmann, Lise Uytterhoeven, and Rachel Fensham

5. Dance Analysis   107
Sarah Whatley

6. Music Always Does Something: Analysing Musical Theatre   125
Millie Taylor

7. A Multimodal Critical Discourse Analysis of Listening   145
Pieter Verstraete

PART II: HISTORIES, CONTEXTS, ECOLOGIES   167

8. Discourse Analysis   169
Sruti Bala

9. Creating Art Ecologies through Contextual Analysis   187
Liesbeth Groot Nibbelink

10. Cultural Materialism and the Politics of Performance   209
Dick Zijp

11. Tracing Histories: An Archaeological Approach   229
Evelyn Wan

12. Archival Research Expanded: Bodily Archives and Embodied Fabulation   247
Lisa Skwirblies

PART III: SITUATED KNOWLEDGES   269

13. Intersectionality   271
Anika Marschall

14. Personal Narratives and Social Constructs through Autoethnography in Performance Studies   293
Wigbertson Julian Isenia

15. Autoethnography in Performance Studies: The Performativity of Queer Parenting   311
Fabiola Camuti and Annemijn van der Schaar

PART IV: EMBEDDED AND PROCESS-BASED APPROACHES   335

16. Practice-led Research: Transversal Ways of Sensing/Knowing   337
Konstantina Georgelou

17. Affective Attunement: Mapping the Invisible   359
Theron Schmidt

18. Doing Performance Philosophy: Thinking alongside Performance   387
Laura Cull Ó Maoilearca

19. Hyphenated Thinking in Performance Processes: Thinking through Performance-pedagogical Entanglements with More-than-human Matter   413
Christel Stalpaert

Index   439

List of Illustrations

2.1	Planes of dramaturgy: composition, spectator, context. ©Liesbeth Groot Nibbelink & Sigrid Merx.	p. 50
2.2	Connecting the vectors: spectatorship, statements, situatedness ©Liesbeth Groot Nibbelink & Sigrid Merx.	p. 54
2.3	Thomas J. Price, *Moments Contained* (2023) Rotterdam ©Lex Prummel.	p. 60
3.1	Tore Vagn Lid/Transiteatret Bergen, *03:08:38 States of Emergency* (2024), performed at Alte Münze/Theater der Dinge, Berlin, 10 November 2024. ©Lea Röver.	p. 73
16.1	An example of the cards used for 'Dramaturgy At Work' with the translated version of Lisa Nelson's Tuning Scores. ©Konstantina Georgelou.	p. 348
16.2	Micro-actions from the course 'Engaged Citizenship': Sleeping strike in the campus. ©Konstantina Georgelou.	p. 352
16.3	Micro-actions from the course 'Engaged Citizenship': printed quotes from @blackliturgies stuck up in public spaces. ©Konstantina Georgelou.	p. 352
16.4	Micro-actions from the course 'Engaged Citizenship': chalk project on the streets of Utrecht about street harassment. ©Konstantina Georgelou.	p. 353
17.1	Lone Twin, *Spiral* (2007). Courtesy of the artists.	p. 368
17.2	Forensic Architecture, *Drift-Backs in the Aegean Sea*, 2023. Screen capture from https://aegean.forensic-architecture.org/ ©Forensic Architecture.	p. 371
17.3	Map detail from Ant Hampton, *Borderline Visible* (2023). Courtesy of the artist.	p. 373
17.4	Readers interacting with *Borderline Visible* (2023). ©Bernard Kalu (www.bernardkalu.com).	p. 374

17.5	Agata Kok, score composed for The City As Stage at Utrecht University (2023). Courtesy of the artist.	p. 381
17.6	Júlia Pejó Vergara, score composed for The City As Stage at Utrecht University (2023). Courtesy of the artist.	p. 382
18.1	Doing Performance Philosophy: an image of the author during *Sheep Pig Goat* by Fevered Sleep (2020), Surrey. ©Malachy Luckie.	p. 405
19.1	State of affairs of the area covered by *STILL HERE* (2023-2025), ©Maria Lucia Cruz Correia, 2024.	p. 417
19.2	Maria Lucia Cruz Correia, *Booklet with Map for Walking-With SZenne River*, Soignies, April 13, 2024. ©Christel Stalpaert.	p. 425
19.3	Natural Contract Lab, *Walking-With SZenne River*, Soignies, April 13, 2024. ©Christel Stalpaert.	p. 426

List of Audio/Video files

18.1	Laura Cull Ó Maoilearca, *An [Interrupted] Bestiary* (2022) [book and film], https://www.academia.edu/104641611/An_Interrupted_Bestiary	p. 407
18.2	Laura Cull Ó Maoilearca, *Bestiary Animation* (2022). Duration: 8.44, https://www.youtube.com/watch?v=WcB9Js2F9SQ	p. 407
18.3	Laura Cull Ó Maoilearca, *An [Interrupted] Bestiary: Climate Imaginaries at Sea*, podcast, 7 episodes, https://podcasts.apple.com/nl/podcast/an-interrupted-bestiary/id1725621904	p. 407

About the Contributors

Sruti Bala is Associate Professor in Theatre and Performance Studies of the University of Amsterdam. Sruti's research interests are at the intersections of performance and politics, which has taken shape in specific research projects on nonviolent protest, participatory art, artistic activism, feminist and postcolonial/decolonial theories and translation. Profile and full list of publications: http://www.uva.nl/profile/s.bala

Maaike Bleeker is Professor of Performance, Science and Technology in the Department of Media and Culture at Utrecht University. She has many years of experience working as a dramaturg with theatre and dance makers. She is interested in how thinking and making, theory and practice, may mutually inform and inspire each other. In her writing, she combines approaches from the arts and performance with insights from philosophy, critical theory, and cognitive science to examine how people make sense of what they encounter in the theatre as well as in daily life and scientific practice. She is the author of *Visuality in the Theatre* (Palgrave 2008) and *Doing Dramaturgy: Thinking Through Practice* (Palgrave 2023) and the (co) editor of (among others) *Anatomy Live: Performance and the Operating Theatre* (AUP 2008), *Performance & Phenomenology* (Routledge 2015), *Transmission in Motion: The Technologizing of Dance* (Routledge 2016), *Thinking Through Theatre and Performance* (Bloomsbury 2019) and the *Routledge Companion to Performance and Technology* (forthcoming).

Fabiola Camuti (she/her) is Professor of Critical Creative Pedagogies at HKU University of the Arts Utrecht. She has been a visiting researcher and practitioner in various countries and institutions (Italy, France, Denmark, UK, US, NL), as well as a researcher and lecturer at the Departments of Theatre Studies (University of Amsterdam) and Media and Culture (Utrecht University), and at the Professorship Art Education as Critical Tactics (ArtEZ University of the Arts). She conducts research, leads projects, and gives seminars on topics including socially just pedagogies and pedagogies of care, participatory arts, politics of arts and cultural education, and artistic research. Additionally, she is chair of the HKU Research Ethics Committee and serves as programme leader of Research in Education for the KUO sector (Dutch Association of Universities of Applied Sciences), where she coordinates a national working group aimed at strengthening the knowledge ecosystem and research culture within art universities.

Laura Cull Ó Maoilearca is Professor of Performance Philosophy by special appointment at the University of Amsterdam and Lector for the Academy of Theatre and Dance, Amsterdam University of the Arts where she leads the research programme. Her latest publications include the book *Interspecies Performance* (2024), co-edited with Florence Fitzgerald-Allsopp for Performance Research Books and the journal issue *With the dead: performance philosophy, dying and grief* (2024) co-edited with Rajni Shah and Will Daddario. One current line of research is *Climate Imaginaries at Sea*, a long-term programme of artistic and participatory research into rising sea levels, including *The Power of Water* project which investigates how young people in the Netherlands, Suriname and Curaçao can explore the relationship between climate change and colonialism using photography and the spoken word. Laura is a founding core convener of the Performance Philosophy network and a co-editor of its journal and book series.

Rachel Fensham has been a Professor of Dance and Theatre Studies at the University of Melbourne and the University of Surrey, and her research fields are performance, cultural history, and digital humanities. She is the author of *Movement: Theory for Theatre* (Bloomsbury, 2021) and the forthcoming *Fabrications: Costume, Dance and Material Culture* (Oxford University Press 2026) and co-author of *Cultural Data: An Intimate Analytics of Cultural Collections* (Routledge 2026). She was founding co-editor of the award-winning book series, New World Choreographies (Palgrave), and other scholarly work includes chapters on digital laboratories (Routledge 2023), on archives (Routledge 2016), and on costume in *Small Data is Beautiful* (GSP 2023).

Andrew Fuhrmann completed a PhD on the works of the Australian choreographer Lucy Guerin, and has published on the affective affordances of postmodern choreography. He is a guest lecturer at the Faculty of Fine Arts and Music, University of Melbourne and co-directed the creation of the Theatre and Dance Platform, a repository of significant Australasian performing arts collections hosted by the University of Melbourne. He maintains research interests in the creation, expansion and maintenance of performing arts archives in the digital realm and is on the management committee of the AusStage database. He writes regularly on contemporary performance as the dance critic for *The Age* newspaper and other publications.

Konstantina Georgelou is a performing arts theorist, dramaturg and researcher. Her field of research is the practice and theory of dramaturgical activity, especially from a political perspective, which is part of her ongoing inquiry on embodied practices of resistance and forms of dis/order as expressed within dance and performance. She studies artistic, discursive and activist practices and researches in-practice collective modes of production in theory and in the arts. Her publications have appeared in several journals such as with *TDR*, *Performance Research Journal*, *Performance Paradigm*, *Maska*, and books published by Presses such as Routledge and Palgrave MacMillan; she co-authored *The Practice of Dramaturgy: Working on Actions in Performance* (Valiz, 2017) and co-edited the issue 'On Names' (*Performance Research Journal*, 2017). Konstantina has worked with several artists including Zhana Ivanova, Chara Kotsali, Genevieve Murphy, Billy Mullaney, Danae Theodoridou, Janez Janša and Efrosini Protopapa. She is an Assistant Professor at Utrecht University and at Amsterdam University for the Arts.

Liesbeth Groot Nibbelink is an Assistant Professor in Theatre and Performance Studies at the Media and Culture Studies Department, Utrecht University. She was the programme coordinator of the Master's programme in Contemporary Theatre, Dance and Dramaturgy (2014–2024) and teaches in various BA and MA programmes. Her research interests include the intersection of dramaturgy and scenography, performance philosophy, ecology and new materialism. She is the author of *Nomadic Theatre: Mobilizing Theory and Practice on the European Stage* (Bloomsbury 2019) and has contributed to (among others) *The*

Routledge Companion to Contemporary European Theatre and Performance (2023), *Rancière and Performance* (Rowman & Littlefield 2021), *Thinking Through Theatre and Performance* (Bloomsbury 2019) and *Intermedial Performance and Politics in the Public Sphere* (Routledge 2018). She currently works on a book on simulation, speculation and futurity in contemporary European dramaturgy (with Sigrid Merx). She is a co-founder of Platform-Scenography and on occasion works as an artistic coach and dramaturgy adviser.

Wigbertson Julian Isenia (they/them) is an Assistant Professor in the Department of Anthropology at the University of Amsterdam. Trained in Cultural Analysis and holding a Ph.D. from the University of Amsterdam, their interdisciplinary work merges ethnography and archival research to explore Caribbean identities, postcolonial conditions, and queer subjectivities, particularly in Curaçao. Their scholarship interrogates the entanglements of gender, sexuality, and (post)colonialism through cultural texts, archives, and performances. Isenia has published in *Tijdschrift voor Genderstudies*, *Feminist Review*, *Theaterkrant*, and *Small Axe*. They have also contributed chapters to *The Routledge Companion to Sexuality and Colonialism*, *Postcolonial Intellectuals in Europe*, and forthcoming anthologies with Oxford University Press.

Laura Karreman is an Associate Professor in Media and Performance Studies in the Department of Media and Culture Studies at Utrecht University, the Netherlands. She teaches in the MA program Contemporary Theatre, Dance and Dramaturgy and the Research MA Media, Art and Performance Studies (MAPS). She is also the programme coordinator of the MAPS programme. She researches the role of embodied knowledge in dance transmission practices, the role of digitization in performance archives, and epistemological questions that relate to new notions of performance knowledge emerging from developments in the area of AI and Human-Robot interaction. Within the research group Transmission in Motion of the Department of Media and Culture Studies (UU), she relates to topics such as dramaturgy, somatechnics and mobilizing the archive. In her current research she continues to investigate the rapid growth of motion capture as a tool for movement research and animation in order to critically evaluate the cultural and ethical implications of such practices, which now often remain invisible. She is co-editor of the volume *Performance and Posthumanism: Staging Prototypes of Composite Bodies* (Palgrave Macmillan 2021). Other recent publications include the book chapters "Breathing Matters: Breath as Dance Knowledge" in *Futures of Dance Studies* (The University of Wisconsin Press, 2020) and "How does motion capture mediate dance?" in *Contemporary Choreography: A critical reader* (Routledge, 2017), and a chapter on "Cultural Dreams of Datafied Bodies" in the *Routledge Companion on Performance and Technology* (forthcoming). In 2024, she was conference director of the 9th International Conference on Movement and Computing (MOCO) at Utrecht University.

Anika Marschall (she/her) works as Assistant Professor in Performance, Institutions and Societal Transformation at the Department of Media and Culture Studies at Utrecht University, where she coordinates the MA Contemporary Theatre, Dance and Dramaturgy programme. Her research focuses on theatre, migration and social justice, and she engages with questions of political representation in/through performance. Her research monograph *Performing Human Rights: Artistic Interventions into European Asylum* was published with Routledge (2023).

Sigrid Merx is an Associate Professor in Theatre and Performance Studies and currently the Director of Education at the department of Media and Culture Studies at Utrecht University. Her research interests include contemporary dramaturgy, socially engaged performance and performance in public space. Her current research focuses on creative research methods. Sigrid is co-lead of the research group [urban interfaces] and the Creative Humanities Academy. She is co-editor of a special issue on Urban Interfaces: Media, Art, and Performance in Public Space (*Leonardo Almanac,* 2019) and on Creative Urban Methods (*Mediapolis,* 2023). She currently works on a book on simulation, speculation and futurity in contemporary dramaturgy, which addresses the re-use and re-valuation of fiction and imagination in contemporary European theatre and performance (with Liesbeth Groot Nibbelink).

Annemijn van der Schaar (they/them) is a researcher, guest lecturer, and trained anthropologist currently pursuing a PhD at the University of Humanistic Studies in Utrecht. Situated within mad studies and trans studies, their work draws on lived experience to examine questions of hermeneutical (in)justice for people with psychiatric diagnoses. Their research critically engages with epistemic marginalisation, exploring how knowledge, power, and care intersect. Annemijn uses a range of methodologies, including autoethnography, narrative research, and arts-based approaches, and has conducted research in the field of Disability Studies.

Theron Schmidt is Assistant Professor at Utrecht University, Netherlands, and works internationally as an artist, teacher, and writer. He is a founding co-convener of the Performance Philosophy network and an Editor of the journal *Performance Philosophy*. He is also an Editor of *Global Performance Studies* and an Associate Editor of *Performance Research*. He was the winner of the 2021 UK Theatre & Performance Research Association Editing Prize for *Agency: A Partial History of Live Art* (Intellect 2019), a collection of interviews with almost 50 artists, curators, and thinkers in the field of contemporary performance, and is the author of *The Theatricalists: Making Politics Appear* (Northwestern University Press 2024).

Lisa Skwirblies is Assistant Professor in Theatre Studies at the University of Amsterdam. Her research interests are on colonial histories, performance histories, and the archive. Lisa holds a PhD from the University of Warwick and between 2018 and 2020 held a Marie-Curie International Research Fellowship (Horizon 2020) at the University of Munich. Some of her most recent publications include the chapter 'Colonial Theatricality' in the *Oxford Handbook of Politics and Performance* (2020), ed. by Rai et al. and the edited collection *Theaterwissenschaft postkolonial/dekolonial* (2023), ed. by Sharifi and Skwirblies. Lisa also works as a dramaturg in the Netherlands and Berlin and has been a board member of the SPRING festival in Utrecht.

Christel Stalpaert is Senior Full Professor at the Department of Art History, Musicology and Theatre Studies at Ghent University (Belgium). She is director of the research centre S:PAM (Studies in Performing Arts and Media) and co-founder of the FWO-funded research network CoDa (Cultures of Dance). She was a Distinguished Visitor at the University of Alberta, Canada in 2023 and publishes widely in the field, in journals such as *Performance Research* and *The Drama Review*. She recently published *Performance and Posthumanism* (with van Baarle and Karreman, Palgrave 2021) and *Violence and Trauma in Contemporary Performance* (with Sofie de Smet, Marieke Breyne, and Pedzisai Maedza, Leuven University Press, 2025), and co-edited the volume 'On Activation' with Eylül Fidan Akıncı for *Performance Research* (28:8, 2023). She is currently writing her monograph on *Hyphenated Thinking: Performance (Studies) Activating Ecological Encounters*.

Millie Taylor holds the Van den Ende Chair of the Musical at the University of Amsterdam. After twenty years as a freelance musical director, during which time she worked on many musicals as diverse as *West Side Story*, *The Rocky Horror Show*, *Little Shop of Horrors* and *Sweeney Todd*, she switched to research and lecturing. Since then, she has written (or co-written or co-edited) eight books and numerous articles and chapters, mostly about musical theatre. She is currently working on the second edition of the textbook *Studying Musical Theatre*.

Lise Uytterhoeven is Chief Academic Officer at The Place, London Contemporary Dance School. Her monograph *Sidi Larbi Cherkaoui: Dramaturgy and Engaged Spectatorship* is published by Palgrave Macmillan in the *New World Choreographies* series. She has published articles and chapters in a range of publications on dance, theatre and performance. She co-authored the study guide *What Moves You? Shaping your Dissertation in Dance*, published by Routledge. Lise was Co-Chair of the Society for Dance Research from 2018–2023 and is a current member of the Associate Board of *Dance Research*.

Pieter Verstraete is a tenured Assistant Professor in Arts, Culture and Media at the University of Groningen. He is Editor in Chief of the *European Journal of Theatre and Performance (EJTP)*, elected member of the Executive Committee of EASTAP, and Chair of the MCAA Benelux Chapter. His work centres around two main topics: the interdisciplinary study of sound and voice in the theatre, including music theatre, and the study of socio-political and activist forms of performance, post-migration and exile, memory and commemoration, with a regional focus on Turkey. Recent publications include articles in *Performance Research* (27:3–4, 2022), *ITI Journal* (3, Feb. 2023), *Red Thread* (6, 2023),

Open Research Europe (3:109, 2023), *Music and Sound in European Theatre* (2024). He co-edited the special issue on 'Activism and Spectatorship' of *EJTP* 4 (2022) with Agata Łuksza, and the issue on 'Exile and (Neo-)Nationalism' of *EJTP* (7.1, 2025) with Yana Meerzon. He is co-editor of *Inside Knowledge: (Un)doing Ways of Knowing in the Humanities* (CSP 2009), *Berberian: Pioneer of Contemporary Vocality* (Routledge 2014), and *Theatre, Performance and Commemoration: Staging Crisis, Memory and Nationhood* (Bloomsbury 2023).

Evelyn Wan is an artist-scholar and dramaturg. She is Assistant Professor in Media, Arts, and Society at the Department of Media and Culture Studies at Utrecht University, where she coordinates the MA Arts and Society programme and works on interdisciplinary curriculum innovation in the domain of Humane AI. Her award-winning research studies historical and contemporary emerging technologies through the lens of decolonial media studies and performance studies. She is the resident dramaturg of Hong Kong-based artistic collective *If Time's Limited*. She currently serves on the Executive Board of Performance Studies international (PSi) and the Supervisory Board of TETEM (Enschede).

Sarah Whatley is Professor and Director of the Centre for Dance Research (C-DaRE) at Coventry University, UK. Her research interests extend to dance and disability, dance and new technologies, intangible cultural heritage, dance archives, and somatic dance practice and pedagogy; she has published widely on these themes. Her research has been funded by the AHRC, UKRI, the European Commission, Leverhulme Trust and Wellcome Trust, and is often interdisciplinary, collaborating with artists, designers and researchers from other disciplines including law, anthropology, psychology, digital media and computing science. Her current projects explore the interface between dance, disability, prosthetics and robotics. She served as panel member for UoA D35/33 in REF 2014/2021, is a member of the AHRC peer review college and Chairs the AHRC-sponsored 'Dance Research Matters' campaign. She was founding Editor of the Journal of Dance and Somatic Practices and sits on the Editorial Boards of several other Journals.

Dick Zijp is an Assistant Professor in the Department of Media and Culture Studies at Utrecht University, the Netherlands. He has a background in theatre and performance studies, philosophy and cultural studies. His research explores the politics and aesthetics of humour and comedy in the late twentieth and early twenty-first centuries. He has published extensively on Dutch cabaret, stand-up comedy and the role of humour in the public sphere. His work has appeared in, among others, the *European Journal of Cultural Studies*, *Comedy Studies* and the *European Journal of Humour Research*. Zijp is currently preparing a monograph on the politics of Dutch cabaret and stand-up comedy for Palgrave. In addition to his academic work, he is active as a freelance comedy critic, and regularly engages in public debate.

Acknowledgments

The creation of this book opened up avenues of exchange that we had not anticipated at the outset. It began with the idea of sharing the research methods taught by the teaching staff at Utrecht University, but its scope soon expanded beyond that initial perimeter—as performance tends to do—driven by our desire to offer readers a broader range of perspectives. These readers are not only our own students at Utrecht University, both in the BA Media and Culture and various MA programmes in Art and Performance Studies. We also hope this book will be useful to many teachers and students involved in studying art, dance and performance studies, both at universities and art academies, as well as to artists involved in practice-research.

When the authors completed their first draft, we organised a peer-review event at Utrecht University. It was a pleasure to bring together colleagues from various universities and engage in meaningful dialogue about research and teaching. The inter-institutional connections this book fostered and rekindled provided genuine support during a time of severe budget cuts affecting higher education in the Netherlands. We are grateful to all the authors who contributed to this book for their insight, commitment, and support.

We would especially like to thank our colleagues in theatre, dance, and performance studies at Utrecht University, also known as the 'Performance People': Irene Alcubilla Troughton, Maaike Bleeker, Konstantina Georgelou, Anika Marschall, Sigrid Merx, Theron Schmidt, Evelyn Wan, and Dick Zijp. Most of them contributed to the book, but their support extended far beyond that. They encouraged us, tested early versions of chapters in their classrooms, and generously shared their thoughts, doubts, and aspirations regarding methods and methodologies in performance research contexts.

We also extend our thanks to, the Department of Media and Culture Studies, our academic home. Working in this department inspires us daily with examples of what interdisciplinary research in the arts and humanities can look like. A special thanks goes to Director of Education Sigrid Merx, whose advice and support throughout this project were invaluable.

We are grateful to the three peer reviewers of the book. In particular, we appreciate the extensive feedback provided by Paul Rae. We had the pleasure of collaborating with Paul again when we were invited to curate a Forum for Discussion on methods together with Tracy C. Davis, organised as part of the International Federation for Theatre Research (IFTR) conference at the University of Cologne (2025). We also presented a Roundtable on Performance Research Methods at the same conference. Several authors of the book participated, marking the first public announcement of the project and offering us valuable feedback.

We sincerely thank Fabiola Camuti, Professor in Critical Creative Pedagogies at HKU University of the Arts, for her financial support during the final stages of preparing the manuscript. Thanks to her support, we were able to enlist the help of Maren Seidel, a recent alumna of Utrecht University, for the final editing. Maren served as a 'pacer' in this final stretch of our run—when we were nearly out of time, energy, and breath at the end of the academic year. Her meticulousness, thoughtful communication, and enthusiasm for the book lifted our spirits immensely. We are extremely grateful for her help, without which we could not have finalised the book in such a short time.

From the beginning, we envisioned this book as an Open Access publication to ensure it would be widely accessible to the audience we had in mind. We found an ideal partner in Open Book Publishers, and we warmly thank Managing Director Alessandra Tosi and the rest of the OBP team for their unwavering support throughout the publication process, but also for their belief in and commitment to making research freely available to readers around the world.

Finally—and most importantly—we want to thank the international community of students, past and present, in the programmes at Utrecht University that inspired the creation of this book: the MA Contemporary Theatre, Dance and Dramaturgy, the MA Arts and Society, and the RMA Media, Art and Performance Studies (MAPS). Their curiosity, enthusiasm, and critical engagement challenge and inspire us in the best possible ways. We dedicate this book to them.

Liesbeth Groot Nibbelink and Laura Karreman

Utrecht, July 2025

Introduction

Liesbeth Groot Nibbelink and Laura Karreman

Why this book?

It is a somewhat painstaking ritual. Each year in Spring, when our BA and MA students start writing their thesis and need to include a methodology section in their thesis plan, they ask: "What are the methodologies in theatre and performance research, actually? And where is the literature that describes these methods?" And each year, we answer: "Well, that is a complicated question". We then continue with carefully explaining that in our field—dedicated to the study of theatre, dance, and dramaturgy—there are numerous ways of studying and analysing contemporary performance events, but, strangely, many of these methods are not described explicitly and at times are hard to recognise as such. Studying in the interdisciplinary department of Media and Culture studies at Utrecht University, our theatre and dance students notice how their peers in film and media studies refer to research methods such as formal analysis, representational analysis, visual data analysis, and more. No wonder they look puzzled: how come that they have not been introduced to similarly clearly articulated methods in theatre and performance studies? Well, we sigh once more, it is complicated—in fact, we do not really know why that is the case. We can only share in your amazement, and in the need for them.

While there is a lack of publications in this area, a wide range of methods are in fact actively used and taught in university classrooms. This academic practice-led knowledge, however, is largely taught by individual scholars, and often remains within singular classrooms, whereas a larger community of researchers may also benefit from such analytical skills. This book renders visible the practical and didactic knowledge as it is used, practised, and developed in university classrooms, both in The Netherlands and beyond, speaking to theatre, dance, and performance studies students as well as students, researchers, and practitioners in related fields, art academies, and artistic practice. The book is about naming and listing these methods, taking an explicit hands-on approach, by describing and contextualising these methods systematically and in detail, and by demonstrating how to use them, by drawing on actual examples from research done by students and scholars in this area.

This book originates from the urgently felt and perceived need for clearly described methods for performance research, a need that is grounded in many years of experiencing scenes such as the ones described above, and that is shared by the many contributors in this book, who work at various institutes for higher education in mostly—but not only—continental Europe. As already observed in the article "Missing Names" (Groot Nibbelink 2017), there is a pressing need to actively name and articulate the research methods currently used in the field of contemporary performance studies, which actively address the societal, technological, ecological, and material contexts in which theatre, dance, and performance operate.

Such methods could also play a vital role in identifying the expertise and knowledge specific to the field of theatre, dance, and dramaturgy, particularly in view of the increasing interest in interdisciplinary knowledge exchange. Handbooks on (current) methods in theatre and performance studies are remarkably scarce, as is also observed by Tracy C. Davis and Paul Rae, editors of *The Cambridge Guide to Mixed Methods Research for Theatre and Performance Studies* (2024). Existing, previously dominant methods such as theatre semiotics, historiography, or phenomenology fall short in addressing the societal dynamic in which contemporary performance operates, and the manifold artistic strategies that emerge in response to that. On top of that, many researchers are hesitant to name their methods as methods and to describe what they do, when they do research. Or, as the editors Rosemary Candelario and Matthew Henley point out, in *Dance Research Methodologies: Ethics, Orientations and Practices*, they use different terms and vocabularies for what is actually a shared practice (2023, 5).

Methods are used to show 'how' you have done your research. We do not look at methods as prescriptive or static 'recipes' ('this is how you should do it' or 'if you follow this method then that will be the outcome') but as tools of communication. By opening up the 'how', it becomes possible to explain to peers the process through which certain findings, observations, or interpretations have been reached. This way, we reach an intersubjective understanding of these findings. We fully agree with Candelario and Henley in *Dance Research Methodologies*, who observe that

> Teaching people how to become researchers is not, we believe, a simple transferal of steps to be followed, a prescriptive imposition of a model, or a straightjacket into which students are put. We argue that becoming a researcher is about joining an active community of practice that seeks answers, frameworks of understanding, and new knowledge about dance, dancers, and dancemaking (2023, 15).

Navigating within a specific community of practice also entails a responsibility to support those who are either new to that community or "implicitly or explicitly made to feel that they are not legitimate members of the community" (2023, 15). This responsibility also involves being transparent about how research 'works', i.e. the practice of doing research itself, the modes of questioning, the dealing with objects, and modes of sharing and presenting research outcomes. A defining characteristic of our community of practice in the field of theatre, dance, and performance studies is that we engage not only with theories and concepts, but also with diverse forms of embodied knowledge that manifest in and through the performative events we study: the affects created by a performance, the kinetic awareness of a dancer, the situated knowledge of an artist, the intuitive way one organises performative walks or practice-led research. This is also the key argument of Dwight Conquergood's essay "Performance Studies: Interventions and Radical Research" (2002) in which he observes the dominance of research approaches such as empirical observation and critical analysis (knowing-that or knowing-about), at the cost of attending to alternative, intimate, and personal hands-on knowledge (knowing-how and knowing-who). Such tacit, embodied knowledges then become subordinate or 'subjugated' knowledges—a term coined by Michel Foucault which designates the type of local, regional, or vernacular knowledges "at the bottom of the hierarchy—the low Other of science" (2002, 146) which are erased because they are seen as illegible, "they exist by and large, as active bodies of meaning, outside of books" (146). Performance studies—and we might include here theatre and dance studies as well—precisely stands out by bringing together both academia and artistic practice, analysis and action, theory and practice:

> Performance studies brings this rare hybridity into the academy, a commingling of analytical and artistic ways of knowing that unsettles the institutional organization of knowledge and disciplines. The constitutive liminality of performance studies lies in its capacity to bridge segregated and differently valued knowledges, drawing together legitimated as well as subjugated modes of inquiry (Conquergood 2002, 151).

This book intends to render visible such implicit, embodied knowledge and to show the richness of knowing that is specific to our field. Knowing how to study and analyse such ephemeral objects as performances and performance practice is also a form of tacit knowledge as it relies on years of experience in doing research (tacit comes from the Latin 'tacitus' which means 'silent' or 'unspoken'). Research experience, in a way, is also privileged knowledge. When scholars do not describe or explicate methods or express their resistance by saying that in this field 'we do not use methods'—in some sort of variation—implicitly exposes that privilege. The main goal of this book is to share this knowledge with students, for whom this knowledge is not always evident.

The attentive reader will have observed by now, that we use the terms theatre and performance in an intertwined way, since we feel the distinction is no longer reflected in the practices we study, and that occasionally, in an attempt to write economically, we use 'performance' as an umbrella term to address theatre, dance, and dramaturgy as fields of study.

Briefly returning to the classroom scene above, how is it that performance research methods are so scarce? Why do they hardly exist, or perhaps more aptly put: how come they are not visible? What does this tell us about our field of study? There are many possible answers, not one exhaustive. One reason could relate to the nature of our research object, that is, the ephemerality of the live event which characterises all performative events. We cannot replay or revisit our object of study, like our colleagues in film, media, or art studies. Despite the occasional support of performance documentation (surely necessary for in-depth analysis), we also rely on subjective experience, as many performance analyses also involve the way that spectators are being addressed by and situated in performance. However, this does not mean that these forms of spectatorial address cannot be studied in a systematic manner. A second reason could be the close affiliation between the studying and making of theatre and dance, as many scholars are theatre and dance practitioners themselves. Perhaps inspired by the freedom of artistic creation processes, and its inherent need for not-knowing and risk-taking, many performance scholars seem hesitant to name what they do and how they do it. Artworks are creative, which may entice creative reflection in return. Rather than (methodologically) repeating what others have done before, perhaps we are lured by the imperative of originality.[1] A third reason is probably the influence of performance studies, a discourse that emerged from the 1970s onwards, and, in line with Conquergood mentioned above, a strong advocate of the interdisciplinary, insubordinate nature of the performance event (and its study), drastically cutting the boundaries across categories of art, culture, and society—also known as the "broad spectrum approach" (Schechner 1988).[2] Performance studies' argument that any cultural utterance or ritual can be regarded as performance is perhaps not really served by the 'rigidity' that often seems associated with methods by scholars in this field. That being noted, we do not believe that methods are rigid—quite the opposite.

A fourth reason is perhaps more an observation than an explanation. Due to the hesitance or resistance to explaining or articulating methods, it is at times difficult to recognise how a scholar positions their research

---

1   Paul Rae presents a somewhat similar argument, in the Epilogue to *The Cambridge Guide to Mixed Methods Research for Theatre and Performance Studies*, observing an 'aesthetics of research' in which the researcher adopts a similar flexible approach to the dramaturg or any other co-creator: "If research activity, as continuous with the phenomena it investigates, has a performative and enactive quality, then there stands to be an area of substantial overlap between what TaPS scholars research and how they research it, making a distinct method discourse all the harder to tease out" (2024, 303).

2   The hesitance towards methods is clearly identifiable if one takes a look into the archive of the widely acclaimed *Performance Research Journal*, where journal issues are organised around themes, topics, and trends, but not around theoretical strands, schools of thought, or concepts, let alone methods.

in a wider academic debate. It seems that many of us seek to carve out our own path, borrowing a few stones or scaffolds from others but mostly figuring it out ourselves. Yet at the same time, this 'figuring out ourselves' is, in fact, often based on or inspired by existing research traditions, such as looking at our continental European context, semiotics, dramaturgical analysis, or concept-based approaches. As indicated above, we think that our field can benefit from making this knowledge explicit, and we hope that this book can support in sharing and making visible the rich knowledge that is present in performance research.

A brief positioning

Many contributors to this volume—though not all—developed their pedagogical and research practices within a continental European context, an environment in which teaching and research on theatre and dance has been strongly influenced by traditions of heuristic and hermeneutic methodologies as well as cultural analysis.[3] This is why various forms of performance analysis are given a somewhat prominent position in the book. This environment also supports a wide array of theatre-making practices, ranging from movement-based works to music theatre, from installation art to critical documentary work, from site-specific and community-based projects to works that critically interrogate colonial histories and legacies. Moreover, the existence of an active international performance touring circuit enables both teacher-researchers and students to engage with a wide array of artistic forms and strategies. These diverging practices call for analytical approaches that are sensitive to the specific dramaturgical and theatrical strategies at play, as is also noted by Maaike Bleeker in *Doing Dramaturgy: Thinking Through Practice* (2023). Consequently, such diversity has led to the development of a broad spectrum of performance-analytical methodologies.

---

3 Hermeneutics describes the 'art' and methodology of interpretation and the careful positioning and grounding of that interpretation, particularly of texts, artworks, and other symbolic utterances. Cultural analysis focuses on the use of theoretical concepts as tools for analysing cultural objects and phenomena, such as language practices, strategies of representation, or use of media.

Theatre and performance studies have a relatively short history. In Europe and the US, they emerged as autonomous academic study programmes—some precursors aside—from the 1960s onwards, roughly. In the following decades of the twentieth century, at least in continental Europe, semiotic analysis was by far the most used method of performance analysis—joined by deconstruction theories and poststructuralist approaches in the late 1970s, and with phenomenology in a kind of continuing minoritarian position, which, partly due to its sphere of inquiry, never translated into a systematic approach.[4] Towards the end of the century, however, many scholars noted the limitations of semiotics in view of contemporary societal developments, digital culture, political upheavals, and more. To some extent, semiotic approaches still play a role, especially in analysing more conventional forms of theatre and dance that rely on symbolic forms of communication, but this is too limited a toolbox when one seeks to engage with, for instance, a dance work inspired by critical theory, a sound installation working with robot-musicians or the politics of drag performance. Methods such as semiotics or theatre historiography are less suited to address societal context at large, the temporality of the live event or the situatedness of the analyst. Highly influenced by adjacent research areas such as gender studies or (continental) philosophy, and emerging discourses such as decolonialism, intersectionalism, or queer theory, theatre and performance studies proliferated in many directions, and so did the methods with which these developments are explored and examined.

This multidirectional interdisciplinarity is not only a result of recent developments in theory and practice but is also intrinsic to performance studies itself. This interdisciplinarity might even be another reason for the invisibility of methods in theatre, dance, and performance studies. Also observed by Conquergood (2002), performances or performative events cut across many spheres of influence and hence constantly escape definition. A similar observation is made by Thomas DeFrantz, this time related to dance, in his introduction to the 'Academic Research' section

---

[4] This concise reflection does not do justice to the richness of the field that also comprises historiographic research, ethnography, theatre anthropology, and much more, see for a much more nuanced overview, Davis (2024, 6–16). However, many of these methods are grounded in the analysis of plays, conventional theatre, or theatre histories, whereas our book focuses on contemporary performance practices and the methods that emerged in response to this.

in *Dance Research Methodologies* (2023). DeFrantz's valuable insights on the interdisciplinarity of dance could easily be extended to encompass theatre and performance as well:

> Dance studies allow humanities researchers to make any manner of connections across disciplines. Historians, cultural theorists, philosophers, anthropologists, religious studies researchers all turn to dance to better understand their own topics and to reconsider method. In this, dance tends to operate as a lever; as evidence of its own ongoing presence in nearly any construction of culture (2023, 107).

Dance (and theatre and performance) research is a discipline that "escapes containment as a singularity because of its rampant diversity" (109). While such diversity is both inspiring and challenging, this book seeks to identify the expertise and knowledge specific to the field of theatre, dance, and dramaturgy. This focus aims to position it as a valuable partner in interdisciplinary knowledge exchange—particularly in collaborating beyond the humanities and continuing our adventure in engaging with the social sciences, creative industries, or science and technology-driven disciplines.

Due to its interdisciplinary nature, performance research almost always relies on the combination of research methods, precisely because performance projects as research objects cut across a range of knowledge fields and disciplines, such as traditions and genre conventions in theatre and dance making, cultural references, societal debates, environmental issues, political systems, and more. As is evident in the title of their book, this is also the key point of Davis and Rae's *The Cambridge Guide to Mixed Methods Research for Theatre and Performance Studies*, where the editors point out that mixing methods is necessary for examining how theatre and performance (and, we might also add, dance) are forms of cultural inquiry, and the wide range of aesthetic forms, cultural meanings, and historical genealogies invites a corresponding variety of research approaches (2024, 4–5).

Davis and Rae depart from similar critical and urgent observations that we have, and their book shows that the field is certainly not entirely devoid of discussion on methods. *The Cambridge Guide to Mixed Methods Research* answers the need via a different strategy than ours, by focusing on the stages of research, working with sections on Planning, Doing and Interpreting, with play analysis and theatre historiography as recurring themes, whereas this book explicitly addresses a student audience, directed at providing concrete 'how to' guidance in how a wide range of contemporary research methods can be operationalised. *Research Methods in Theatre and Performance*, edited by Baz Kershaw and Helen Nicholson (2011), presents a wide range of approaches, with contributions by scholars, practice-based researchers, and arts practitioners, yet due to the strong emphasis on creative and innovative strategies (like "creative approaches to the archive" and "the usefulness of mess") it does not provide the more systematic approach to methods that we are looking for. Instead, our book aims to position and unpack methods pedagogically, so that it exceeds an author's personal research practice and is opened to be used by others. A final title worth including here is the *Routledge Handbook of Interdisciplinary Research Methods* (2018), edited by Celia Lury, Rachel Fensham, and five others, which organises its contributions around keywords, especially verbs, such as assembling, drawing, explaining, archiving, or scaling. This is certainly an inspiring approach, since these words expose what researchers do, and the flexibility of terms matches well with our interdisciplinary agenda. However, our book seeks to ground methods specifically in a genealogy of theatre, dance, and performance studies, to articulate (and appropriate) the knowledge specific to this field.

Method and methodology

When preparing a book on methods in performance research, it is difficult to overlook the fact that the term method itself is highly contested—if not actively avoided—in this field of study. There is not only a lack of shared understanding about what is meant by method; as indicated above, there is also a tendency to avoid discussing or explicitly naming a method as such. Instead, terms like approach or perspective are often preferred. This reluctance to use the term method in performance research, which is also evident more broadly in the humanities, can partly be attributed to a resistance to the epistemological principles that underpin other research areas, such as the STEM disciplines (science, technology, engineering, and mathematics) and the social and behavioural sciences.

In mathematics and logics, methods often rest on a set of axioms—principles assumed to be true and used as the foundation for further reasoning. Other scientific research in STEM disciplines tends to adhere to positivist paradigms, which view the world as a collection of observable events and measurable facts that can be tested and understood through experimentation. In contrast, humanities research—including art and performance studies—does not use axiomatic frameworks and favours qualitative and heuristic modes of analysis over quantitative methods. Broadly speaking, performance scholars investigate how meaning or knowledge is produced through a wide range of performance practices. To do so, they draw on theories, concepts, and insights from a diverse array of academic debates and disciplines. Despite these differences, it is also important to acknowledge that this is a rather general epistemological distinction between STEM disciplines and performance research. In reality, this distinction is rarely clear-cut. Moreover, interdisciplinary research that combines insights and approaches from the humanities and sciences has been flourishing in the early twenty-first century.[5]

In performance research, methods are usually less transferable than those in the sciences. One reason for this is that the cultural objects or phenomena being studied are often examined through theoretical frameworks informed by multiple academic debates originating from diverse disciplines. This interdisciplinary approach is a distinctive feature of performance research. This plurality and diversity give rise to a great variety of research practices, as evidenced by the work showcased at large annual international conferences in this field such as Performance Studies international (PSi), the International Federation of Theatre Research conference (IFTR), and the Dance Studies Association conference (DSA). The methods at the heart of performance research in such settings are each a unique constellation shaped by the interplay of theories and concepts underpinning the study, the cultural phenomenon or material under investigation and the situatedness and perspective of the researcher.

Methods in performance research often take the form of unique constellations shaped by the triangular relationship between object,

---

5   There is growing openness to acknowledging the benefits of fostering such collaborations. To give just one example, in *After Method: Mess in Social Science Research* (2004), John Law advocates for acknowledging the role of embodiment, agential objects, and performativity in social science research, as the phenomena studied in that field become increasingly "complex, diffuse and messy" (2). This is precisely the expertise of performance researchers.

theory, and researcher. This offers a useful entry point for understanding another common source of confusion in this field: the distinction between the terms method and methodology. In its broadest sense, method refers to the way in which answers to a research question are sought. It denotes an approach to solving a problem or gathering data. But how, then, can method be distinguished from methodology? A key complication lies in the fact that, in English, the term methodology is sometimes used interchangeably with method. This creates confusion because at the same time it is also common to draw a distinction between method and methodology in research design. However, the way in which this distinction is understood is far from universally agreed upon.

A research survey examining the use of the terms methodology and method in academic textbooks on research methods revealed significant inconsistencies (Mackenzie and Knipe 2006). According to the findings, "a large number of texts provided no definition for the terms methodology or method, some texts use the terms interchangeably, and others use them as having different meanings" (2006). Based on this survey, which focused primarily on the area of social sciences, the authors concluded that: "The most common definitions suggest that methodology is the overall approach to research linked to the paradigm or theoretical framework while the method refers to systematic modes, procedures, or tools used for collections and analysis of data" (2006). However, when considering the diverse research practices of performance scholars, it quickly becomes evident that maintaining such a distinction is challenging. This difficulty arises from the profound entanglement of theory and method that characterises performance research. Theories are usually not merely 'linked' or 'applied' to the methods that are being used, they are part and parcel of the perspective shaping the analysis of the cultural phenomenon under investigation.

An example of how method and methodology can be distinguished, as well as a definition of these terms more attuned to performance research, is presented by performance scholar and theatre historian Davis in *The Cambridge Guide to Mixed Methods Research for Theatre and Performance Studies* (Davis and Rae 2024). Davis conceptualises research as comprising two distinct parts. The first part, she explains, involves "a set of activities involving intentional effort to seek and identify stuff" (2). This corresponds to methods, defined as "ways to gather information relevant to the project, whether that information is just data or, conversely, will later become evidence (data in service of claims)" (2). Methodologies are part of the second part of conducting research, where they are used to interpret and analyse the collected material, informed by existing academic debates and theories, which Davis refers to as "traditions of interpretation" (3). This distinction underscores the importance of carefully considering the relationship between method and methodology during the research design phase. What type of data needs to be gathered to enable a methodological approach based on a specific intellectual tradition or theoretical framework? Additionally, Davis asserts that a single research project often employs multiple methods and multiple methodologies.

Many titles of the contributions to this book include the term 'analysis', which, following Davis, seems to emphasise the aspect of methodology. However, in the 'how to' sections of the chapters, it also becomes clear that these various modes of analysis often imply or incorporate specific methods, distinct types of data gathering. Additionally, John L. Austin's problematisation of the distinction between the "constative" (descriptive) and the "performative" reminds us that the activity of describing material can never exclusively be descriptive, let alone "neutral" (Austin [1962] 1975). Selections and descriptions of data always already produce a certain degree of interpretation about what was perceived.

The complexities relating to method and methodology, including the entanglement of theory and method, and the unique object-theory-researcher constellations in performance research do not however mean that we should steer clear of distinguishing methods in performance research. On the contrary, a primary aim of this book is to not leave emerging researchers in the dark because of such concerns but instead illuminate a selection of methodological approaches that contribute to the contemporary field of performance research, which connects the creative with the critical in abundant ways.

In the understanding of method and methodology that we propose in this book, we acknowledge the deep entanglement of how they operate. Methodology encapsulates the extended theoretical framework of a research project—which may consist of references to multiple academic disciplines and debates—that informs how the main research question can be answered. Method or—usually plural—methods denote the different ways of *doing* research that are involved in answering a research question. Methods structure how research objects and data are found and how researchers make sense of them. Since this 'making sense' is always informed by the chosen theoretical framework, method and methodology are intrinsically connected.

The organisation of the book

A core characteristic of this book is its explicit hands-on approach, which systematically describes and positions methods in detail, showing how they can be used through brief demonstrations. Starting from the observed necessity of naming and articulating the research methods that we use in our field and teach to our students, the book aims to make practical and share the didactic knowledge we use in our classrooms, rendering these methods visible to both humanities students at research universities, as well as to students in related fields, at art academies and in other forms of artistic and creative practice. With this agenda in mind, we have asked all contributors to write down how they teach methods, which are often connected to their personal research agendas but not exclusively so, how they explain these methods in class, and how they help students to actively work with these methods.

We also asked the contributors to organise the text in a specific way. Drawing on many years of teaching experience and thorough insights into what students need or are asking for, we wanted to make sure that each chapter provides the student with information on not only where to use this method for, but also to place the method in a wider tradition of theatre, dance, and performance research. Additionally, each chapter seeks to actively 'open up' the method, encouraging flexible and creative use. We will briefly explain the various elements of the format below.

Each chapter starts with a concise introduction of the method and what one can use it for. It introduces the type of object that is suitable for this approach. This helps raise awareness of the close relation between (research) object and method, as not any object can be researched by using any method. It is rather that the object and method mutually inform each other. If one wants to analyse a debate on a controversial performance, for instance, the method of movement analysis or archival research will be of less assistance, but methods of discourse analysis or cultural materialism certainly do.

This introduction is then followed by a 'context' section, which elaborates on some core ideas or concepts inherent in this method while describing the historical and/or theoretical lineages of this method. Where does this method stem from? This section helps to position this method in a theoretical debate and also provides further insights into details of this method.

Up next is the 'how to' section which explicitly stands in line with our hands-on approach: How does one work according to this method? What are the core elements of the method? What are the main concepts associated with this method? Some chapters present a step-by-step approach, whereas others introduce a set of questions, and again others elaborate on certain key themes or concepts to work with. These variations on the one hand correspond to different research or teaching styles of the contributors, and different ideas about what constitutes a method, but also relate to the type of object that is explored. Sometimes an object is not a clearly pinpointable 'object' but rather a process, a type of engagement, a durational work, and so on. This invites rather different, often more flexible or exploratory methods and ways of working in comparison to object-centred methods in which, for example, a dance or music theatre performance operates as a centrifugal point in multimodal forms of analysis.

Continuing the hands-on approach is the 'demonstration' section in which a concrete demonstration of the method is provided, discussing a specific case study and showing how core elements of the method can be used, and how this yields specific, method-driven results. This gesture of demonstration is followed by an 'expanding the method' section, for which we have asked the contributors to reflect on or demonstrate an interdisciplinary translation of the method: What else can be done with this method? In what other field could this method be used as well? This can be a general reflection with some brief examples or demonstrated by means of a second case study. Many contributions are already interdisciplinary in their theoretical grounding or in the practices discussed, yet all these methods are highly flexible and easily transferable to other contexts. This renders the book useful for other research areas beyond that of performance studies as well. This section helps to show not only the interdisciplinary potential of theatre, dance, and performance methods, but also underlines again the flexibility of method, as it is not a clear-cut recipe that always yields the same results.

Each chapter ends with some suggestions for further reading, a motivated selection of relevant titles, that helps to further elaborate on and deepen the reflection on the research method.

Despite the many resonances between the chapters, we have organised the contributions in this book into four sections. Part I is dedicated to object-oriented modes of analysis and presents methods that are developed to analyse a certain cultural object, and to a certain extent are also inspired by its object e.g. the dramaturgy of a performance, or relations between movement and meaning in dance and movement analysis. This part starts with a chapter on Concept-Based Analysis (cultural analysis), since a concept-based approach undergirds many subsequent chapters. The methods in this section are: Dramaturgical Analysis, Spectatorship Analysis, Movement Analysis, Dance Analysis, Musical Theatre Analysis, and Multimodal Analysis of Listening.

Part II presents methods that pivot around the social, historical, or material contexts in which the object of study is or can be situated. These methods are Discourse Analysis, Contextual Analysis, Cultural Materialism, Theatre Archaeology, and Embodied Fabulation as a mode of archival research. Part III continues this line of enquiry yet is even more firmly grounded in situated knowledges, with contributions on Intersectionality and two chapters on Autoethnography (including decolonial and queer theory). Part IV, finally, focuses on methods with a strong affiliation with (performance) philosophy and ways of thinking through performance, grounded in embedded, experiential, and process-based research. Contributions in this section involve Practice-Led Inquiry, Affective Attunement, Performance Philosophy, and Hyphenated Thinking.

Of course, this is an artificial division of the contributions. As pointed out above, humanities research can be identified by its unique way of combining multiple approaches, in dialogue with the research object. Subsequently, in any type of research, objects, contexts, concepts, and matters of situated embodiment are always intertwined. This is why there are many resonances between the chapters. Discourse analysis, for instance, as described by Sruti Bala, is intrinsically interested in archaeological approaches, which is the focus of the chapter by Evelyn Wan, an approach which in turn engages deeply with historiographical questions, described by Lisa Skwirblies, who explores these questions through the concept of 'embodied fabulation'. All these methods address the power and politics of knowledge, which is close to Anika Marschall's reflections on intersectionality and Dick Zijp's approach to cultural materialism. These chapters expose how methods facilitate a critical engagement with research objects, a criticality that also echoes in Pieter Verstraete's multimodal critical discourse analysis of listening.

Explorations on performance *as* a form of research, as introduced by Theron Schmidt, not only bring about site-specific awareness (via topics such as performative cartography, situationist 'drifting' and grounded theory) but also affiliate with practice-led research and transversal thinking as described by Konstantina Georgelou, Laura Cull Ó Maoilearca's chapter on performance philosophy and Christel Stalpaert's introduction to 'hyphenated thinking' as a way of listening and relating with landscapes and durational work. All these chapters demonstrate and reflect on the use of (collaborative) exercises, scores, and directives as ways of organising experimental, process-based projects. Such methods of attunement also address the social and environmental situatedness of the researcher and/ or the research object; this embeddedness of the (experiencing) subject is equally key to intersectionality and autoethnography. This book includes two contributions on autoethnography, a method which combines autobiography with ethnography. Prompted by the autobiographical component in this method, which always relies on the author's culture or belonging to certain communities, the two contributions show the versatility of auto-ethnographic approaches in diverse research settings. Wigbertson Julian Isenia focuses on queer identities in relation to his fieldwork in Curaçao, whereas Fabiola Camuti and Annemijn van der Schaar address the (performance of) social roles and identities in queer parenting.

Terms like 'attunement', 'embodied fabulation', or 'hyphenated thinking' can also be seen as examples of a concept-based approach in performance studies, a method that is at the core of many performance analyses, as is demonstrated and described by Laura Karreman. This concept-based approach returns in the method of contextual analysis, described by Liesbeth Groot Nibbelink. In this chapter it is suggested that contextual analysis produces art ecologies. This method derives its thinking from ecological and new materialist approaches to research, as does Evelyn Wan in her work on theatre and media archaeology, in her tracing of how various physical materials produce layered meanings, and as emerges as well in Christel Stalpaert's hyphenated thinking, which explicitly addresses our entanglements with more-than-human matter. Whereas Stalpaert relates this entanglement mostly to natural environments, other chapters actively engage the role of digital technology, for instance, in Evelyn Wan's media-archaeological tracings, in Laura Karreman's discussion of the 'motion capture imaginary' as a concept or in the analysis of holographic characters, in Andrew Fuhrmann, Lise Uytterhoeven, and Rachel Fensham's chapter on movement analysis.

Various authors explicitly argue for the need of combining methods, such as in Sarah Whatley's chapter on dance analysis, Millie Taylor's approach to musical analysis or Pieter Verstraete's analysis of multimodal listening. Other methods implicitly combine methods: contextual analysis also draws on dramaturgical analysis, as described by Liesbeth Groot Nibbelink and Sigrid Merx. The chapter on movement analysis, by Andrew Fuhrmann, Lise Uytterhoeven, and Rachel Fensham offers a multi-scalar approach to movement which brings together concepts from various historical, cultural, and ideological contexts. Which would bring us back to Sruti Bala's discourse analysis, and so on.

This book is far from comprehensive. We fully realise that there are many more methods used in performance research, yet we hope that the ones described in this book contribute to increasing the visibility of methods currently used in the performance research field. We wish the book to be of benefit for students, in that the detailed descriptions will provide them with knowledge and insight on methods and methodological choice-making, and also support them in deciding on and using methods in their research design. On the other hand, this book might inspire members of our academic community to more often share and make explicit their knowledge and expertise on working with methods as well. In this sense, we hope this book invites others to join in the effort to reach a more common discursive ground. This way, both students and more experienced scholars can participate in this community of practice, which helps support and fuel the thriving of a community of all those involved in theatre, dance, and performance research.

References

Austin, John L. [1962] 1975. *How to do Things with Words*. Edited by James O. Urmson and Marins Sbisà. Second edition. Harvard University Press.

Bleeker, Maaike. 2023. *Doing Dramaturgy: Thinking Through Practice*. Palgrave Macmillan. https://doi.org/10.1007/978-3-031-08303-7

Candelario, Rosemary, and Matthew Henley, eds. 2023. *Dance Research Methodologies: Ethics, Orientations and Practices*. Routledge. https://doi.org/10.4324/9781003145615

Conquergood, Dwight. 2002. "Performance Studies: Interventions and Radical Research." *TDR/The Drama Review* 46 (2): 145–56. https://doi.org/10.1162/105420402320980550

Davis, Tracy C., and Paul Rae, eds. 2024. *The Cambridge Guide to Mixed Methods Research for Theatre and Performance Studies*. Cambridge University Press. https://doi.org/10.1017/9781009294904

DeFrantz, Thomas. 2023. "Introduction to Research in Dance Studies: Dance as Humanity." In *Dance Research Methodologies: Ethics, Orientations and Practices*, edited by Rosemary Candelario and Matthew Henley, 107–12. Routledge. https://doi.org/10.4324/9781003145615-11

Groot Nibbelink, Liesbeth. 2017."Missing Names." *Performance Research* 22 (5): 128–37. https://doi.org/10.1080/13528165.2017

Kershaw, Baz, and Helen Nicholson, eds. 2011. *Research Methods in Theatre and Performance*. Edinburgh University Press. https://doi.org/10.1515/9780748646081

Law, John. 2004. *After Method: Mess in Social Science Research*. Routledge. https://doi.org/10.4324/9780203481141

Lury, Celia, Rachel Fensham, Alexandra Heller-Nicholas, Sybille Lammes, Angela Last, Mike Michael and Emma Uprichard, eds. 2018. *Routledge Handbook of Interdisciplinary Research Methods*. Routledge.

Mackenzie, Noella and Sally Knipe. 2006. "Research Dilemmas: Paradigms, Methods and Methodology." *Issues in Educational Research* 16 (2). http://www.iier.org.au/iier16/mackenzie.html

Schechner, Richard. 1988. "Performance Studies: The Broad Spectrum Approach." *TDR: The Drama Review* 32 (3): 4–6. https://doi.org/10.2307/1145899

I

OBJECT-ORIENTED DRAMATURGIES AND CULTURAL ANALYSIS

1. Concept-Based Analysis

Laura Karreman

Summary

This chapter introduces concept-based analysis as a method in performance research, grounded in cultural analysis as developed by Mieke Bal (2002), a Dutch scholar in literature, art history, and cultural theory. It highlights Bal's notion of theoretical concepts as "searchlight theories"—tools that illuminate specific layers of meaning in an object of study. The chapter also emphasises the potential of "travelling concepts" for interdisciplinary work. Such concepts retain core theoretical insights from their original disciplines but can be adapted and operationalised in new contexts.

A step-by-step guide is proposed for conducting concept-based analysis, including selecting and contextualising the concept and object, formulating guiding questions, and reflecting critically on the method and the researcher's positionality.

The method is illustrated through a student project on queer presence in the work of Sasha Velour, a genderfluid drag artist (Van der Vegt 2023). This project uses the concept of the "shimmer" to explore visibility and identity. Another example employs "the imaginary" to analyse motion capture technology in dance, as in Karreman (2017). The chapter concludes by showing how concept-based analysis can be applied in interdisciplinary and pedagogical contexts, such as using concepts from performance studies to examine and develop social robotics.

Introduction

This chapter explains how a concept can be used as a theoretical lens to analyse a chosen cultural object. What are concepts, and how can concepts originating from various academic debates serve as useful analytical tools to investigate performance practices and other cultural phenomena? This chapter situates concept-based analysis within its roots in cultural analysis, as proposed by Bal (2002), and within more recent academic discourse where it has been used in performance research.

Performance practices often have a history of being viewed from a specific perspective. By using theoretical concepts as analytic lenses, researchers can challenge such established interpretations and shed light on dimensions of such practices that have to date remained hidden. This constitutes the critical potential of this approach. What meaning is revealed by looking at performance through the lens that a specific concept offers us that was not visible to us before? How does this perspective help us understand complex phenomena from a different vantage point? How does the narrative that emerges differ from those told thus far?

Creating such a new understanding is part of the project of performance research, but it also—more broadly—aligns with the objectives of cultural analysis, a field of study whose main goal is to interpret cultural practices in order to gain new knowledge. The method described in this chapter is first and foremost based on the work of a key scholar in this field: Dutch cultural theorist and critic Mieke Bal. "Doing theory" (2006, 162) for her takes place in the dynamic interaction between researcher, concepts, and objects. This is the theoretical practice that Bal has termed cultural analysis. In her foundational book *Travelling Concepts in the Humanities* (2002), Bal proposes a "concept-based methodology" (5) as a central approach in the research area of cultural analysis. The core of this method lies in the use of theoretical concepts as tools to analyse cultural objects.

Working with this method entails contextualising concepts within academic debates and justifying their relevance to the cultural phenomenon that is being studied. When concept-based analysis is used as a method in performance research, researchers articulate how using concepts as analytic tools enhances their understanding of the subject matter, while also critically reflecting on how the interaction between the concept and the performance practice that is being analysed has consequences for the concept's meaning and potential use.

While this approach is suitable for studying a wide range of cultural objects, practices, and phenomena, this text will specifically focus on how such concept-based analyses can be used as a method in performance research. It contextualises this approach within the field of cultural analysis, highlighting the interdisciplinary orientation and potential of the method. Additionally, it outlines the various steps typically involved in applying this method, which are useful when developing research design. Finally, several examples of concept-based analyses in performance research will be discussed to demonstrate the value of using concepts as an analytic lens in making sense of theatre, dance, and other more broadly defined practices of performance that we encounter in the world beyond the stage of the performing arts. These examples range from student work to more advanced research projects.

Context

To provide a better basis for understanding of how concepts can be understood as a tool for analysis, it is helpful to first address the question: what do we mean when we use the term concept? The word concept comes from the Latin verb 'concipere', which translates to the English 'conceive', or 'to form in the mind', and the Latin 'conceptum', 'something conceived'. From these etymological roots, in the late fifteenth century, the English term concept emerged, which meant 'thought' or 'idea'.

Today, in everyday language, the term concept still carries 'idea' as its primary meaning. But the term concept may also refer to an overarching theme, or an initial design or prototype. For instance, in the art field, conceptual art refers to a movement emerging in the 1960s in which the idea behind the art mattered more than the physical object itself. This was a response to the increasing commercialisation of the art world. Conceptual artists were not concerned so much with the aesthetics of the object itself nor the craft needed to create the art; instead they focused on other ways of engagement with audiences, often creating installations, performances, videos, and text-based works. An example is the work of Yoko Ono, who often worked with scores. Consider for instance her score-based installation *White Chess Set* (1966) which invites the reader to "play as long as you can remember where all your pieces are". Another use of the term can be found in today's urban environments in which 'concept stores' offer varied collections that are carefully curated around a specific theme, for instance relating to new trends in art, design, or technology, whilst creating a specific, often immersive, experience for their visitors.

In various academic disciplines, the notion of a concept carries different meanings and implications. In the sciences, concepts are often abstract, generalised ideas that help make sense of natural objects and phenomena. For example, the idea of a "system" is used when we refer to ecosystems or solar systems. In cognitive science, concepts are understood as mental constructs that help us navigate and interpret the world around us. For instance, we have a mental image of what a chair looks like and how it functions. This mental concept enables us to recognise a chair as a chair, despite the vast variety in the appearances of chairs. In philosophy, concepts are often employed to explore abstract ideas in the realms of ethics or behaviour, such as the question, "What is justice?", which is discussed in Plato's *Republic*.

The type of conceptual analysis that this text focuses on, however, is not aimed at an analysis of the concept itself, at least, not solely. In the method that is described here, a concept is used as a theoretical lens to analyse a chosen cultural object. This concept-based analysis is proposed by Bal and forms a methodological approach in the field of cultural analysis. Bal is a literature and art scholar, a video artist, and the founder of the Amsterdam School for Cultural Analysis (ASCA) in 1993, where she was director till 1998. The main fields of study that her work relates to are literary studies, visual analysis, postmodern theology, and interdisciplinary methodology (Bal 2006).

The main thesis of Bal's book *Travelling Concepts in the Humanities: A Rough Guide* (2002) is that "interdisciplinarity in the humanities, necessary, exciting, serious, must seek its heuristic and methodological basis in *concepts* rather than *methods*" (2002, 5). For Bal, working with concepts to analyse cultural objects forms an answer to the question of how to establish intersubjectivity in the field of the humanities.

Intersubjectivity is a term that refers to a shared understanding and agreement among different researchers regarding the meaning of, for instance, data, objects, and phenomena. Bal argues that interdisciplinary research is vital when striving for intersubjectivity. Theoretical concepts can play an important role in this. "Concepts are the tools of intersubjectivity", Bal writes, "they facilitate discussion on the basis of a common language" (2002, 22). Because concepts have the capacity to 'travel' across boundaries of academic disciplines, she argues, they have the potential to become methodological agents that enable interdisciplinary research that is conducted with academic rigour.

Bal has proposed to understand concepts both as "miniature theories" (Bal 2002, 22) as well as "searchlight theories" (Bal 2006, 158). First of all, through Bal's notion of a concept as a "miniature theory" it becomes clear what the difference is between a term as 'just' a noun or a term that is a concept. Regular words or terms can be used to describe or label something, whereas concepts can be used to analyse something. Note that this does not exclude the fact that some terms may potentially function both as a regular term as well as a concept. Secondly, the metaphorical notion of a concept as a "searchlight theory" draws attention to the capacity of concepts to illuminate specific layers of meaning in the object of analysis. What is highlighted here is the perspectival dimension of a concept. The concept functions as a theoretical lens through which an object is viewed, creating a dynamic relationship between the two. Following the searchlight metaphor, the object is sought through a beam of light, and the way in which the object subsequently catches and reflects this light may reveal specific elements but may also hide or downplay others.

In *Travelling Concepts*, Bal's understanding of concepts as theories is informed by the ideas of several philosophers. Gilles Deleuze and Félix Guattari play an important role here because in their book *What is Philosophy?* they define philosophy explicitly as "the art of forming, inventing, and fabricating concepts" (Deleuze and Guattari 1994, 2). Indeed, as Deleuze and Guattari suggest, concept-based analyses may utilise existing concepts, but they may also propose new ones. This will be further elaborated upon in the 'How to' section of this chapter.

Additionally, Bal builds on the notion of the (French) 'concept nomade' (a term which may be translated as 'nomadic concept' or 'travelling concept') that was proposed by philosopher of science Isabelle Stengers (1987) to call attention to the usefulness of concepts as theoretical tools that make phenomena "askable" (Bal 2006, 159) and that enable interdisciplinary scholarship in the sciences. Concepts make phenomena 'askable' because the perspective they offer gives rise to a specific set of questions that are prompted by the object. In this sense, concepts give shape to a research agenda related to the object at hand.

Finally, Bal also supports her proposal to understand concepts as theories by referring to philosopher of science Thomas Kuhn who states that "accuracy, consistency, scope, simplicity, and fruitfulness—are all standard criteria for evaluating the adequacy of a theory" (Kuhn 1986, 103). All these criteria, Bal writes, hold true for concepts as well. She writes: "Concepts can be judged according to the same norms" (2006, 159).

Working with concepts first requires reflection on what meanings they have acquired whilst travelling between disciplines over time. As Bal writes: "[B]ecause they are key to intersubjective understanding, more than anything they need to be explicit, clear, and defined. In this way everyone can take them up and use them" (2002, 22). Such a shared understanding of the meaning of concepts, however, is not easily achieved. What makes this difficult is that the meaning of concepts is never fixed, but ever-changing and transforming. Bal acknowledges the complexity of striving for a precise definition and explanation of the concepts researchers are working with. The meaning of concepts is never finite. At the same time, however, this is in itself a vital part of how concepts work. Bal argues that the methodological strength of concepts is formed precisely through their being in constant development. "[T]he travelling nature of concepts", she writes, "is an asset rather than a liability" (2002, 25). The meaning of a concept is continuously being renegotiated by being brought to bear on the objects that are being analysed. Bal writes: "It is only through a constant reassessment of the power of a concept to organise phenomena in a new and relevant way that its continued productivity can be evaluated" (2002, 32).

In this constant reassessment that Bal refers to, the interaction between the concept and the object of analysis plays a vital role: "The counterpart of any given concept is the cultural text or work or 'thing' that constitutes the object of analysis. No concept is meaningful for cultural analysis unless it helps us to understand the object better *on its*—the object's—*own terms*" (2002, 7). Bal understands theoretical practice as a dynamic process in which both an object and a concept are meaning-making agents that are subject to change: "The confrontation between concept and object is a kind of rubbing of two forms of language use against each other which changes both" (2006, 162).

This dynamic interaction between concept and object also means that a concept is never just applied *to* an object. Instead, Bal argues for an "empowerment of the object" (2002, 10) and posits that "sustained attention to the object is the mission of *analysis*" (2002, 9). This means that for researchers, it is important to spend time with the material. The cultural object itself poses questions and evokes complex meanings and in that sense also has the potential to contribute to academic debates. In the words of Bal: "[Images] can entice viewers to theorise. They are performative. They do something; they act. I call such 'speaking images', which speak back, resist (parts of) my interpretation of them, and make me think, 'theoretical objects'" (Bal 2013, 51–52).[1][2]

Bal's view of the theorising power of objects of analysis is informed by philosopher Hubert Damisch's notion of "theoretical object" (Bois et al. 1998, 8). Damisch explains this term as follows:

> [A] theoretical object is something that obliges one to do theory (...) but also furnishes you with the means of doing it. Thus, if you agree to accept it on theoretical terms, it produces effects around itself. (...) It is posed in theoretical terms; it produces theory and it necessitates a reflection on theory (1998, 8).

Similarly, Bal regards theoretical objects as "active participants in the performance of analysis in that they enable reflection and speculation [...] and thus constitute a theoretical object with philosophical relevance, whether materially embodied or not" (Bal 2013, 53).

Through a concept-based analysis, then, a theoretical argumentation emerges from the confrontation of a concept and an object. This happens by analysing an object through the lens of a concept and vice versa: by

---

1 With "theoretical objects" in this quotation, Bal cites Hubert Damisch (1988, 3–17).
2 Bal refers to "images" in this example but note that objects of analysis may include a wide range of cultural phenomena including, but not limited to: theatre and dance performances, music concerts, films, computer games, literature, but also events and practices such as rituals, protests, and interactions on social media.

re-imagining a concept through the confrontation with an object. It is not only the concept that helps us to 'conceive', or 'form things in the mind', a theoretical object does so too. This interactivity between objects and concepts continuously tests and reassesses the critical productivity of concepts in a specific area of research. "By *selecting* an object", as Bal puts it, "you *question* a field" (2002, 4).

As has become clear previously, an important advantage of working with concepts is that they are flexible. Concepts can travel between different disciplines, which means that they can encapsulate key theoretical findings in a specific field in such a way that these can be mobilised and operationalised as methodological tools beyond the borders of the discipline from which they originated. Performance studies is a field that from its emergence in the late 1970s has been characterised by its interdisciplinary approach. This explains the appeal of Bal's concept-based methodology to various scholars in this area. In her book *Visuality in the Theatre* (2008), Maaike Bleeker uses concepts such as perspective, theatricality, absorption, and focalisation to analyse different modes in which theatre performances construct spectatorship. Liesbeth Groot Nibbelink's *Nomadic Theatre* (2019) introduces the concept of nomadic theatre to position and analyse mobile theatre performances, while Marijn de Langen's *Dutch Mime* (2022) uses the concept of 'zéro', which was introduced by the founder of 'mime corporel' ('corporeal mime') Étienne Decroux, as a lens to illuminate the tradition and identity of this specific cultural strand of physical theatre.

In *Critical Concepts for the Creative Humanities* (2022), Iris van der Tuin and Nanna Verhoeff show the broader importance of concepts for critical inquiry in the creative humanities by presenting an extensive list of conceptual entries situated "at the intersection of contemporary design, art, culture, philosophy, and critical and cultural theory today" (ix). A collection of concepts that more specifically relate to performance research can be found in the PSi Lexicon (2013–ongoing), a project by the organisation Performance Studies international, which constitutes a dynamic and fruitful ground for debate for performance studies as well as for various intersecting disciplines.

How to

How does one conduct a concept-based analysis in a research project? In this section, an overview is provided of the elements typically included in a research design that incorporates this approach. This explanation draws on Bal's ideas, my own experience teaching this analytical method, and observations of the diverse ways students have worked with concepts in their research over the years.

It is important to note upfront that the elements mentioned here are not intended to serve as a strict step-by-step plan that must be followed in a specific order. For example, a research project might begin with an observation of a performance that intrigues or puzzles the researcher. Alternatively, it might start with an encounter with a concept that sparks the researcher's curiosity. In some cases, a concept might only emerge after significant progress has already been made in analysing the object of the research. Ultimately, however, as the research develops, the researcher will likely engage with each of these elements at some point.

1. Choosing an object

Identify the object that will be the focus of the research. This object of analysis can take various forms: it can be an artwork, such as a dance or theatre performance, visual artwork, media object, or music concert. Alternatively, it could be a specific cultural phenomenon, a ritual, or other cultural practice.[3] Motivate this choice: determine whether the object has sufficient complexity to warrant analysis and explain the academic relevance of studying it.

2. Object description

Describe and contextualise the object or phenomenon under scrutiny. Other research methods, such as dramaturgical analysis, discourse

---

[3] To give some examples, students writing their MA theses have used concepts such as necropolitics to study femicide (Hernandez 2020), attunement to explore human-robot interactions (Jang 2024) and expanded scenography to analyse digital memorial sites (Karjalainen 2022). It also happens that concepts are adapted, or new concepts are introduced.

analysis, or contextual analysis (also discussed in this book), may serve as helpful tools to support this process.

3. Selecting a concept

Identify the concept that will be worked with.[4] What concept could help open the complex narrative that the object is intuitively held to possess? Does the concept have the capacity to adequately address different layers of meaning of the object in question?

4. Positioning the concept

Trace the journey of this concept. How has it evolved over time? Can its origins be identified? What connotations has it accumulated as it has traversed one or more knowledge discourses? How is the concept currently situated within these discourses?

5. Analysis

Conduct the analysis. What insights emerge from the critical interaction between the object and the concept? What can be observed by examining the object through the theoretical lens of this concept? What meanings does the concept reveal when used as a 'searchlight' or 'miniature theory'? And how does the analysis affect or add to the concept's meaning(s)?

6. Critical reflection on method

Reflect critically on the strengths and potential limitations of the argumentation that arises from the object-concept encounter as it emerges in this research. Are there significant aspects of the object that remain unaddressed? What further research does this call for?

7. Researcher identity

A critical reflection on method may also involve a reflection on the identity of the person who conducts the research. How do knowledge, experience, and cultural situatedness shape the way a researcher views

---

4 It may also occur that an existing concept is rephrased or added to, or that a new concept is introduced. For instance, Zwinkels (2023) introduces the concept of "affective passing" to analyse trans* fictional gender performances.

and approaches the concepts and objects in their research? What are significant elements to acknowledge and convey in their particular research context?

The following brief example shows how these elements of a concept-based analysis can be identified in a graduate research project. In her MA thesis *Hiding in Plain Sight* (2023), Chris van der Vegt examines the artistic work of Sasha Velour, a genderfluid drag queen based in New York, who gained widespread fame and recognition after starring in an Emmy Award-winning television series in 2017, where Velour was crowned America's Next Drag Superstar. This research demonstrates how the concept of 'the shimmer' can function as a theoretical tool to reveal the ways in which Velour's artistic strategies are deeply connected to queer presence and visibility in this work.

The phenomenon or object (#1) that Van der Vegt focuses on is the intricate use of light projections in Sasha Velour's performance oeuvre, where her own body frequently serves as a screen. Van der Vegt argues that fully understanding what is happening here requires an argument grounded in insights from drag performance history, queer theory, theories of visibility and presence, and the use of light projection as a dramaturgical tool. She provides an overview of drag history to contextualise (#2) Velour's artistic practice and maps various debates that relate to this topic, such as queer visibility, political activism, and theatrical production.

The central concept (#3) that Van der Vegt works with in her research is "the shimmer", which denotes "a rapid, fleeting movement in the space between binaries [which] questions the binary's validity" (Van der Vegt 2023, 56). This concept was introduced and developed by Eliza Steinbock, in their book *Shimmering Images: Trans Cinema, Embodiment, and the Aesthetics of Change* (2019). Van der Vegt traces (#4) Steinbock's use of the term "the shimmer" back to philosopher Roland Barthes, who briefly mentions the shimmer in association with "the neutral", to resist the inherent binarism of paradigms and offer a third, unexplored option capable of disrupting existing frameworks (Barthes [1978] 2005; Van der Vegt 2023, 55). Steinbock's notion of "the shimmer" is also informed by Michel Foucault's (1978) and Gilles Deleuze's (1988) perspectives on visibility. Van der Vegt then translates Steinbock's concept of the "trans-cinematic shimmer" into the "drag shimmer" (Van der Vegt, 61).

In her final analysis (#5), Van der Vegt argues that Velour uses projections to create a shimmering queer presence that emerges in relation to societal (queer) visibility, sensory visibility, and theatrical presence. She identifies five dramaturgical strategies that render ambiguous "Velour's visibility and presence on stage: reimagining the spotlight, using the body as a screen, transforming through projection, duplicating presence through pre-recorded material, and drawing parallels between the virtual and the actual" (Van der Vegt, 2). This research thus demonstrates a new affordance of the shimmer as a concept that may support analyses within performance studies, and, more specifically, queer dramaturgy and scenography.

Reflecting on her method (#6) in the conclusion, Van der Vegt points out that "this framework could be beneficial to those writing about drag in order to avoid the pitfalls of thinking about drag primarily as the crossing of a binary opposition" (102).

Lastly, reflecting on her research identity (#7), she writes that due to a sensory processing disorder, it has been difficult for her to access live drag performances, as the performances as well as the environments in which drag typically takes place tend to be sensory-heavy. She acknowledges this as a challenge, noting that "drag is best experienced in person" (15). Because the performances were accessible to her through recordings, she was able to engage with them without the sensory load of attending in person. However, as she notes, "this methodology, combined with my situatedness as a Dutch disabled scholar who discovered Velour's work in 2017, may produce a different type of knowledge than what might be produced by an able-bodied New Yorker who has been able to attend her shows from the beginning of her career" (15).

Demonstration

To further illustrate how to work with concepts in performance research, I draw on my own research, in which I have examined the use of motion capture in dance.[5] In the dance field, motion capture has been used

---

5   Motion capture (often abbreviated to mocap) is a digital technology that can translate human movement into motion data. In optical motion capture, reflective markers are attached to a tight-fitting motion capture suit. Cameras can record the three-dimensional trajectory of such markers in submillimetre detail. This

to notate, document, and transmit dance. It also has been used as an artistic tool, for instance to mediate the kinaesthetic quality of dance movement in different ways. I have studied a broad range of applications of optical motion capture in various dance and performance practices, whilst trying to retrace the roots, motivations, and convictions behind these projects, asking the question: How does motion capture invite us to know dance differently? This research was primarily led by a concept that I titled "the motion capture imaginary" (Karreman 2017), which was based on the already existing concept of 'the imaginary'.

To explain why I chose to work with this concept, it is necessary to provide some contextualisation in the debate on dance and motion capture (#2). It is not self-evident that one would use motion capture to record dance. After all, through the translation of human movement to motion data, much of the phenomenological complexity of embodied movement is lost. Visual renderings of data points coming from the reflective markers on a body suit do not give us immediate access anymore to elements that seem vital to dance performance, such as the volume and weight of a dancer's body, how dancers breathe and sweat, what clothes or costumes they are wearing, to name but a few aspects. In other words, motion capture heavily abstracts dance performance. This creates a significant representational gap between dance as motion data and dance as performance. This raises the question: how to render or communicate dance motion data in a way that makes sense? Or, more simply put: how to make motion data speak?

Despite these critical observations and challenges, it is undeniable that motion capture experiments in the dance field flourished during the early twenty-first century. This growing interest in exploring motion capture as a new form of dance documentation stood out especially when compared to video and other traditional documentation methods, such as cumbersome and costly dance notation systems, such as Labanotation.[6] For the first time, via motion capture the three-

---

technology has been applied in a wide variety of fields, including biomechanics, medicine, and robotics, as well as in creative industries, in which motion capture is used to map human movement onto virtual avatars to make the characters in film and games more 'lifelike' or believable.

6   Symbolic dance notation systems are ways of representing human dance movement through symbols and methods like graphic figures, path mapping, numerical systems, words, or letters. These notation systems may be highly

dimensional trajectory of dancing bodies in performance could be remediated via visual and computational modes in sub-millimetre detail. The curiosity and experimentation surrounding motion capture within the dance field, manifesting in various forms, became the central observation (#2) that motivated my research.

Using research methods such as media archaeology and discourse analysis, I identified motion capture practices in the dance field as an emerging cultural phenomenon that manifested itself in ways that could not be easily explained (#1). I selected various examples of such dance capture practices, which functioned as theoretical objects in my research (#1). These objects included the performance *Emergence* (2014) by John McCormick and Steph Hutchison, the project Capturing Stillness by Gibson/Martelli, the digital score *Using the Sky* (2011) by Deborah Hay and Motion Bank, and the now classic work *Ghostcatching* (1999) by OpenEndedGroup.

The perspective that was offered to me by using the concept of 'the imaginary' as an analytical tool (#3) allowed me to hear the stories that these objects were telling me. This concept shifted the focus from the traditional emphasis on the technological affordances of motion capture to an analytical approach that created space to explore the cultural-historical context of motion capture, and the poetics associated with its practices. As I have stated elsewhere:

> Focusing solely on what a technological apparatus (Agamben 2009) consists of and how it operates does not give us an adequate picture of how such apparatuses produce meaning. If we want to understand how technologies act as part of a larger cultural phenomenon, we must determine which ideas, intentions, and fantasies have dreamed them into being (Karreman 2025).

The imaginary is a well-travelled concept. It has been used in areas of study as diverse as psychoanalysis, phenomenology, philosophy, social political theory, culture studies, and history of science. Recently, the terms 'cultural imaginary' or 'technological imaginary' have become increasingly common in the field of media and culture studies (#4).

---

personal, but they also have been set up as systems that have been more widely used, such as the thirty-five dance notation systems discussed by Ann Hutchinson Guest (1984; 1989).

In her book *Gods and Robots: Myths, Machines and Ancient Dreams of Technology* (2018), science historian Adrienne Mayor narrates how ancient Greek mythology already imagined robot-like automata and other forms of artificial life. Myths show that imagination can give rise to new ways of knowing, doing, and creating in the real world, and thus, to new paradigms of thought. As a concept, the technological imaginary helps to see the profound entanglement between our imagination and the technological realms that have emerged therefrom. This specific meaning of the imaginary as a concept informed the media archaeological part of my research. My analysis (#5) of motion capture experiments conducted in the late nineteenth century by photography pioneers such as Eadweard Muybridge and Étienne-Jules Marey showed the significant role their work played in the growing belief that empirically capturing movement could reveal an ultimate truth about the nature of human motion, which is still present in motion capture practices today.

The notion of the imaginary can also be traced back (#4) to psychoanalytic theory, in which Jacques Lacan starts using the term ('l'imaginaire') in 1936 to describe the mirror stage in the development of the child in which it learns to identify with the image that it perceives outside of itself, which is a crucial step in the formation of its ego (Lacan [1936] 1966). It is about the ability to render the experience of a body in pieces into a body as a whole (Miller 1988, 54). In response to Lacan, Gilles Deleuze described the imaginary as defined "by games of mirroring, of duplication, of reversed identification and projection, always in the mode of the double" (2004 [1972]).

In my analysis (#5) of dance capture practices, these connotations of the imaginary highlighted the inherent segmentation involved in motion capture, where optical markers divide a 'body in pieces' to reconstruct a virtual body elsewhere based on this input. Digital renderings of motion capture data create 'mirror images' of dancers that may well be recognisable but are simultaneously highly unstable and manipulable as indexical references to the phenomenological bodies they represent. This nature of motion capture settings also influences how dancers perform in such environments, with many reporting that they experience performing *with* motion capture rather than *for* motion capture. This posthuman entanglement of human and technological agents reveals that such settings cannot objectively capture movement in any straightforward way, but rather use various strategies of staging to capture movement. "In this sense", I conclude elsewhere, "motion capture should perhaps better be understood as motion *creation*" (Karreman, forthcoming).[7]

Expanding the method

Concepts always originate from specific fields of knowledge, but their application is not limited to those areas of debate. On the contrary, as Bal proposes, travelling concepts precisely create the conditions for interdisciplinary research. In the previous sections, I explored examples of research that employ concepts from various disciplines, such as philosophy and gender studies, to provide new insights into drag performance and digital dance data. But what if we reversed this approach? How might terms and concepts from dramaturgy and performance studies serve as analytical tools for phenomena outside the performing arts?

A compelling example is found in the article "Dramaturgy for Devices" (2021), where Maaike Bleeker and Marco Rozendaal suggest using concepts from dramaturgy and theatre studies to analyse smart objects. One such object is the Mokkop, a cup designed by Josje van Beusekom to support caregivers of hospital patients (Vermeeren et al. 2014). Visiting loved ones who are gravely ill often involves feelings of fear, uncertainty, sadness, and fatigue. This may also lead to experiences of social isolation. The Mokkop aims to alleviate these challenges by glowing at intervals throughout the day, encouraging caregivers to take a break and connect with others facing similar situations over coffee or tea.

To explain how the Mokkop functions, Bleeker and Rozendaal employ dramaturgical concepts such as 'presence' and 'performativity'. Analysing the Mokkop through the lens of presence as a concept highlights specific design choices made for this smart object. Bleeker and Rozendaal note that in theatre studies "having presence" has been defined as the ability to "captivate the audience" (Pavis 1998, 285).

---

7   An explanation on the element of research identity (#7) is provided in a section on "The identity of the dramaturg-researcher" in "The Motion Capture Imaginary" (Karreman 2017, pp. 14–16).

While the designer of the Mokkop could have used sound or movement to attract the user's attention, opting for soft light creates a gentler approach, particularly in contexts where a patient is resting. When the cup begins to glow, its presence changes, serving as a cue for caregivers to step away, take a break, and recharge.

In this way, the presence of the cup also co-creates the conditions for its performativity, its capacity to change the situation. "The performativity of Mokkop", Bleeker and Rozendaal write, "is the result of a combination of the choice for a cup, the design of the cup, its specific way of performing and the situation in which this happens (including the availability of the coffee machine, the material arrangement of the refreshment room and the presence of more than one caregiver)" (2021, 49). By looking at the Mokkop through the lens of dramaturgical concepts like presence and performativity, this smart object can now be recognised and analysed as an actor or agent capable of effecting changes in both the spatial and social dynamics of its environment.

The understanding that concepts from performance theory provide a valuable perspective for design also underpins the research project Dramaturgy for Devices: Designing Sustained Relationships with Robots and Other Smart Technologies, which is being conducted from 2024 to 2028 at Utrecht University in the Netherlands. This project aims to demonstrate how the performing arts can inform innovative design tools and methods, emphasising the importance of skills and knowledge derived from theatre practice for technological innovation in the field of social robotics (NWO 2024).

In an educational context, this approach is applied in the MA course Expanding Performance at Utrecht University (UU), where students from various arts and humanities MA programmes collaborate with students from the MA Artificial Intelligence programme at Vrije Universiteit Amsterdam (VU) to work on design solutions for human-robot interaction challenges using NAO robots. Drawing on their expertise in performing arts concepts and theories, the UU students contribute to the design process by offering dramaturgical insights, effectively supporting and inspiring the VU students in their work on robot design.[8]

---

8   A selection of final student papers written for this course can be found in the Dramaturgical Aid for Designing Robots (DADeR) database at https://

Suggestions for further reading

Bal has elaborated on her concept of using concepts as methodological tools in several texts, but her book *Travelling Concepts in the Humanities: A Rough Guide* (2002) remains the most comprehensive demonstration of cultural analysis, where each of the chapters in this book is an example of how such an analysis can take shape, using concepts such as framing, image, and mise-en-scène. In her more recent publication, *Moments of Meaning-Making* (2025), Bal presents an abecedarium that explores the key concepts underlying her analytical work.

Bleeker's book *Visuality in the Theatre* (2008) demonstrates how concepts coming from art history ('perspective') and narratology ('focalisation') can be used to create a relational view on how meaning is produced in dance, theatre, and performance.

The edited volume *Concepten en Objecten* ('Concepts and Objects', Bleeker et al. 2009, with chapters in Dutch and English) provides several other examples of concept-based research in the field of performance studies in the Netherlands and Belgium.

Available in open access, *Critical Concepts for the Creative Humanities* (2022) by Iris van der Tuin and Nanna Verhoeff offers a relevant selection of concepts that may inform contemporary interdisciplinary research in the broader field of the humanities, including performance studies. In the introduction to this book, when addressing the criticality of concepts, they observe how analysis can mobilise a concept toward an argument. The concise yet rich entries on concepts as varied as cartography, curation, gesture, randomisation, situatedness, and tracing invite readers to use the book as a source of inspiration during the research design phase.

References

Bal, Mieke. 2002. *Travelling Concepts in the Humanities: A Rough Guide*. University of Toronto Press.

Bal, Mieke. 2006. "Scared to Death." In *A Mieke Bal Reader*, edited by Mieke Bal, 149–68. University of Chicago Press.

Bal, Mieke. 2013. "Imaging Madness: Inter-Ships." *InPrint* 2 (1): 51–70. http://arrow.dit.ie/inp/vol2/iss1/5

Bal, Mieke. 2025. *Moments of Meaning-Making: On Anachronism, Becoming, and Conceptualizing*. Valiz.

Barthes, Roland. (1978) 2005. *The Neutral*. Translated by Rosalind E. Krauss and Denis Hollier. Columbia University Press.

Bleeker, Maaike. 2008. *Visuality in the Theatre: The Locus of Looking*. Palgrave Macmillan. https://doi.org/10.1057/9780230583368

Bleeker, Maaike, Lucia van Heteren, Chiel Kattenbelt and Rob van der Zalm, eds. 2009. *Concepten en Objecten*. Amsterdam University Press. https://library.oapen.org/handle/20.500.12657/35227

Bleeker, Maaike and Marco Rozendaal. 2021. "Dramaturgy for Devices: Theatre as Perspective on the Design of Smart Objects." In *Designing Smart Objects in Everyday Life: Intelligences, Agencies, Ecologies*, edited by Marco C. Rozendaal, Betti Marenko and William Odom. Bloomsbury Press. https://doi.org/10.5040/9781350160156.ch-002

Bois, Yve-Alain, Denis Hollier, Rosalind Krauss and Hubert Damisch. 1998. "A Conversation with Hubert Damisch." *October* 85: 3–17.

de Langen, Marijn. 2022. *Dutch Mime*. Amsterdam University Press and DAS Publishing.

Deleuze, Gilles and Félix Guattari. 1991. *What is Philosophy?* Columbia University Press.

Deleuze, Gilles. [1972] 2004. "How Do We Recognize Structuralism?" In *Desert Islands and Other Texts, 1953–1974*, edited by David Lapoujade, translated by Martin McMahon and Charles J. Stivale. Semiotext(e), pp. 170–92.

Deleuze, Gilles. 1988. *Foucault*. Translated and edited by Seán Hand. University of Minnesota Press.

Foucault, Michel. 1978. *The History of Sexuality: Volume I: An Introduction*. Translated by Robert Hurley. Pantheon Books.

Groot Nibbelink, Liesbeth. 2019. *Nomadic Theatre: Mobilizing Theory and Practice on the European Stage*. Methuen Drama.

Hernandez, Aline. 2020. "Images that Leap in the Dark: Feminicide Photography and Necropolitics of Gender in Contemporary Mexico." Master's thesis, Utrecht University.

Hutchinson Guest, Ann. 1984. *Dance Notation: The Process of Recording Movement on Paper*. Dance Horizons.

Hutchinson Guest, Ann. 1989. *Choreo-Graphics: A Comparison of Dance Notation Systems from the Fifteenth Century to the Present*. Gordon and Breach.

Jang, Soyun. 2024. "To Attune to a Robot Arm: A Moving Body's Perspective of Speculating, Programming, and Dancing with the Robot." Master's thesis, Utrecht University. https://studenttheses.uu.nl/handle/20.500.12932/46703

Karjalainen, Eedi. 2022. "150,000 Ways of Saying Goodbye: Constructing the Space of Ritual Mourning in Digitalised Memorial Sites." Master's thesis, Utrecht University. https://studenttheses.uu.nl/handle/20.500.12932/42871

Karreman, Laura. 2017. "The Motion Capture Imaginary: Digital Renderings of Dance Knowledge." PhD diss., Ghent University. https://www.researchgate.net/publication/316428528_The_Motion_Capture_Imaginary_Digital_renderings_of_dance_knowledge

Karreman, Laura. Forthcoming. "Cultural Dreams of Datafied Bodies: Motion Capture as a Technological Imaginary." In *The Routledge Companion on Performance and Technology*, edited by Maaike Bleeker and Norah Zuniga Shaw. Routledge.

Kuhn, Thomas. 1977. "Objectivity, Value Judgment, and Theory Choice." In *The Essential Tension: Selected Studies in Scientific Tradition and Change*, edited by Thomas Kuhn. University of Chicago Press.

Lacan, Jacques. 1966. *Écrits*. Éditions du Seuil.

Mayor, Adrienne. 2018. *Gods and Robots: Myths, Machines and Ancient Dreams of Technology*. Princeton University Press.

Miller, Jacques-Alain, ed. 1988. *The Seminar of Jacques Lacan. Book 2: The Ego in Freud's Theory and in the Technique of Psychoanalysis 1954–1955*. Translated by Sylvana Tomaselli. Cambridge University Press.

NWO (Dutch Research Council). 2024. "Dramaturgy for Devices." https://www.nwo.nl/en/projects/nwa151822080

Pavis, Patrice. 1998. *Dictionary of the Theatre: Terms, Concepts, and Analysis*. University of Toronto Press.

Performance Studies International. 2024a. *PSi Lexicon*. https://lexicon.psi-web.org/.

Performance Studies International. 2024b. "PSi Lexicon". https://www.psi-web.org/psi-lexicon/

Steinbock, Eliza. 2019. *Shimmering Images: Trans Cinema, Embodiment, and the Aesthetics of Change*. Duke University Press.

Stengers, Isabelle. 1987. *D'une Science à l'Autre: Des Concepts Nomades*. Éditions du Seuil.

van der Tuin, Iris and Nanna Verhoeff. 2022. *Critical Concepts for the Creative Humanities*. Rowman and Littlefield. https://dspace.library.uu.nl/handle/1874/420043

van der Vegt, Chris. 2023. "Hiding in Plain Sight: Shimmering Queer Presence in Sasha Velour's Lip-Sync Performances." Master's thesis, Utrecht University. https://studenttheses.uu.nl/handle/20.500.12932/49949

Vermeeren, A. P., J. van Beusekom, M. C. Rozendaal and E. Giaccardi. 2014. "Design for Complex Persuasive Experiences: Helping Parents of Hospitalized Children Take Care of Themselves." In *Proceedings of the 2014 Conference on Designing Interactive Systems*, 335–44. https://dl.acm.org/doi/10.1145/2598510.2598548

Zwinkels, Elle. 2024. "From Trans* as Impasse to Affective Passing Exploring Gender Identification in and Through Fictional Performance." Master's thesis, Utrecht University. https://studenttheses.uu.nl/handle/20.500.12932/47698

2. Dramaturgical Analysis: A Relational Approach

Liesbeth Groot Nibbelink and Sigrid Merx

Summary

In this contribution, the authors present a relational approach to dramaturgical analysis. Dramaturgical analysis is a particular form of performance analysis, used to examine performances from a dramaturgical perspective, with the aim to highlight and analyse dramaturgical strategies at work in performances, installations, artworks, and other events. This methodology of dramaturgical analysis has been developed in the context of research and teaching at the Department of Media and Culture Studies at Utrecht University, and in response to nearby dramaturgical practices in contemporary theatre and dance. In their approach to dramaturgical analysis, the authors distinguish three planes of dramaturgy, namely: principles of composition, modes of addressing the spectator and ways in which a performance relates to wider social and artistic contexts, while also emphasising the inherent relationality of these aspects. In combining these elements, dramaturgical analysis launches another triad of terms, which supports further inquiry into aspects of spectatorship, situatedness, and how a performance event may deliver a certain 'statement'. This contribution advocates for an understanding of dramaturgy as an extremely useful perspective for analysing not only artistic processes but also societal or even behavioural processes; the proposed approach also supports the analysis of, for instance, the dramaturgy of urban spaces, classrooms, climate conferences, or presidential elections.

Introduction

In this contribution we present a relational approach to dramaturgical analysis, in which we distinguish acts of composition, the address to the spectator and the immanent context as key elements in any performance event.[1] Dramaturgical analysis is a particular form of performance analysis, used to examine performances from a dramaturgical perspective, with the aim to highlight and analyse dramaturgical strategies at work in performances, installations, artworks, and other events. When explaining what a 'dramaturgical perspective' entails, it is helpful to acknowledge from the start that dramaturgy is a multifaceted and somewhat elusive term as it is used for many different activities and processes, at times emphasising the creative making process of theatre or dance while at other times focusing on the structural coherence or artistic strategies of 'finished' work. Historically, dramaturgy is often associated with playwriting or literary research (Turner and Behrndt 2016, 23–29). Looking at mostly European contemporary staging practices, which inform our approach, dramaturgy is not only concerned with the knowledge of composition and storytelling principles, but also with exploring how theatrical means and strategies are put to use to position, situate, or manage the attention of the audience, and how theatre, dance, and performance relate to the 'world at large'. Such layered acts of performance-making then become dramaturgical strategies, in which specific compositional tactics, modes of audience address, and social or artistic contexts that resonate from within a performance collaborate in creating meaning and experience. We look at dramaturgy as an extremely useful perspective for analysing not only artistic processes but also societal or even behavioural processes; we can also analyse, for instance, the dramaturgy of urban spaces, classrooms, climate conferences, or presidential elections.

Within the context of this chapter, we focus on the dramaturgy of performances, installations, or other performative events presented to an audience, and less on the function of dramaturgy as a reflexive component

---

1   This chapter draws on an earlier text in which we describe this method, published in *Forum+*, see Groot Nibbelink and Merx (2021). In this version we have extended the discussion on dramaturgy discourse (in the Context section), kept one out of three brief case studies (in the Demonstration section), and added a new case to demonstrate the method's interdisciplinary potential (in the Expanding the method section).

in artistic making processes—although the creation process can never be isolated from its moment of presentation, of course. Dramaturgy, as we understand it here, concerns the meaningful coherence of all theatrical means employed, of their organisation and structure in time and space, and how their interplay generates meaning and experience. 'Theatrical means' is an umbrella term which includes the multiple methods and tools for creating theatre and dance, referring to the use of bodies, spaces, objects, text, media, gesture, acting, or movement styles, light and sound design, music, cameras, screens and other technologies, and more. Dramaturgy revolves around asking questions such as: how is a work composed or constructed, and what theatrical means does it use? How does a performative event engage its audience? How does a performance relate to the 'outside' world, that is, to everyday life, to historical events or actual phenomena, to anything that is present within the theatre but not 'of' the theatre? Dramaturgy may be a slippery and multidimensional term, yet it can perhaps be boiled down to a single question, once asked by artist Edit Kaldor: "Does it make sense?" The question is itself multifaceted, subsequently inquiring into the inner logic, structure, or cohesiveness of a given event (does the performance make a point in a convincing way?); to what is its purpose (what is this text, action, or gesture trying to say or do?); and to how a work engages the senses (what does this performance make you see, feel, hear, or smell?).

Our methodology of dramaturgical analysis has been developed in the context of our work as dramaturgs, teachers and theatre and performance scholars at the Department of Media and Culture studies at Utrecht University. In our approach to dramaturgical analysis, we distinguish three components, or planes of dramaturgy, namely: principles of composition, modes of addressing the spectator and ways in which a performance may relate to a wider social and artistic context. Composition, briefly put, entails the arrangement of space, time, and action, and the employment of all theatrical means available to create and activate that arrangement. Such aspects of composition may generate specific meanings or experiences when presented to a spectator, through varying modes of audience address and responses to that address, and through the different ways that sociocultural or artistic contexts reverberate within the performative event. Our triad is fundamentally relational; dramaturgical analysis necessarily pays attention to all three components. One cannot discuss one component without evoking the other two.

Our take on dramaturgy is closely connected to the innovative and experimental Dutch and Flemish theatre and dance practice that surrounds us—which also is home to many international makers—and that inspires our work. This practice can largely be characterised as postdramatic, which explains why audience address and spectatorship play a prominent role in our approach. It is precisely the relationship between the stage and the spectator (who sometimes can be found *on* the stage) that is a key theme in postdramatic theatre (Lehmann 2006). This is not to say that our approach only suits a postdramatic take on theatre; rather, we wish to present an inclusive approach, as our dramaturgical analysis accommodates both conventional and experimental work.

Context | Dramaturgical analysis—a brief positioning

Dramaturgy has been a topic of debate since its inception in the eighteenth century, when the German playwright and artistic consultant G. E. Lessing wrote *Hamburgische Dramaturgie* (1769), advocating innovations in play composition, repertoire, institutional politics, and art criticism. Histories of dramaturgy often jump-step from Lessing via Bertolt Brecht's dramaturgical research in the early twentieth century, to 1960s innovations in theatre and dance towards the emergence of 'open', process-based, or 'new' dramaturgies in the 1990s. This is not the space to reproduce that history here, but we do notice, similar to Cathy Turner and Synne Behrndt in their informative and revised edition of *Dramaturgy and Performance* (2016), a remarkable increase of studies on dramaturgy, both in theatre and dance, in the first decades of the twenty-first century, as is evidenced by publications such as Gritzner et al. (2009), Trencsényi and Cochrane (2014), Hansen and Callison (2015), Profeta (2015), Romanska (2015), Trencsényi (2015), Turner and Behrndt (2007, 2016), Eckersall et al. (2017), Georgelou et al. (2017), Bleeker (2023), Eckersall (2024), or Lotker (2024). Many of these studies consider the changing role of dramaturgy on par with innovations in contemporary theatre, dance, and performance, where the (postdramatic) shift away from theatre as the staging of texts has paved the way for post-mimetic, process-based, and devised forms of theatre-making, with ample attention for the societal context, technological innovations, collaborative work, and other developments that all profoundly impact the practice and theory of dramaturgy.

Some of these publications focus on the creative process, such as Katalin Trencsényi (2015) or *The Practice of Dramaturgy: Working on Actions in Performance* (2017), where the editors Konstantina Georgelou, Efrosini Protopapa, and Danae Theodoridou develop an understanding of dramaturgy as a "catalytic type of operation" (2017, 39), identifying three key principles in inspiring creative processes, namely 'mobilizing questions', 'alienating', and 'commoning'. Other works pivot around the term 'new dramaturgy' to account for how post-representational theatre and work-in-progress methods have altered dramaturgical practice. Trencsényi and Bernadette Cochrane use the term, for instance, to identify the fluctuating role of the dramaturg who, rather than a distant and critical 'third eye', becomes an involved facilitator and curator in process-based, intercultural, and interdisciplinary processes, who helps negotiate cultural values and knowledges. In the book *New Media Dramaturgy: Performance, Media and New Materialism*, the 'new' primarily refers to how the incorporation of technology and non-human matter changes theatre making processes (Eckersall et al. 2017, 4–11).

In *Doing Dramaturgy: Thinking Through Practice* (2023), Maaike Bleeker prefers the idea of a paradigm shift to the use of the term 'new dramaturgy', as new developments in theatre making also invite a reconsideration of how we understand the term across both 'old' and 'new' forms of dramaturgy (2023, 3). In this book, Bleeker brings together theory and practice, thinking and making, process and product: "Rather than opposing thinking and making, theory and practice, we better look at what kind of thinking making is, and how thinking and making, theory and practice, may mutually inform and inspire each other" (2023, 10). By means of the concept of 'reverse engineering' and in relation to several case studies, Bleeker presents dramaturgy as a process of engaging with performances as constructions, which emerge as the result of intricate processes of choice-making, with how these constructions work and what they do to audiences.

Along this paradigm shift one can also notice an increasing attention for dance dramaturgy (Profeta 2015, Hansen and Callison 2015), which can partially be explained by dance practices growing closer to the attention for movement, space, time, and the body in postdramatic theatre and new materialist dramaturgies, but which also springs from choreography's increasing interest in collaborative, participatory, and self-reflexive creation processes (Noeth 2015, 415). With the rise of non-hierarchical, research-informed creative processes, contemporary dance dramaturgy increasingly engages with scholarly discourses, drawing upon fields such as cultural memory, materiality, or somatic knowledge (Hansen and Callison, xi).

Central to our relational approach to dramaturgical analysis is the emergence of the term 'relational dramaturgies'. The term is used, however, in diverse contexts. In some instances, it specifically refers to relations with the audience (Boenisch 2014), while in others it highlights collaboratively generated and site-responsive practices (Pewny, Callens and Coppens 2014). Our understanding of relationality is more theoretically grounded, inspired by the triadic thinking of scholars such as Henri Lefebvre (1991) and Chiel Kattenbelt (2018) and the network-oriented frameworks of poststructuralist and new materialist theorists, including Gilles Deleuze and Félix Guattari (2004) and Jane Bennett (2010). Our approach also affiliates with Mike Pearson and Michael Shanks' conceptualisation of dramaturgy-as-assemblage (2001), but foremost relies on our own (field) experience.

While some studies highlight the close connection between dramaturgical practice and performance analysis, or emphasise an artwork's relation to broader societal contexts (e.g. Turner and Behrndt 2016, 29–41), the majority of reflections on dramaturgy do not provide concrete methods for dramaturgical analysis.[2] As most texts on dramaturgy are not intended as methodologies for dramaturgical analysis, it is not surprising that they refrain from offering any systematic

---

2   An exception, perhaps, is Maaike Bleeker (2023) who introduces a six-question model aimed at operationalising a dramaturgical mode of looking, drawing on Elinor Fuch's "EF's Visit to a Small Planet" as well as Marianne van Kerkhoven's concepts of micro- and macro-dramaturgy.

models. Our approach, which may be understood as a dramaturgical take on performance analysis, occupies a space between established models of performance analysis and dramaturgy studies. In both fields of inquiry, scholarly discussions tend to concentrate on one or two key components (composition, spectator, context), whereas we argue for the value of addressing all three components in an integrated manner—which is why we put emphasis on the relationality of our approach. Many performance analysis handbooks—particularly the structuralist and semiotic models that predominated in the European context during the 1980s and 1990s—place a strong emphasis on compositional aspects of theatre texts or performances. These models aim to teach students how to systematically observe and analyse the various theatrical elements and the relationships between them as signifying systems (e.g. Aston and Savona 1991; Fischer-Lichte 1993, Pfister 1991, Whitmore 1994, Pavis 2003).[3] Less attention, however, is given to audience address or to the process of moving from such a systematic analysis to a motivated interpretation of a work's dramaturgy—specifically, how particular compositional strategies and organising principles relate to, or engage with, broader societal and cultural contexts.

How to

A dramaturgical triad: composition, spectator, context

In our dramaturgical analysis we distinguish between three planes of dramaturgy.[4] These planes relate to, respectively, matters of composition, ways in which the spectator is being addressed in or through this composition and the social and artistic context immanent within a work (see Fig. 2.1). These planes continuously inflect and interfere with each other. In this section, we will briefly describe and discuss these planes, demonstrating their use later in the essay.

---

[3] Pavis attends to performance-as-process but his methodology of analysing transitional 'vectors of performance' still relies on a separation of (sign) systems and hardly addresses matters of dramaturgy.

[4] We opt for 'plane' rather than 'layer' to evoke a sense of spatiality. For us, a 'plane' indicates a domain, area, or 'denkpiste' as the Flemish so aptly put it; a 'thinking arena' for playing around with ideas and observations, which is open to interference by other planes.

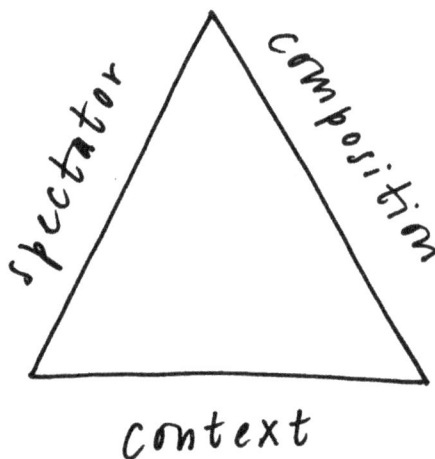

Fig. 2.1 Planes of dramaturgy: composition, spectator, context. ©Liesbeth Groot Nibbelink & Sigrid Merx.

The first plane, that of 'composition', comprises all the tactics and strategies used to create and structure a performance, organising and arranging space and time so that the performance is carried across from beginning 'a' to endpoint 'z'. Such strategies may be derived from certain creation principles or methods deployed for generating text or movement material, (interdisciplinary) teamwork dynamics, or preparatory research. This compositional component is often addressed in dramaturgy studies. In *Dramaturgy and Performance*, for instance, Turner and Behrndt refer to composition as the "internal fabric" or texture of the performance event (2016, 4). Equating dramaturgy with architecture, they observe that both elicit structural coherence. Drawing on the writings of architect Bernhard Tschumi, they note that dramaturgy, like architecture, involves the "deliberate deployment of structure in order to provoke or enable live events" (6). Such a take on composition accommodates traditional as well as non-conventional forms, from well-made plays to conceptual dance. We can think of Aristotelian or classical plot structures, or the fragmentary episodic structures of many absurdist plays, the repetitive patterns of minimalist dance or sequences organised through chance or algorithms. These structures and organisational principles are meaningful in themselves; they often suggest a certain worldview, for instance teleological or, on the contrary, fragmentary, or without a centre. Marianne van Kerkhoven qualifies this internal structure as the "soul" of the performance (1994a, 7). Structural principles like (a)symmetry, mirroring, play-within-the-play, or seriality are equally significant. The compositional plane also pertains to the means and tools with which a work is made and staged, whether theatrical means (like acting or movement styles, proxemics, text, objects, costumes, set, sound, music, or lighting), or 'extra-theatrical' elements (such as film, social media, mobile phones, VR headsets, etc.).[5]

The second plane of dramaturgical analysis pertains to the spectator and to specific modes of spectatorial address. Spectators, whether in groups or as individuals, do not just look at or participate in a performance. They are addressed in particular ways and are positioned through that address: perhaps they are confronted, warmly welcomed, or aroused, treated as guests or as outsiders, as sensitive organisms, as democratic citizens, and so on. We focus on the single spectator rather than the collective audience, as our primary interest lies in examining spectatorial address rather than audience reception research.

As previously noted, the address to the spectator is seldom examined in a systematic manner. Although valuable for the detailed analysis of composition principles, semiotic models prove less suitable for analysing how a composition produces specific forms of spectatorial address. These models do acknowledge the relation between performance and the spectator yet often reduce the spectator to a decoding 'recipient'. From the 1990s onward, post-semiotic theory began to conceptualise the act of spectating as an active, embodied form of participation in the process of meaning-making (Boenisch 2014). However, when it comes to analysing these new dramaturgies, we align with Helen Freshwater's critical observation that post-semiotic and phenomenological approaches often rely heavily on the affective and emotional experience of the analyst—and regularly fall short in actively connecting the performance to its broader social context (2009, 23–25). Our focus, instead, lies on how the spectator's experience is deliberately structured and on the dramaturgical strategies through which particular sensations and meaning-making processes are invited.

Many genres and theatre conventions have developed specific modes of address. Think of Naturalism, Absurdism, or classical ballet,

---

5   This brief inventory presumes some basic experience in play or performance analysis. Readers unacquainted with this could consult handbooks such as Fischer-Lichte (2014), Balme (2008), Pavis (2003), Pfister (1991).

the fourth-wall convention or the aside, the use of dramatic irony or Brecht's defamiliarisation techniques. In *Visuality in the Theatre* (2008), Bleeker lucidly analyses the function of address in the theatre. 'Address' means that spectators are invited to adopt a particular point of view from which to look at what is being presented on stage. Bleeker terms this presented viewpoint the 'subject of vision', to be distinguished from the subject seeing and the performance event as the subject seen (2008, 80). Bleeker's subject of vision does not imply that spectators (the subjects seeing) always accept or identify with the presented or implicated perspective (the subject of vision) in the performance (the subject seen). In fact, Bleeker's theory helps to explain precisely how experiences of frustration, annoyance, or displacement arise from the tension between the subject seeing and the subject of vision.

The plane of 'context' is the third building block in our approach. Obviously, performances do not exist in a vacuum. In trying to understand and interpret what performances communicate to their audiences and how they do so, a dramaturgical analysis attends to the social and artistic contexts in which a work is made and embedded. 'Societal context' is an umbrella term for the social, cultural, economic, or political world(s) that somehow resonate within the work. Such broader contexts invariably reverberate within a work—even when they are obscured, or when a performance pretends not to. This resonance is also alluded to by Alan Read, in *Theatre, Intimacy and Engagement* (2008), when he describes the relationship between artworks and the 'outer world' as two surfaces, characterising their connection as "the crossing and re-crossing of intensities across and between these surfaces" (2008, 37). Another 'intensity' moving across that surface is the specific artistic biotope within which a work is created. This artistic context works its way through an artwork as well. This context or biotope refers to a given artist's oeuvre, preferences for certain styles, sources, or working methods, sets of design principles or parameters identified in specific creation processes, recurring themes or motifs, affinities with other artists, thinkers, political ideas, working conditions, and so on. All these elements add up to a work's communicative potential and may inspire certain interpretations.

We argue that these contexts are as integral to the dramaturgy of a performance as compositional elements or modes of spectatorial address and are therefore immanent within the work itself. Kerkhoven's famous distinction between 'minor' and 'major' dramaturgy is helpful here. 'Minor dramaturgy', for Van Kerkhoven, is the dramaturgical work that situates itself around a concrete artwork, referring to "that zone, that structural circle, which lies in and around a production" (1994b). Within our framework, minor dramaturgy primarily aligns with the planes of composition and spectatorial address. However, as Van Kerkhoven continues, "around the production lies the theatre and around the theatre lies the city and around the city, as far as we can see, lies the whole world and even the sky and all its stars" (1994b). This is what she terms 'major dramaturgy', which for us activates the plane of context. For Van Kerkhoven, the circles of minor and major dramaturgy are inseparable: "The walls that link all these circles together are made of skin, they have pores, they breathe" (1994b). This is why we argue for a relational approach that allows for analysing the interaction between work, spectator, and world.

Although we distinguish between these three planes, we ultimately wish to emphasise their relationality. A performance event always involves the triad of composition, spectator, and context, and so, necessarily, must a dramaturgical analysis. As Van Kerkhoven aptly points out, "a production comes alive through its interaction, through its audience, and through what is going on outside its own orbit" (1994b). Similarly, dramaturgical analysis comes alive through actively tracing such interactions. We envision the three sides of our triangle as flexible bases from which one can start the analysis at any point, facilitating a movement back and forth between these planes of meaning-making.

Connecting the vectors: spectatorship, statements, situatedness

Exploring the different sides of the triangle creates different perspectives from which to analyse a performance dramaturgically. Which starting point to choose and which plane to emphasise depends both on what the performance itself seems to foreground and on the position of the analyst-researcher, i.e. what it is you want to show in the analysis. Moving between these planes, our triadic approach helps to discuss, respectively, elements of spectatorship, the possible statements conveyed, and matters of situatedness (see Fig. 2.2).

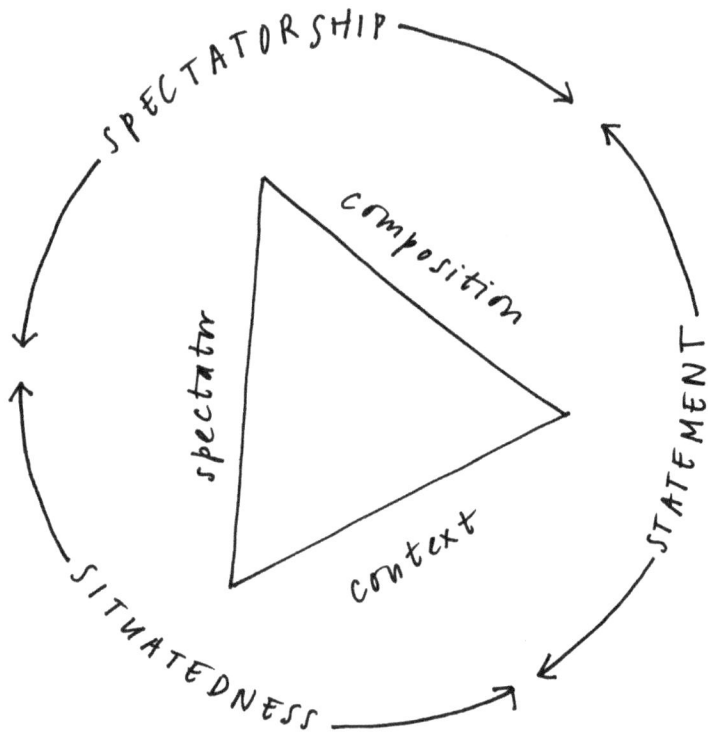

Fig. 2.2 Connecting the vectors: spectatorship, statements, situatedness ©Liesbeth Groot Nibbelink & Sigrid Merx.

When emphasis is on the address to the spectator, this often leads to an analysis of spectatorship that can reveal how the performance constructs a position for the spectator and, importantly, how spectatorship itself becomes a theme in the work. In the previously mentioned *Visuality in the Theatre*, Bleeker distinguishes two often recurring modes of audience address. 'Theatricality', on the one hand, is about rendering visible how theatre addresses and positions a spectator, illuminating how the means of theatre are deployed to present a specific argument and to expose how the spectator is actively involved in processes of meaning-making. 'Absorption', on the other hand, is the mode of address in which the spectator is drawn into the world on stage, precisely because the traces of mediation are erased (2008, 21). These modes are not fixed or static phenomena, they are two poles on the same axis of spectatorship. They can alternate within a performance or even appear to be present simultaneously, as is in the case in *Phobiarama* (2017), a performance installation by Dutch theatre maker Dries Verhoeven. *Phobiarama* is conceived of as a twenty-first-century haunted house which enquires into collective social fears. Seated in small carriages, and driving around in a pitch-dark space, the spectators are startled by unexpected sounds and bodies of various kinds which suddenly appear. They are alternatively confronted by media footage full of populist rhetoric, hairy bears, creepy clowns, and ultimately, and rather unexpectedly, muscular men of colour, of various cultural backgrounds. Much of Verhoeven's work is about spectatorship, as he confronts spectators with their own biases and prejudices. On the hand the spectators are absorbed in the installation, casted in the role of anxious visitors, feeling fear and enjoying fearing at the same time. In this sense, *Phobiarama* fully embraces the logic of a haunted house. On the other hand, the work's composition (the space and audience seating, the logic of the haunted house, the order of appearances) lays bare *how* this sense of fear is being produced, which illuminates the work's theatrically.[6]

In this act of disclosure, *Phobiarama* can also be read as a firm societal critique, which is an example of how performances can express or present a certain statement. By using the word 'statement', we certainly do not aim for extracting a clear-cut 'message' or a single-focused meaning from an artwork. On the contrary, a statement can be many things and can take numerous shapes. As previously mentioned, a performance event always relates to an outside world, as both a reflection *of* and a reflection *on* that outside world. Van Kerkhoven once beautifully described how the composition of a work is "a provisional or possible arrangement which the artist imposes on those elements he gathers from a reality that appears to him chaotic" (1994a). The theatrical world of a performance thus emerges as the result of an artist's attempt to work his or her way through and make

---

6   See for a much more nuanced and detailed analysis, Merx (2018) or Groot Nibbelink and Merx (2021).

sense of the outside world. In doing so, a 'statement' is conveyed, that is, the performance affirms, questions, or criticises that world, or maybe proposes an alternative. *Phobiarama* can be seen, for instance, as a dissection of how fear of 'foreigners' is created and manipulated through populist rhetoric. In our view, answering the question of what the performance 'says' or is trying to do, and how this is achieved, is crucial to dramaturgical analysis. This is not just a matter of reflecting on how a performance thematically relates to and references a social context, be it a contemporary or historical one. It is equally relevant to explore how the artistic context shapes the work, and how a choice for certain genres, styles, or working methods may reveal specific perspectives, strategies, assumptions, or propositions.

Previously, we remarked that the outside world always reverberates within the work. This 'echoing' or interference pertains to the maker as well as the spectator who engages with that performance. Dramaturgical analysis, therefore, also facilitates inquiries into the situatedness of both the work and the spectator. Situatedness acknowledges that knowledge and expertise is not universal but precisely particular, informed by one's specific local and social position and circumstance. The term 'situated knowledges' was coined by feminist scholar Donna Haraway, to question biases and claims of objectivity or neutrality, accounting for a pluralism of knowledges instead (Haraway 1988; Rogowska-Stangret 2018). Widely used in feminist debates thereafter, the term is equally relevant for theatre, dance, and performance. Not only makers but also spectators are situated in specific social, economic, and political contexts; they are defined by race, ethnicity, gender, age, social class, and physical capacities, which allow or limit each spectator to act within these contexts. Obviously, situatedness has an impact on how spectators make sense of a performance and how they look at the statements a performance may convey. A spectator to *Phobiarama*, who involuntarily has been subjected to being seen as a 'foreigner' despite having lived in the Netherlands all their life, will likely experience the performance rather differently than when this has not been the case. Subsequently, we can start to see how it is not at all self-evident that a spectator is willing or able to identify with the point of view or 'subject of vision' offered by the performance. We can imagine how radical differences between the 'conceived' subject position constructed by the work and the 'lived' subject position of the spectator can produce tensions that become tangible and therefore meaningful in the performance event. Or, alternatively, how being able to fully identify with a presented point of view might produce a sense of empowerment, especially when this viewpoint relates to a minority perspective. A performance thus can become active as a political agent. Dramaturgical analysis may help render visible such politics of perception.

Demonstration | Radical re-enactment in Florentina Holzinger's *Apollon*

Now that we have outlined the core components of relational dramaturgical analysis, let's put these tools to work, in a brief analysis of Florentina Holzinger's dance performance *Apollon* (2017), which is a radical re-enactment of George Balanchine's ballet *Apollon Musagète* from 1928. Balanchine's ballet tells the story of the young Apollo who becomes a god after meeting the three Muses of Poetry, Mime and Dance. Balanchine's ballet marked an important point in the tradition of classical ballet in the United States, as it challenged then-current views on ballet technique and movement (Joseph 2002). Holzinger, an Austrian-born performance artist and choreographer with a background in sports, specifically challenges the gender roles in Balanchine's ballet, reclaiming space for the female bodies in the ballet. As a re-enactment, the performance invites an analysis of how the context of the original ballet and its particular gender codes resonates within compositional choices, which is a starting point for exploring how Holzinger's re-contextualisation of Balanchine's ballet ultimately proposes a radically different view on femininity, a statement which provokes spectators to think about what they believe femininity is and confronting them, inevitably, with their own situatedness.

Starting with the plane of composition, Balanchine's *Apollon Musagète* depicts how Apollo, through his encounter with the Muses, discovers and takes up his calling as god of music, evolving into being their mentor in the arts. At the end of the ballet, he humbly assumes his new stature and ascends Mount Olympus. The Muses in Balanchine's composition are dainty waif-like figures, elegant and beautiful, dancing around Apollo like he is the centre of their world. They balance upon his muscular arms and are stripped of their unique personalities as they march identically behind him to the final balancing pose on the staircase to Mount Olympus. Balanchine allegedly said that it is the woman's task to inspire the man with her beauty, and he is commonly seen as a choreographer who glorifies women in his dances—albeit from a clearly patriarchal point of view. His choreographies literally stretched ballerinas' bodies to new physical extremes, which is why his work has been qualified as "sadomasochistic" (Daly 1987, 8).

Against this artistic context, in Holzinger's version of the ballet, Apollo and the three Muses are replaced by six naked female performers, all equally representing Apollo and the Muses—to the point that the roles collapse into one another. The strict hierarchy of the original has given way to a radical equality of collective 'sisterhood', turning the original inner logic of the work upside down. In the composition of this "freak show" (according to one of the performers) notions of strength, beauty, and technique are all radically redefined in a wild mix of short scenes that reference a gamut of artistic and cultural contexts, including fitness culture, bodybuilding, Western movies, pornography, bull fights, and body art. The performers shamelessly and confidently showcase their naked bodies and ironically indulge in performing male stereotypes: working on a six-pack, playing a cowboy, riding a rodeo bull. These scenes are interrupted by short re-enactments of movement sequences from the original ballet, including dancing *en pointe*. The manifestations of what a woman can do and achieve with her body in Holzinger's version are diverse, ranging from impressive, to daring, absurd, carnal, and banal—but certainly none of it qualifies as what Balanchine considered aesthetically pleasing or beautiful. Fuelled by this emancipatory, societal context, the performance playfully cracks open the role and technique Balanchine (or ballet) etched out for the ballerina and gives the performers the freedom to present their bodies and their skills radically differently.

According to dance critic Fransien van der Putt, more than simply critiquing Balanchine's sadomasochism or the patriarchal order, *Apollon* seems to want to do away with female masochism as well, that is, the passive suffering of patriarchy by women (van der Putt 2017). And indeed, the performance makes a powerful statement about how female suffering and pain can be transformed into a source of power and strength, to be enjoyed. The actions clearly offer the performers a kind of pleasure which also informs the performance's take on spectatorship. It is precisely because of that pleasure, and the performers' ease and self-awareness on stage, that this performance forces spectators to consider what they feel or think while watching these women. Is their (the women's) pleasure also the spectator's? Are these indeed Muses, inspiring and empowering role models of femininity? Or the opposite? Does the spectator feel empowered, intrigued, shocked, appalled? Spectators thus are invited to reflect on their own responses to the performance.

What *Apollon* might mean to evoke in the spectator is very much dependent on the spectator's situatedness. The performance makes an active appeal, confronting each spectator through its extreme provocations, triggering immediate and uncensored responses (people applaud, walk out, scream, shut their eyes, become nauseous, laugh, sigh, etc.). Because the feminine world on stage is not presented as one that is up for debate or discussion but as a reality, and since it is so clear that the performers truly don't care about what the audience thinks about them and do not ask for either positive or negative judgment or in fact any sort of identification, the spectators are thrown back on themselves and their sensations—leaving nothing more than their own situatedness as the context within which they need to come to terms with what they are seeing. Classical ballet fans may think it outrageous, those critical of patriarchy may embrace it, visitors who tend not to like provocation may be pleasantly surprised by the omni-present humour, followers of Holzinger's work may recognise her style, and so on. Situatedness is thus not always contingent upon concrete locations or sites, but foremost on being embedded in specific socio-cultural environments.

Fig. 2.3 Thomas J. Price, *Moments Contained* (2023) Rotterdam ©Lex Prummel.

Expanding the method | Dramaturgy in public space

As indicated in the introduction, dramaturgical analysis can easily be expanded beyond the theatre. To demonstrate this, we will briefly discuss a work of art in public space, and analyse *Moments Contained* (2022), a sculpture by Thomas James Price of a young woman of colour, dressed casually, placed on the square in front of Rotterdam Central Station. Price is known for his large bronze sculptures of Black contemporary figures he calls 'everymen' and 'everywomen'. They present fictional characters. His work engages with politics of representation and the dismantling of power structures in society as well as in the arts.

Starting with aspects of composition, the scale, pose, appearance, and site-specificity of the sculpture call for attention. The sculpture is larger than life, nearly four meters tall, made of black bronze, with a soft-shiny coating. Yet, in spite of the scale, her presence is modest. The girl is not standing on a pedestal, but on the same level as the onlookers. It is not suggested in any way that she is more special or important than we are.

At the same time, she is huge. Precisely this combination of modesty and scale triggers questions about who or what is worth to take up space and to attract attention, which already points forward to aspects of spectatorship and statement. In a short online report on the making of the sculpture, Price remarks: "The scale is to challenge our current understandings of monuments, to critique this idea of status and value within society: who gets to be seen, to be represented" (Price 2022).

To return to compositional elements, also in relation to the address to the spectator, her appearance and pose are remarkable too. The young woman is casually dressed, wearing a T-shirt, tracksuit bottoms, and a pair of sneakers. Indeed, she is an 'everywoman'. There is nothing spectacular about her. Many people who have seen her characterise her as "soft" and "chill" and "recognisable"—which Price also explicitly aims for. People like to take selfies with her, lean against her, or mimic her pose.[7] She stands still, her pose seemingly relaxed, hands in her pockets, self-contained, precisely as the title of the work suggests. She is just there, with a sense of self-evidence: why should she not be here? Yet this pose is an important steppingstone to address aspects of situatedness, which calls upon the plane of context as well. Self-containment, for a person of colour in (Western) public space, is not at all evident. In an artist talk, Price explains how Black people are mostly cultured to laugh and to act obligingly, to show they are harmless, civil, unarmed, unthreatening.[8] In an online, two-part essay entitled "Operatic stillness/Unbothered, still" (2023), Simone Zeefuik, an Afro-Dutch writer and cultural programmer, points to the preciousness of seeing a woman who is busy with herself, not paying attention to others, which she beautifully describes as 'unbotheredness'. She quotes a 'twenty-something' attending the placement ceremony who remarks: "It is so nice to see that we can also just chill, that we don't always have to engage with whatever seeks our attention and demands something from us" (Zeefuik 2023b). Zeefuik reports on the many tears and other emotional responses flowing amongst the participants in the ceremony, as they finally feel recognised. She adds herself that "it's exactly because

---

7   See for an impression the footage available at https://www.sculptureinternationalrotterdam.nl/collectie/moments-contained/
8   Thomas J. Price, Artist Talk at Kunsthal Rotterdam, moderated by Simone Zeefuik, 6 October 2024.

she's not looking at anyone that I know we're seen. Not watched but understood in our desires to see ourselves in the sceneries of the cities that we're part of" (2023a).

The site-specificity of the urban environment is also an aspect of situatedness here. Many state that a statue of a Black body was long due in a multicultural city like Rotterdam, a bustling port city where 55 percent of the population has migrant origins—especially placed so centrally as on the busy square in front of the Central Station. Zeefuik refers to the work as "a highly anticipated marker on a map that's still too blank" (2023b). Rotterdam is known for its extensive art collection in public space and has a tradition of 'anti-monuments'. Although Price purposely refers to his works as sculptures rather than monuments, *Moments Contained* too asks questions about what is deemed important or who 'deserves' a monument—making us aware that our public space is mostly occupied by statues of once-powerful men.

The sculpture raised quite some debate, including negative responses. One that attracted much attention was a column by white publicist Rosanne Hertzberger, who called the statue 'insulting' because "this young woman has not achieved anything" (Hertzberger 2023, our translation). She also critiqued its inherent activism: "Just being a woman, having a disability, wearing a headscarf, a dark skin colour, or preferably a combination of these is enough to be hoisted on the shield, and especially in the cultural sector" (2023). This comment sits across the axis of spectatorship and situatedness. It implicates that statues or monuments ask for reflection on what is seen and who deserves to be seen (spectatorship). It also presents a rather biased and also privileged answer to those questions, namely that only people who have "achieved" something are entitled to receive attention (situatedness).

Despite Herzberger's complaints, this young woman is here to stay, and she is not going anywhere soon. For many this is more than hopeful, which brings us to a close with some remarks on the statements that *Moments Contained* brings about. The sculpture is about recognisability, about representation in public space; it raises discussions of who deserves a monument. The sculpture has also become a physical and symbolic marker for anti-slavery or racial injustice demonstrations,[9] and played an

---

[9] The sculpture was the starting point for a demonstration against court ruling in the case of Sanda Dia, a Black young man who died in 2018 after a brutal hazing

important role in rejecting and rethinking Western arts standards of size, scale, materiality, and subject matter. We call upon Zeefuik once more: "When you think statues are about status, grandeur and value ... and you believe that the honour of your awe must never be bestowed upon a young, Black woman wearing casual clothing and sneakers ... yet she still appears, refusing to give you even a fraction of the attention that she put into those baby hairs ... mad things rearrange" (2023a).[10]

Suggestions for further reading

A work fully in tune with actual developments in contemporary theatre is Bleeker's *Doing Dramaturgy: Thinking Through Theatre* (2023), which draws on case-studies and interviews with makers working with digital technology, choreographic, plant-based and post-humanist thinking, and much more. Where Bleeker explicitly focuses on the dramaturgy as a practice of making, in the extensive *The Routledge Companion to Dramaturgy* (2015), edited by Magda Romanska, the emphasis is on the (many) professional roles of a dramaturg in an increasingly diverse field, while also attending to subgenres such as devised and collaborative processes.

For those readers eager to get a 'view from the ground', Katherine Profeta's *Dramaturgy in Motion: At Work on Dance and Movement Performance* (2015) provides delightful reading. Although explicitly targeting a US context, the book gives an insightful introduction to the work of a (dance) dramaturge, as Profeta generously shares many rehearsal room stories, while her professional experience springs from every page. For a wider overview of developments in dance dramaturgy, featuring many prominent dance studies scholars, Pil Hansen and Darcey Callison's *Dance Dramaturgy: Modes of Agency, Awareness and Engagement* (2015) is a good starting point. Of particular interest is the attention for 'dramaturgical agency', as agency is located not only in individual dancers but also in-between creative collaborations, in task-based improvisation, and other action-based systems.

---

he had to endure to join a Belgium student society. Currently it also marks the start of a walking tour inspired by anti-slavery writer Anton de Kom.

10 For a rich and moving account of the many statements this sculpture may convey, we warmly recommend reading Zeefuik's two-part essay "Operatic stillness/ Unbothered, still" (2023) in full.

References

Aston, Elaine and George Savona. 1991. *Theatre as Sign System: A Semiotics of Text and Performance*. Routledge. https://doi.org/10.4324/9781315002576

Balme, Christopher B. 2008. *The Cambridge Introduction to Theatre Studies*. Cambridge University Press. https://doi.org/10.1017/CBO9780511817021

Bennett, Jane. 2010. *Vibrant Matter: A Political Ecology of Things*. Duke University Press. https://doi.org/10.2307/j.ctv111jh6w

Bleeker, Maaike. 2008. *Visuality in the Theatre: The Locus of Looking*. Palgrave Macmillan. https://doi.org/10.1057/9780230583368

Bleeker, Maaike. 2023. *Doing Dramaturgy: Thinking Through Practice*. Palgrave Macmillan. https://doi.org/10.1007/978-3-031-08303-7

Boenisch, Peter. 2014. "Acts of Spectating: The Dramaturgy of the Audience's Experience in Contemporary Theatre." *New Dramaturgy: International Perspectives on Theory and Practice*, edited by Katalin Trencsényi and Bernadette Cochrane, 225–41. Bloomsbury. https://doi.org/10.5040/9781408177075.ch-015

Daly, Ann. 1987. "The Balanchine Woman: Of Hummingbirds and Channel Swimmers." *The Drama Review* 31 (1): 8–21. https://doi.org/10.2307/1145763

Deleuze, Gilles and Félix Guattari. 2004. *A Thousand Plateaus: Capitalism and Schizophrenia*. Translated and introduced by Brian Massumi. Continuum.

Eckersall, Peter, Helena Grehan and Edward Scheer. 2017. *New Media Dramaturgy: Performance, Media and New Materialism*. Palgrave Macmillan. https://doi.org/10.1057/978-1-137-55604-2

Eckersall, Peter. 2024. *Dramaturgy to Make Visible: The Legacies of New Dramaturgy for Politics and Performance in Our Times*. Routledge. https://doi.org/10.4324/9781003163879

Fischer-Lichte, Erika. 2014. *The Routledge Introduction to Theatre and Performance Studies*. Routledge. https://doi.org/10.4324/9780203068731

Fischer-Lichte, Erika. 1992. *The Semiotics of Theater*. Translated by Jeremy Gaines and Doris L. Jones. Indiana University Press. https://doi.org/10.1017/S0307883300019623

Freshwater, Helen. 2009. *Theatre & Audiences*. Palgrave Macmillan.

Georgelou, Konstantina, Efrosini Protopapa and Danae Theodoridou, eds. 2016. *The Practice of Dramaturgy: Working on Actions in Performance*. Valiz.

Gritzner, Karoline, Patrick Primavesi and Heike Roms, eds. 2009. *Performance Research: A Journal of the Performing Arts* 14 (3): On Dramaturgy.

Hansen, Pil, and Darcey Callison, eds. 2015. *Dance Dramaturgy: Modes of Agency, Awareness and Engagement*. Palgrave Macmillan. https://doi.org/10.1057/9781137373229

Haraway, Donna. 1988. "Situated Knowledges: The Science Question in Feminism and the Privilege of Partial Perspective." *Feminist Studies* 14: 575–99.

Hertzberger, Rosanne. 2023. "Het standbeeld van een jonge, zwarte vrouw op Nikes in Rotterdam is een belediging." *NRC*, 3 June.

Joseph, Charles M. 2002. *Stravinsky and Balanchine: A Journey of Invention*. Yale University Press. https://doi.org/10.12987/yale/9780300087123.001.0001

Groot Nibbelink, Liesbeth and Sigrid Merx. 2021. "Dramaturgical Analysis: A relational approach." *FORUM+* 28 (3): 4–16. https://doi.org/10.5117/FORUM2021.3.002.GROO

Kattenbelt, Chiel, ed. 2018. *Maske und Koturne* 16.4: Warum Drei?.

Lessing, Gotthold Ephraim. 1769. *Hamburgische Dramaturgie*. Hamburg.

Lehmann, Hans-Thies. 2006. *Postdramatic Theatre*. Translated and introduced by Karen Jürs-Munby. Routledge. https://doi.org/10.4324/9780203088104

Lefebvre, Henri. 1991. *The Production of Space*. Translated by Donald Nicholson-Smith. Blackwell Publishing.

Lotker, Sodja Zupanc. 2024. *Devised Theatre Dramaturgy: A Practical Handbook*. AMU Press.

Merx, Sigrid. 2018. "Facing Fear: The Radical Reversal of Narratives of Risk." In *The Routledge Companion to Theatre and Politics*, edited by Peter Eckersall and Helena Grehan, 250–53. Routledge.

Noeth, Sandra. 2015. "On Dramaturgy in Contemporary Dance and Choreography." In *The Routledge Companion to Dramaturgy*, edited by Magda Romanska, 414–19. Routledge.

Pavis, Patrice. 2003. *Analyzing Performance: Theatre, Dance and Film*. Translated by David Williams. University of Michigan Press. https://doi.org/10.3998/mpub.10924

Pearson, Mike and Michael Shanks. 2001. *Theatre/Archaeology*. Routledge. https://doi.org/10.4324/9780203995969

Pewny, Katharina, Johan Callens and Jeroen Coppens, eds. 2014. *Dramaturgies in the New Millennium. Relationality, Performativity and Potentiality*. Narr Verlag.

Pfister, Manfred. 1991. *The Theory and Analysis of Drama*. Translated by John Halliday. Cambridge University Press. https://doi.org/10.1017/CBO9780511553998

Price, Thomas James. 2022. "Thomas J Price on 'Moments Contained'". *Hauser & Wirth—Art Gallery YouTube*. https://www.youtube.com/watch?v=Cs5C3JgHTww

Profeta, Katherine. 2015. *Dramaturgy in Motion: At Work on Dance and Movement Performance*. The University of Wisconsin Press.

Putt, Fransien van der. 2017. "Feministisch exorcisme anno 2017." *Theaterkrant*, 14 December 2017. https://www.theaterkrant.nl/recensie/apollon-musagete/campo-florentina-holzinger/

Read, Alan. 2008. *Theatre, Intimacy and Engagement: The Last Human Venue*. Palgrave Macmillan. https://doi.org/10.1057/9780230273863

Rogowska-Stangret, Monika. 2018. "Situated Knowledges." *COST Action IS1307 New Materialism Almanac*. https://newmaterialism.eu/almanac/s/situated-knowledges.html

Romanska, Magda, ed. 2015. *The Routledge Companion to Dramaturgy*. Routledge. https://doi.org/10.4324/9780203075944

Trencsényi, Katalin. 2015. *Dramaturgy in the Making: A User's Guide for Theatre Practitioners*. Bloomsbury. https://doi.org/10.4324/9780203075944

Trencsényi, Katalin and Bernadette Cochrane. 2014. *New Dramaturgy: International Perspectives on Theory and Practice*. Bloomsbury.

Turner, Cathy and Synne K. Behrndt. 2016. *Dramaturgy and Performance*, second edition. Palgrave Macmillan.

Van Kerkhoven, Marianne. 1994a "On Dramaturgy." *Theaterschrift*, no. 5/6, February 1994. http://sarma.be/docs/3108

Van Kerkhoven, Marianne. 1994b "The Theatre is in the City and the City is in the World and its Walls are of Skin." [State of the Union speech Theater Festival 1994]. Translated by Gregory Ball. *Sarma*. http://sarma.be/docs/3229

Whitmore, Jon. 1994. *Directing Postmodern Theater: Shaping Signification in Performance*. University of Michigan Press. https://doi.org/10.3998/mpub.23644

Zeefuik, Simone. 2023a. "Operatic stillness." *Sculpture International Rotterdam*. https://www.sculptureinternationalrotterdam.nl/en/operatic-stillness/

Zeefuik, Simone. 2023b. "Unbothered, still." *Sculpture International Rotterdam*. https://www.sculptureinternationalrotterdam.nl/en/unbothered-still/

3. Spectatorship Analysis

Maaike Bleeker

Summary

Analysing spectatorship involves examining how performances affect spectators and how they are invited to make sense of this address. How do shows direct attention, play into (and play with) expectations, desires, conventions, habits, and frames of reference? How do they engage spectators as bodies via various sensory dimensions? How do they trigger associations and invite interpretations? How do experience and meaning emerge from this address and the audience's responses to it? This text looks at spectatorship in *03:08:38 States of Emergency* (2019–2022) by Tore Vagn Lid and Transiteatret Bergen (Norway) to show how this performance engages the audience in a collective and embodied working through of a traumatic historical event, namely the blowing up of a Norwegian government building in Oslo and the massacre of sixty-nine young social democratic politicians at a summer camp on the island of Utøya in 2011. Spectatorship analysis can also be used to unpack real-life events. This will be demonstrated with an analysis of the arrival of the remains of the victims of the MH17 (the Malaysian Airlines flight shot down in 2014) at Eindhoven Airport and the procession through the Netherlands that followed.

Introduction

The term spectatorship refers to the state of being a spectator. In theatre and performance studies, this term describes how performances engage audiences in modes of perceiving and making sense of what they encounter. Analysing spectatorship involves examining how performances affect spectators and how they are invited to make sense of this address. This involves examining how performances engage their audiences in various modes of perception, including sight, sound, touch, association, and interpretation of what they encounter. This may include asking questions like: how do performances position spectators in relation to what is shown, and how does this affect their understanding of the show? How do shows direct attention, play into (and play with) expectations, desires, conventions, habits, and frames of reference? How do they engage spectators as bodies via various sensory dimensions? How do elements of a performance resonate with the context in which the audience encounters it, and how does this affect their understanding? How does the order of events mediate a succession of experiences, and how does this become part of how audiences make sense of what they encounter?

Spectatorship analysis thus directs attention to the experiential basis of performances as compositions of various elements (including performers, texts, movements, spatial arrangements, sounds, music, props, costumes, and more) that unfold in time and space, bringing about experiences, triggering associations, and inviting interpretations. Spectatorship analysis acknowledges the spatial, processual, and embodied nature of performance, and how what makes performances meaningful is a function of this nature. It unravels how experience and meaning emerge as a result of specific characteristics of the composition of the performance, how this composition evolves over time, and how the performance is situated within social, cultural, and historical contexts. Performances themselves may direct attention to this processual nature and make such coming about of experience and meaning the subject of the performance. An example is *03:08:38 States of Emergency* (2019–2022) by Tore Vagn Lid and Transiteatret Bergen (Norway).[1] This show consists of a minute-by-minute reconstruction of the blowing up of a Norwegian government building in Oslo and the massacre of sixty-nine young social democratic politicians at a summer

---

1   See https://www.transiteatret.no/kopi-av-now

camp on the island of Utøya in 2011. Using miniature sets placed on table-height wooden structures amidst the audience, a group of singers, musicians, set designers, and film artists take the audience along in a real-time (i.e. three hours, eight minutes, and thirty-eight seconds long) reconstruction of the chain of events and how media, police, politicians, and others tried to make sense of them. Spectatorship analysis helps to understand how the meaning of this performance is a matter of how it engages the audience in a collective and embodied working through the course of events. Spectatorship analysis similarly provides a perspective on real-life events and 'stagings' and how their meaning resides in how they take the audience along in a collective working through of experiences. Here, my example will be the staging of the arrival of the remains of the victims of the MH17 (the Malaysian Airlines flight shot down by Russia in 2014) at Eindhoven Airport and the procession through the Netherlands that followed.

Context

The object of spectatorship analysis is not actual audiences and their reception of a show (this would be the subject of reception research), nor what a show represents or means per se, but how experiences and interpretations result from how performances are constructed as compositions of elements in time and space, and how their construction addresses the audience and mediates experiences. A helpful concept here is that of the apparatus. This term is used to describe the modes of operating of the totality of all human and non-human elements that are part of performances, as well as the evolving relationships between all these elements, between them and the audience, and between them and the broader context of the performance. This includes the performers and what they do, objects, set design, space, costumes, sound, music, lighting, and everything else in the performance (Bleeker 2023, 82–84).

Elements of such apparatuses may serve as signs for other things outside the performance proper. A chair on stage can stand for a chair in Prince Hamlet's castle. A twinkling light moving about can represent the character Tinkerbell in *Peter Pan*. A small cardboard car moved along models of a city and the surrounding countryside can come to stand for Anders Brevik's vehicle on its way to the summer camp that would become the site of carnage, as in *03:08:38 States of Emergency*. Such relationships between signs and their meanings are the subject of semiotic analysis. Spectatorship analysis, too, may involve examining how elements of performances and their combinations represent aspects of real or fictional worlds outside the theatre. However, whereas semiotic analysis approaches performance as a set of signs to be decoded, spectatorship analysis directs attention to how the performance makes it possible for this cardboard car to be experienced and become meaningful in this way as a result of, among others, how the title of the show and information made available beforehand sets expectations and invites this interpretation.

Questions of spectatorship are closely connected to those of dramaturgy. Analysing spectatorship involves understanding how experiences and interpretations emerge between performances and spectators, and as a result of the construction, or dramaturgy, of the performance. Spectatorship describes how spectators and spectating are implicated within the dramaturgy of the performance, and how this dramaturgy invites modes of perceiving, experiencing, and interpreting. This may involve narrative, characters, and dramatic representation, as well as montage-like compositions of what at first may seem unrelated materials, ritual-like events that take audiences along in associative experiences and many other modes of structuring materials. Like dramaturgy, spectatorship analysis draws attention to the durational and processual character of performances, highlighting how the specific nature of the performance's composition takes audiences along in a succession of experiences. Like dramaturgy, spectatorship analysis is interested in how these experiences may affect the audience and how performances are constructed to achieve this effect.

Spectatorship analysis shares this interest in how audiences are addressed and taken along, with narratology, which offers many concepts for analysing how narratives are constructed and understanding how narrative structure affects human perception. Especially useful for spectatorship analysis is the concept of focalisation, as introduced by

Gerard Genette and operationalised by Mieke Bal (1997). Focalisation describes the relationship between what is shown and the point of view from where that which is shown is seen in that particular way, and how this relationship is set up by, for example, a performance.[2] This relationship is part of how a performance mediates modes of looking at and listening to what is shown on stage. Such mediation may happen in ways that go unnoticed, resulting in us seeming to see things 'as they are'. Naturalist and realist traditions of staging explicitly strive for such 'visions from nowhere', absorbing spectators into worlds on stage. Other staging practices more explicitly reveal their 'being theatre', and thus alert spectators to the fact that what they are witnessing is staged. This may destabilise the self-evidence of ways of looking at what is there, and confront the spectator with their cultural and historically specific point of view. The conceptual pair of absorption and theatricality thus describes two different strategies for engaging the spectator (Bleeker 2007, 2008; Zijp 2025).

This interest in how experiences are brought about and become meaningful also provides a point of connection between spectatorship analysis and phenomenology. Phenomenology examines how our physical and social environments, as well as the things within these environments, influence our experience and cognition. Spectatorship analysis examines how the mattering of experience and cognition is shaped by the specificities of the performance's composition. It draws on insights from diverse theoretical fields that help explain how spectators respond to what they encounter, including theories of embodied perception and cognition, cultural analysis, narratology, theatre, dance, and performance studies and media theory. Furthermore, spectatorship analysis shares with new materialism an understanding of meaning and matter as fundamentally entangled. Performances come to matter in the double sense observed by Judith Butler (1993): their concrete materialisation is inseparable from how they come to signify. Spectatorship analysis looks at how spectators are implicated in how performances thus come to matter.

---

2   For a further discussion of the concept in relation to theatre, see Bleeker (2008).

How to

Spectatorship analysis examines how modes of seeing, hearing, feeling, experiencing, associating, and interpreting are implicated in performances and how they are constructed. This involves looking at how this construction implies positions for the audience. Performances are made to be seen from a specific position, literally. In the tradition of Western dramatic theatre, this is often a fixed position in the dark (marked by a seat in the auditorium), where the audience can attend the performance as an invisible outside observer absorbed in what is presented on stage. Actors perform as if they cannot see the audience and are unaware of their presence (the convention of the so-called fourth wall). Other types of performances explicitly acknowledge the audience's presence, with actors speaking directly to the audience or about them, thereby alerting them to the staged nature of the event. Furthermore, audience positions are not necessarily static and fixed. Performances may take audiences along through successions of spaces or on a tour through public space. They may also invite audiences to walk around and choose from which position to watch the performance, as in *03:08:38 States of Emergency*. In this performance, the reconstruction of the 22 July 2011 events took place on wooden constructions across the performance space, with chairs placed between and around them. Spectators were invited to choose their seats and were encouraged to move around and change seats during the performance.

Understanding how performances position their audiences provides a starting point for unravelling how they bring about experiences and become meaningful. Such positioning involves more than the actual position in space in which spectators find themselves. It also includes how performances mediate ways of relating to what is presented, inviting audiences to look in certain directions rather than others, utilising, for example, scenography, mise-en-scène, choreography, and lighting. Narrative structures, costumes, or the ways performers behave may invite audiences to sympathise with certain characters rather than others. The way people, relationships, and events are portrayed can make them appear self-evident or questionable, and in ways that either confirm or destabilise beliefs and worldviews.

Fig. 3.1 Tore Vagn Lid/Transiteatret Bergen, *03:08:38 States of Emergency* (2024), performed at Alte Münze/Theater der Dinge, Berlin, 10 November 2024. ©Lea Röver.

How things are shown inevitably implies a perspective, even if, at first, it may seem that things are shown 'as they are'. Analysing spectatorship involves finding indicators of such perspectives and how they mediate ways of relating to what is presented. This is where the notion of focalisation comes in handy. What is shown always implies one or more points of view. This point of view may be related to one or more agents within the performance. This is called internal focalisation. An example is how, in *03:08:38 States of Emergency*, the behaviour of the performers—on the spot constructing and manipulating the scale model of Oslo city and its surroundings—directs the attention of the audience towards what they are working on as if they are inviting the audience to become attentive with them and share their efforts of reconstructing the tragic course of events. The spatial setup with the audience reinforces this sense of being part of the investigative efforts, spread around the tableaus on which the reconstruction is executed, and with the invitation to walk around and view from different angles. This sense of being made part of the investigation (rather than observing from a distance) and the invitation to take a position similar to that of the performers is also reinforced by the use of cameras and projections. The reconstruction is filmed from close by and projected on large screens, thus giving the impression of zooming in on the events being reconstructed together with those working on it, as if seeing it from close by and through their eyes.

The audience is thus placed in the position of (almost) being part of the reconstruction being executed and invited to experience the events from there and not from the position of (for example) the protagonist of the story. Although the reconstruction follows in real time the trajectory of the person who committed the horrible crimes being reconstructed, the performance at no point takes his perspective. Although his name is probably known to everybody in the audience, it is not mentioned throughout the performance. This choice, in combination with the strategy of internal focalisation via the reconstructors, shifts focus away from him and his motivations and towards the activities of the reconstructors as the central focus. This strategy of constructing spectatorship is crucial to what the performance does and how it becomes meaningful.

This strategy of not mentioning the name of the perpetrator reminds of New Zealand's Prime Minister Jacinda Ardern's choice, in the aftermath of the 2019 Christchurch mosque shootings, not to mention the name of the gunman to avoid amplifying his cause and giving him the recognition he sought. The makers of *03:08:38 States of Emergency,* however, do mention the name of the killer in the materials accompanying the performance, for example, on their website. Not mentioning his name during the performance seems to be part of their strategy to transport the audience back to a moment in time when it was not yet known what the events would lead to and who this person was.

Another example of internal focalisation is the excerpts from historical radio broadcasts that are part of the reconstruction of the events, featuring reports on the bomb explosion in Oslo and the attempts of officials and commentators to explain these events. These messages take the audience back to the moment before it was clear what had happened and before they would become aware that the biggest tragedy (the massacre at the summer camp) was yet to come. The excerpts from historical radio broadcasts also include other news items and announcements, as well as excerpts from songs that, at that moment, featured in the hit parade, thus further immersing the audience in a particular historical moment, as if being taken back to the time it was happening. These examples demonstrate that focalisation is not only a visual or textual phenomenon but can also have auditory dimensions.

Apart from one or more internal focalisers, performances always feature external focalisation, which can be harder to detect. Whereas internal focalisation involves a point of view that can be marked within what is shown, the point of view of external focalisation (the external focaliser) lies outside what is presented. It is the point of view implied by how things are shown. In the case of *03:08:38 States of Emergency*, the external focaliser is the point of view of someone who is still unaware of what has happened and is not yet aware of the tragedy that the trajectory reconstructed in the show will lead towards. The performance is constructed around the tension between these two positions: not yet knowing and already knowing. This tension is not merely a matter of actual audiences already knowing where this will end. The show actively gives the perspective of already knowing part of the experience, for example, through the show's title, which indicates the total duration of the reconstructed events. The title thus implies an overview and viewpoint that were not yet available during the moments being reconstructed.

This use of focalisation in *03:08:38 States of Emergency* exemplifies how creating spectatorship also has temporal and processual dimensions. Performances have a specific duration during which there is usually some development. Later moments build on earlier moments, and audiences take the experience of earlier moments with them, and these earlier experiences will affect their experience and understanding of later moments. The conceptual pair of story and plot helps distinguish between the chronological sequence of events that the performance is about (the story) and how the audience encounters the story through what is presented on stage (the plot). The story of *03:08:38 States of Emergency* is that of how Anders Brevik became radicalised and how this inspired him to bomb the government building in Oslo and kill the youngsters in a summer camp on the island of Utøya. The plot of *03:08:38 States of Emergency* begins only after all of this has happened and consists of the step-by-step reconstruction of what happened between the bombing and the moment Brevik was caught. So, although the plot includes a chronological reconstruction of the story's course of events, it does not begin at the same moment that the story starts, but only after all that is being reconstructed has already happened. Such differences between the story and plot are instrumental in how this and other performances evoke experiences. Furthermore, the plot of *03:08:38 States of Emergency* also includes songs and creative expressions that do not serve to reconstruct the course of events on 22 July 2011. Instead, these elements seem to be part of commemorating what happened and finding ways to express feelings toward it. This suggests that the story being told does not end with Brevik's capture, but also includes the mourning that happened afterward and the attempts to make sense of the events through (among others) the performance the audience is attending. Seen this way, the performance itself (as an expression of sense-making and mourning) is part of the story, like an inside-out version of a play in a play.

The difference between story and plot is helpful for spectatorship analysis in how it supports unpacking the distribution of information over time (what do spectators know at what moment, and how do they get to know things?) and how this contributes to setting expectations and building tension. The conceptual pair originates from the theory of the kind of dramatic narrative that aims to create representations of fictional worlds on stage. The example of *03:08:38 States of Emergency* shows that we may also use these terms in a broader sense to refer to the distinction between the real or imaginary events that performances are about and how this is addressed in a performance. The relationship and difference between the story and plot indicate the performance's perspective on what is presented to the audience.

Demonstration

Usually, a good starting point for spectatorship analysis is tracing how performances provide spectators with a point of entry, how this positions them in a specific way and sets expectations. This may involve examining the show's title, information from publicity and the programme, where the performance is presented, how audiences encounter the performance, and what happens during the show's initial moments. The title *03:08:38 States of Emergency* triggers associations with a stopwatch and counting down, but does not directly mention the

22 July 2011 events. Still, from the publicity, the programme, and the director's introduction at the show's beginning, it is clear what 'states of emergency' this performance is about. Shortly after entering the theatre room, the spectators are addressed by a male voice welcoming them in Norwegian and introducing himself as Tore Vagn Lid, the director. "It has already become history", he says, thus stressing the perspective 'after the fact' and how the performance is a reconstruction in which "a timeline stretches through a framework built up as an installation of wood, cameras, instruments, track strings, tape players, and small and large loudspeakers". He refers to the track strips with small lights marking the killer's trajectory. Every 15 seconds, the next light switches on, indicating where on this trajectory the killer found himself at each moment. Small notes with numbers on them mark the passing of minutes. Around this succession of lights that slowly crosses the space, "second-by-second, minute-by-minute, a team of sketch artists, singers, musicians, and film artists shall reconstruct the time it took a young man to blow up a Norwegian government building and then massacre young social democratic politicians at a summer camp. *03:08:38*. Three hours, eight minutes, and thirty-eight seconds".

The director enacts the role of a focaliser, setting the perspective in a way that hovers between internal and external focalisation. His introduction is part of the construction of the performance, but at its very margin. The director is not physically present but only as a disembodied voice-over, preparing the audience for what is to come, indicating what the audience can expect and also how the perspective taken is

> Different from films about the terrorist's attacks in Oslo and Utøya or theatre plays that read aloud from the manifesto, we do not work in retrospect, rather in a sense prospectively. The events are attempted to be reconstructed 'from the beginning' from the chain of events—when nothing was yet clear and no one among us, and no one of you, quite knew what was about to happen; what was important and not important and who's behind it all and what the outcome of this Friday would be.

The introduction invites the audience to go back with them to this moment 'before', when the news was about "circus elephants" and "a holiday guest who had fallen asleep on the bathroom floor, clogging the shower drain at a hotel in Grimstad". At this moment, in a warm office in a rainy city in western Norway, a still relatively young director prepared his next theatre performance. At the same time, on Utøya in eastern Norway, a former Norwegian prime minister left the island ahead of schedule. "Then at 15:25:22 it explodes".

The director's introduction also addresses the role of the media, both in relation to the historical events and as part of what is being reconstructed. He observes that "different broadcast editors, financed in different ways, respond differently. [...] There are speculations, first in Norwegian, then in English, German, French, and Spanish. In this web of reactions, national and supernational, one can sense the contours of a dramaturgy of a state of emergency". This state of emergency is what is being reconstructed. Including these media speculations in the reconstruction, he points out,

> can tell us something about our reactions, not afterward, but in the middle of such a state, when nobody can know for sure about the extent, for what reason and motivation; when speculations go in all directions because the world needs answers, where Facebook photos are replaced by Norwegian flags, national symbols that later on are replaced by the old ones; where suppressed political ideas can thrive on the street and on the couch, where choices big and small have to be made—there and then.

The temporal distance between internal focalisation (taking us back to the moment 'in the middle' of the unfolding of the events) and external focalisation (looking at the events from a position afterward) is instrumental in exposing the focalisation at work within these media reports and speculations: the point of view and assumptions underlying them and how these give shape to the images they paint of what has happened.

Near the end of the introduction, the performers enter and position themselves around the wooden constructions, amidst the spectators. While they take their positions, the director ends with some instructions to the audience: "Dear all, please turn off your mobiles and pads. Feel free to get up, walk around, and look at our work along the way. We will now turn back the time to 22 July 2011. The time is 15:19:55, and we will start now". At that moment, a digital clock with red numbers begins to tick, and the first light on the track strip illuminates.

Another critical moment to consider is the show's ending and, from there, what has changed between the beginning and the end. What kind of spectatorship position is the audience offered at the end? Is there closure, or are things left open? Are expectations met or not? How does this position differ from where they started? How did these differences come about? *03:08:38 States of Emergency* ends at the island of Utøya when, after what seems to be an endless length of time, it finally becomes known to the outside world what is happening. Police arrive on the island. The reconstruction traces their trajectory as well. The moment the two lines—the one marking the killer's trajectory and the other marking that of the police—meet, the performance ends. This ending offers some relief in that the killing finally stops, but it does not provide closure in the sense of an answer to help make sense of it and put things in perspective. Instead, the reconstruction leaves us where that what the performance attempts to do (making sense of what happens) begins.

As a spectator, I was emotionally exhausted. It felt as if the three hours, eight minutes, and thirty-eight seconds of minute reconstruction had been a collective reaching out to something that could not be reached, an answer that was not there, only this unsettling and ungraspable magnitude of what had happened unfolding in a clock-like manner. Yet, having gone through it felt nevertheless meaningful as an honouring of the people who lost their lives in this terrible terrorist attack, as if our collective attention was a form of paying respect, acknowledging them, acknowledging the terror of these events, and giving a place to this horror beyond imagination.

Such personal experiences, obviously, cannot answer questions about spectatorship. Yet, they may provide a starting point. The trick, then, is to move beyond describing your personal experiences and see what they may reveal about the performance's construction and what this construction does to the spectators. For example, my experiences made me realise the importance of the care and attention of the performers and how internal focalisation (described above) made this part of my experience. I noticed how the tension between internal and external focalisation (between progressive reconstruction and already knowing the outcome) increasingly puts the audience in a Cassandra-like position, where they see the future while being unable to prevent the horror from happening. The marking of the killer's trajectory in real-time (i.e. each step taking the exact same amount of time it took him) makes us witness the clock's ticking toward the inevitable, horrible outcomes already known. I also noticed how, in this respect, a difference could be observed between the relatively cool earlier part of the performance (tracing the period the killer travelled from the site of the bombing in Oslo to the island of Utøya) and the later part (tracing how the killer moved around the island, killing people wherever he encountered them). This second part of the performance adds elements to the clock-like marking of the passing of time that contribute to increasing awareness of all the time that passes without anyone stopping the killer. Just before crossing to the island, the killer parks his car and waits for thirty minutes. Nothing happens. This, too, is reconstructed in real-time, taking what seems to be an endless amount of time in which he could have been stopped but isn't. During the final part, on the island, a performer traces the killer's trajectory in real-time on a paper copy of a map of the island. The extremely slow motion of his marker on the paper, making several rounds around the island without anyone stopping the killer, is suffocating. Music, choral singing, and a collectively created paper sculpture evoke a sense of mourning about the killings while they are still happening, adding to the feeling of inevitability and the sense that whatever this reconstruction can help us understand will always already be too late.

Expanding the method

17 July 2014, flight MH17 of Malaysia Airlines, on its way from Amsterdam to Kuala Lumpur, was shot down close to the Ukrainian village of Hrabove. All 298 people on board died. The bodies of the victims were transferred to the Netherlands in 10 flights, the first arriving on 23 July 2014. The military planes arrived at Eindhoven Airport with a ceremonial welcome. From Eindhoven Airport, the bodies were transported in hearses to the Korporaal Van Oudheusden Barracks in Hilversum, where they would be identified.

The arrival of the airplanes, the offloading of the coffins, the transferring of the coffins to forty hearses waiting on the platform, the lining up and departure of the hearses, the ride through the Netherlands from Eindhoven to Hilversum, and the arrival at the Barracks were all meticulously choreographed in an ongoing performance for three different audiences: those present at the airport (including the King, the Queen, the Prime Minister, and relatives of the deceased), audiences at home watching television and live stream and audiences along the route who, standing silent, clapping and throwing flowers, in turn became part of the performance for the camera. Their performance was not scripted but a spontaneous response to how the choreography of the event invited them to participate as active spectators.

Theatre director Ivo Van Hove (in an evening-long interview for Dutch National Television) praises this choreography of national mourning as a "perfect staging" and "a grand ritual" for people to feel what hurt so much at that time. He refers to the notion of catharsis in Greek tragedy, which he understands as the process by which performance allows you to fully experience the emotions raised by something like the MH17 disaster in a way that enables you to continue living afterward. His appreciation highlights spectatorship as a key factor in what made this staging meaningful: it engaged audiences across the Netherlands in a shared emotional experience. The point here was not what the ceremony meant or the message it conveyed. The point was what it did to audiences, how it allowed them to be part of the experience and how this resonates with Greek tragedy, which is characterised by the enactment and collective working through of moments of shared history and mythology.

Like *03:08:38 States of Emergency*, this real-life staging set the stage for shared mourning in the wake of loss and violence of a magnitude that was hard to grasp. Whereas *03:08:38 States of Emergency* does so through a reconstruction that draws attention to the dramaturgy of this state of emergency, the MH17 ceremony was itself part of the giving of shape to this event as a dramaturgical intervention in the collective imagination. This intervention shifted perspective on what had happened, turning it from a military casualty (as it tended to be represented in debates about Russia's involvement) into an act of violence against civilians. The presence of the King, the Queen, and the Prime Minister underlined the national character of the loss, inviting the audience to identify with their emotions as an expression of a nationally shared feeling (internal focalisation). Although the victims arrived on military airplanes and coffins were offloaded by soldiers and transported to military barracks in Hilversum, they were not transported in military vehicles, and the police, not the military, escorted the procession. Thus, the procession invited audiences to relate to it as a funeral procession rather than a military convoy. The length of the procession made the magnitude of the loss palpable, transforming the victims from numbers on a page into a long row of individuals to whom audiences nationwide paid their respects. While thus mediating a shared experience of grief among live and online spectators, the choreography of the ceremony also implied a perspective on what had happened (external focalisation), presenting it as the killing of a great number of innocent individuals by a foreign nation.

Suggestions for further reading

Spectatorship has been a central theme in my work from the outset. My *Visuality in the Theatre* (2008) elaborates a comprehensive framework for analysing spectatorship. It demonstrates how spectatorship analysis helps to understand the culturally and historically specific, as well as embodied, nature of how performances engage spectators. "What do Performances Do to Spectators?" (2019) is a more condensed demonstration of spectatorship analysis. In *Doing Dramaturgy* (2023), I develop a dramaturgical mode of looking at performances as apparatuses that evoke experiences and invite interpretations. Many of my other articles elaborate on different aspects of spectatorship. Pieter Verstraete (2009) proposes a model of auditory spectatorship in the theatre. For a general introduction to questions raised by the encounter between performers and audiences, see Helen Freshwater (2009). For more on spectatorship and ethics, see Helena Grehan (2009); for more on embodied spectatorship and affect, see Rachel Fensham (2009). Miriam Felton-Dansky's "The Algorithmic Spectator: Watching Annie Dorsen's Work" (2019) is a beautiful example of using personal experiences and observations as a starting point for an analysis that demonstrates how these experiences are shaped by the performances themselves and their situatedness in cultural-historical contexts. Dick Zijp (2025) demonstrates the usefulness of the conceptual pair of theatricality and absorption for unpacking spectatorship in stand-up comedy and for questioning the perception of authenticity.

References

Bal, Mieke. 1997. *Narratology: Introduction to the Theory of Narrative*. 2nd edition. University of Toronto Press.

Bleeker, Maaike. 2007. "Theatre of/or Truth." *Performance Paradigm* 3: 6–22. http://www.performanceparadigm.net/journal/issue-3/articles/theatre-ofor-truth/

Bleeker, Maaike. 2008. *Visuality in the Theatre: The Locus of Looking*. Palgrave. https://doi.org/10.1057/9780230583368

Bleeker, Maaike. 2019. "What Do Performances Do to Spectators?" In *Thinking Through Theatre and Performance*, edited by Maaike Bleeker, Adrian Kear, Joe Kelleher and Heike Roms, 33–47. Bloomsbury. https://doi.org/10.5040/9781472579645.ch-002

Bleeker, Maaike. 2023. *Doing Dramaturgy: Thinking Through Practice*. Palgrave. https://doi.org/10.1007/978-3-031-08303-7

Butler, Judith. 1993. *Bodies That Matter: On the Discursive Limits of "Sex"*. Routledge.

Felton-Dansky, Miriam. 2019. "The Algorithmic Spectator: Watching Annie Dorsen's Work." *TDR: The Drama Review* 63 (4): 66–87. https://doi.org/10.1162/dram_a_00875

Fensham, Rachel. 2009. *To Watch Theatre: Essays on Genre and Corporeality*. Peter Lang.

Freshwater, Helen. 2009. *Theatre & Audience*. Palgrave. https://doi.org/10.1007/978-0-230-36460-8

Grehan, Helena. 2009. *Performance, Ethics and Spectatorship in a Global Age*. Palgrave. https://doi.org/10.1057/9780230234550

Lid, Tore Vagn/TransiteatretBergen. n.d. "03:08.38—States of Emergency." *Tore Vagn Lid/TransiteatretBergen*. https://www.transiteatret.no/kopi-av-now

Verstraete, Pieter. 2009. *The Frequency of Imagination: Auditory Distress and Aurality in Contemporary Music Theatre*, PrintPartners Ipskamp B.V.

Zijp, Dick. 2025. "Deconstructing Comic Persona: Theatricality and Absorption in Bo Burnham's *Make Happy* (2016) and Hannah Gadsby's *Nanette* (2018)." *Comedy Studies*. https://doi.org/10.1080/2040610X.2025.2463255

4. Movement Analysis

Andrew Fuhrmann, Lise Uytterhoeven, and Rachel Fensham

Summary

This chapter proposes a layered framework for analysing movement in performance, combining multiple historical, theoretical, and cultural perspectives. Rather than prescribing a fixed method, it introduces six key concepts (movement dynamics, gesture, transposition, social choreography, rhythmic milieu, and algorithmic performance) distributed across three analytic levels: individual, ensemble, and ecological. Case studies of *small metal objects* by Back to Back Theatre and the virtual concert *ABBA Voyage* demonstrate how this conceptual framework can reveal the political, ethical, and affective dimensions of movement, including the challenges posed by neurodivergent embodiment and algorithmically generated choreography. The chapter also situates movement within wider socio-technical and historical contexts, examining how performance reflects and reshapes systems of power, identity, and attention. By engaging with traditions such as Laban effort analysis, Brechtian gestus, and Lefebvre's rhythmanalysis, the authors insist that movement analysis can be both rigorously attentive and adaptable to contemporary hybrid performance environments. The aim of this chapter is therefore to attune researchers to the layered textures of motion, human and non-human, live and virtual, so as to develop bespoke analytical strategies responsive to the specific affordances and meanings of each performance.

Introduction

A man stands on the busy concourse of a metropolitan train station. It is rush hour, but he remains still, staring at the floor, his hands by his side. At first, sitting in the audience at the other end of the concourse, all you see is this stillness. He does not move his arms, his legs, or his torso. He is, apparently, motionless. As the seconds pass, however, and then the minutes, you notice more. It becomes possible to bracket out the hustle and bustle of commuters coming and going. You become attuned to the persistence of movement, even in stillness. You see the performer make subtle adjustments of weight to alleviate discomfort. You see a momentary quavering of his hands. You see his body sway and his head tilt. And you see the slight expansion and contraction of the chest, which registers in small ripples in the gathered folds of his sweatshirt around the shoulders and arms.

These first moments of Back to Back Theatre's *small metal objects* can be imagined as a sort of prelude: a performance composed of the smallest voluntary and involuntary movements, exposing the intelligence of the body and its capacity to act autonomously while keeping the body upright. Conscious volition is suspended and yet the muscles still respond, still move the body. Crucially, these movement processes are opened not only to the performer but also to the careful observer. Like turning the knob on a radio, trying to find the right frequency to listen to a particular radio station, we must find the right mode of noticing, of observing what happens in a performance. Once attuned, the public performance of this minimally sustained verticality reveals, in the words of Gabriele Brandstetter, the "tumult in the heart of standing still" (Brandstetter 2013, 177).

This example, which recalls what pioneering postmodern choreographer Steve Paxton calls the small dance of a body at rest, is a reminder that even in apparent stasis, a multitude of subtle dynamics are at play (Paxton 2018).[1] There is no such thing as an absolutely static system. It is always possible to apply a frame of reference in which movement appears. In this sense, it is possible to say that all

---

1   A sound recording of Paxton guiding the "small dance" is at
    https://contactquarterly.com/cq/rolling-edition/view/the-small-dance-stand-audio

performance can be understood in terms of movement. The recognition of this possibility not only enriches our understanding of stillness and the appearance of the human body within the performative space but also invites the wider application of movement—broadly construed—as a paradigm for analysis.

In this chapter, we propose a multi-scalar approach to movement analysis that outlines three distinct levels at which movement can be conceptualised: the movement of a single body, the movement of multiple bodies in concert and the movement of relational and material elements within the larger ecology or habitat of a performance. Instead of naming and describing one or several existing methods of movement analysis that might be deployed at each level, this chapter aims to facilitate the development of an original methodology appropriate to a given performance. Every performance will require its own specially attuned method of movement analysis. What we offer in this chapter are six key movement concepts applicable to these three levels of analysis, which operate as prompts for thinking about how movement works in a given performance. We will then return to *small metal objects*, demonstrating the practical application of these concepts to an immersive, site-specific performance by a company of actors with perceived disabilities. The chapter concludes with discussion of a second case study, the *ABBA Voyage* virtual residency, a stadium concert experience featuring digital avatars, depicting the famous Swedish pop group as they appeared on their 1979 North American and European tour.

Context

The study of movement in any given performance must consider the specific historical, cultural, and ideological contexts in which the performance is situated. Consider, for example, the formal poses of medieval Noh dancers, the gestures of ancient Roman rhetoricians, or the robust realism of twentieth-century American stage actors: their techniques of acting are responsive to what Jennifer Martin has called a "period movement score" indicative of the movement choices and physical vocabulary of an historical or cultural milieu (Martin 1996, 31). Similarly, when analysing contemporary performance, it is only by attending to the specific traditions in which the work is situated that researchers can begin to appreciate the complex ways in which human bodies express and enact cultural meanings through movement.

As the French social anthropologist Marcel Mauss noted in 1934, there is not one technique of the body, but many; humans engage with their bodies in a multiplicity of ways, and movement emerges not just as a physical act but as a cultural construct (Mauss 1973, 70). Societal norms influence basic physical actions like walking or swimming, acting or dancing, and these techniques vary across cultures and over time. This is why Mauss argued for the importance of studying movement techniques from concrete examples, rather than starting with abstract theorisation.

In the early twentieth century, for instance, an anatomical approach to movement analysis was introduced into theatre and dance training as a significant shift away from rhetorical gestures and poses towards a more scientific understanding of the body in motion. This approach required the virtual dissection of the moving body into distinct parts in order to precisely describe their position, relation, structure, and function, and an understanding of functional anatomy became a cornerstone of movement training systems, such as Meyerhold's Biomechanics, Dalcroze Eurhythmics, and the Feldenkrais Method (Evans 2019). These methods all required thinking of the body as a complex geometry and balancing of forces, such as weight, distributed by the joints and muscles. This approach to performance contrasts with a more intuitive approach that emphasises emotional expressiveness over mechanical function.

At a macro scale, the industrial revolution and global modernity also profoundly altered human interaction with the physical world, fragmenting what French dance theorist Laurence Louppe describes as the "global body-subject" into discrete, repetitive tasks defined by mechanical efficiency (Louppe 2010, 27). The transformation of movement systems through mechanisation spurred theories in Europe that aimed to understand and counteract these changes, and a creative exploration and unmaking of movement patterning was seen as a medium with liberatory and revelatory potential. The rise of physical theatre, shaped by Jerzy Grotowski's 'via negativa' and Antonin Artaud's radical views on performance, led to forms of performance demanding extreme physical exertion. The Japanese dance form Butoh reflected, for instance, a visceral response to post-war existential angst. Moreover, contemporary dance practices, notably by Pina Bausch, alongside the introduction of non-Western performance methods, pushed the boundaries of how movement communicates and transforms theatrical space, narrative, and audience engagement.

The focus on physicality as a system of meaning contrasts with culturally specific practices that provide important concepts for the analysis of movement. The *Natyashastra*, for example, is a Sanskrit text compiled more than 2000 years ago that articulates the theoretical foundations of classical Hindu performance. It profoundly influenced the development of Indian theatre, as well as dance forms such as Bharatanatyam and Kathakali, and integrates perspectives on the use of movement, music, emotion, architecture, costume, and narrative within stage performance. Concepts, such as 'rasa', that combine the sensuousness of rhythmic articulation with the pleasure of audience reception, remain applicable not only for the analysis of Indian performance but also in contemporary performances that draw upon or critique traditional forms. Rasa, often translated as 'taste', might resist the linearity or semiotic interpretation of physical action and replace it with a way of knowing that is more disturbingly felt (Fensham 2021, 41–42).

Of course, treatises and systems in a living performance tradition are always entangled with complex social and political realities. Contemporary performing arts practices predictably promote and assert movement norms; particularly given ideological discourses of authenticity, classicism, tradition, and identity in the performing arts. Even ideas that have been deemed progressive, such as anatomical alignment or gestural expression, can produce exclusions that limit the range of movements visible within a performance. If performance includes more diverse bodies, and theatre expands to include inter-species interactions and technological mediation, so too then will movement become imbricated in new perceptions and values. Of increasing importance to intermedial, virtual, or immersive contexts of performance are ideas of hybridity, mutability, and computation that disrupt the emphasis on body-to-body transmission that has determined the coordination of human movement for centuries. The semi-autonomous performances of non-conscious machine cognition and emergent AI pervading contemporary life suggests that other logics of movement are applicable. In what follows we examine some alternative approaches that question and redetermine the scale, orientation, intimacy, and velocity of movement in performance studies.

How to

With access to so many rich and varied understandings of movement—so many frames of reference—how does the contemporary researcher approach movement analysis? There is tremendous transhistorical value in utilising these systems and approaches to analysis when thinking about how movement affects our experience of a performance. With that in mind, rather than identify a single methodology of movement analysis, in this chapter we frame an approach to movement analysis in terms of three scales of analysis, suggesting some key concepts that may prompt creative thinking about the function or significance of movement in a given performance. At the level of an individual body in movement, we discuss movement dynamics and gesture. And at the level of ensemble movements, or the movement of multiple bodies, we introduce transposition and social choreography.

A third, more abstract, level of analysis is that of holistic movement ecologies. This refers to movement as the environment or surrounding context in which a performance occurs. When analysing a movement ecology, we are not only analysing the place of the performance, but also the set of relations and interactions—understood in movement terms—that shape and are shaped by the entities within it. In that sense, a movement ecology is an intermediary space, operating between the performers and the environment. This space can be thought of in terms of physical factors, but also in terms of changing social, cultural, and political forces. This means that movement ecologies have multiple registers: from the biological to the climatic, the technological to the economic. In this chapter, we introduce the rhythmic milieus and the algorithmic as exemplary concepts for thinking about these connections between performances and larger movement contexts.

The movement of a single body

Movement dynamics

This concept invites us to look not only at what moves but how it moves. Movement might be smooth and controlled or jerky and sharp. A performer might sway when they walk or propel themselves forward at speed. The way an arm is held out might be stiff or tremulous. An actor might abruptly collapse into a chair or carefully lower themselves. These dynamic attributes of movement can provide important details about a character's emotional state and narrative intentions, as well as enriching the overall aesthetic texture or style of the performance.

There are a number of frameworks for analysing the dynamic qualities of movement, but the effort system of Rudolf Laban is the most widely known (Laban and Ullman 1950). This system allows for a close description of movement in individual body parts, as well as the phrasing of longer movement sequences, drawing attention to the selection, arrangement, and coordination of movement factors and their respective attributes. There are four basic factors in Laban's system: time, space, weight, and flow. These factors can be thought of as distinct aspects or ways of looking at movement and can be qualified as either more or less intense. For example, the use of weight can be categorised as either forceful or yielding. Or, when analysing the timing of a movement, you might ask whether it is performed with a sense of urgency or leisure. Is it a sudden movement or a sustained movement?

More complex movement attitudes that evoke specific psychological or emotional states can also be analysed in terms of the coordination of these effort factors. For example, an actor might focus on the timing of their movements and their use of space and weight, while focusing less on whether their movements are free or constrained.

Effort analysis

Movement Quality	Space	Time	Weight	Flow
Punch	Direct	Quick	Heavy	Bound
Wring	Indirect	Sustained	Heavy	Bound
Press	Direct	Sustained	Heavy	Bound
Slash	Indirect	Quick	Heavy	Free
Dab	Direct	Quick	Light	Bound
Float	Indirect	Sustained	Light	Free
Glide	Direct	Sustained	Light	Free
Flick	Indirect	Quick	Light	Free

According to Laban, the use of effort also produces movements that suggest a specific goal or clear purpose, directed or indirect with intention. Movement attitudes that emphasise the factors of space, weight, and flow, but not timing, are often associated with an immersive, meditative quality, where the performer appears suspended in time, deeply absorbed in the movement itself, as if in a trance or waking dream. Changes in dynamics within a performance are important signs of shifts in attitude taking place either within the actions of a single performer or the overall pacing of a narrative. Attending to the uses of effort reminds us that communication of bodily attitudes can be varied by the effects of movement qualities.

Gesture

In its most basic sense, the term gesture refers to the positioning and shaping of the arms and hands in relation to the body in the performance of a discrete action. Gesture, however, can also be thought of as a kinesic sign or movement that is invested with a special definition and purpose. Indeed, the word comes to us from the Latin 'gerere', meaning to carry or bear, which is also the root of the word 'gestate'. This etymological connection underlines the capacity of gestures to hold and communicate a deeper, contextual significance—as if pregnant with meaning.

Many theatrical traditions, particularly dance, rely on codified movement languages to identify character types and to advance the narrative, and these can be understood in gestural terms. In other performance contexts, less formal movement dialects can be used to reveal the nuances of a character's personality, background, and development, adding depth to the portrayal. A character's gait, posture, and gestural repertoire are key to understanding their inner world and narrative import.

Gestures connect characters not only to a larger social and cultural background but also to a network of political relations. The German director, playwright, and theorist Bertolt Brecht frequently used stylised gestures, which he called 'gestus', as a way of activating and drawing attention to the "social relationships prevailing between people of a given period" (Willett 1964, 139). Whenever we move together, whenever we gesture toward one another, we shape a relationship. The space between us is transformed by such movements: it becomes not only a political space, but an ethical one.

Gesture continues to stimulate research and to provide the basis for new theoretical approaches not only to the analysis of performance but also the analysis of performative behaviours such as political protests and demonstrations (see Noland and Ness 2008; Manning 2016; Dutt 2017). It is useful for researchers to practise identifying and analysing significant gestures, exploring how these movements, when excerpted from their motive context, convey information about social relationships, emotions, and ideological positions. Because gesture is such an important marker of subjectivity in performance, it is also interesting to think about the way these gestural moments either connect or disconnect performers with the roles they are playing.

The movement of an ensemble

Transposition

The term 'transposition' is borrowed from music theory, where it traditionally refers to the movement of a piece to a different key while retaining its harmonic and melodic structure. In performance analysis, however, a transposition might be plotted as a vector, "a trajectory inscribed in space as a temporal and rhythmic itinerary" that displaces a singular gesture, action, or scene (Pavis 2003, 165). In this sense, the term invites researchers not only to compare rhythmic states, dynamic qualities, and modes of energy expenditure, but also to reflect on the trajectories of actors and objects as they move through and create the space of the stage, establishing connections as well as disjunctions and variations.

It is a term that indicates not only the difference between two positions on the stage, but also the process of navigating that difference. In this sense, the scene on the concourse of a metropolitan train station described at the beginning of this chapter might be imagined as an exemplary transpositional space: commuters drift from the gates to the platforms, marking out passages from one habit of energy expenditure to another, weaving a web of connections, creating a spatial body—which is the concourse itself—through the incorporation and folding together of so many crossings.

Transposition also offers a way of thinking about mobility and variation between situations or states of being. In this expanded sense, the concept resembles what the feminist philosopher Rosi Braidotti, in her book on transposition, calls an analytical method for thinking the positivity of difference in spatial terms: "[Transposition] is thus created as an in-between space of zigzagging and of crossing: nonlinear, but not chaotic; nomadic, yet accountable and committed; creative but also cognitively valid; discursive and also materially embedded—it is coherent without falling into instrumental rationality" (Braidotti 2003, 5). Remaining on the concourse, we can imagine distinct figures as concentrations of significant difference. The teenagers kissing on one side of the concourse are transformed into an elderly woman brushing past a man handing out coupons on the other side. Meanwhile, the three police officers near the ticket machines are displaced by the man in sandals bounding down the steps to the platforms.

Researchers applying a transpositional analysis might begin by plotting the movement vectors of performers through a scene: for example, plotting the trajectories of an ensemble as unison movement gives way to oscillations along alternative pathways. Once the terrain has been mapped, it becomes possible to ask how character movements and ensemble formations are transformed to meet the emotional and narrative contexts of the performance. For instance, in Braidotti's terms, what happens when the fixed locations within a situation become chaotic or are disrupted by an intruder? The significance of such transpositional moments is ramified from scene to scene, influencing the dramaturgical development of the performance.

Social choreography

Social choreography is a concept developed by American literary scholar Andrew Hewitt to describe the political relationship between aesthetics and social order. When applied to the analysis of movement in a performance context, it draws attention not only to the ideological and political structures reflected in the disposition of bodies in space, but also to the way in which performance helps to shape those structures. Thinking about the social order as movement, as Hewitt writes, "derives its ideal from the aesthetic realm and seeks to instill that order directly at the level of the body. In its most explicit form, this tradition has observed the dynamic choreographic configurations produced in dance and sought to apply those forms to the broader social and political sphere" (Hewitt 2007, 46)

In other words, the orchestrated and disciplined movement of dance formations—whether the military precision of the ballet corps or the improvisatory potential of a social dance such as the jitterbug—produces not just symbolic representations but active articulations of social order. Such ensemble movements can be used—and have historically been used—to rehearse and perform regimes of social order, serving both as a model for social regulation, and as a means of subcultural resistance. The dance scholar André Lepecki, augmenting Hewitt's concept, has termed these two regimes choreopolicing, which is the controlling of movement, and choreopolitics, which is "the experience and practice of movement as freedom" (Lepecki 2013, 15).

This framework can be applied not only to dance but to ensemble movements in other aesthetic forms. Methodologically, social choreography invites researchers to ask what norms, values, hierarchies, and behaviours are somatically produced—rather than simply referenced or otherwise reflected—in a given performance. It invites us to think about performance as the enactment of social possibilities, of social critique and transformation, or as a proposal for new ways of thinking about social order and interaction.

Movement ecologies

Rhythmic milieu

The consideration of movement ecologies encourages us to cultivate relationships with places through embodied practices, fostering a sense of belonging and responsibility towards an environment. It suggests that movement is not merely physical but also a form of communication and connection within ecological networks. This reflects the idea that all beings—human and non-human—are part of dynamic systems, where movement facilitates resilience and adaptation to environmental and technological changes.

The rhythmic milieu of a performance can be imagined across multiple levels. It must include the corporeal rhythms of the performers, the material rhythms of the production and the life rhythms of the contemporary reality in which the performance is embedded. It acknowledges that a performance does not exist in isolation but forms part of the external and fluctuating rhythms of the world around it.

The concept of the rhythmic milieu extends Henri Lefebvre's theory of rhythmanalysis to the study of movement in live performance. Lefebvre's rhythmanalysis explores how rhythm, which he defined as the interaction between place, time and energy expenditure, shapes and is shaped by social, cultural and environmental contexts. He posits that rhythm is present wherever there is repetition, interference of linear and cyclical processes, and phases of development and decline (Lefebvre 2004, 25).

In the realm of live performance, the concept of the rhythmic milieu can be applied to the interplay between the corporeal rhythms of the performers and the external rhythms of the performance space and audience. It can also be applied to the interplay between the performance and larger cultural contexts, such as when the rhythm of contemporary life, its sounds and patterns, intrudes into performance in novel and interesting ways.

In developing her concept of the 'kinaesthetic imagination' of the dancer and choreographer, Dee Reynolds connects rhythmic movement both to individual expression and collective cultural practices, focusing on how the body dynamically responds to and negotiates "patterns of energy usage that are culturally dominant" (Reynolds 2007, 1). For example, Reynolds identifies a "punctual" rhythmic tendency in the early work of Merce Cunningham, which she associates with his celebration of individuality in response to the pressures of social conformism.

Innovative rhythmic patterns can also develop critical or alternative uses of energy from everyday movement and behaviours. In an analysis, we might ask if the performers are reflecting conventional energy expenditures or challenging them by constituting an alternative rhythmic milieu.

Algorithmic performance

Algorithmic performance refers to an emerging field of practice that recognises the datafication of performance elements including movement and text in technologies that mingle the digital, the virtual, and the live. In contemporary theatre works, algorithms have been invited by artists into the creative process in the role of co-writer, co-director, or even performer, as Annie Dorsen has proposed in her 2012 essay in which she coined the term 'algorithmic theatre'. Since the late-twentieth century, movements have been extracted from the human body through motion capture technology and transposed onto avatars, with applications developed simultaneously in theatrical performance as well as immersive media experiences and computer games. Motion capture is the ultimate anatomical approach to analysing, recording, and manipulating movement, as markers are placed on the different joints. The body's movements are then captured by different cameras and fed into digital models that create realistic animations.

More recently, extended reality (XR) experiences have explored AI-driven interactions between the work of art and the audience. For example, *LILITH.AEON* (2024) by British-based dance company AΦE, co-directed by Aoi Nakamura and Esteban Lecoq, seamlessly combines technologies like Unreal Engine, motion capture, AI, machine learning, and 3D animation with live performance. The digital character Lilith, inspired by the story of the youngest person to be cryogenically frozen, is able to see the audience and interact with them in real-time, for example by following someone around or avoiding them. The narrative unfolds on a large LED cube through Lilith's dynamic engagement with the immersed audience. Prior to this particular work, a dedicated channel on the social platform Discord was used by the artists to enable Lilith to speak and co-write a script. This led to a live dance work called *ORPHEUS* (2023) for two dancers and two musicians, co-written by Lilith and choreographed by the company, which was then motion captured and used to train Lilith to learn the artists' movement. In *LILITH.AEON*, Lilith generates new movements in real-time based on the *ORPHEUS* choreography that was also co-authored by her. This marks a shift in Lilith's role, from 3D animated character, to digital performer, to artistic co-author. Through the one-on-one interaction, audience members are moved by Lilith's story in a way that sharpens their emotional involvement, and personalises their connection to the character and the themes of the performance as a unique and distinctive experience.

With the transformation from physical being as actor into data as agent, audience members often willingly participate in emotionally compelling immersive XR works. In such performances, they simultaneously bear witness to, and are an active part of, changes taking place in representations of movement across the human life cycle. As with gaming and other genres of immersive performance, the 'performance' or algorithmic enactment/resurrection of movement by digital technologies no longer relies on the presence of a living body and its applications can proliferate without the bounds of space and time upon which in-person performance is predicated. The shifts in how algorithmic movement is created, perceived, experienced, and understood by users/consumers have become fundamental sites for inquiry about the human-non-human. For the moment, however, let us assemble these layers of movement analysis into a demonstration case study.

Demonstration

The premiere season of *small metal objects* took place on the concourse of Flinders Street Station, Melbourne's busiest train station. Audience members, equipped with headphones, watched from temporary tiered seating at one end of the station. The four performers, located some twenty or thirty metres away at the other end, were wired with microphones. The first season of performances was scheduled during the afternoon rush hour, so that hundreds of commuters appeared as unwitting extras, passing through the concourse, between the performers and the audience, moving from the gates toward the platforms below. In this way, the irregular flow of bodies sometimes obscured the audience's view of the performers, but never for long.

The show, created by Back to Back Theatre, a much-lauded ensemble of actors perceived to have intellectual disabilities, has since toured to dozens of metropolitan locations around the world (Grehan and Eckersall 2013, 264–67). The company has staged *small metal objects* in the Staten Island Ferry terminal, on the third floor of the largest shopping mall in Singapore, on Queen Street in Cardiff and in the Ikebukuro Nishiguchi Park in Tokyo, to name just a few locations. All these places have their own special ambience and distinct architectural and urban design features. There are also differences in climate and social behaviour that make these places unlike one another. What they share, however, is the constant movement of human bodies. The show is usually, if not always, staged in places with a high volume of pedestrian traffic: transit zones through which people move on their way to somewhere else.

At Flinders Street Station, streams of commuters move across the concourse, the complex patterning of their circulation corresponding to the larger rhythms of the streets outside the station and to the arrival and departure of the trains. Before the performers begin speaking, the action has already started: the audience is invited to sit and observe the choreography of the city at its busiest time and also to observe themselves being observed.

The play is about two street dealers, Steve and Gary—played during the premiere season by ensemble members Simon Laherty and the late Sonia Teuben—who are about to close a deal with a lawyer in a hurry called Alan—played by guest performer Jim Russell. Gary and Steve are met on the concourse by Alan where a large amount of money in a white envelope is handed over. All that is needed is for the three of them to walk over to the station's locker room and the transaction will be complete. This never happens, however, because Steve—who is in a contemplative mood—refuses to leave the concourse. Gary, in turn, cancels the deal, unwilling to leave his melancholy friend alone.

At first Alan tries to reason with Gary. He then addresses Steve directly and tries to convince him to move from the concourse, offering more money. In terms of its movement dynamics, his attitude is indulgent but intense. He does not want to offend Steve, and he cannot force him to move, but he is determined to make his point. His demeanour suggests focus and control as he leans forward, shoulders squared and eyes locked on Steve, literally looking down on him. The lean is sustained, held over time to maintain pressure in the conversation. The tension in the body expresses strength and bound energy, reflecting a habit of authority and communicating his resolve. This energy, however, begins to shift, and to dwindle as Steve remains unmoved.

Indeed, lack of movement is a feature of Laherty's performance. He walks about the concourse with slow deliberation, following patterns in the tiles, then pauses, falling into suspension. He is contained but not relaxed. His back is straight and his face is minimally expressive. Steve becomes a counterpoint to the nervous intensity of Alan and the rocking and shuffling of Gary. Whatever happens around him, Steve remains impassively upright, withdrawn but disconcertingly present, resistance held in the angle of the spine.

A signal moment occurs when Alan, still leaning forward but with less intensity, asks Steve if he is 'stable'. With one hand Alan clutches a cup of coffee to his chest, with the other he holds his mobile phone: as he speaks, he gestures toward Steve with the phone, but his focus is beginning to falter. He vacillates, pointing first at Steve, then himself, then Steve, then himself. It is a gesture of indecision. Through this repeated action, it is as if he wants to implicate himself in the question. There is a pause before Steve answers with a calm but resolute 'no'. Alan's gesture indexes the disruptive potential of Steve's presence at this moment. In other words, the gesture makes visible one of those exchanges described by disability activist Petra Kuppers as "a shift in the status quo": a moment in which the presence of a disabled person manifests the possibility of the spectator's own difference (Kuppers 2003, 6). It is as if Alan suddenly feels, to some degree, the vulnerability that comes with being othered.

Steve's refusal to move from the concourse can be connected with his desire to be seen and acknowledged: a recurring theme in disability theatre. "I want people to see me", he tells Gary. "I want to be a full human being" (Grehan and Eckersall 2013, 66). And yet, the disruptive potential of Steve's obstinacy, which is registered in the equivocation of Alan's gesture with the phone, inevitably provokes a violent reaction.

In desperation, Alan calls a colleague, Carolyn, a psychologist who works in the corporate sector—played by Genevieve Morris during the premiere season. Carolyn agrees to come down to the concourse and talk to Steve. It is Carolyn who explicitly connects the physical movement in the station, the people coming and going, with the smooth work rhythms of corporate capitalism: "CAROLYN: Once a person shuts down it affects everyone else on that team. Sometimes when you're stuck here, it's good to move, physically" (Grehan and Eckersall 2013, 71). Shutting down is a refusal to be moved, or to move along, to keep up with the pace of a city where daily rhythms are contoured by corporate forms of capitalist production. By remaining on the concourse, by refusing to pass through in order to complete the deal, Steve places himself in opposition not only to the wishes of Alan and Carolyn, but the broader rhythmic milieu.

As *small metal objects* reaches its crescendo, Carolyn moves very close to Steve, enveloping him with her arm. In a tense whisper, she begs him to relent, making crude and patronising suggestions, which transition into abuse when Steve still does not respond. Carolyn's movements are not expansive, and her whole body is rigid in that last moment, as if held in a vise of disgust. The sudden escalation is shocking. Her injunction—start walking!—must be understood as a form of choreopolicing: Steve is ordered to move along, to enter back into the circulation of commuters, workers, and deal makers. Carolyn insists on this conformity of movement; Steve cannot be allowed to loiter in the liminal space of the concourse.

Faced with Steve's absolute intransigence, Alan and Carolyn do not linger. They hurriedly exit the space, disappearing into the flow of human traffic. Gary and Steve are left behind, facing one another. At this point there is an opportunity for audience members to reflect on their participation in this moment of stillness. We thus return to the image with which we began this chapter, although now the small dance of the body at rest is not a solo but a duet: there are two performers, moving with their individual corporeal desires and limitations witnessed by the spectators, who have also through the mediated technology of the headphones been party to a disturbance, a violent intercession in the everyday. In these final moments, a transposition is created: the audience is invited to see that it was never a question of refusing to move. It was, rather, a question of Steve moving in his own way, and not according to the normative and constraining economies of energy urged on him by Alan and Carolyn.

If this Back to Back performance exemplified qualitative differences in human movement and the social choreography activated in the rhythmic milieu of the city, the increasing range of digital explorations at the intersections of algorithms and live performance in large-scale mainstream entertainment warrant scholarly attention as our second movement case study will suggest.

Expanding the method

In a promotional video for the virtual residency *ABBA Voyage* (2022), a useful example of algorithmic performance, the ABBAtars—digital avatars—clap their hands and step and gently sway from side to side.[2] These holographic figures, projected onto a transparent LED screen, contribute towards creating an immersive experience for the audience. The ABBAtars' movements, like Paxton's small movements of the spine introduced at the start of this chapter, are driven by the feet stepping in time to the disco beat, which in turn have an undulating effect on the hips, spine, and upper body. The movement dynamics embody and enhance the energy and emotional content of ABBA's songs. Sometimes synchronised, sometimes individualised, the movements highlight both the unity of the band and the relationships between its members. The ABBAtars interact with each other through virtual gestures, glancing, smiling, and exchanging banter about each other's costumes. On the enormous screens surrounding the stage, audience members can see the smallest details, such as the feminine, flirty fluttering of eyelashes and the hyperreal vibrating of little hairs on the back of a leg.

The ABBAtars, lifelike representations engaging in interactions and delivering speeches, were created in collaboration with Industrial Light & Magic using advanced motion capture technology, by capturing the movements of the band members in a studio. British choreographer Wayne McGregor translated ABBA's movements into digital avatars, ensuring that the performance captured familiar components of individual movements within the ensemble while also incorporating contemporary elements. He emphasised the importance of allowing

---

2   The promotional video for the ABBA Voyage experience is at https://www.youtube.com/watch?v=iEikjzZO2N8.

the 'reconstituted' band to express themselves by blending iconic dance moves from the 1970s with new choreographic material informed by his background in ballroom and Latin dance that was performed by body doubles. The data collected from these different movement sources was used to model, animate, and render the singers as avatars, a process involving testing and simulating of gestures enhanced by the alacrity of AI technologies. The holographic figures were then projected onto a sixty-five-million-pixel LED screen, utilising transparent display technology.

Replication of the historical movements of the real performers raises questions about the complex interplay between technology, memory, and the embodiment of performance in a contemporary digital context. If the concept of transposition in music refers to moving a melody to a different key while retaining its fundamental structure, *ABBA Voyage*'s movement material can be considered a digital transposition of the band's historical embodiments to the present day. The style of a singer's gestures at the microphone—an intimate leaning in and hovering as she looks across at her singing partner—that may be familiar from earlier video recordings, suddenly becomes registered at a different scale in the enlarged swooping arms created on the screen. An inherent choreographic structure for the band's embodied expressions and anatomical shapes has been preserved, but enlivened, reinterpreted, and made accessible and relevant to present day audiences.

ABBA Voyage somatically creates a social choreography of artists in the prime of their life, their youthful bodies seemingly cryogenically preserved, yet not fully frozen in time. The use of technology here produces a choreopolicing that foregrounds eternally young, energetic, and sexually attractive performers as the pinnacle of enjoyable entertainment, notwithstanding the odd self-referential, tongue-in-cheek comments regarding the virtuality of the experience. Hidden in the algorithm logic is a complex mixture of live band, recorded sound, reproduced film, and archival gestures that ask audiences to evaluate the affective experience of watching this virtual performance, their relationship to history and to the value systems that prioritise youthful performers.

Finally, *ABBA Voyage* invites us to consider the twenty-first-century neoliberal entertainment economy. Paying attention to the rhythmic milieu in which *ABBA Voyage* is situated is not limited to the screen but extends from the whole spectacle to the city surrounding the performance. A purpose-built ABBA Arena significantly boosts the evening economy of post-Olympic regenerated East London. After its second birthday, the production has generated ticket sales worth more than the initial $175 million dollar investment and its London run has been extended until at least 2025, after which it may go on a world tour. *ABBA Voyage* connects energies of this performance across generations. For older fans, *ABBA Voyage* enables them to reconnect to memories of ABBA's alluring live physical performances of the late 1970s, while younger people can become immersed with (almost) all their senses in the electrifying 3D physicality of the band. Feelings of connectedness abound in the audience, both with the ABBAtars and within the crowd as they unite in a temporary community through algorithmic performance in this spectacular celebration of music.

In these two case studies, movement analysis precipitates a close attunement to layers of potential meaning to be revealed within a performance. Neither of these events operate without some displacement of our attention, perhaps some level of adjustment to the micro-gestures, or a more generalised awareness of the rhythmic structures that constitute its social choreography. Using recognised systems for movement analysis can be a starting point for research but we affirm also the necessity of allowing attention to wander, to return to that which might be moving in the small dance—such as ethical or political gestures—before observing what occupies the expanded or virtual horizons of algorithmic performance.

Suggestions for further reading

Mark Evans' book *Performance, Movement and the Body* approaches movement as a set of systems or exercises for training the performer. With a focus primarily on methods or practitioners relevant to Western-European styles of theatre-making, it includes useful sections on how different methods condition or prepare the body to utilise movement in performance, as well as providing a vocabulary of terms that can be used in identifying movement styles in performance analysis.

Stanton Garner's book *Kinesthetic Spectatorship in the Theatre: Phenomenology, Cognition, Performance* builds upon contemporary interest in cognitive psychology and its concept of mirror neurons (Garner 2018). The idea that affective responses to movement are mirrored in the mind of a spectator has been important to performance studies, helping us to affirm 'kinesthetic resonance' or 'empathy' (also in Brandstetter et al 2013), which is the capacity to feel what it might be like to move like someone else. Garner develops his study in a way relevant to this chapter because he also discusses performances involving bodies with diverse abilities.

Rachel Fensham's book on *Movement* in the Methuen *Theory for Theatre Studies* series provides an overview of theories relating to the use of movement in traditions and contexts ranging from the ancient Greeks to Chinese political theatre (Fensham 2021). With contemporary case studies of selected works, it introduces details of how movement systems establish conceptual frameworks around the work of the actor in performance as well as critical responses to mass mobilities and collective social formations.

References

ABBA Voyage. 'Your Official First Look at ABBA Voyage. Only at the ABBA Arena, London, UK.' Promotional video. Posted June 2, 2022. YouTube, 00:01:00. https://www.youtube.com/watch?v=iEikjzZO2N8

Braidotti, Rosi. 2006. *Transpositions: On Nomadic Ethics*. Polity. https://doi.org/10.3366/e1750224108000408

Brandstetter, Gabriele, Gerko Egert and Sabine Zubarik, eds. 2013. *Touching and Being Touched: Kinesthesia and Empathy in Dance and Movement*. Walter de Gruyter. https://doi.org/10.1515/9783110292046

Dorsen, Annie. 2012. "On Algorithmic Theatre." *Theater Magazine*, May 1. https://theatermagazine.org/web-features/article/algorithmic-theater

Dutt, Bishnupriya. 2017. "Performing Gestures at Protests and Other Sites." In *The Oxford Handbook of Politics and Performance*, edited by Shirin Rai et al. Oxford University Press. https://doi.org/10.1093/oxfordhb/9780190863456.013.20

Evans, Mark. 2019. *Performance, Movement and the Body*. Bloomsbury.

Fensham, Rachel. 2021. *Theory for Theatre Studies: Movement*. Methuen Drama. https://doi.org/10.5040/9781350026407

Garner, Stanton B., Jr. 2018. *Kinesthetic Spectatorship in the Theatre: Phenomenology, Cognition, Performance*. Palgrave Macmillan. https://doi.org/10.1007/978-3-319-91794-8_1

Grehan, Helena and Peter Eckersall, eds. 2013. *'We're People Who Do Shows': Back to Back Theatre* (Inside Performance Practice Series). Performance Research Books.

Hewitt, Andrew. 2007. "Choreography is a Way of Thinking About the Relationship of Aesthetics to Politics." *Frakcija Performing Arts Journal* 42: 45–51.

Kuppers, Petra. 2003. *Disability and Contemporary Performance: Bodies on Edge*. Routledge. https://doi.org/10.4324/9781315016214

Laban, Rudolf and Lisa Ullman. 2011 [1950]. *Mastery of Movement*. Dance Books.

Lefebvre, Henri. 2004. *Rhythmanalysis: Space, Time and Everyday Life*. Translated by Stuart Elden and Gerald Moore. Continuum.

Lepecki, André. 2013. "Choreopolice and Choreopolitics: Or, the Task of the Dancer." *TDR: The Drama Review* 57(4): 13–27. https://doi.org/10.1162/dram_a_00300

LILITH.AEON. 'LILITH.AEON Trailer—AI driven XR and Dance Production by ΑΦΕ' Promotional video. Posted April 2024. Vimeo, 00:01:10. https://vimeo.com/925210197

LILITH.AEON. 'LILITH.AEON Documentary Video—AI driven XR and Dance Production by ΑΦΕ' Promotional video. Posted March 2024. Vimeo, 00:08:13. https://vimeo.com/922037571

Louppe, Laurence. 2010. *Poetics of Contemporary Dance*. Translated by Sally Gardener. Dance Books.

Manning, Erin. 2016. *The Minor Gesture*. Duke University Press. https://doi.org/10.1515/9780822374411

Martin, Jennifer. 1996. "The Period Movement Score: Embodying Style in Training and Performance." *Theatre Topics* 6 (1): 31–41. https://doi.org/10.1353/tt.1996.0003

Mauss, Marcel. 1973. "Techniques of the Body." Translated by Ben Brewster. *Economy and Society* 2 (1): 70–88. https://doi.org/10.1080/03085147300000003

Noland, Carrie and Sally Ann Ness, eds. 2008. *Migrations of Gesture*. University of Minnesota Press.

Paxton, Steve. 2018. *Gravity*. Éditions Contredanse.

Pavis, Patrice. 2003. *Analyzing Performance: Theater, Dance, and Film*. Translated by David Williams. University of Michigan Press. https://doi.org/10.3998/mpub.10924

Reynolds, Dee. 2007. *Rhythmic Subjects: Uses of Energy in the Dances of Mary Wigman, Martha Graham and Merce Cunningham*. Dance Books

Willett, John. 1964. *Brecht on Theatre*. Methuen.

5. Dance Analysis

Sarah Whatley

Summary

Dance analysis is a method that encompasses a wide range of approaches that have developed over time to aid researchers, teachers, students, and practitioners to understand and appreciate dance. These approaches have continuously evolved to reflect advances in the discipline of dance, taking account of the influences of cultural perspectives and of developments in wider theoretical frameworks. Advances have also acknowledged the diversity of dance, which includes dance made for theatrical performance, dance as a social or cultural practice, and how dance has developed in new directions due to the impact of digital technologies. This continuing evolution of methods, which have often emerged concurrently rather than sequentially, has led to a rich and dynamic field of dance analysis. This chapter explores a range of approaches to demonstrate how they can be applied to dance in myriad forms, providing tools that can help to see dance 'from the inside' and support meaning making, whether the analysis is located in dance performed live, on screen, online, or in documented forms, such as images, scores, and notations.

Introduction

Dance analysis is a method that encompasses a wide range of approaches that have developed over time to aid researchers, teachers, students, and practitioners to understand and appreciate dance. These approaches have continuously evolved to reflect advances in the discipline of dance, taking account of the influences of cultural perspectives and of developments in wider theoretical frameworks. Advances have also acknowledged the diversity of dance, which includes dance made for theatrical performance, dance as a social or cultural practice and how dance has developed in new directions due to the impact of digital technologies. This continuing evolution of methods, which have often emerged concurrently rather than sequentially, has led to a rich and dynamic field of dance analysis.

This chapter explores some of these different approaches and demonstrates how they can be applied to dance in myriad forms, providing tools that can help to see dance 'from the inside' and support meaning making, whether the analysis is located in dance performed live, on screen, online, or in documented forms, such as images, scores, and notations.

Context | The development of dance analysis

Critical aesthetic analyses can be traced back to the classical philosophers of the fifth century BC and dance was frequently referred to in these. Through the centuries, dance found more presence within the critical discourses of the arts in Europe. During the fifteenth and sixteenth centuries, dancing masters began to sow the seeds for a critical analysis of dance by developing various scores to document dance in diverse forms of notation, with symbols and drawings of spatial floor patterns and so on, that became the foundation for classical ballet. Fast forward to the twentieth century and the Diaghilev period (1909–1929) stimulated more critical engagement with theatrical dance although the writings that emerged were not yet developing specific models for dance analysis.[1] The records of dance until and during this time were also limited to a few volumes documenting specific periods of theatrical dance, primarily located in Western societies, and written largely by dance aficionados, as well as dance reviews, photographs, a limited number of notated

---

1 Led by the impresario Serge Diaghilev, the 'Diaghilev Period' is generally referred to as a twenty-year timeframe in which the world of ballet was radically changed through a shift from narrative structures to more expressionistic or abstract works, and brought together world leading choreographers, dancers, artists, and composers at the time; see Sjeng Scheijen (2010) for further reading.

scores, and some very early filmed records. It was later in the twentieth century when the arrival of postmodern dance, in the late 1960s in the US and Europe, led to a new paradigm in dance criticism which began to establish a framework for dance analysis, reflecting the growth of dance within the academy as a discipline in its own right. Dance then needed to develop its own discourse, literature, and robust methods for analysing dance. Initially, dance studies as a subject within the educational context looked to other disciplinary fields, notably anthropology, philosophy, psychology, gender, and feminist studies and the other performing arts, to 'borrow' relevant approaches. These relationships have supported dance building frameworks and methodologies for analysis that continue to draw on relevant connections, which are now operating in reciprocal ways, expanding the kinds of dances that are being analysed. The integration of diverse perspectives has served to enrich the understanding of dance as a complex phenomenon, encompassing cognitive, emotional, cultural, and embodied dimensions.

In the latter stages of the twentieth century, dance analysis became established as a serious aspect of dance studies within the academic field. In the US, Susan Foster, who created the first doctoral-level programme in dance studies in the US, examined how structural and syntactical principles contribute to the dance's internal consistency and integrity in her influential text *Reading Dancing: Bodies and Subject in Contemporary American Dance* (Foster 1986, 96). Another of the first texts that emerged as a guide for 'doing' analysis was Janet Adshead's edited volume *Dance Analysis: Theory and Practice* (1988).[2] At the root of Adshead's and her co-authors' contribution is a framework for analysing dance that focuses on the stages of appreciation: discerning and describing the components of the dance, interpretation, and evaluation. The framework offered a valuable resource for teaching dance analysis, providing a clear and systematic procedure that is still a useful reference point. It served the wider development of dance studies towards being a serious academic subject, providing a language and discourse to support critical engagement with dance performance and choreographic practice.

---

2   This book emerged from an earlier article (Adshead et al, 1982), co-authored by those who contribute to the later book, which sets out some of the principles of dance analysis, with the aim to make clear the distinction from movement analysis.

The focus on a descriptive analysis as the first and most important stage soon generated discussion about the influence of context and the reader's own positionality in relation to the dance. However, Adshead's contribution is part of a longer evolution that reaches back to the much earlier work of the movement analyst Rudolf Laban (1879–1958), whose work continues to have a significant impact on the analysis of dance, and many other fields. Born in Austro-Hungary, Laban moved across Europe, notably Germany, before arriving in the UK in 1938 where he spent the rest of his life.

Laban developed a scientific analysis of what constitutes human movement and his theories have been applied across fields as diverse as actor training, human-computer interaction, occupational therapy, anthropology, design, and architecture. His work has been the subject of many critical studies and publications, and whilst his influence is wide, his major contribution is to dance. In 1928, his study *Kinetographie Laban* laid the ground for the development of his movement notation system, Labanotation, and for his related analytic method, Laban Movement Analysis (LMA), otherwise known as Labananalysis. [3] Labanotation continues to be used today to record movement on paper, or on a computer program equivalent such as LabaNotator, using a complex set of symbols, allowing for the dance to be documented and analysed in depth. [4] Sequences of movement, choreographic structures, and rhythmic patterns can be studied through examining a notated score although it requires a deep level of expertise to be able to read and write the notation. Laban also devised systems he named choreutics and eukinetics to analyse the dancer's relationship with space, and the dancer's control of dynamic and expressive movement, respectively. Labananalysis, as a collective set of procedures, continues to be used quite widely in developing observational and analytical skills in the dancer. Movement qualities can be analysed by assessing how weight, space, time, and flow are connected, combined, and expressed through the moving body.

Labanotation is one of several notation schemes devised to record the complexity of dance. Whilst some schemes were devised with particular dance styles in view (e.g. Benesh for ballet), Labanotation was intended

---

3   See Ann Hutchinson Guest (2015).
4   See https://www.labanotator.com/

to be applicable for recording and analysing any dance style and has been adapted for a wide range of theatrical, popular, social, and folk dance forms.[5] However, originating from within a European context, Labanotation tends to be located in the analysis of Western cultural forms and, as dance anthropologist Brenda Farnell noted, at that time there was almost nothing known of movement writing systems in areas of the world outside of Europe and North America (Farnell 2005, 145).

In more recent times, Labanotation has been drawn upon to document and analyse other dances beyond the Global North, such as Doris Green's study of traditional African dances (2018) which looks at how Labanotation can accompany her Greenotation system for notating African percussion music. However, there is more progress needed to consider how the specifics of dance epistemologies in African cultures, as well as cultures in many parts of the Global South, can shape new notation systems, and to avoid the problem of regarding dance as a singular, homogenised label (Mabingo 2022).

Elsewhere, Labanotation has been a base for many experiments in computing science whereby different dance forms and dance styles have been the focus for representing dance in various animated forms (see for example, Tongpaeng et al 2017; Ryman 2000). The digital environment has also led to an expansion of digital modes for processing related analogue notational forms such as annotation. Technological advancements have contributed new approaches to dance analysis more generally: a plethora of studies and related publications have promoted the value of machine learning in supporting methods of dance analysis. These studies have often employed motion tracking/capturing devices to extract information about dancing bodies to attempt to model, classify, and "for the analysis and semantic representation of choreographic patterns" (Rallis et al 2020, 103). These developments are welcomed for the attention they have brought to dance as a multifaceted artform, and to support more ways to analyse, interpret, document, and archive dance. But in looking for patterns and correlations they may occlude the individual dancer's 'felt

---

5   Other systems have been less widely adopted, for example Noa Eshkol and Avraham Wachman's, published in *Movement Notation* (1958), which is based on a mathematical record of the degree of rotation made by each of the moving parts of the body.

experience' and may overlook the way dancing bodies are culturally and socially shaped. The identity of the individual dancer, which may become fixed through the process of 'capture', may be obscured and lead to attempts to stabilise findings. Dance analysis is thereby richer if computational methods intersect with analyses of bodily techniques and choreographic structures drawn from the researcher's direct observation and embodied knowledge of the dance. This point will be elaborated in the demonstration section below.

How to | Core elements and main concepts

Laban's contribution to dance analysis extends further into influencing other systematic approaches to analysing dance, and some of these have led to many different analytic paradigms, including methods of structural analysis, semiotics, choreographic, and choreomusical analysis, and those that have drawn from adjoining fields, such as biomechanics and physiology, and as noted earlier, anthropology. The range of approaches thus expands to include somatic and ethnographic methods and the exercise of detailed study of dance may well mean that different approaches are combined and adapted to construct an analytic framework. The following section will provide a detailed example of how to combine methods as a dialogic analytic process, but first, each of these different approaches will be outlined.

A structural analysis is concerned with a close reading of the way in which dances are constructed and can draw on literary theory and linguistic models to identify the structural elements. Focussing initially on how the dance is formed means giving time to examine the relationship between actions, time, and space, before attributing meaning to the dance. For example, dance ethnologist Adrienne Kaeppler's development of linguistic analogies (defining small pieces of movement, analogous to phonemes and morphemes in speech as 'kinemes' and 'morphokines') enabled her to determine a view of the structure of the Tongan movement system (1972). This semantic approach has found close connections with semiotics, which considers the dance as a system of signs or signifiers that form a basis for developing interpretations and to create meaning that is in the dance set within its wider context.[6] Closely related to Adshead's model, the dance is thus encountered as a complex matrix of constituent features that together transmit meaning through a detailed observation of the dance actions, use of time and space, relationships between dancers and with non-choreographic elements including sound, and design aspects such as stage, lighting and costume, together with genre, dance style, and subject matter where relevant.

These structuralist approaches find links with ethnochoreologists, such as Anca Giurchescu (1984), who have developed methods to show how the morphological laws of language could be applied to understanding more about the structures of Eastern European folk dance. Their studies, as part of a wider cross-disciplinary commitment to rigorous analytic methods, demonstrate the way in which ethnographic approaches, alongside methods drawn from cultural studies and critical theory, can become integral to dance analysis. Consequently, dance scholars show how interacting and coexisting semiotic properties of the dance reveal more about how dance functions as a cultural text. Observations may shed light on how dance operates at a ritual level, or has symbolic or mythical meaning, reflecting and influencing societal norms, power dynamics, and identity. In this way, a focus on the dance from a structural, 'objective' perspective considers the dancer and her lived experience as fundamentally important in the analysis. Thus, by recognising how the dance operates intertextually, meaning is rooted in who dances (their gender, age, social status, etc.), indicating dance's place within a society. Dance analysis has thus successfully integrated these broader methods, reflecting how dance is the sum of all its parts: whilst individual parts may be in focus, the dance is the whole.

As dance is often choreographed into performable entities, choreographic analysis is a related core element in identifying structural properties of dances. Harmony Bench offers an astute commentary on how choreographic analysis manifests underlying structures, saying:

---

6   See De Saussure (2011), Pierce (1991) and Barthes (1986), for the origins of semiotics as an academic study of how signs and symbols (visual and linguistic) create meaning.

> Giving movement weight as evidence affirms how bodies are articulate—they are not merely reacting to environments and conditions as 'dumb' matter, they are actively reading the scene and making choices. But at the same time, choreographic analysis demonstrates how those choices are circumscribed. In other words, choreographic analysis offers a way to hold the agential and articulate in productive tension with the nonvoluntary and coerced (Bench et al 2023, 116).

Bench is drawing attention to the importance of recognising that the agency of the dancer in any analysis goes hand in hand with the importance of cultural, historical, and social contexts in shaping dance practices. These elements have also influenced the development of choreomusical analyses.

Dance scholars, notably Stephanie Jordan, have discussed how dance and music, as two distinct disciplines, have become more "mutually permeable, and in relation to their shared interdisciplinarity" (Jordan 2011, 1). Jordan's research has furthered the dialogue around choreomusical analysis and demonstrated its potential for examining the interrelations between dance and music, conducting several projects since, situated primarily within the context of Western theatre dance (examples include analyses of the works of Mark Morris, Pina Bausch, George Balanchine, Bronislava Nijinska, and Richard Alston). Jordan examines the connecting threads between the history of musicology and the growing interest in pluralistic approaches to music and dance analysis, reflecting on how the body plays a core role in how music is performed and understood.

Methods of choreomusical analysis have also influenced researchers who challenge what some see as the problematic binary of music-dance practices which could undermine the experiences of dance practices located within the Global South where the "choreomusical worlds are fundamentally different ones" (Hood and Hutchinson 2000, 73) when compared to the Global North. Moreover, in some cultures there may be no distinction between dance and music; "in many cultures performing arts are entities which are ontologically integrated into the fabric of holistic and integrated social, cultural and religious contexts" (Hood and Hutchinson 2000, 76).

Advocating for the importance of doing embodied research, scholars point to how choreomusicology suggests that "the music I hear and respond to bodily is likely different from the music others hear and respond to bodily: observing and analysing bodily responses to music might be one way of getting closer to a description of these multiple musics" (Hood and Hutchinson 2000, 73). Choreomusical analysis has thus expanded to find relevance beyond dance within the Euro-American theatrical tradition. As an analytic method it has informed ethnographic methods including field research to deepen understanding of bodily expression and bodily behaviours, which point to how much dance points to the inseparability of dance and music.

Modes of analysis are continually expanding, and some emphasise the analysis by experiencing from 'inside' the dance rather from understanding the dance through external observation. Many somatic practices (for example, Ideokinesis, The Feldenkrais Method, Alexander Technique and Body-Mind Centering®) emphasise the internal experience and sensation of moving. These approaches often look to consciousness studies and philosophies such as phenomenology to analyse the role of subjectivity in the analysis, and which integrates some of the more ineffable aspects of dance, such as mind, body, and emotion connections. Analyses may be located primarily within making sense of dance from the mover's point of view, leading to a wide range of dissemination methods, such as first-person narratives, poetic descriptions, drawings, and other forms of visualisations. Writing from the researcher's own bodily experiences thus aims to find a performative writing style that transmits the corporeal and sensorial nature of dance.

Whilst a somatic-informed analysis is usually rooted in direct human experience and looks towards post-positivist methods for understanding, dance analysis is also benefitting from the relatively recent developments in dance science.[7] These analytic methods incorporate kinetic and mechanical approaches from biomechanics, physiology, sports medicine, and neuroscience to develop empirical observations and measurements of the physical aspects of movement (Hawke and Bredin 2023). Methods often require specific technologies such as motion capture (which uses camera, sensors, or markers to record movement in three-dimensional space), force plates, and electromyography. These technologies support

---

7   In simple terms, post-positivism critiques positivism (which views the study of objects as something that cannot be influenced by the reader) and views findings as contextually bound, constructed based on our own perceptions, rooted in our own lived experiences and culture.

focused investigations that quantify specific activities such as providing insights to safe dance practice, optimising performance, and how dancers may avoid injury through collecting data of movement parameters such as pressure on joints and joint angles, muscle activation, velocities and accelerations, and forces on different parts of the body. Dance science studies provide analyses that generate models that can be applied to a wide range of different dance forms and dance practices, ranging from ballet to contemporary, jazz, and Latin American dance (see, for example, Lampe et al 2019).

Technologies that have had a significant impact on methods of dance analysis are not confined to dance science. Digital processes such as motion capture, video analysis software, 3D modelling, and annotation tools can open new ways to examine gestures, movement patterns, spatial configurations, timing, dynamics, and choreographic structures/elements. They can also generate insights into the physiological, cognitive, and socio-cultural dimensions of dance performance and choreographic practice.

Demonstration

As has been outlined, dance analysis is a very broad term and there are multiple methods that comprise dance analysis. There is no single method or standardised system, so researchers often develop their own frameworks that best serve the dance or dances in view. Doing dance analysis means engaging directly with the dance in question, whether live, on film, online, or recorded through other modes. Whichever approach or approaches are selected, new analyses will help to build a valuable store of dance 'texts' that will support the understanding of dance as a complex and dynamic artform, and facilitate the communication of analytical findings to diverse audiences. However, one of the ongoing challenges for dance analysis is access to the dance work. Relatively few dances are recorded in a way that makes them readily accessible. Analysis is thus based largely on filmed records (where they exist) and the experience of seeing the work 'live', but the need for repeated viewing tends to limit what is available for in-depth analysis, and in turn, access to those analyses for reference. The example that will be discussed here combines several of the methods described previously, to demonstrate how combining a structuralist, choreomusical, ethnographic, and somatic approach can uncover meaning in the dance in question.

The work of British choreographer Siobhan Davies (b. 1950) provides a useful case study for how to draw on different methods to form interpretations and draw out meaning in her work. Davies has been choreographing since the 1970s and her work has both influenced and reflected the shifts and turns in dance over this period. Davies' choreography until the late 1980s was primarily concerned with complex formal structures, requiring a close reading of the 'building blocks' of the dance. After a study trip to the US in 1987, Davies returned to the UK and developed a release-based approach to movement, concerned with imagery and 'internalised' movement, but the complexity in structure persisted. Her choreography continued to evolve as she moved through different creative phases and company structures calling for an analytic process that could identify what makes her dance distinctive.

My own analysis of Davies' movement vocabulary (Whatley 2002) developed an analytic method that combined approaches as outlined previously. It was primarily structuralist in orientation, emphasising the form, structure, and morphology of the dance to uncover structural units and how clusters of units are formed (Whatley 2002, 46). A focus on an analysis of the structural elements of the dance drawing on Labananalysis, choreutics, and ethnochoreology, in dialogue with an ethnographic study of Davies' rehearsals and my own somatic experience of the dance, led to claims about Davies' signature practice, and the distinctive aspects of her movement vocabulary and choreographic style. So how did this work in practice? The following considers how modes of analysis were combined in two different projects by Davies.

Davies choreographed *The Art of Touch* in 1995. For my own analysis I could access the broadcast version of the dance supplemented by viewing the dance live in performance and observing the dance in rehearsal as part of an extended ethnographic study.[8] This privileged 'insider' view enabled me to combine first-hand observations of the dance in development, enriched by somatic knowledge from my own experience as a dancer and choreographer working at the same time, with a more 'distant' encounter of the dance in performance. The dance is structurally

---

8 The film version of *The Art of Touch* was directed and edited by Ross MacGibbon and broadcast by the BBC at the end of 1998.

complex, so my first task was to create a hierarchical structural diagram to make sense of how the dance unfolds, allowing comparisons to be made between the density of compositional units, which I categorise (drawing on Laban scholars and ethnochoreologists) from Part (at the macro level), to section, phrase, motif/clusters, cells, and elements (at the micro level).

Davies' inspirational sources are also drawn into the analysis. For example, Davies has an ongoing interest in the anatomical 'stop start' frames of human movement from the work of the nineteenth-century scientist and photographer, Eadweard Muybridge, whose morphological analysis links well to the morphological nature of Davies' vocabulary. The music, a combination of eighteenth-century composer Scarlatti juxtaposed with new music by Matteo Fargion, informed ideas of 'touch' (touch on keys), breaking up the musical phrasing, isolating movement frame by frame and how feet pound the floor. A choreomusical analysis of the relationship between the rhythm in the dance and the music reveals how the dance vocabulary is concerned with rhythmic complexity and fragmented, 'interrupted' movement. My analysis involved aligning sections of the musical score with specific dance motifs, notated with Labanotation, creating a score that visualised the intersecting points between dance and music. The interrelationship between dance and music reveals more about how the perception of speed is conveyed through the dance.

Dance motifs in *The Art of Touch* can be identified as core units of composition, small and significant 'chunks' of movement that recur across this work and can also be identified in other Davies' works. By examining the complex relationship between bodily action, how those actions create spatial pathways, and rhythmic structures in these motifs, motifs can be clustered into those with shared features. The motifs form the basis for determining the core characteristics and properties of Davies' movement vocabulary in the dance, which points to an emphasis on countertension and the pull of opposing forces in the body, and a body that is fragmented, unbounded and unfixed. These properties may be particular to *The Art of Touch* but by identifying the recurring concern with dynamics, a dynamic motif is consistent across her works, serving to confirm that dynamics are the primary structure at play in Davies' vocabulary, highlighting the way in which several different accents appear in different body parts at any one time. The analysis then considers how these perform metaphorically and convey broader thematic ideas. *The Art of Touch* is not a narrative work: its meaning lies in its structural organisation, at the level of the dance as a whole, and in the microunits within the different sections of the dance. Detailed structural analysis can thus uncover affinities, or broken affinities, between rhythmic and spatial properties and point to how these might help to define Davies' movement vocabulary.

Whilst the study including *The Art of Touch* was conducted prior to the arrival of digital technologies, the research formed the basis for developing a digital archive of Davies' choreographic works: *Siobhan Davies RePlay*.[9] The digital environment meant being able to bring together multiple videos of Davies' dance works, including *The Art of Touch*, along with other materials, thus addressing the challenge noted earlier of being able to access filmed records of full dance productions. The digital platform also enabled experiments with graphic visualisations that emerged through a close analysis of compositional dance structures.

Two visualisations, which we named 'kitchens', were designed to be a kind of digital score in *Siobhan Davies RePlay*. They offered tools to enable users to develop their own analyses of the dances through several lenses, encountered either at an individual item level, or across multiple component parts. The digital score thus operates in the same way as the score I created in the analysis of *The Art of Touch*, to identify intersecting elements of the choreography, but here the score is able to incorporate many different 'ingredients', layering videos of the dance with extracts from the sound score, examples of source materials, and dancers' commentaries, providing a flexible organisational structure in response to the enquiry of the user.

For example, the kitchen for *Bird Song* (2004) could be analysed at the structural level by examining how the dance was organised spatially through several concentric circular pathways, and its setting 'in the round' in the performance space. Further, the filmed records of the solos, duets, and group sections that comprise the dance, organised through time, reveal different levels of structural elements, such as motifs and dance phrases, which can be analysed and compared to explore each dancer's individual movement style, and to understand how meaning is

---

9   *Siobhan Davies RePlay* was created with funding from the UK's Arts and Humanities Research Council. The archive is currently offline but it is hoped to relaunch it in the near future.

formed. The constituent elements of the dance itself are supplemented by the inclusion of some of the source materials that Davies drew upon for the dance, lighting, and costume designs, sound scores as well as reflective notes from the dancers. Together, the interactive aspects of the digital visualisation, which enable the user to develop their own route through the many 'ingredients' that make up the dance, support a different kind of engagement, and a richer multimodal analytic experience and method of analysis.

Whilst rooted in the same method of combining approaches as adopted in *The Art of Touch*, in this case structural, semiotic, somatic, and choreomusical, the analysis is enriched by access to materials that describe the choreographic process and videos that track the stages of the rehearsal through to the final performance. The structural analysis is thus more layered. For example, the kitchen includes information about how the dancers were tasked with visualising the sound score of *Bird Song*, the irregular patterns, stresses, lines, rests, and dots on the page. These were then taken into the dancers' bodies as an improvisational 'score'. A close reading reveals how danced motifs reflect the sound's structure and rhythmic shape. The same affinities, or broken affinities, between rhythmic and spatial properties are evident in motifs where a looping swing in the upper body is punctured by a jutting drop backwards in space through the pelvis, as an insistent syncopated rhythm is stomped through the feet. The kitchen design is organised to draw the eye to the centre of the circular structure, the solitary song of the Australian Pied Butcher bird of the title mirrored in Henry Montes' shaking, twitching solo. Structurally, this is where Davies started the work and so the solo dance and bird song marks how the dance spirals inwards to and outwards from this central point. The analysis exposes how spirals are visible in the spatial patterns throughout the dance and further echoed in the dancers' individual movement.

As Davies' choreography is principally concerned with structural complexity, a structural analysis serves well to make sense of her choreography. Davies rarely focuses on narrative ideas but the focus on the single bird song and circular structure suggests a semiotic reading of the interconnectedness and precarity that shapes human/

nature relationships. Moreover, the digital score has the potential to be reconstructed through dance so a somatic analytic process can involve re-embodying extracts from the dance to gain an embodied understanding of how motifs 'feel' when danced and how dance and sound interrelate.

Expanding the method

Just as the development of dance analysis has benefitted from integrating perspectives and methods from other disciplines, approaches to analysing dance have had influence on other fields. A close reading of choreographic structures, of how different dance practices embody principles related to spatial, temporal, and other dynamic properties, such as those discussed earlier, can inform research in other areas. Dance, as method, is often recruited into studies assessing the health benefits of dance. Whilst some of these studies develop a mixed-methods approach, combining quantitative and qualitative methods (e.g. Houston 2011; Chappell et al 2021), and some basic analysis of different dance forms might determine the focus for the study (e.g. the role of flexibility, balance, strength, etc. in analysing benefit or change), findings in the health domain are almost always limited to what can be measured and compared using statistical models.

Otherwise, methods of dance analysis have made at least some intervention in the field of sports science. For example, dance scholar Susanne Ravn has advanced the integration of ethnography, phenomenology, and somatic dance practice to demonstrate how modes of dance analysis can participate in interdisciplinary research, crossing dance and sport, to find out, as Ravn asks, "what a moving body can be like" (2023, 107). Ravn develops interdisciplinary research enquiries to explore ways to "use specialised forms of movement practice as factual variations in a phenomenological analysis by integrating qualitative research methodologies and phenomenology" (2023, 109). The emphasis on phenomenology as a principal mode of analysis, which foregrounds the dancers' sense experiences, connects well with analysis that focuses on a somatic, sensorial, first-person, and bodily-based analysis.

Suggestions for further reading

Adshead's introductory book (1988) provides an exploration of the theoretical underpinnings and practical applications of dance analysis. Each chapter provides a different example, drawing on a range of theories including aesthetics, anthropology, criticism, and choreographic and movement theories. There are many texts that offer insights to Laban's theory and Eden Davies (2007) provides a useful overview of how his methods of analysis have influenced research in a range of fields, within and beyond dance. For an insight into choreomusical analysis, Jordan demonstrates the ways in which the disciplines of dance and music can learn from each other's histories and practices to support analyses in both fields (2011, 2019). Recent scholarship has looked to how other frames of reference can support methods for uncovering meaning in dances through developing complex analyses. An emphasis on the decolonial possibilities in the context of choreographic analysis is the focus for a conversation between dance researchers (Bench et al, 2023), which makes clear why dance analysis is never a neutral process and always needs to be situated within its historical, cultural, and political context. This conversation is included in Rosemary Candelario and Matthew Henley's collection (2023) offering multiple perspectives on dance research methodologies.

References

Adshead, Janet, Valerie Briginshaw, Pauline Hodgens and Michael Huxley. 1982. "A Chart of Skills and Concepts for Dance." *Journal of Aesthetic Education* 16 (3): 49–61. https://doi.org/10.2307/3332192

Adshead, Janet, ed. 1988. *Dance Analysis: Theory and Practice*. Dance Books.

Barthes, Roland. 1986. *The Rustle of Language*. Blackwell.

Bench, Harmony, Rosemary Candelario, J. Lorenzo Perillo and Christina Fernandes Rosa. 2023. "Choreographic Analysis as Dance Studies Methodology: Cases, Expansion, and Critiques." In *Dance Research Methodologies*, edited by Rosemary Candelario and Matthew Henley. Routledge.

Candelario, Rosemary, and Matthew Henley, eds. 2023. *Dance Research Methodologies*. Routledge. https://doi.org/10.4324/9781003145615

Chappell, Kerry, Emma Redding, Ursula Crickmay, Rebecca Stancliffe, Veronica Jobbins and Sue Smith. 2021. "The Aesthetic, Artistic and Creative Contributions of Dance for Health and Wellbeing Across the Lifecourse: A Systematic Review." *International Journal of Qualitative Studies on Health and Well-Being* 16(1): 1–21. https://doi.org/10.1080/17482631.2021.1950891

De Saussure, Louis. 2011. "Discourse Analysis, Cognition and Evidentials." *Discourse Studies* 13 (6): 781–88. https://doi.org/10.1177/1461445611421360b

Davies, Eden. 2007. *Beyond Dance: Laban's Legacy of Movement Analysis*. Routledge. https://doi.org/10.4324/9780203960066

Eshkol, Noa and Abraham Wachmann. 1958. *Movement Notation*. Weidenfeld and Nicolson.

Farnell, Brenda. 2005. "Movement Notation Systems." *Journal for the Anthropological Study of Human Movement* 13(3): 145–88.

Foster, Susan, 1986. *Reading Dancing: Bodies and Subjects in Contemporary American Dance*. University of California Press.

Giurchescu, Anca. 1984. "European Perspectives in Structural Analysis of Dance." In *Dance—a multicultural perspective. Report of the third study of dance conference at the University of Surrey*, edited by Janet Adshead. University of Surrey.

Giurchescu, Anca. 2001. "The Power of Dance and its Social and Political Uses." *Yearbook for Traditional Music* 33: 109–22. https://doi.org/10.2307/1519635

Green, Doris. 2018. "The Creation of Traditional African Dance/Music Integrated Scores." *Journal of Movement Arts Literacy* 4 (1): Article 4.

Hawke, Jamie and Shannon Bredin. 2023. "Examining the Preferences and Priorities of Dance Educators for Dance Science Information: A Pilot Study." *Journal of Dance Medicine & Science* 27(2): 107–15. https://doi.org/10.1177/1089313X231178079

Hood, Made Mantel and Sydney Hutchinson. 2020. "Beyond the Binary of Choreomusicology: Moving from Ethnotheory Towards Local Ontologies." *The World of Music* 9 (2): 69–88.

Houston, Sara. 2011. "The Methodological Challenges of Research into Dance for People with Parkinson's." *Dance Research* 29 (supplement): 329–51. https://doi.org/10.3366/drs.2011.0023

Hutchinson Guest, Ann. 2015. "Early Development and Publications in Kinetography Laban/Labanotation." *Library News from the Dance Notation Bureau* X (1): 1–3. http://dancenotation.org/news/Library_News/library_v10_n1.pdf

Jordan, Stephanie. 2011. "Choreomusical conversations: Facing a Double Challenge." *Dance Research Journal* 43 (1): 43–64. https://doi.org/10.1353/drj.2011.0013

Jordan, Stephanie. 2019. "Choreomusicology and Dance Studies: From Beginning to End?" In *The Routledge Companion to Dance Studies*, edited by Helen Thomas and Stacey Prickett. Routledge.

Kaeppler, Adrienne. 1972. "Method and Theory in Analyzing Dance Structure with an Analysis of Tongan Dance." *Ethnomusicology* 16 (2): 173–217. https://doi.org/10.2307/849721

Lampe, Jasmin, David Alexander Groneberg, Bernhard Borgetto, Daniela Ohlendorf and Eileen Wanke. 2019. "Assessment of Musculoskeletal Pain in Dance Focusing on dance-style related differences." *The Physician and Sportsmedicine* 47 (4): 433 440. https://doi.org/10.1080/00913847.2019.1613120

Mabingo, Alfdaniels. 2022. "'African Dance': The Dangers of a Homogenizing Label." *International Journal of Education & the Arts* 23 (1.2): 2–13. http://doi.org/10.26209/ijea23si1.2

Peirce, Charles Sanders. 1991. *Peirce on Signs: Writings on Semiotics,* edited by James Hoopes. University of North Carolina Press.

Rallis, Ioannis, Athanasios Voulodimos, Nikolaos Bakalos, Eftychios Protopapadakis, Nikolaos Doulamis and Anastasios Doulamis. 2020. "Machine Learning for Intangible Cultural Heritage: A Review of Techniques on Dance Analysis." *Visual Computing for Cultural Heritage*: 103–19. https://doi.org/10.1007/978-3-030-37191-3_6

Ravn, Susanne. 2023. "Integrating Qualitative Research Methodologies and Phenomenology—using Dancers' and Athletes' Experiences for Phenomenological Analysis." *Phenomenology and the Cognitive Sciences* 22 (1): 107–27. https://doi.org/10.1007/s11097-021-09735-0

Ryman, Rhonda, ed. 2000. *Reading Southeast Asian Dance: Selected Labanotation Scores*. Unipress for SPAFA, Centre for the Arts, National University of Singapore.

Scheijen, Sjeng. 2010. *Diaghilev: A Life*. Profile Books.

Tongpaeng, Yootthapong, Mongkhol Rattanakhum, Pradorn Sureephong and Satichai Wicha. 2017. "Implementing a Tool for Translating Dance Notation to Display in 3D Animation: A Case Study of Traditional Thai Dance." In *Advances in Artificial Intelligence: From Theory to Practice,* edited by Salem Benferhat, Karim Tabia and Moonis Ali. Springer. 22–26. https://doi.org/10.1007/978-3-319-60045-1_3

Whatley, Sarah. 2002. "Beneath the Surface: The Movement Vocabulary in Siobhan Davies' Choreography Since 1988." PhD diss., University of Surrey Roehampton.

6. Music Always Does Something: Analysing Musical Theatre

Millie Taylor

Summary

Because of the interdisciplinary nature of musical theatre, researchers often put together a group of methods to create a framework within which to analyse a musical performance across disciplines. The strategy proposed in this chapter has three steps.

First, consider the context within which the work was first created and analyse the conditions within which its performance was produced. Second, through analysis of chosen moments within the work, explore the ways in which the music, its signification, repetitions, and genres, casts light on the narrative and characters. Third, reflect critically on the performance in relation to context, politics, and theoretical frameworks.

By analysing the recent Dutch production of *Jesus Christ Superstar* (directed by Ivo van Hove) using this method, it was possible to identify ways in which the musical narrative and the staged production presented different approaches to the work, such that the performance text appears unclear, and the press expressed criticism of the work. A second case study, a production of *The Tempest* at the Royal Shakespeare Company in the UK, reveals a more cohesive political concept that can be discerned not just in the direction of the actors, but in the signification of music, voices, sounds, and silence.

Introduction

Musical theatre is a very new subject for academic study. With some important exceptions, the majority of published writings about musical theatre before the early 2000s were journalistic rather than academic. In about 2003, a group of scholars from theatre and music—myself included—gathered at Bristol University, invited by Stephen Banfield who was a pioneer in this field: in 1993 he had published an important musicological study of the works of Stephen Sondheim. Following this introduction to each other and the potential new field, the subject area has developed. In 2006 two British scholars, Dominic Symonds and George Burrows, established the first academic conference series devoted to musicals, *Song, Stage and Screen* (SSS), that hops annually across the Atlantic between the UK (or continental Europe) and the US. Alongside this, in 2007, they also inaugurated an academic journal, *Studies in Musical Theatre*, which is the home of musical theatre research. As the subject developed, many other journals, especially in drama, opera, and music, began accepting articles about musicals and there has been a veritable boom in the number of edited collections and books about musicals especially in the last decade. Finally, after two American scholars, Jessica Sternfeld and Elizabeth Wollman, inherited the editorship of the journal and conference series, they set about inaugurating a formal organisation for the discipline. In June 2024, at the SSS conference hosted by the Lincoln Center branch of the New York Public Library, the International Society for the Study of Musicals was inaugurated.

I begin with this short history because, while there are now many excellent academic scholars, and some methods for analysis are widespread, our subject area is young and our analyses tend to arise from a combination of disciplinary sources. In many cases this results from the sub-discipline in which we trained; since the number of graduate courses in the study of musicals is still relatively small, many people arrive at research in musicals from different disciplines. There is now a continuity of overall methods even though the level of detail in each part of the analysis and the focus of the argument might differ profoundly. So, people from a background in opera studies or musicology are likely to consider the music as the central part of the analysis, while those from a theatre studies or cultural studies education might focus on the narrative content or performative elements in their analysis, though it is likely that all will at least mention how the disciplines intersect. The advantage of our young and developing field is that we are a small community, in which everyone is aware of diverse theoretical practices, and we celebrate many different approaches. Consequently, the field is becoming increasingly interdisciplinary.

Given this background, many scholars draw from a constellation of theoretical approaches that result from an initial consideration of what they are trying to discover and their interest in the work in question. These can be drawn from voice studies, popular music studies, musicology, sound studies, film studies, narrative theory, cultural studies, dance studies, and performance studies. Even in this collection there are chapters on visual performance analysis, sound analysis, and movement/dance analysis, any or all of which could be used to analyse parts of a musical theatre text.

All that makes it very difficult to suggest a single method for analysing musical theatre. Instead, this chapter will introduce a method in fairly common use for analysing the dramaturgy of a musical. It combines theoretical materials from several disciplines and consists of three main steps. First is to provide some background to the work giving a political and historiographical context. Then, the narrative, dramatic, and musical elements in the work, and how they intersect in performance, are analysed. These elements consist of the lyrics/libretto (called 'the book' in musical theatre) and the musical score, as well as consideration of how the written elements were transformed in the development of the first performances. The third step is to critically reflect on the work and its production, which might include a certain amount of critical judgement alongside evaluation. Following this model, the three steps are condensed as follows: historical context; analysis of the work; reflection on dramaturgy and politics. Finally, if there has been a recent new production some reviews and analysis might be included commenting on how a different interpretation of the work speaks within a changed context.

Such a method is useful for all types of musicals, from through-composed (without spoken scenes) to musical comedy (light and entertaining song and dance musicals), jukebox musicals (that use previously existing music), and book musicals (that contain scenes and songs), on film or on stage. On this occasion, this method will be used to analyse the musical *Jesus Christ Superstar* (music Andrew Lloyd Webber, libretto Tim Rice, 1971), since it is widely available in concert versions, films of stage performances and films, and has also recently been revived in the Netherlands directed by Ivo van Hove (2024).

This method can also be used in other works where narrative performance and music are combined, so the final section of this chapter will introduce the application of this method to a production of a Shakespeare play, with a focus on how its original music score and sound design contributed to a contemporary political interpretation.

Context

Although there are differences in perspective between scholars who come from different disciplines, there is one important feature of the dramaturgical and critical analysis of an interdisciplinary work—which is that the researcher needs at least to be aware of all the disciplines that comprise the dramatic work or performance text. In order to find models for interdisciplinary analysis that incorporate music, musical theatre scholars initially drew on film music studies and opera studies, alongside narrative and reception theory. An example from one leading scholar is Jessica Sternfeld, whose book *The Megamusical* (2006) draws on her background in opera studies so is centred around music, but always in relation to the narrative and characters. She commented (in an email conversation) that she focusses on identifying compositional elements such as motivic repetitions, the musical construction of scenes and the musical signification of character types and relationships. All of these elements are then reflected on in relation to the narrative/book and with reference to reviews, interviews with the creators and other archived materials, but crucially, this approach to musical analysis relies on informed listening rather than score reading.

Film studies and opera studies are particularly relevant as models for the analysis of musical theatre because they deal with the interaction of music with a visual performance of what is often a linear narrative. Michel Chion, in his book *Audio-Vision*, describes the "audiovisual illusion" of film music as "added value" (1990). He explains the term: "I mean the expressive and informative value with which a sound enriches a given image so as to create the definite impression [...] that this information or expression 'naturally' comes from what is seen and is already contained in the image itself" (1990, 5). Claudia Gorbman's analysis of how music functions in narrative cinema, *Unheard Melodies* (1987), introduces the term "mutual implication" (1987, 15), continuing: "Whatever music is applied to a film segment will *do something*, will have an effect". Later in the same chapter she outlines a compositional process (similar to the operation of leitmotif) when she argues that "a theme is by definition a musical element that is repeated during the course of a work; as such it picks up narrative associations, which, in turn, infuse themselves into each new thematic statement" (1987, 17). When writing about opera in *Unsung Voices*, Claudia Abbate includes reference to the congruence and non-congruence between the narrative and the music and what effects they each have on the signification of the potential meanings of the text (1991, xii).

I will turn to the 'book' for a moment, to consider with what music is interacting. Narrative theory is traced back to Aristotle and the Greek dramas, reappeared in the work of the Russian Formalists and in recent theory provides a means of analysing narrative in all kinds of media. Gérard Genette's structuralist model divides a narrative into two basic elements: the story ('histoire') and the plot or order and mode of the telling ('discours'). These are important when thinking about musical theatre because of two frequently used descriptions of musicals as 'integrated' or 'concept' musicals. Although both terms are the subject of debate, in broad terms, the integrated or 'book' musical attempts to smooth the disruptive moment between speech and song or dance, so that audiences become involved in the plot and empathise with characters. Such musicals are often largely chronological versions of the plot (examples are the golden-age musicals of Rodgers and Hammerstein, and, more recently, many of the Disney musicals). Concept musicals are those musicals that might have a more fragmentary or non-linear narrative structure, and whose structure arises from a thematic and/or political catalyst. The material of these musicals arises from a theme or concept sometimes alongside, and sometimes instead of, a linear plot, and strategies of distancing are often incorporated into the structure, the content and/or the performance (examples are *Cabaret* (1966), *Hair* (1967), *Company* (1970), *Chicago* (1975) and *Assassins* (1990)).

Scott McMillin draws together thinking on the interaction of narrative and music in his book *The Musical as Drama* (2006). First, he problematises the concept of the integrated musical, speaking of "the crackle of difference" between the book and the numbers (2006, 2). He argues that in a musical, no matter how the creative team attempts to heighten the illusion of continuity or realism, it is always an illusion that relies on the audience's suspension of disbelief (2006, 2). This, he argues, is because the abstract language of music is constructed motivically, in repeated phrases, and therefore differently from verbal grammar, and that because of this, book time (the chronology of scenes) and lyric time (the melodic and harmonic construction of musical numbers) cannot ever be entirely integrated. Thus, a musical is always disruptive, and this feature is crucial to its ability to entertain (Taylor 2012, 7–11). Furthermore, film music theorists remind us that in the musical, frequency and duration as well as the perception of pace are affected by music (for example Chion 1990, 13–18). In this way music influences the difference, distance and perception of real time and 'diegetic' or story time, and that between song time and spoken scenes.

Following on from Genette's consideration of issues of narration, McMillin introduces the idea that the musical itself might have a voice—effectively pitching the music score as a kind of narrating entity or storytelling voice (2006, 67) even though there might also be a narrator onstage whether within or without the diegesis. Finally, McMillin introduces what he refers to as "the ensemble effect" (2006, 78–101). This is a device that also features in opera in which many voices come together at key moments, each expressing their own different perspectives or revealing their harmonious togetherness. It is argued to demonstrate similarities and differences among and between characters, and to express the experience of community and diversity among the characters.

In summary, one of the earliest analyses of musical theatre texts, Banfield's book *Sondheim's Broadway Musicals* (1993), follows the strategies of film music and opera studies, focusing on repetition of materials, use of leitmotifs, effects of pace and dynamics and their interactions with narrative and character. Clearly, all these disciplines are drawing on similar approaches to analysing the interactions, affects and effects of interdisciplinary works, with the key elements being signification, repetition, pace and congruence.

How to

This section will demonstrate the three phases of the analysis as outlined above: first the historical context, then the analysis of the work, before concluding with a critical reflection on the dramaturgy and politics. In addition, the analysis is subdivided into three sections that take as starting points the three features identified by Sternfeld and noted in the Context section above. They are: motivic repetitions; the musical construction of scenes; the musical signification of character types. Finally, a short consideration of how Van Hove's production interacts with the historical context and the musical/sonic features of the work offers an opportunity for reflection to conclude the case study.

Since *Jesus Christ Superstar* is a historical work about which much has been written, one of the first tasks was to gather the main body of materials relating to it. This collection included the Norman Jewison film from 1973 and clips of several stage productions in New York or London, the script/score of the musical (as the work is through-composed this is one document), interviews and journalistic writings about the production practices and sound design, as well as several academic sources that analysed the work and its history. Finally, reviews were added to the list of sources, specifically those of the recent Ivo van Hove production in the Netherlands (2024). This diverse body of accessible resources provided a good reason for the choice of this musical, as most of the materials would be available to students.

Having gathered these materials, the next task was to consider what the aim of this analysis was—beyond demonstrating a method. Hearing and seeing *Jesus Christ Superstar* (JCS) again recently in Ivo van Hove's new production was a reminder of what a good score this is. The musical and narrative materials interact to shape the work, focus the narrative and open up moral questions for interpretation. So, a through line for this case study emerged around the question: how does a musical score guide the interpretation of a theatrical work? Since the recent Amsterdam production was the catalyst for the choice of this work, a sub-question also emerged: how does this new production engage with the historical materials?

Demonstration | Music and narrative interactions in *Jesus Christ Superstar*

Historical context

Conceived and first produced as a concept album in 1970, this rock opera or concept album was extraordinarily successful. The terms 'rock opera' and 'concept album' were being used at the time to describe studio recorded rock albums that engaged with one body of musical materials in a unified manner—such as The Beatles' *Sgt Pepper's Lonely Hearts Club Band* (1967), Pink Floyd's *Dark Side of the Moon* (1973) or Mike Oldfield's *Tubular Bells* (1973). Notably the term is predominantly applied to rock albums that use new electronic instruments, synthesised sounds, electronic amplification and were mixed, edited and produced in a recording studio.[1]

The concept album of *JCS* was extraordinarily successful.[2] Producer Robert Stigwood believed the album's enormous popularity could be used to generate sufficient interest to adapt the work as a Broadway musical, but because of the popularity of the album, the music would need to remain intact, which meant it would be through-composed and it needed to achieve an equivalent sound quality to the album. Having appointed Tom O'Horgan as director, Stigwood began work on a tour that would serve as out-of-town try-outs for the Broadway run. With several tours launched and the success of the album generating money and interest, the show opened on Broadway in 1971 with advance ticket sales of over one million dollars (Sternfeld 2006, 24).

The story is presented as a linear narrative relating the last seven days of Jesus's life according to the Christian bible. However, it tells the story from Judas's perspective. He is a friend and follower of Jesus with

---

1 The term 'concept' in concept album is used differently than when applied to concept musicals.
2 It reached number one in the Billboard charts in February 1971 and hovered in the top five places for months, only slipping from the top one hundred albums more than a year later in May 1972.

whom he has built a movement, but Judas has now become an outsider as he sees Jesus's control of the situation slipping away, and the crowds and the authorities becoming more dangerous. As Sternfeld remarks, "the result is a largely character-driven show, one which spends its time examining the thoughts and actions of its players and sketches events only in a general way" (2006, 19).[3] John Snelson also comments on the focus of the work on Judas because by "dropping the Resurrection and stressing the dilemma of Judas, the work moved from religious morality play to a play about morals, thus also open to a secular reading", which meant it was likely to have a much wider resonance among diverse audiences (2004, 64).

Wollman notes that the stage adaptation had only moderate success, perhaps because the anticipation generated by the album could not be transcended, but also because there was insufficient narrative clarity even while the materiality of a stage production eradicated many of the potential interpretations suggested by the audio recording (2006, 90). She makes two other suggestions for its initial relatively short run of 711 performances (less than two years). Firstly, since the work was conceived as an album, the writers took liberties with the subject matter; the characters' thoughts and motivations were the primary content, whereas a stage performance required action. Secondly, Stigwood's appointment of O'Horgan as director seemed appropriate because he had successfully developed an earlier rock musical, *Hair*, that transferred from the small Off-Broadway Public Theatre to Broadway. However, to provide the necessary action for *JCS* he "developed a grandiose concept comprised of spectacular scenery, special effects, and costumes" (2006, 97) that overwhelmed the nuanced approach to characters in the album.

Meanwhile, the album had not been as successful in the UK, but a new production of *JCS* directed by Jim Sharman (who had previously directed *Hair* in Sydney in 1969) opened at the Palace Theatre in London and ran for eight years. Wollman implies that the lack of awareness of the album in the UK may have contributed to the show's much greater

---

3   The full story of the development of this production, director Tom O'Horgan's mistakes and the protests that followed is available in Jessica Sternfeld (2006) and Wollman (2006). A book written just after the first film was released, that focuses on the development of the work, is Nassour and Broderick's *Rock Opera: The Creation of Jesus Christ Superstar from Record Album to Broadway Show and Motion Picture* (1973).

success, since audiences had fewer preconceptions of it before arriving at the theatre (2006, 102), though alternatively, Sharman's version of the work may have been more suitable to the complex characters the writers had created. Subsequently, there have been at least two film versions, the best known of which is by Norman Jewison, and numerous restagings in concert and theatrical contexts.

The second issue in the show's development is that since the work had begun as a concept album, the creative team needed to recreate studio sound in a theatre. The show was initially staged to be performed with radio mics, but when the sound team arrived in the theatre they discovered they were getting interference on the radio frequencies the mics were using (Thomas 2008, 32). The first preview performance was cancelled, and by the next day the original sound team had been sacked and Abe Jacob, a rock music sound designer who had sorted out similar issues on *Hair*, was installed. He abandoned the radio mics and in the next three days the show was re-choreographed so that performers used hand-held microphones with cables. He also moved the PA system forward and opened the pit to allow the acoustic sound to energise the live performance (Thomas 2008, 33–34). This was a turning point in the development of sound design and technology since the cost of the sound system had risen from an average of £1400 to £20,000 for this show (Collison 2008, 215). But most importantly for this analysis, this investment underpins how different the sound world of this show was from almost everything that had gone before. Even now, over fifty years later, the opening riff on electric guitar in this score is distinctive and dramatic.

Analysis of the work

As noted above, the analysis is subdivided into three sections that take as starting points the three features identified by Sternfeld and noted in the Context above: motivic repetitions; the musical construction of scenes; the musical signification of character types. The focus on how the music informs the narrative has been chosen for this analysis because this is the area many non-musicians are most uncertain about. This demonstration relies only on elements that can be heard in the music rather than by analysing a score.

a. Musical repetitions

Sternfeld discovers many kinds of repetition in the score: short motifs carry emotional or character-related meaning and recur with the character or situation; sung melodies return in new contexts where they take on additional interpretive potential; songs or themes are sometimes introduced in short form (in the Overture as well as within the work), only being fully developed later (2006, 27–28). All these features help to generate a sense of continuity and cohesion through the musical.[4] They also give the music a narrating, or even a directing, voice within the musical, even though Judas also has the function of a traditional narrator onstage.

This is particularly noticeable when the two forms of narration combine in Judas's opening song "Heaven on their Minds" (Webber and Rice Vocal Score (n.d.)), which is a scene-setting song that precedes any action. Judas explains his concern that the crowd thinks it has "found the new Messiah" (9), singing of Jesus "you really do believe this talk of God is true" (8) and later, "they'll hurt you when they find they're wrong" (10). This narrative information sets the scene for Judas's attempts to subdue the excitement about Jesus, and for his later betrayal, because he believes that, since they are living in a state that is occupied, they and their followers must "keep in our place" for "we are getting much too loud" (12). Judas explains these sentiments further in "Damned for all Time" when he goes to the priests to make a deal because "Jesus can't control it like he did before" (105). At the end of the scene Judas sings in the priest's musical language when he tells them where to find Jesus (113).

In some productions Judas is seen repeatedly overseeing the action, so that the story can more clearly be seen as the embodiment of the actor's narration/the dead character's memory. In this way, the musical score shapes and directs audience attention and emotional engagement to Judas's perspective. This is particularly evident in the annexation of Mary Magdalene's song "I Don't Know How To Love Him" by Judas shortly before his death. Both characters love Jesus in their own ways, but their ways of expressing that in their actions differ dramatically,

---

[4] Although this work was written as a concept album, these are patterns that recur in many musicals.

as Judas betrays Jesus supposedly to save the movement, while Mary continues to support him. This difference, that is highlighted when Judas appropriates Mary's melody, accentuates his moral dilemma and explains his suicide.

b. Musical construction of scenes

There are many examples of scenes built from short sections of repeated musical material. "The Last Supper", for example, begins and ends with the gentle lyrical melody of "Look at all my trials and tribulations", but the scene shifts to listen to Jesus meditating about the future he knows awaits him. Here the tempo alters from the regular 4/4 to the unsettling 5/4 and becomes increasingly heavy rock as Jesus responds in an angry confrontation with Judas. Jesus screams at Judas to go and betray him, before the Apostles resume their lilting melody—as though nothing has happened. What is presented as two emotional journeys (the fight and the Apostles' lullaby), that follow one another in reality, becomes a simultaneous representation because of the continuity provided by the musical structure. The scene therefore reveals the obliviousness of the Apostles to what is happening between Jesus and Judas, and ignorance of Judas's betrayal that will follow. This construction makes clear the contrast between the leaders and followers: the emotional disparity is highlighted. Here is a moment where the musical structures are those of film and opera, where the perception tends to be that the scene runs smoothly though it is made so by the music that compresses the perception of time. The different viewpoints and musical languages of the chorus and protagonists reveal the tension between these different positions and presage the tragedy.

In the Ivo van Hove production (2023) the placement of part of the audience onstage surrounding the action can also be seen as an attempt to implicate them as members of the crowd that gets out of control. However, it is not particularly effective since the conflict outlined in the music is between Jesus and Judas, and the music articulates that the crowd is ignorant of the betrayal whereas this placement seeks to implicate them in it.

c. Musical character types

Many musicals and operas signify character types through the association with music, musical genre or voice type. In this work, the extreme range of Caiaphas (bass) and the priests (high tenor), and the dissonant angular melodies they sing, contrasts with the mid-range gentle folk rock melodies of the Apostles and Mary. The priests' music, since it is outside the accepted parameters of the musical genre, paints them as extraordinary—different from the rest of the community in their musical and vocal sounds. Further, this music is outside the bounds of easily singable and harmonically consonant tonality, and so the characters become culturally signified as separate and unpleasant. Then their actions support this reading and they are understood as the villains, reinforced at each appearance by similar music and by their subsequent actions. I have also noted above that Judas takes on their musical language when he betrays Jesus. The Apostles, meanwhile, sing their upbeat melodic, harmonically tonal and rhythmically regular "Hosanna" and "Everything's Alright", signifying a simple direct communication from a happy community. Both of these examples demonstrate what Abbate refers to as "congruent music", where the music signifies character consistently (1991, xii).

Of most note here, though, are the songs of Herod and Pilate. The vaudevillian Herod is a comic buffoon with a cruel disposition. Abbate's "non-congruent music" (1991, xii) or Chion's "anempathetic music" (1994, 8) both describe the dissonance between the semi-comic vaudevillian music and lyrics, and the cruelty portrayed. This song has also become a stand-alone moment, and often a cameo appearance by a star performer that demonstrates the gap between the narrative integration of the plot and its disruptive theatricality. In such performances an extra layer of intertextuality is contributed by such a cameo for audiences to enjoy disentangling. In the case of Van Hove's production this star turn was performed (on the night I saw the show) to great effect by Alex Klaassen, who is well known to Dutch musical theatre audiences, adding an interesting layer of intertextuality.[5]

---

5   Klaasen is an award-winning musical theatre actor, television and cabaret star. He is perhaps best known to musical theatre audiences for a series of revue-style

"Pilate's Dream", on the other hand, given its very straightforward AABA structure, folk ballad style and guitar accompaniment, signifies the 'authentic' expression of emotion in a simple and direct way. It, therefore, allows audiences to perceive Pontius Pilate as an intelligent and moral man in an impossible situation. Meanwhile, even the rock music has different colours for each character, and by identifying the musical styles—Judas often singing hard rock with extended and very high ornamentation, Mary singing folk rock within a comfortable speech-like pitch and Jesus moving between them—can identify characteristics based on cultural expectations.[6] Snelson, for example, speaks of rock as "hierarchical in that it believes in geniuses and heroes" (Harron quoted in Snelson 2004, 64). This is, he argues, the gesture of *Jesus Christ Superstar* with the hard rock riffs driving Judas's songs "Heaven on Their Minds" and "Damned for All Time" as well as the Temple scene which together signify Judas's search for the genius and the heroic revolution.

Critical reflection

The analysis of the music and context reveals that the focus of the work centres on the complex relationship between Jesus and Judas, related mostly from Judas's perspective, as explained in his opening number "Heaven on their Minds". In Van Hove's production this relationship became lost in Judas's one-dimensional anger and Jesus's rather passive style. Houman Barekat, writing in *The New York Times*, noted that Jesus was lacking the charisma needed to be believable (Barekat 2024), and Jeroen van Wijhe, writing in *Theaterkrant*, commented that Judas was too clearly a villain, and that the lack of complexity in his characterisation meant that the nuanced relationship and the moral dilemmas between the two protagonists were lost (2024). Meanwhile, Mary's excessively tactile relationship with Jesus, made her seem like an over-protective, somewhat suffocating mother rather than an independent and fulfilled woman, and gave her no sense of identity or agency. There is little opportunity for her

---

productions he co-created and starred in called Showponies, Snowponies and No Ponies that focus on the theme of identity.

6 See also Wollman's (2006) discussion of "Rock 'Authenticity' and the Reception of the Staged Rock Musical", 24–41.

in the score, but this version failed to introduce a more contemporary reading of her character or her relationship with Jesus.

Building on the discussion of sound design above, this production—over fifty years after the original staging—benefitted from head-worn radio mics for all the performers and a well-mixed design that allowed the energy of the electronic instruments and rock sound to be revealed. However, the close micing of performers led to many of them giving low-energy vocal performances, relying on the mics rather than projecting voices and character. The notable exception was the cameo appearance of Alex Klaassen as Herod. Moreover, a filmic, realistic aesthetic in the acting style of all the cast except Klaassen, that suited the vocal style, seemed to be incompatible with the setting in a kind of amphitheatre with some of the audience seated around the stage. Rather than playing as if in the theatrical, or even the gladiatorial arena, the performances were televisual in scale.[7]

In addition, the presence of the onstage audience around this arena, which had the potential to implicate us all as bystanders, was almost never really explored, and instead, simply created problems. In his review, Barekat noted that "when the cast hand out wine bottles and glasses to audience members during the Last Supper, it's not immersive, it's just awkward" (2024). While not able to expand on Barekat's comment, as an audience member I found the sharing of food and wine was a distraction that had no advantages; the recipients of the gifts appeared confused as to what to do with the offerings, and were often ignored by the cast during the rest of the performance.

At other times the motivations of the ensemble characters and Apostles, that are confusing in this work because it was written as an album where it is unnecessary to characterise consistently, have not been visually clarified in this production sufficiently. In this production, the ensemble appeared to change loyalty for no reason, and to go from supporting Jesus singing the beautiful "Could We Start Again, Please" to smearing blood over his whipped body in a rather confusing and instant transformation. Further, as Barekat noted, "smearing blood over each

---

7   In line with the close micing that has led to a tendency among performers to sing lightly on the breath, which has the consequence of creating a characterisation that fails to reach audiences beyond the first row, acting in a televisual style assumes audiences are as close as the camera is in a studio.

other's torsos in a heavy-handed metaphor for their [the ensemble's] moral complicity in Jesus's demise" was "overwrought and trite" (Barekat 2024), though it chimed with the gladiatorial amphitheatre. In addition, the scenes of Jesus being tortured and mutilated were not only violent but beautifully lit to the extent that they appeared to glorify the violence they might have been expected to critique.

Some of this is, of course, the result of the history of the work's creation as an album that does not make the actions and motivations of the ensemble clear, but this difficulty has been dealt with differently in other productions. While the work continues to resonate very strongly with contemporary issues of occupation, rebellion and war and has huge potential for reworking, this production seems to miss the exploration of human relationships and tragedy that is at the heart of the work. On the other hand, in my opinion, the musical score has stood the test of time and guides the dramaturgy of the work, if one only listens.

Expanding the method | *The Tempest* (2016) at the Royal Shakespeare Company: sound and music in a literary theatre

Moving beyond the analysis of musical theatre, one can apply similar methods to the study of theatre music and sound in the production of a literary text. As an example, here I will refer to a chapter I wrote in *Music and Sound in European Theatre: Practices, Performances, Perspectives* (2025), which analyses the music and sound of a 2016 production of *The Tempest* (William Shakespeare 1610) directed by Gregory Doran and composed by Paul Englishby with sound design by Jeremy Dunn. This production has previously been much discussed because of its technological innovations: Ariel was played by an actor who appeared live onstage in a computer-connected bodysuit that generated an avatar that could shape-shift, while his voice was technologically enhanced and accompanied by offstage sopranos. I wanted to explore what the sound and music were contributing to this modern staging, or whether since the visual elements were so dramatic, the music was almost mundane in its reflection of the performance text.

Beginning from the premise that theatre music comprises the combination of music and sound, and that discussing their interaction with narrative and visual texts is essential to interpretation, I argue that this production is revealed to be deeply political, and, in fact, contributes to debates about colonisation and enslavement. Although music and sound are often designed to be 'unheard' they impact on audiences in ways that can be political and are often underestimated.

The chapter begins by discussing the details of the production before considering the historical context of *The Tempest*, the commission for which was as a court wedding masque in the English Jacobean court in 1610. Highlighting this context, its narrative contains a wedding masque before the nuptials of the play's young lovers. After discovering the correspondence between the director and composer of the 2016 production along with the sound designer's notes in the RSC's archives, I began to analyse the extent to which the team was exploring how hierarchies and class structures could be revealed through musical and sonic language.

The main characters mentioned in this analysis are: Prospero, a dispossessed Italian duke shipwrecked on the island with his daughter Miranda; Caliban, the indigenous resident of the island whom Prospero has enslaved and tortured and and Ariel, a magical fairy sprite whom Prospero has also enslaved. There is always a debate in this play as to whether the magical control of the environment and the creation of the storm, that shipwrecks the other characters (who were responsible for Prospero's dispossession and banishment many years earlier) on the island at the start of the play, is caused directly by Prospero's magic, or indirectly by Ariel who seeks his own freedom by carrying out Prospero's instructions.

Since there are several songs as well as the masque in the play, these instances of diegetic music and sound were analysed to reveal how certain aesthetic qualities are employed to reveal character. While the magical Ariel and the fairy sprites are accompanied by high pitched voices and bell sounds, Caliban has no music on which to draw, singing unaccompanied except for his own stamping and a drumbeat, and the drunken sailors sing with him completely unaccompanied. The "effect is to create a context for the performance that uses quite conventional signifiers of magic, ethereality, otherness and the historical context of the early modern" period, which gradually slips from Prospero's control (Taylor 2025, 179). In this way the historical setting of the play and the status of the characters is revealed, and the politics of the decolonial reading of the play begins to appear. The power to enslave is linked with music—those who have it have magical power, natural or usurped.

Subsequently, in a discussion of soundscape and atmosphere, it is the use of silence that becomes notable, particularly in the final scene when Ariel—who, in this interpretation, was constrained by Prospero to generate the island's music and magic—is released from his servitude, and Prospero (the occupier of the island) is left facing Caliban, its other earthly inhabitant who he has enslaved, now powerless and in silence. Conceptually, this contemporary production uses traditional musical hierarchies and sonic signifiers (the magic bells and voices of fairy music, the absence of music and raucous voices for the 'lower' characters) that draw attention not just to the history of enslavement, but its politics. Prospero's usurpation of the island and enslavement of its indigenous peoples is revealed once his magic staff and musical control are relinquished. Then, finally, Ariel flies freely away and Caliban stands tall and stately before the diminished and music-less Prospero.

In a similar fashion to the case study addressed above, I conclude that "just as in the integrated musical, and in keeping with Chion's concept of added value in film, the music and sound design in mainstream literary theatre adds, shapes, manoeuvres and interacts with the other elements of the performance […] that is designed to be unobtrusive and whose true value and impact is often underestimated" (2025, 185). In this case, it is through music and its absence that the decolonial reading of the director, composer and sound designer is fully revealed.

Suggestions for further reading

Banfield's *Sondheim's Broadway Musicals* (1993) set the precedent for methods for analysing the interaction of music and narrative in musical theatre. It is still the most comprehensive book of its kind with excellent case studies. Sternfeld's *The Megamusical* (2006) outlines what constitutes a megamusical and then analyses many of those produced before 2006. In "In Defence of Pleasure" (2007), an article about teaching a course on musical theatre, Stacy Wolf adds an appendix that lists "Some Elements of Music Analysis", designed to encourage non-musicologists not just to realise how much they understand through their experience and interpretation of music, but how they might discuss and describe it. I have not mentioned dance in my analysis, not least because there is no dance in these case studies, but when dance is included in a musical, the clearest explanation of how to analyse it is Phoebe Rumsey's "Reading Dance: The Body in Motion Onstage" (2024).

References

Abbate, Carolyn. 1991. *Unsung Voices: Opera and Musical Narrative in the Nineteenth Century*. Princeton University Press.

Barekat, Houman. 2024. "Searching for the Superstar in Ivo van Hove's Jesus Christ." Review. *New York Times*, January 22.

Banfield, Stephen. 1993. *Sondheim's Broadway Musicals*. University of Michigan Press.

Chion, Michel. 1994 [1990]. *Audio-Vision: Sound on Screen*, edited and translated by Claudia Gorbman. Columbia University Press.

Collison, David. 2008. *The Sound of Theatre: A History*. PLASA.

Gorbman, Claudia. 1987. *Unheard Melodies: Narrative Film Music*. Indiana University Press.

Lloyd Webber, Andrew and Tim Rice. n.d. Jesus Christ Superstar [Vocal Score]. The Really Useful Group Limited.

McMillin, Scott. 2006. *The Musical as Drama*. Princeton University Press.

Rumsey, Phoebe. 2024. "Reading Dance: The Body in Motion Onstage." In *Dance in Musical Theatre*, edited by Dustyn Martincich and Phoebe Rumsey. Methuen.

Snelson, John. 2004. *Andrew Lloyd Webber*. Yale University Press.

Sternfeld, Jessica. 2006. *The Megamusical*. Indiana University Press.

Sternfeld, Jessica. 2024. Email Communication. March 19 2024.

Taylor, Millie. 2016 [2012]. *Musical Theatre, Realism and Entertainment*. Routledge.

Taylor, Millie. 2025. "*The Tempest* (2016) at the Royal Shakespeare Company: Music and Sound in a Literary Theatre." In *Music and Sound in European Theatre: Practices, Performances, Perspectives*, edited by David Roesner and Tamara Yasmin Quick. https://doi.org/10.4324/9781032678214

Thomas, Richard K. 2008. *The Designs of Abe Jacob*. United States Institute for Theatre Technology.

Van Wijhe, Jeroen. 2024. "Superstar herrijst door cast en mooie beelden." *Theaterkrant*. January 23 2024. https://www.theaterkrant.nl/recensie/jesus-christ-superstar-2/albert-verlinde-producties/

Wolf, Stacy. 2007. "In Defense of Pleasure: Musical Theatre History in the Liberal Arts [A Manifesto]." *Theatre Topics* 17 (1): 51–60. https://doi.org/10.1353/tt.2007.0014

Wollman, Elizabeth Lara. 2006. *The Theater Will Rock: A History of the Rock Musical, from Hair to Hedwig.* University of Michigan Press. https://doi.org/10.3998/mpub.119496

7. A Multimodal Critical Discourse Analysis of Listening

Pieter Verstraete

Summary

This chapter introduces a multimodal Critical Discourse Analysis model well-tuned to the analysis of sound and music in the theatre in relation to other impulses like gestures, images, texts and spaces. This methodology facilitates discussion of the connections between direct auditory perceptions and other sense perceptions in narrativising music and sound. It combines analysis of listening modalities, as introduced by R. Murray Schafer and Barry Truax, with theories of music and sound as communicative affordance in discourse, like Lyndon Way and Simon McKerrell's. One critical aspect of the method is that it can reveal the ideological aspects lurking behind the power of music and sound. For that purpose, the methodology incorporates Stuart Hall's encoding/decoding differentiation which explains how we consent to certain dominant, hegemonic ideas in which both processes of encoding (intentional meanings at the production side) and decoding (possible interpretations) take place in line with national and geopolitical interests, or in other words, the dominant cultural order. The method is well-suited for the discussion of music(al) theatre in all its forms, but it has been also developed for other audiovisual media, like music videos or the use of music in TikTok reels.

Introduction

There resides great communicative power in music and sound. Yet *to mean* something, sounds, including musical sounds, are very weak signifiers in themselves. They are more semantically ambiguous than any other signifier (Moore 2013, 14; Way & Mc Kerrell 2017, 3). Hearing and listening are imbued with a fundamental insufficiency that needs to be complemented by signification and discourse in such a way that it makes the auditory experience meaningful. First of all, listening is 'insufficient' in that sensory stimuli always present an uncontrollable form of excess to the perceiving system, which is filtered out for self-protection. The ear needs to be selective or biased, because the ear is vulnerable in the absence of ear lids, while sound is omnidirectional and pierces directly through into our inner ears. Secondly, listening always needs the connection with other sense perceptions to stimulate our ability to process our experiences into something meaningful. The eye-sight is the culturally preferred sense but the imagination also plays a role, as we will see, in the theatre, and a lot depends then on memory or familiarity.

Narrativisation is a powerful mode to make sense of the world. But Theodor Adorno once mentioned in a comment to Mahler that music can only constitute "a narrative which relates nothing" (Nattiez 1990, 245) as music can never produce a clear narrative on its own as text does. It can only simulate a sense of narrative through impulses in the listener to imagine their own. In a representational context, be it in opera, musical theatre or experimental 'music theatre', but also in theatre in general, sonic or musical narratives can be triggered and channelled but always in relation to other signifiers, like lyrics, dialogues, images, bodies or gestures on stage, but also linguistic texts outside the performance, like brochures, programme notes etc. In the absence of them, we would relate the music or the sounds to what we do know, or what we can imagine as far as the (musical) sounds afford triggering certain modes of listening in us. This calls for attention to the role of our auditory imagination and how it is called upon in a specific theatre production.

This chapter proposes then a multimodal method of analysis that discusses the connections between our direct auditory perceptions and other perceptions for sense-making in narrativising music and sound in the theatre in a critical way. One critical aspect of that process and method is that it can reveal the ideological aspects lurking behind the power of music and sound to muddle or obscure the possible meanings with their ambiguity. This will prove to be a method well-suited for the discussion of music(al) theatre in all its forms, despite its many different traditions. This method sits between analysis of the modalities of our listening habits and music as communication and discourse, between a phenomenology and semiotics of listening.

Context | Multimodality, discourse and the listening subject

The core of the method I am proposing here is to study the power issues at hand arising from sonic situations in the theatre. Before I explore the method, it is important to understand the reasons and origins of the power relations within sound and music perception, as well as the critical environment in which the method has originated.

A key principle of sound that explains the need for auditory imagination and its narrativisation is 'acousmatisation'. Acousmatisation is today ubiquitous with all the sound technology that splits recorded sound from its origins, even when the production of sound is simultaneous. The acousmatic listening situation, which is most central to the theatre although we are often not aware of it, opens the road to imagination and with that, ideology. When sounds are detached from their originating bodies, they give rise to affordances of listening positions: we feel we need to position ourselves towards these sounds, we feel 'interpellated' or addressed by them.[1] Listening perspectives to the sounds are traditionally described as 'points' of listening/audition (Beck 1998; Rodero Antón 2009) within the spatial and semiotic design of the play. The true phenomenal reality is, however, that sound comes

---

[1] An affordance is the quality or property of an object that defines its possible usage or actions by its user/agent as shaped by the relationship between the latter and its environment. J.J. Gibson (1997) developed the concept of *affordance* in his study, *The Ecological Approach to Visual Perception* (Vol. 1), yet it has been also widely applied to music and sound.

to us rather as atmospheric in a zone of attention, not necessarily clear points in space, calling for our active attention: "Above all, when we 'attend' the theatre we are necessarily required to make an effort, to do something, to *stretch ourselves*" (Home-Cook 2015, 1).

This need for stretching and relating to sounds happens when sounds are detached from their originating bodies, which in their turn give rise to affordances of listening positions. Later I will discuss how these positions give rise to listening modes depending on how our attention is steered, like causal listening, listening-in-search (analytical listening), semantic listening, representational and concert modes, but also other semiotic modes of listening—narrativisation is a very potent one. I will return to these terms in the 'How to' section. Modes of listening have been discussed ever since the 1970s, particularly centred around Soundscape Analysis, associated with the World Soundscape Project (WSP) initiated by R. Murray Schafer (1977), and *Acoustic Communication* by Barry Truax (1984) which found its way into film studies (Doane 1980; Metz 1980; Chion 1983/1994) and very limitedly in theatre studies (Verstraete 2009, Home-Cook 2015), as well as (New) Musicology (Dell'Antonio 2004; Sloboda 2010). My contribution is to consider these modes of listening together with a larger multimodality of the stage. Moreover, these listening positions as 'affordances' can also be enhanced by technology on the stage, which gives a certain media opacity to the experience of the music or the sound(scape) but often make us unaware of our positionings. The use of popular music on the stage, as is particular to musical theatre, also needs extra scrutiny due to its power to promote socio-political interests and cultural values in ways that often go unreflected.

It is then crucial to find clues in the performance as to how the spectator, as part of an audience, may be addressed (or 'interpellated', following Althusser 1970) by the codes in the performance which, through steering their listening attention, incite specific responses in the audience, and with that, specific discursive interpretations. A multimodal approach would allow for a dynamic model that is aware of the switching between many possible modes depending on these affordances and a dynamic processing of communicative meanings (as signs) because or in spite of the listeners' persuasive address and their own agency.

There are two more caveats to this all. One is the realisation that 'the' spectator or 'the' listener does not exist; there must be room for different interpretations by audience members with diverse backgrounds. The cognitive processing as a result of the modes of listening depends on the specific situation, time, place and sociocultural conditions. Second is the critique that not all experiences in the theatre are semiotic; particularly sound and music contribute to phenomenological experiences in a more embodied, somatic sense that does not always contribute to decodable or verbalised meanings in the audience's minds. The method needs to acknowledge music's ability to stimulate general, 'unnuanced' emotions as well as more nuanced memories, associations and emotions (Cook 2001; Way & McKerrell 2017, 9).

This brings me to the need for a Multimodal Critical Discourse Analysis (MCDA). The latter has been proposed by several authors in the 1990s up to the 2010s like Theo van Leeuwen (1999) and David Machin (2010), mostly out of a dissatisfaction with an overemphasis on language in Critical Discourse Analysis. Ever since *Reading Images* was published in 1996 by Gunther Kress and Theo van Leeuwen, the focus has shifted from written language to meanings in texts that have other semiotic sources such as visual codes, material objects, architecture and sound, as well as music. In his discussion of multimodal analysis, Lyndon Way approaches music as a communicative affordance. Way's model allows us to understand musical sound for its communicative power in relation to other modes and thus, signifying systems, though he focuses on audiovisual media like YouTube (Way 2021). I propose to extend Way's approach to theatre as another multimodal text.

In MCDA, multimodality refers to "the use of several semiotic modes in the design of a semiotic product or event, together with the particular way in which these modes are combined" (Kress and van Leeuwen 2001, 20). MCDA studies then how these different semiotic modes, like images, texts and sounds work together to convey meaning in order to understand how they interact with issues of power, ideology and identity. MCDA finds its origins in Critical Discourse Studies and functional grammar (Halliday 1985). These studies suggest that linguistic and visual choices reveal broader discourses articulated in texts (Kress and van Leeuwen 2001), and we should add to that: auditory and musical choices. Discourse can be thought of as a 'model' of how we understand and have access to the world. It projects certain social values, attitudes and ideas that contribute to the (re)production of social life. The aim of analysis is then to reveal what kinds of social relations of power, inequalities, and interests are generated, reproduced and legitimised in texts, be it explicitly or implicitly (van Dijk 1993). 'Texts' should of course be understood here in the wider semiotic project as any constellation or assemblage of signs.

Multimodality has been proposed for the study of narratives too, particularly in post-classical Narratology. One such new perspective was on music as narrative, which also brought in new cognitive approaches to comprehend and analyse the listener's ability to 'narrativise' auditory stimuli even in the absence of a clear, traditional narrative. According to Allen Moore (2013), certain types of music or musical sounds afford certain meanings in a society—some more than others, yet not all meanings are equally plausible. Usually, the interrelationship between music and language restricts the meanings in a particular way, while 'undercoded' musical sounds, particularly in a situation where the source is ambiguous (aka acousmatic sound), may afford many more possible meanings (Way & McKerrell 2017, 3).

In the 'Demonstration' section, I will discuss how a theatrical context with its multiple semiotic modes may restrict the affordances of (musical) sounds, yet they may also imbue new, unexpected meanings in the spectator's imaginations due to their ambiguity. Inspired by social and cultural semiotics, we could say that discourse has moulded and keeps shaping the way the listener responds, makes sense of and thereby positions oneself as listening subject, and that positioning shapes in turn the very (listening) culture that it is part of. It is key then to study how these ambiguities caused by sound and music in the theatre play into hidden ideologies, not just to make sense but also to sustain power relations and interests through the ways we position ourselves to the discourse of a theatre performance. In the next section, I will introduce the key terms of the conceptual toolbox to analyse our listening modalities in the theatre while teasing out the often unreflected, ideological bearings of sound and music.

How to | Modes of listening and ideology

In my classes on 'Music, Theatre and Sound' in the MA programme of the University of Groningen, I usually start with "ear cleaning" and "deep listening" exercises, as developed in the 1970s by R. Murray Schafer and Paulina Oliveros, to make students aware of their listening modes in relation to the ubiquity of sound in their everyday environments and in controlled spaces like the theatre.[2] Among those modalities are background listening (more precisely, secondary, absorbed or distracted listening, and global perception or evenly hovering attention), causal listening, listening-in-readiness, listening-in-search, reduced listening and semantic listening (Truax 1984; Chion 1994), which can be put on a horizontal scale ranging from low to high attention levels. These are ingrained modalities as part of our cognitive system to filter out noise and perceptual redundancies. They are usually triggered by the context and the sounds themselves, depending on the listening perspectives they afford to, or as Truax suggests: "The way in which a sound *functions* for the listener depends on its social and environmental contexts" (1984, 24).

In the theatre, different from the everyday, more specific semantic and discursive modes play a role as the attention is steered in more controlled ways. The same holds for radio drama or as Alan Beck (1997) calls it, somewhat misleadingly, "fictional soundscapes", as opposed to real-life soundscapes (Ferrington 1994), where the director "fills the role of ideal 'ears', selecting, focusing and designing" while "the audience actively play their part in the construction of the 'second play' in their heads" (section 1.2). The latter I have termed the *auditory imagination* (Verstraete 2009), which determines the extent to which we can discursively associate feelings, memories, images, or in short,

---

2 'Ear cleaning' is a term and set of exercises that Schafer introduced in an experimental music course he offered at the Simon Fraser University at the end of the 1960s, with which he brought awareness to his students around environmental sound and our listening modes. He published his lecture notes in a book, *Ear Cleaning: Notes for an Experimental Music Course* (1967). Similarly, by the beginning of the 1970s, Oliveros developed her therapeutic methods in 'sonic meditations' for weekly gatherings with a women-only group, the '♀ Ensemble', in her home in San Diego. In the 1990s, she would extend her methods and organise 'deep-listening' retreats for 'ear-minded people'. The scripts of her instructions were collected in handbooks, like *Sonic Meditations* (1971) and *Deep Listening: A Composer's Sound Practice* (2003). Both Schafer's and Oliveros' methods are rooted in a deep engagement with everyday soundscapes.

meanings to the sounds that we perceive. Cultural discourse including learned associations as well as personal, idiosyncratic memories play a role in this. The theatre production combines and shapes the listening perspectives, and ultimately the modes that are afforded for, in relation to other sign systems of which it makes use. The context of (representational) theatre sharpens our analytical and semantic modes of listening besides representational and "concert or recital" modes (Kivy 1994), which allows us, for instance, to both enjoy beautifully executed songs for their musicality and artistry while attending to the world represented in the fiction or 'diegesis' (extramusically): "[W]e are in a mode of attention that is both—and very *strongly* both—one of attending to a singer giving a 'performance' (remember how the action comes to a full stop for the applause!), and attending to a character in a drama making an expressive utterance" (Kivy 1994, 68). Kivy's two modes of listening attention are perhaps not exclusive to the theatre or concert stage only. Ruth Herbert (2011), for instance, remarks that everyday music listening constitutes "a series of binarisms on the theme of 'special' and 'everyday' musical interaction: aesthetic pleasure or functional resource; complex or basic emotions; music-focused or listener-focused experience" (2). In that regard, everyday listening (according to Gaver 1993, listening to events) and specialised musical listening (listening to sound characteristics) might perhaps not create such an incommensurable gap as Pierre Schaeffer (1966) once saw it. Yet the theatre and concert hall create an aural context where one simply has to listen, or as Peter Szendy remarks: "[M]usical listening that is aware of itself has always been accompanied in me with the feeling of a duty. Of an imperative: you have to listen, one must listen" (Szendy 2008, 1).

Besides this double mode of attention to music there is also the possibility of narrativisation of music as one of the most attentive but complex semiotic modes of listening. According to Monika Fludernik (1996), narrativisation constitutes a way for readers to solve inconsistencies in a text, which would otherwise be "unreadable" (34). As musical sounds are semantically ambiguous, there might be extramusical, contextual clues or affordances in the structure of the assemblage of sound itself that stimulates a narrative impulse in the listener-spectator. Narrative is then a "basic pattern-forming cognitive system bearing on sequences experienced through time" (Meelberg 2018, 847).

There is, however, a semantic confusion in the modes that we can analyse in MCDA. In Way's model, discourse is studied critically as reproduced through different modes in a multimodal text, like a music video. With 'mode' he explicitly means a socially agreed-upon channel of communication, like a medium or means of expression that would bring in its own code, rather than a channel of human perception (Way & McKerrell 2017). He includes, for instance, lyrics, visuals and musical sounds as modes (2018, 22). Yet what I want to underline is that depending on how our attention is steered, the meanings afforded by these means of communication are heavily dependent on our modes of perception, particularly in listening. So, I propose to include modes of listening as equally embedded in discursive practices of meaning making than signifiers like lyrics, visuals or sounds. My model is then moving from an objectivist approach to a more performative one, encompassing affective, somatic and cognitive aspects of perception and interpretation of these channels of communication.

How these discursive practices of meaning making are connected to ideology still needs our attention. After Gramsci, Raymond Williams defined ideology as "a more general predominance which includes, as one of its key features, a particular way of seeing the world and human nature and relationships" (1988, 145; qtd. in Way 2022, 12). Way follows this definition of ideology as the basis for his MCDA method, noting that multimodal texts do also take part in the ongoing hegemonic battles for re-winning the consent of a societal majority. Within British Cultural Studies, the Birmingham School in particular has offered tools and terms to discuss how we consent to certain dominant, hegemonic ideas through our ways of reading popular cultural messages. Stuart Hall (1973; 1999) speaks of a "complex structure in dominance" in which both processes of encoding (intentional meanings at the production side) and decoding (possible interpretations) take place, namely in line with national and geopolitical interests, that is, the dominant cultural order. His model, though meant to analyse broadcasting messages, can still inspire us today to analyse ideological positions in other multimodal texts such as theatre and performance.

Hall sees encoding and decoding as distinctive or 'determinate' moments, each with their own set of modalities, forms and conditions of existence (1999, 508). They do not need to correspond necessarily, and the intentionality of both has been critiqued numerous times. Yet Hall's three "codes" or positions in the interplay of presumed intentions or affordances and the reader's responses to them can still be useful to discuss ideological positions. The terms that Hall proposes are: dominant-hegemonic, negotiated and oppositional positions. When we try to decipher the codes inside a multimodal text as close as intended "in terms of the reference code in which it has been encoded" (515), then we are dealing with a possible dominant-hegemonic code or position. A second possible position, the negotiated position, happens when we acknowledge the legitimacy of the hegemonic "definitions of situations and events which are 'in dominance' (*global*) ... while, at a more restricted, situational (situated) level, it makes its own ground rules—it operates with exceptions to the rule" (516). Here the decoding deviates somewhat from intended, presumably encoded meanings, yet it does not challenge the structure in dominance it is part of. The third possible position is oppositional in that it decodes "in a *globally* contrary way" (517).

For Hall, these three major positions are entrenched in—thus 'afforded' by—the codes at hand and can be revealed through MCDA. For our analysis, we should then also discuss the interplay between certain codes and their affordances in the multimodal text, and the modes of listening that are elicited and that are complicit in the ideological positions the spectator ultimately takes. The analytical model of MCDA for listening in the theatre that I propose here includes then the integrated analysis of the following four aspects:

1. the functions of sound and music, including their properties, besides other signifiers in a performance, like images, lyrics, texts, but also scenography and other significant stage properties;

2. the afforded listening modes, including background, causal, acousmatic, reduced, semantic listening, more specialised modes like listening-in-readiness, listening-in-search, representational, concert or recital modes;

3. narrativisation as a more elaborate semiotic mode specific to music (but also 'sonic narratives') often incited by a narrative point-of-audition;
4. the cultural discourse of the reception and audience context, including cultural references and ideology, as manifesting in the afforded positions by the listener-spectator as 'dominant-hegemonic', 'negotiated, or 'oppositional'.

I will demonstrate this model further in the next section. Let's apply and discuss this through an example: the longest-running musical in the Netherlands, *Soldaat van Oranje* (2010–today) by producers Fred Boot and Robin de Levita with compositions by Tom Harriman and lyrics by Pamela Phillips Oland, set to Dutch by Frans van Deursen.

Demonstration | A multimodal critical discourse analysis of *Soldaat van Oranje*

The Dutch musical *Soldaat van Oranje* (trans. Soldier of Orange) is a good case study to analyse ideological underpinnings due to its success as popular musical entertainment and its mythologising effects of its subject matter. It has all the elements of a state-of-the-nation play, where the nation—in this case the Netherlands—becomes the real protagonist in order to reflect on national identity and the state of its culture today.[3] The musical narrates the story of resistance fighter Erik Hazelhoff Roelfzema who collaborated with the exiled Queen Wilhelmina during the Second World War, based on his 1970 autobiography and even more so, Paul Verhoeven's movie of the same name from 1977. In the musical, the protagonist becomes the prism through which one can process the trauma of war while also invoking patriotic pride and reinforcing Dutch national identity.

The musical has already been scrutinised by critics for its 'selective' patriotism which makes it "a blind spot for race and a rather selective history of Dutch heroism in wartime" (van Wijhe & Mikołajczyk 2022, 408) as well as for its playing into emotions of white supremacy through

---

3 The 'state-of-the-nation play' is a British tradition of playwriting that has disappeared. It indicates play texts that engage with the nation. The term appears in Michael Billington's 2007 book, *The State of the Nation: British Theatre since 1945*.

cultural memory in times of an upsurge of far-right populism in the Netherlands (van Hulst 2024). Jeroen van Wijhe Jacez and Mikołajczyk base their criticisms predominantly on the narrative and the overall perspective through the eyes of those characters that are in the anti-Nazi resistance, which would underline the *dominant-hegemonic* reading of the musical play:

> Although several characters in Soldaat van Oranje look away or support Nazi Germany, Holland's involvement in the war is seen through the eyes of its resistance heroes. This emphasis on heroism is as telling of its success as its exciting staging and historical weight. Rather than a history lesson, it can be read as a myth in the vein of David and Goliath: a young everyman confronting the might of the Third Reich (2022, 407).

The "myth" here turns into interpellation in the song "Morgen is Vandaag" ("Tomorrow Is Today") in the third scene of the first act, after we are introduced to Erik and his friends in their student association where it is made clear that if they, and thus "by extension, the audience want to fight oppression, they need to act now" (idem). This myth is not entirely innocent as the musical's main narrative line—as well as some of the idyllic images of the Netherlands that are projected right in the beginning of the show—is in line with current right-wing parties' celebration of a glorious, 'typically Dutch' past, which anti-racist mainstreaming would expose today as white supremacist. Van Hulst digs deeper into the myth by revealing how narrative and an all-white cast work together to perpetuate a "white innocence" (Wekker 2016), particularly by omitting references to Erik's and Queen Wilhelmina's roles in the occupation of Indonesia.

Notwithstanding the fair analyses that reveal a deeper ideological shadow looming over the dominant-hegemonic positions of the play, what these criticisms lack, however, is a multimodal critical approach that analyses listening modes in context. One key principle in this musical drama is the shifts of listening modes from immersive historical soundscapes as background listening—where the script speaks of 'drone' music—to semantic listening to the speech and lyrics, while also enacting shifts between representational realms of listening between film and theatre. The documentary-style projections are clearly meant to give the fiction an aura of authenticity, while the immersion of the spectacle cancels out any critical judgement on the veracity of the events as *pars pro toto* for the Dutch war situation.

One such moment is the transition to scene 6 when the stage wall closes, while Erik and his friend Bram drive away on a motorbike and a projection of a historical montage is shown with images of the battle of Grebbeberg and the German attack on the Valkenburg airport. The latter is actually the place where the audience is located, as they are seated in an old airplane shed ('hangar'). The audience is drowned in patriotic brass music while the text of "Day Two and Three" appears with the sound of strikes on an old typewriter. Another moment of such immersion happens between scenes 11 and 12, where a historical mash-up of old news reels are sonically mixed with Hitler's voice, the sound of breaking glass and gunshots, accompanied by an emotional, symphonic musical score. The images we see are from 1941, as the script reveals: "arrests of resistance fighters, razzias against Jews, the February strike" (45). The background music with its surround sound in both instances cinematises the experience, calling for a more absorbed, 'secondary' listening (Frith 1996), while it also incites narrativising the projected images and on-stage events, blending history with fiction in the spectator's auditory imagination.[4]

Sonic immersion in *Soldaat van Oranje* is often overlooked as just being part of the rock music aesthetic in this genre of theatre—a megamusical—and its volume politics, but it is a great catalyst for ideological ideas, like an uncritical Dutch patriotism based on historical inaccuracies, that go unnoticed.[5] The immersion is enhanced even further by the intricate SceneAround system, a 360-degree rotating auditorium which makes the seamless transitions between the static sets around the audience not

---

4   Simon Frith uses the term 'secondary listening' for situations in which the act of listening is not the primary focus of the experience.
5   As part of global expansion since the 1980s, 'megamusicals' were developed and popularised by producers like Andrew Lloyd Webber and Cameron Mackintosh. They are typically large-scale musical theatre productions that concern large investments for large commercial profit, international audiences, higher stakes, and follow therefore an industrial logic through the cultivation of a particular commercial aesthetic model of production that ensures replication at a greater number of international venues (Burston 1998, 205–06). Although *Soldaat van Oranje* is a specifically Dutch-language musical for the Dutch national context, it follows those same production models and was said to be replicated on the London stage.

just 'cinematic' but also dynamic—as if the audience is moving along with the dramatic characters in the action. The first time this happens is right before scene 5, "Day One", when the auditorium starts to rotate while the audience sees projections on the wall of marching soldiers. The audience moves along as the war unfolds. They are moved to celebrate the heroism of individual resistance fighters as representative of the Dutch anti-war attitude, without acknowledging other, politically organised forms of resistance. It is all part of that same interpellation of the individual through a collective experience described earlier: act now before it is too late.

In MCDA, the affects created by this dynamic spatial setup and scenography can take prominence besides the textual input from the character conversations and lyrics, and the other semiotic codes of the theatre. Not only does the visceral sense of movement turn the musical spectacle into a theme park experience, but it also cancels out any critical judgement as one is forced to move along with the system. The Italian (protofascist) Futurists or even Antonin Artaud could only dream of such a theatre where the spectator is totally immersed into the machinery of the auditorium. This is particularly ironic in a context of an unreflective, dominant-hegemonic reading of the play which equates anti-fascism with Dutch nationalism and patriotism, and by extension, an exclusively white Dutch national identity. The war machine it purports to critique, and that drives all the characters, in fact immerses the audience, leaving no escape or distancing possible.

However, the multimodality of the scenes in combination with the rotating auditorium can also afford a resilient position against the representation of a rigid hegemony, be it of the German enemy and its Dutch collaborators, or the 'good old'—Christian/royalist—Dutch nation that celebrates its patriotism against the Germans. Such a compelling, oppositional reading is precisely made possible by the interplay of sensuous modalities, musical narrativisation and context, delivered by text and action but also spatial cues on the stage. It is sustained in the moments when we see our main protagonist Erik resisting the image of a post-War Netherlands that goes back to being a Christian-royal abiding nation: instead, he gives us a powerful image of a hero driving away from it all on a motorcycle in true *Top Gun* style, a topos in Hollywood cinema that is also not without ideology. MCDA can reveal here how the music and its listening modalities can call for a more critical, oppositional reading, while this state-of-the-nation musical poses the question to its audiences: in what kind of country do we want to live?

This is particularly clear in scene 33, when Erik arrives at Anneville where liberation festivities are going on. In the background, a waltz is playing (in the script it is called a "freedom waltz"), which is in fact Johannes Brahms' Waltz in A-flat Major (Opus 39, no.15) performed by the Budapest Strings. Erik invites Queen Wilhelmina to the dance, which is a bit awkward as the queen is seemingly uneasy. The dance breaks up abruptly when Queen Wilhelmina asks him to become her personal adjutant (assistant), which Erik respectfully rejects. All the while, the waltz music keeps playing. For the observant listener with a sense of history, the waltz could remind them of the 'good German music' that the Nazi Reich Chamber of Music defined against the degenerate music (*Entartete Musik*) between 1933 and 1945, although it is not clear if the producers were aware of this.[6] Brahms was on that list as a main representative of traditionalist classical music against modern music, reflecting traditional German values, which made his music particularly prone to political appropriation: "Brahms's music was ideal for bolstering the trustworthiness of the Nazi state, showing its high cultural standards as well as the great tradition of the German cultural heritage" (Petersen 2019, 343). Such appropriations can be meaningful also in this particular scene of the musical, where the liberated Netherlands did not look particularly more (culturally) progressive than its German counterpart in the post-War era, when "only the enduring culture of earlier times could provide comfort and renewed self-esteem" (345). Through the codes of music, we get an impression of how post-War Netherlands has exchanged its more contentious NSB milieu and its exuberant parties (which we observed earlier in the musical drama) for

---

6   Producer Fred Boot explained in an email to me (29 May 2024) that the plan was to use a waltz composed by Tom Harriman (potentially based on the song "The Queen Does Not Tolerate a No" as a musical *leitmotif* earlier in the production). But circumstance had it that the music was never composed, and they have been using the same music that was used in the rehearsals of 2010.

a more toned-down environment that re-establishes permanence with the past, albeit one that still recycles nationalistic parts in its culture.

On an affective level, the waltz's triple meter typically expresses continuous movement and consistency, which a background listening would only confirm in the spectator's mind. On an unconscious level, a musical narrative supports the dominant-hegemonic position, in which the SceneAround system also helps to situate the listener. Yet here, the Dutch celebrations have a distinctive nationalist flavour that welcomes back old ideas of an establishment and hierarchy with the queen as her most ardent advocator: the image of the nation's future as a unitary state is no different from what it tries to escape from, hence Erik's refusal to be a part of it (although in reality, he did accept the queen's offer). Seconds later, the auditorium turns again, while Erik walks by the Kurhaus and onto a jetty to reveal an impressive sunset. Erik's point of view in this awe-inspiring scenography is heralding a heroic individualism against a fascistic system and hegemony, although its intended message is probably more negotiated, as Erik does not reject the nation and national identity that is promoted here as a whole. Despite all the affective manipulations through musical narrative and scenography, the vigilant spectator does have a choice for a third way: to 'act now' is to resist the imposed dominant-hegemonic and negotiated positions.

Despite the hegemonic-dominant and negotiated positions that this visual spectacle offers to the spectator in terms of its brazen patriotism and nationalism, our MCDA method, by focusing on music and sound, revealed possible positions to oppose them, be it mildly. MCDA helps us then to critique the underlying ideological positions in the modes of address and their affordance structure of the multimodal text of this musical state-of-the-nation play.

Expanding the method | From music theatre to audio-visual media analysis

The MCDA method, in combination with ideology criticism, offers a fitting approach to a theatre and performance analysis that tries to incorporate performative aspects of sense modalities in a discussion of both affects and signifiers in context. The method is not only useful to discuss popular forms of musical theatre, which are often neglected and misunderstood as merely 'entertainment', but also opera and new music theatre—to emancipate them from their literary and musicological approaches, as I have shown elsewhere with the *La Didone* (2007) production by the Wooster Group, for instance (Verstraete 2010).

In that production, the multimodality of the theatre was played out to juxtapose two sonic environments in a sound montage by Matt Schloss, namely that of Francesco Cavalli's baroque opera *La Didone* from 1641, and of Mario Bava's cult science-fiction film *Terrore Nello Spazio* (1965) better known as *Planet of the Vampires*. The proposed method would not only allow us to analyse how these distinct sonic narrative worlds start to blend in the spectator's auditory imagination, but it also reveals a deeper ideology criticism of how our mediatised listening cultures evoke a colonial "hungry listening" (Robinson 2020), like the point of view/audition of Aeneas arriving on the shores of Carthage in the baroque opera and the American astronauts crashing on the zombie planet Aurora. The continuous narrativisation can thereby lead to questions of our own desires to make sense of these complex sonic worlds through our modes of listening.

The scope of MCDA can also be productively expanded to the experience of sound and music in other audiovisual media, like popular music clips for their potential to communicate socio-political interests and cultural values. The method as presented in this chapter could be expanded to encompass insights from cultural materialism, as Dick Zijp advocates (see Chapter 10), to address larger contextual, socio-historical and technological frames as connected to the material conditions not only of the work itself but of its experience as well. To do so would allow further discussion of how multimodal experiences in the theatre, be it on a scale of narrowcasting, but also of audiovisual media on a bigger scale, help to shape our societies.

Suggestions for further reading

As mentioned before, semiotic analyses always need to be seen in tandem with somatic and emotional layers in the phenomenological experience of sound and music. Machin's *Analysing Popular Music* (2010) offers a whole range of parameters of sound that are not necessarily 'heard' or perceived by the listener upon first hearing but that may stimulate the shaping of experiential meaning for both unnuanced emotions and nuanced associations. Machin focusses on how popular music came to mean so much, which is often overlooked in theatre analyses of listening.

To expand on the different modes of listening I recommend the conference proceedings *Listening to Music: People, Practices and Experiences* (2017), edited by Helen Barlow and David Rowlands, which is also a rich online resource for teaching. Simon Frith, for instance, discusses the potential of participatory listening, where the listener is a co-creator in music-making. Many contributors acknowledge cultural differences in (active) listening and suggest further research methods to find more empirical evidence of the listener's individual experiences, like qualitative interviews and the Listening Experience Database.[7]

For those who want to read further on the ideological nature of music, I recommend "Why is Music so Ideological…" (2007) by Marcello Sorce Keller. His insights can strengthen the basis of MCDA in discourse, as he explains how music can nurture certain values and attitudes that are tied to the identity construction of individuals and social groups ('sound groups'), with a special focus on its functions in patriotism, nationalism and totalitarianism.

Finally, MCDA could benefit from recent efforts to decolonise sound studies like Dylan Robinson's *Hungry Listening* (2020). Through music ethnography, the book focusses on the need for bringing forward forgotten indigenous listening practices in the Canadian context. It problematises the epistemic violence in colonial, hungry listening positions in Western music (theatre) traditions by recognising their ideological underpinnings. Negotiated and oppositional positions in producing music—through participation, collaboration, adaptation and "co-existence of differences" (123)—can then lead to a more inclusionary listening awareness that helps to critique our auditory experiences in our theatres today.

---

7   This online resource can be accessed via https://led.kmi.open.ac.uk/.

References

Althusser, Louis. [1970] 2006. "Ideology and Ideological State Aparatus (Notes Towards an Investigation)." In *Lenin and Philosophy and Other Essays*, translated by Ben Brewster. Aakar.

Barlow, Helen and David Rowland, eds. 2017. *Listening to Music: People, Practices and Experiences*. The Open University. http://ledbooks.org/proceedings2017/

Beck, Alan E. [1997] 2024. "Listening to Radio Plays: Fictional Soundscapes." *eContact!* 5 (3): n.p. https://econtact.ca/5_3/beck_listening.html

Billington, Michael. 2007. *The State of the Nation: British Theatre since 1945*. Faber and Faber.

Burston, Jonathan. 1998. "Theatre Space as Virtual Place: Audio Technology, the Reconfigured Singing Body, and the Megamusical." *Popular Music* 17 (2): 205–18. https://doi.org/10.1017/S026114300000060X

Chion, Michel. 1994. *Audio-Vision: Sound on Screen*. Edited and translated by Walter Murch and Claudia Gorbman. Columbia University Press. https://doi.org/10.7312/chio18588

de Vries, Edwin, book; Tom Harriman, Pamela Phillips Oland and Frans van Deursen, music; Fred Boot, producer. 2010. *Soldaat van Oranje*. Musical production.

Dell'Antonio, Andrew, ed. 2004. *Beyond Structural Listening? Postmodern Modes of Hearing*. University of California Press. https://doi.org/10.1525/california/9780520237575.001.0001

Doane, Mary Ann. 1980. "The Voice in the Cinema: The Articulation of Body and Space." *Yale French Studies* 60, Cinema/Sound: 33–50. https://doi.org/10.2307/2930003

Ferrington, Gary. 1994. "Audio Design: Creating Multi-Sensory Images for the Mind." *Journal of the International Visual Literacy Association* 14 (1): 61–67. https://doi.org/10.1080/23796529.1994.11674490

Fludernik, Monika. 1996. *Towards a 'Natural' Narratology*. Routledge. https://doi.org/10.4324/9780203432501

Frith, Simon. 1996. *Performing Rites: Evaluating Popular Music*. Oxford University Press. https://doi.org/10.1093/oso/9780198163329.001.0001

Gaver, William W. 1993 (online since 17 Sept. 2010). "What in the World Do We Hear? An Ecological Approach to Auditory Event Perception." *Ecological Psychology* 5 (1): 1–29. https://doi.org/10.1207/s15326969eco0501_1

Gibson, James J. 1979. *The Ecological Approach to Visual Perception*. Houghton Mifflin. https://doi.org/10.4324/9781315740218

Hall, Stuart. 1999. "Encoding, Decoding." In *The Cultural Studies Reader*, edited by Simon During. Second edition. Routledge.

Halliday, Michael A. K. 1985. *An Introduction to Functional Grammar*. Edward Arnold.

Herbert, Ruth. 2011. *Everyday Music Listening: Absorption, Dissociation and Trancing*. Ashgate. https://doi.org/10.4324/9781315581354

Home-Cook, George. 2015. *Theatre and Aural Attention: Stretching Ourselves*. Palgrave Macmillan. https://doi.org/10.1057/9781137393692

Keller, Marcello Sorce. 2007. "Why is Music So Ideological, and Why Do Totalitarian States Take It So Seriously? A Personal View from History and the Social Sciences." *Journal of Musicological Research* 26 (2–3): 91–122. https://doi.org/10.1080/01411890701361086

Kivy, Peter. 1994. "Speech, Song, and the Transparency of Medium: A Note on Operatic Metaphysics." *The Journal of Aesthetics and Art Criticism* 52 (1), The Philosophy of Music: 63–68. https://doi.org/10.2307/431585

Kress, Gunther and Theo van Leeuwen. 2001. *Multimodal Discourse*. Bloomsbury Academic.

Machin, David. 2010. *Analysing Popular Music: Image, Sound and Text*. Sage. https://doi.org/10.4135/9781446280027

Meelberg, Vincent. 2018. "Narrative Sonic Ambiances: Designing Positive Auditory Environments Using Narrative Strategies." Proceedings of the Euronoise 2018 Conference, Reduce Noise to Improve Life, Crete, 28–31 May 2018. https://www.euronoise2018.eu/docs/papers/145_Euronoise2018.pdf

Metz, Christian. 1980. "Aural Objects." Translated by Georgia Gurrieri. *Yale French Studies* 60, Cinema/Sound: 24–32. https://doi.org/10.2307/2930002

Moore, Allan. 2013. *Song Means: Analysing and Interpreting Recorded Popular Song*. Ashgate. https://doi.org/10.4324/9781315609898

Nattiez, Jean-Jacques. [1987] 1990. *Music and Discourse: Toward a Semiology of Music*, translated by Carolyn Abbate. Princeton University Press.

Oliveros, Paulina. 1971. *Sonic Meditations*. Smith Publications.

Oliveros, Paulina. 2003. *Deep Listening: A Composer's Sound Practice*. iUniverse.

Petersen, Ulrike. 2019. "The Era of National Socialism." In *Brahms in Context*, edited by Natasha Loges and Katy Hamilton. Cambridge University Press. https://doi.org/10.1017/9781316681374.034

Robinson, Dylan. 2020. *Hungry Listening: Resonant Theory for Indigenous Sound Studies*. University of Minnesota Press. https://doi.org/10.5749/j.ctvzpv6bb

Rodero Antón, Emma. 2009. "Point of Audition in a Radio Fiction: The Eternal Problem." *Observatorio Journal* 10: 242–52. https://www.academia.edu/363009/Point_of_listening_in_a_radio_fiction_the_eternal_problem

Schaeffer, Pierre. 1996. *Traité des objets musicaux*. Éditions du Seuil.

Schafer, R. Murray. 1967. *Ear Cleaning: Notes for an Experimental Music Course*. BMI Canada.

Schafer, R. Murray. 1977. *The Tuning of the World*. McClelland and Stewart.

Sloboda, John A. 2010. "Music in Everyday Life: The Role of Emotions." In *Handbook of Music and Emotion: Theory, Research, Applications*, edited by Patrik N. Juslin and John A. Sloboda. Oxford University Press. https://doi.org/10.1093/acprof:oso/9780199230143.003.0018

Szendy, Peter. 2008. *Listen: A History of our Ears*. With a Foreword by Jean-Luc Nancy. Translated by Charlotte Mandell. Fordham University Press. https://doi.org/10.2307/j.ctt13x002m

Truax, Barry. 1984. *Acoustic Communication*. Ablex Publishing Corporation. https://doi.org/10.5040/9798216955412

van Dijk, Teun A. 1993. "Principles of Critical Discourse Analysis." *Discourse and Society* 4 (2): 249–83. https://doi.org/10.1177/095792659300400

van Hulst, Yente. 2024. "Staging Whiteness: A Critical Examination of National Identity in Dutch Musical." Unpublished Thesis to obtain the degree in MA Contemporary Theatre, Dance, and Dramaturgy, Utrecht University.

van Leeuwen, Theo. 1999. *Speech, Music, Sound*. Palgrave Macmillan https://doi.org/10.1007/978-1-349-27700-1

van Wijhe, Jeroen and Jacek Mikołajczyk. 2022. "Pilots and Peticoats: Original Musicals in Continental Europe." In *The Routledge Companion to Musical Theatre*, edited by Laura MacDonald and Ryan Donovan. Routledge. https://doi.org/10.4324/9780429260247-36

Verstraete, Pieter. 2009. *The Frequency of Imagination: Auditory Distress and Aurality in Contemporary Music Theatre*. PrintPartners Ipskamp BV.

Verstraete, Pieter. 2010. "The Listener's Response." *Performance Research* 15 (3): 88–89. https://doi.org/10.1080/13528165.2010.527213

Way, Lyndon. 2021. *Analysing Politics and Protest in Digital Popular Culture: A Multimodal Approach*. Sage. https://doi.org/10.4135/9781529753158

Way, Lyndon and Simon McKerrell. 2017. *Music as Multimodal Discourse: Media, Power and Protest*. Bloomsbury. https://doi.org/10.5040/9781474264419

II

HISTORIES, CONTEXTS, ECOLOGIES

8. Discourse Analysis

Sruti Bala

Summary

This contribution presents a Foucauldian approach to discourse analysis as a framework that is suitable for analysing the connections between performance and its political dimensions. The case of a performance that is cancelled due to accusations of it being blasphemous is used to broadly introduce both the concept of discourse as well as the basic tenets and points of departure of a Foucauldian discourse analysis. The contribution then contextualises the discipline's approach to the methodology, by highlighting the role of discourse analysis in shaping the way the concept of performance is currently used in theatre and performance studies, referring to the work of Jon McKenzie and Judith Butler. Following an elaboration of the working principles and practical steps in conducting a discourse analysis, the contribution demonstrates how the author adapted and implemented these in her own research on participatory art. The contribution concludes with a discussion of Edward Said's *Orientalism* as an instance of expanding discourse analysis.

Introduction

Consider the following situation: a performance by an experimental theatre collective is cancelled because of its purportedly inappropriate content, resulting in fierce debates on freedom of expression and state repression, expressions of support for the artists as well as protests outside theatre venues. The controversy concerns the portrayal of a mythical religious figure in the performance as an ordinary human with flaws and desires, making use of satire and exaggeration in its depiction of this figure. Critics accuse the performance of being blasphemous and offensive to the religious sentiments of one of the powerful demographic communities. Ruling party leaders join the condemnation of the performance, using the occasion to mobilise their own constituency as victims, thereby invoking a sense of threat from and animosity toward members of other religious communities. The theatre group and its director in particular face online attacks targeting their personal lives and religious backgrounds. Cultural institutions remain either silent or extremely cautious in their responses to the cancellation.

This is a hypothetical but nonetheless realistic instance of a theatrical problem that could potentially lend itself to a discourse analysis. It is fundamentally concerned with questions of power. It invites connections between performance and its political dimensions. It requires paying attention to not only what occurs on stage or during the broader production process, but also and especially to what is left unsaid and remains invisible, by following its traces and reading between the lines. It calls for an inquiry into how something came about, what created the conditions for it to be such and not otherwise. It suggests that there is more to the event than what is self-evident or immediately perceptible, and that making sense of it requires attention to how power is manifested and materialised in dynamic ways. When it comes to disentangling controversies, grappling with differing interpretations and viewpoints or contested claims on truth, discourse analysis can be a useful methodological framework. It engages with the ways in which meaning is produced and contested in society, shedding light on the processes by which something comes to be seen as true or meaningful or is mobilised for specific ends.

The term 'discourse' has been theorised in different ways by scholars in various disciplines. Common to these conceptions is the rejection of a literal or descriptive understanding of language and communication and an emphasis on how language in all its facets is part of the construction of social life (Gill 2018). Subsequently, there are several distinct approaches to discourse analysis, ranging from a sociolinguistic understanding of discourse, which is broadly interested in linguistic interactions between communities, as well as rituals and modalities of text, speech and communication (van Dijk 1985), to a media studies approach to discourse analysis which adopts a multimodal and multimedia engagement with language in relation to image, sound and interactive media.

In the present contribution, discourse analysis refers to a methodology derived from Michel Foucault's theory of discourse, honed through his life-long interest in the history of ideas and the sciences. The Foucauldian conception of discourse is an epistemological and simultaneously a political one, i.e. it understands discourse as inseparable from the process of creating or gaining knowledge, which is in turn inseparable from power struggles. In this sense it can be distinguished from the common, linguistic definition of discourse, which refers to a particular, ordered mode of speech or a unit of conversation (e.g. as evident in the phrases 'holding a discourse' or 'media discourses').

In his studies on madness, on sexuality and the prison system, Foucault puts forward an understanding of discourse in terms of being "an institutionalised way of speaking or writing about reality that defines what can be intelligibly thought and said about the world and what cannot" (Longhofer and Weinberg 2023). He further elaborates discourse as "a historically contingent social system that produces knowledge and meaning" and, in doing so, masks itself as objective and stable (Adams 2017). Following this, we can argue that the discourse of the body that circulates in the field of performance studies is significantly different from theological discourses of the body. This implies that an idea, such as that of a divine body, may make perfect sense within theological discourses of the body, yet not be intelligible in the discourse of artistic performance. This unintelligibility might become evident when, for instance, the costumed or visually embellished stage appearance of a holy figure evokes contradicting responses among audiences who bring to the performance very different associations and emotions related to 'the body', shaped by social, cultural or religious factors.

Discourse is thus knowledge that is formed not only through spoken or written language, but also through material realities that are systematically organised with their own constraints and regularities and have specific histories. There are thus conditions and criteria for a body to come to be regarded as 'divine' or as 'offensive'. Foucault's conception of discourse thus emphasises the power relations that govern the relationship between discourse and social reality.

The analysis of discourse should not be reduced to a linguistic reflection or representation of reality. Rather, it considers discourse as a material reality of its own kind (Jäger and Maier 2016, 112). Foucault speaks of 'discursive practices or formations', indicating that discourse is not a sign or language system with abstract grammatical rules, but rather the conditions and effects as well as the material manifestations of sign or language systems (Leezenberg 2021, 68). Discourse analysis is therefore based on a constructivist epistemology. This means that it is not simply about analysing how meanings are allocated and interpreted through sign systems, but rather about the generative and constructive dimensions of discourse, i.e. how discourse produces and generates reality and diversifies knowledge. Some scholars thus refer to it as 'critical discourse analysis', whereby 'critical' refers not only to a criticism of power in relation to discourse, but also to an analysis of its effects and how it materialises and manifests itself (Foucault 1997, 58–59).

Although Foucault neither uses the term 'discourse analysis' nor prescribes how to conduct such an analysis, his influential, cross-disciplinary conception of discourse offers valuable principles and directions for the study of the systems of thought and material practice that shape and enliven a particular field. The present contribution thus approaches discourse analysis as the study of underlying patterns and power relations in terms of how they are manifested in language, objects, practices and other expressions. Discourse analysis often departs from that which is declared as self-evident or taken for granted and destabilises this object of study through processes of historicisation and comparison and contrast. Rather than aiming to uncover some ultimate universal truth, discourse analysis sheds light on how something comes to be regarded as true or significant, and what this reveals or implies.

Context

Discourse analysis includes divergent approaches and has been adapted in different disciplines of the social sciences and humanities, such as in sociolinguistics (Blommaert 2005), communication studies

(Fairclough 2010) and political theory (Laclau and Mouffe 1985). The present contribution suggests possible avenues for adopting a discourse analytical framework in studying theatre and performance, departing from Foucault's conception of discourse, especially as outlined in his inaugural address at the Collège de France in 1970 (1981), and subsequently developed by scholars of media, migration and social-political conflict, such as Siegfried Jäger and Florentine Maier (2016).

Discourse analysis is relevant to the theorisation of theatre and performance at two interconnected levels. It seeks to understand on the one hand the conditions under which a particular field (a genre, a practice, any kind of theatrical activity) came to be formed, what Foucault refers to as discursive formations. On the other hand, it examines the conditions under which it is transformed, challenged or discarded. This is what Foucault terms discursive ruptures. Take the case of the cancellation of the music theatre performance *Aïsha and the Women of Madina* by Rotterdam's Independent Theatre (Onafhankelijk Toneel) in 2001 because of protests and fears of violence around the stage depiction of the Prophet and his wife. A discourse analysis of the politics of the cancellation of a performance would ask what factors influenced the choices in the staging of the mythical religious figure, what factors led to the call for its cancellation, and what were its direct and indirect effects in the aftermath of the cancellation. An inquiry into discursive formations and ruptures might include a discussion of how certain kinds of representations of religious figures came to be associated with obscenity or sacrilege. Lonneke van Heugten's discourse analytical study (2013) examines how perceptions of the play were entangled with public debates on 'multiculturalism' and growing hostilities toward Muslim Dutch citizens.

In this sense, discourse analysis is intrinsically interested in historiographical questions. A discourse analytical view of theatre fundamentally approaches it as a historically and geographically contingent and fluid object of study. In terms of its etymological roots in Greek, theatre is 'a place of looking' that is intrinsically tied to theory, 'contemplation and speculation'. The fact that the term theatre was used with reference to a space such as an anatomical theatre ('theatrum anatomicum') in the sixteenth century is not only relevant as a historical fact, but also invites us to probe into how theatre became shaped as a means of producing and disseminating knowledge, a means of speaking about, perceiving and presenting bodies, and how this knowledge ties to power struggles. The analysis of discourse probes its fault lines and contradictions. It reflects on how this meaning-making changes, sometimes assuming radically different forms across times and geographies. This refers not only to language usage and the linguistic aspects of discourse, but equally also to the institutions, practices, objects, subjects, architectures, infrastructures and material manifestations of discourse. The web of relations connecting all these aspects of discourse are also called 'dispositives' (Foucault 1980, 194; Jäger and Maier 2016, 113–14). In the example introduced earlier, the dispositive would include the web of relations connecting theatre, religious communities, the state, political parties and local or regional histories.

Viewed in this manner, discourse analysis helps us comprehend 'performance' as a dynamic set of organising principles rather than as a fixed object of study, thus steering our attention to the conditions under which something comes to be regarded as performance or is excluded from the category. To view performance not as a stable object of study but as a 'lens' through which social practices may be understood, is to thus signal the possibility of a different kind of knowledge emerging from a particular shift in discursive formation, an insight that has been foundational to the field of performance studies (Taylor 2003).

Jon McKenzie's *Perform or Else* (2001) is one such instance of the use of discourse analysis, inquiring into what distinguishes the discourse of performance in the artistic and cultural context (with its focus on experimentation, creativity, aesthetic experience) from discourses of performance in neoliberal business and technology (emphasising efficiency, normativity, output). In doing so, McKenzie pays attention to those elements that coincide between discourses of performance in business, management or technology on the one side, and cultural performance on the other. It de-objectifies performance as a stable object of study by comparing and contrasting it to other domains wherein performance has an entirely different valence.

Following Foucault's approach to discourse, the methodological framework of discourse analysis is important not only as a diagnostic tool, i.e. to offer an incisive analysis of the effects and mechanisms of discursive activities, but also as a tool of critique, resistance and thus social transformation (Hook 2001, 522). By revealing the socially or historically constructed nature of a phenomenon, it becomes possible to develop ways of transforming what might otherwise appear to be given and thus unchangeable.

Judith Butler's foundational work on gender is an outstanding example of a critical deployment of discourse analysis as a tool of resistance to the seemingly all-powerful mechanisms of the gender binary. In "Performative Acts and Gender Constitution" they argue that "what is called gender identity is a performative accomplishment compelled by social sanction and taboo. In its very character as performative resides the possibility of contesting its reified status" (Butler 1998, 520). Butler decodes gender here in terms of enactment, thus mobilising theatre and performance into a consideration of philosophical conceptions of the body. In doing so, they lay bare the social mechanisms of sanctioning or admitting certain kinds of gender transgressions. In a telling example, Butler analyses how the act of cross-dressing may well be welcomed and applauded when it is practised on stage in the framework of an artistic performance, but nevertheless ostracised and punished when it takes place in a day-to-day social situation, such as a transgender person who is ridiculed and discriminated against while walking down the street (1998, 528). In fact, what Butler does here is to identify what Foucault describes in "The Order of Discourse" ([1970] 1981) as the external procedures of discursive formations, in this case gender discourses. These include procedures of exclusion and prohibition, such as those determining when gender cross-dressing is acceptable and when it is penalised, procedures of dividing and categorising certain gendered behaviours as 'decent' or 'transgressive', as well as procedures that make it possible for subjects to be imbued with authority or privileges, such as through being seen as 'respectable' or 'proper'. Butler's reading of gender, however, pushes beyond describing how gendered performance plays out in daily life. They instead use the analysis of gendered discourse to argue that "there is nothing about a binary gender system that is given" (Butler 1998, 531). This should not be misconstrued as implying that everything about gender is relative or a matter of perspective. In fact, following a Foucauldian approach, Butler argues that gender discourses are constructed in specific and historically situated ways that cannot simply be altered by will or by swapping interpretive frameworks.

However, by understanding the complex web of conditions that make gender both restrictive as well as generative as a discursive practice, Butler offers a good example of using discourse analysis to not only capture the historical 'formations' of gender discourse but also, in doing so, challenges its foundational categories—in this case gender binaries—revealing them in their contingency, thereby paving the way for their potential 'rupture' and transformation. In their recent book *Who's Afraid of Gender?* (2024) they extend this critique to the category of sex as well.

How to

Although there are no formulae or fixed steps for using the discourse analytical method, Foucault identifies four abstract principles, namely the principles of reversal, discontinuity, specificity and exteriority ([1970] 1981, 67). These principles challenge widely accepted epistemological norms in a counter-intuitive fashion.

The analytical principle of 'reversal' refers to looking beyond the level of the individual text or authorial voice to the broader undercurrents and operations of power. Foucault reverses the widespread assumption that subjects produce discourses, instead proposing that it is discourse that produces subject positions. Such a view would, for instance, reject the idea that an incident such as a performance cancellation was motivated by ill intentions or moral flaws, instead examining how religious conservatism, sexism, liberalism and political authoritarianism crystallised into conflicting positionalities and identities. The principle of 'discontinuity' rejects the idea of the stable and linear origins of discourse, instead studying discourse as a moment, an event, a slice of history, as it were. In van Heugten's study of *Aïsha and the Women of Madina*, directed by Gerrit Timmers, it is not the performance itself that forms the focus of analysis, as it was cancelled prior to its premiere. Rather, the discourse analysis emphasises the public perceptions and discussions of the performance and the way in which the cancelled performance became the site for a public debate on free speech and censorship. The principle of 'specificity' similarly rejects the idea of there being a universal or general explanation for discourse, instead preferring an analysis of the specificity of a discursive moment or event.

A core challenge from a Foucauldian standpoint is that "the effect of discursive practices is that it is virtually impossible to think outside of them; to be outside of them is, by definition, to be mad, to be beyond comprehension, and therefore beyond reason" (Hook 2001, 522). Discourse analysis therefore doesn't presume a neutral or objective standpoint, but rather departs from the assumption that the work of analysis consists of tracing the contours and limits of discourses. The epistemological attitude of discourse analysis is thus not one of unveiling a truth that is internal to a discourse but one of charting the external conditions of the possibility for truth on the one side, as well as the effects of this discourse on the other. Foucault refers to this as the principle of 'exteriority' ([1970] 1981, 67). Doing discourse analysis is thus about exploring what kinds of realities are made possible, and significantly, not possible, by a specific discursive formation. In researching a performance deemed as blasphemous or offensive to particular communities, it is thus the task of the discourse analyst not to judge audience responses from the standpoint of artistic freedom or morality, but rather to unpack how notions of freedom and morality become attached to a particular scene or act.

In terms of practical guidelines, the steps proposed by Siegfried Jäger and Florentine Maier (2016) provide a useful and flexible starting point, though care should be taken not to adopt them in a formulaic manner. Jäger and Maier visualise a discourse as subdivided into strands, fragments and knots. The first step in analysing discourses is to identify and specify one or more 'strands'. These are "flows of discourse that centre on a common topic" (Jäger and Maier 2016, 121). This could be issues such as the discourse of victimisation or the discourse of blasphemy in performance. Jäger and Maier suggest limiting the discourse strand in terms of diachronic and synchronic dimensions, i.e. identifying which historical period will be covered in the study and which geographical region or linguistic group. Researchers may decide to narrow down the study to one single performance or expand it to a comparative exploration of various instances of performances that were cancelled due to their allegedly offensive content around the same time, in other parts of the world, such as Habib Tanvir's *Ponga Pandit* in the 1990s in India, which was accused by right-wing groups of offending religious sentiments for its portrayal of a morally corrupt Hindu priest (Deshpande 2005).

The next step is to identify the discursive 'fragments' that are relevant to a particular discourse strand. According to Jäger and Maier, these can be texts, objects or expressions in whole or part (122). In the case of the cancelled performance, examples of discursive fragments could include social media posts related to the cancelled performance, reviews, panel discussions, but also rumours or gossip. Advertisements or news items, though unrelated to the performance, may reference the topic of victimisation or religious offence in ways that enrich the analysis. Costumes may be equally relevant as a discursive fragments as they may suggest or offer commentaries on how members of a religious community perceive issues such as decorum, sacrilege or 'proper' behaviour. Paying attention to one's own discursive position and attitudes toward the topic is also part of this process of linking various discursive fragments and strands. In her study of theatre censorship in Turkey, Burcu Yasemin Şeyben investigates changes in theatre legislation in the wake of performances that satirically depict politicians. Extracts from legal and cultural policy documents are treated here as discursive fragments that reveal modalities of censorship and surveillance (Şeyben 2021).

Having identified the discursive strands and fragments that are pertinent to the research, the next step is to analyse the strands in-depth. Jäger and Maier identify three dimensions of analysis: a structural analysis of the discourse strand, a detailed analysis of fragments and a synoptic analysis (128–31). The structural analysis involves capturing the overarching characteristics, based on the frequency of their occurrence or the conspicuousness of their absence. For instance, it could be noteworthy that there is a correlation between the portrayal of religious or mythical figures on stage and societal conflicts or tensions between (religious) communities.

Jäger and Maier propose the concept of a 'discursive knot' as a way to describe the detailed analysis of discursive fragments. A discursive knot is the entanglement of different discursive strands or fragments into one event, moment or utterance (122). For instance, religious sentiments of offence often carry implicit gendered dimensions, as in the case of the public controversy around the play *Behzti* (2004) by British South Asian playwright Gurmeet Kaur (Ahmed 2020). By unpacking references to women's bodies or gender relations in the performance, a researcher might be able to elaborate on how religious discourses employ gender categories, such as the honour of women or the duty of men to justify the adherence to religious norms. The woman's body on stage may thus serve as the contentious discursive knot through which power struggles over religion, race and representation are enunciated. In a synoptic analysis, the findings from the broader structural analysis are interpreted and compared with the findings of a detailed analysis.

Demonstration

My own use of a Foucauldian-influenced discourse analysis is undertaken in a study titled *The Gestures of Participatory Art* (2018). The study grappled with conceptions of participation in different academic disciplines and brought these to bear on the analysis of participatory artworks. A Foucauldian discourse analytical approach primarily helped me determine what *not* to study. Following the principles of discontinuity and specificity, I chose not to attempt to trace a history of participatory art as originating from a singular moment, movement or artistic genre, but rather as emerging in response to or rejection of specific circumstances in the art world. I refrained from attempting to define or fix the characteristics or features of participatory art as a genre, but instead paid attention to the discursive formations and ruptures of participatory art, i.e. the ways participatory practices emerge as differentiating or distancing themselves from other genres. Foucault's discourse analytical principle of exteriority allowed for an expansive historicising of participatory art, attending to the external factors that made it possible for participatory practices to emerge. I applied this principle by investigating the objections that proponents of participatory artworks implicitly or openly raise about the insufficiencies of conventional theatre and performance forms, such as the absence of audience agency, or democratic deficiencies in performance creation processes, or lack of interaction between performers and spectators. These tend to be put forward as reasons necessitating the adoption of participatory methods or approaches, and thus serve as an indication of the external conditions influencing them.

I identified different discursive strands of participation, such as the deployment of the concept of participation in movements for grassroots democracy and citizen participation, in international development policy and practice, in museums and cultural institutions, in community theatre and in performance art. Each of these strands revealed different entanglements of the idea of participation with institutions, social tensions and disparities, as well as the transversal connections between political aspirations and how these translate onto the aesthetic register. I also compared and contrasted approaches to audience participation in the visual arts in a museum or installation setting, and in theatre and performance, such as immersive performance and community art practices. I delved into the contradictions and commonalities between these diverse understandings of participation. I paid attention to the concepts or ideas to which participation is implicitly tied, such as claims of democratisation or horizontality, examining how these effectively mask practices of pacification or manipulation and thus risk a co-optation of the concept into neoliberal governance models. These strands provided the basis for a broad structural analysis of discourses of participation in the arts.

One of the discursive knots I identified, although I did not use the terminology proposed by Jäger and Maier, revolved around the question of how people (audiences or communities at large) participate in artworks on their own terms, i.e. in unexpected and unscripted ways. The discursive fragments I chose for this purpose were wide-ranging: from site-specific installations to community theatre workshops to conceptual performance art. The focus on unsolicited or non-obvious forms of participation steered me toward the question of non-participation or refusals to participate, i.e. moments or aspects of performance that may not be at the centre of conventional performance analyses, such as what happens at the para-theatrical margins of a performance, during after-talks or audience reactions during a show that might be deemed as disruptive or disturbing.

This bottom-up focus on the terms and conditions of (non-)participation allowed me to analyse in detail forms of participation outside of the boundaries of genre and artform, forms that may not have been taken into consideration because of their peripheral or marginal status. To conduct a synoptical analysis, I interwove the structural analysis of the discourse strands with the detailed analysis of the chosen fragments. This made it possible to centre power relations between artists, art institutions and their audiences or broader communities and to then assess contradictory positions or viewpoints, situating them in a broader historical perspective. To conclude, a discourse analytical approach to participatory art led me to challenge widespread assumptions about participation being a benign and necessarily socially impactful practice in performance. It stimulated me to re-examine the terms of participation, to challenge their neoliberal appropriation in the arts and to suggest how practices of participation may be re-politicised by foregrounding minor gestures of (non-)participation.

Expanding the method

To conclude this contribution by broadening the horizon of what is possible with the discourse analytical methodological framework, I turn to one of the most widely cited and influential examples of Foucauldian discourse analysis: Edward Said's seminal work *Orientalism* (1978). This work is of relevance to performance studies, not least because of the detailed attention that Said pays to the question of the representation of 'the Orient' in Western iconography, travel writing, maps, poetry or paintings. Said argues that Orientalism is a discourse, i.e. it is an assemblage of theory and practice, which produces the pervasive idea of an Orient as an object of knowledge, and ultimately serves the project of imperialist expansion. By presenting the Orient as an imperial construct, Said highlights the discursive nature of Orientalism:

> Orientalism, therefore, is not an airy European fantasy about the Orient, but a created body of theory and practice in which, for many generations, there has been a considerable material investment. Continued investment made Orientalism, as a system of knowledge about the Orient, an accepted grid for filtering through the Orient into Western consciousness, just as that same investment multiplied—indeed, made truly productive—the statements proliferating out from Orientalism into the general culture (Said 1978, 6).

In the above quote, Said firstly makes clear how Orientalism, as a pursuit of knowledge production about a place demarcated as 'the Orient', is not a disinterested pursuit, but is enmeshed in and buttressed by imperial interests. Second, it regulates how the Orient can be imagined or depicted, thus generating stereotypes and fantasies about Arabs or Asians, which, while inconsistent with reality, nevertheless remained durable and hegemonic, i.e. it was a discourse that implicitly rendered certain representations admissible or thinkable and others unthinkable. Third, and following from this, it would be inaccurate to simply dismiss orientalist scholarship as a bunch of lies. It is rather a generative web of institutions and practices that effectively creates facts on the ground through its influence on imperial rule and foreign policies.

Said's discourse analysis reads the historical body of knowledge known as Orientalism not as empirically given, but as a discursively produced tradition of thought-practice, a "dynamic exchange between individual authors and the large political concerns shaped by the three great empires" (1978, 15). One of the direct methodological implications of this approach is that the scope of the study is expansive, covering examples from philology, history, travel writing, novels, poetry, painting and cartography. However rather than attempting a comprehensive, encyclopaedic coverage, Said limits his study to the British, French and American empires and a selection of orientalist works dealing with Islam and Arabs. Another methodological choice in the study is to not analyse the contents or arguments of each text, but to focus, following Foucault, on "the text's surface, its exteriority to what it describes" (Said 1978, 20). For example, Said reads Aeschylus's play *The Persians* with a specific interest in how the play deals with Otherness and how it represents oriental figures. He peels away at the veneer of objectivity in scholarly writings about Egypt or Mesopotamia. He identifies recurring devices or common tropes used by orientalist writers and studies them in terms of what they reveal, less about the actual Orient and more about how power and knowledge intertwine in the discourse of Orientalism. Following Jäger and Meier, we might call these tropes discursive knots, which involve the entanglement of different strands. The trope of "the hyper-sexualised Arab" is one example of a discursive knot, where gendered and racial stereotypes are entangled with condescending geopolitical assessments of Arab defeatism and lack of political acumen (Said 1978, 311–16). Finally, Said addresses his own place as being a product of orientalist discourse, linking his observations on Orientalism in the nineteenth century to his own experience as a Palestinian-American scholar and the enduring legacy of Orientalism in the present, including its influence on geopolitics and the longstanding occupation of Palestine.

Said's *Orientalism* deploys discourse analysis as a methodological framework, within which a number of methods are combined, chosen according to their suitability to the object of study, i.e. the discursive fragments, such as close readings of literary texts, commentaries on current affairs, inventories of cross-references and repeated citations of texts, as well as visual analyses of paintings. Such a bricolage is, more broadly speaking, a common feature of discourse analysis, which must be recalibrated in its methods according to the subject of inquiry.

Returning to the earlier stated examples of theatre censorship and accusations of blasphemy, Said's *Orientalism* offers a way to approach discourse analysis that is not reductive to identifying blame or morally right or wrong positions. Indeed, public discussions around what is representable or unrepresentable on stage, especially in the European or Western context, can often be traced to a legacy of Orientalist categories.

Said's study is an inspiring example of discourse analysis with the goal of not simply offering a diagnosis of orientalist practices but in doing so also offering a tool of critique and resistance. *Orientalism* is considered to be one of the founding texts of postcolonial studies, as it provided a model for scholarship that critically studies imperialism by reading against the grain and in between the lines of imperial documents and writings.

Suggestions for further reading

Foucault's analysis of the prison ([1975] 1979) is arguably his clearest enunciation of the discourse analytical method. His inaugural lecture ([1970] 1981) lays out the principles and approach in the study of discourse. *Methods of Critical Discourse Studies*, edited by Wodak and Meyer (2016), provides an overview of discourse analysis across various disciplines (communication studies, sociolinguistics, media studies and other fields). Jon McKenzie's *Perform or Else* (2001) offers a good entry point into a Foucauldian view of performance as a concept that cuts across the arts, media and neoliberal governance. Noteworthy in the Dutch context are two studies developed as postgraduate dissertations at the University of Amsterdam: Lonneke van Heugten's 2013 study of a cancelled performance of *Aïsha and the Women of Medina* by Rotterdam's Independent Theatre in 2001, cited earlier in this contribution, and Rosa van Kollem's 2024 study of the social value of culture in Dutch cultural policy, interrogating the grounds on which the notion of culture's social value gains legitimacy.

References

Adams, Rachel. 2017. "Michel Foucault: Discourse." *Critical Legal Thinking*, November 17. https://criticallegalthinking.com/2017/11/17/michel-foucault-discourse/

Ahmed, Rehana. 2020. "Space, Symbols, and Speech in Gurpreet Kaur Bhatti's *Behzti* and Its Reception." *Modern Drama* 63 (3): 354–72. https://muse.jhu.edu/article/772934

Bala, Sruti. 2018. *The Gestures of Participatory Art*. Manchester University Press. https://doi.org/10.7765/9781526107695

Blommaert, Jan. 2005. *Discourse. Key Topics in Sociolinguistics*. Cambridge University Press.

Butler, Judith. 1988. "Performative Acts and Gender Constitution: An Essay in Phenomenology and Feminist Theory." *Theatre Journal* 40 (4): 519–31. https://doi.org/10.2307/3207893

Butler, Judith. 2024. *Who's Afraid of Gender?* Penguin Random House.

Deshpande, Sudhanva. 2005. "Upside-Down Midas: Habib Tanvir at 80." *TDR/The Drama Review* 48.4 (184)): 71–80. https://doi.org/10.1162/1054204042441991

van Dijk, Teun. 1985. *Handbook of Discourse Analysis*. Academic Press.

Fairclough, Norman. 2010. *Critical Discourse Analysis: The Critical Study of Language*. Routledge.

Foucault, Michel. 1979. *Discipline & Punish: The Birth of the Prison* [1975]. Translated by A. Sheridan. Penguin.

Foucault, Michel. 1980. "The Confession of the Flesh." In *Power/Knowledge: Selected Interviews and Other Writings 1972–1977 by Michel Foucault*, edited by Colin Gordon. Pantheon Books.

Foucault, Michel. 1981. "The Order of Discourse" [1970]. In *Untying the Text: A Post-Structuralist Reader*, edited by Robert J. C. Young. Routledge & Kegan Paul.

Foucault, Michel. 1997. *The Politics of Truth*. Edited by Sylvère Lotringer. Introduction by John Rajchman. Semiotext(e).

Gill, Rosalind. 2018. "Discourse." In *The Craft of Criticism: Critical Media Studies in Practice*, edited by Michael Kackman and Mary Celeste Kearney. Routledge.

van Heugten, Lonneke. 2013. *Theatre as a Vortex of Behaviour in Dutch Multicultural Society*. AGent: New Theses in Performance Research. Tectum.

Hook, Derek. 2001. "Discourse, Knowledge, Materiality, History: Foucault and Discourse Analysis." *Theory & Psychology* 11 (4): 521–47. https://doi.org/10.1177/0959354301114006

Jäger, Siegfried and Florentine Maier. 2016. "Analysing Discourses and Dispositives: A Foucauldian Approach to Theory and Methodology." In *Methods of Critical Discourse Studies*, edited by Ruth Wodak and Michael Meyer. Sage Publications.

van Kollem, Rosa. 2024. *De maatschappelijke waarde van cultuur: Een discoursanalyse van het Nederlands cultuurbeleid van 2013 tot en met 2020*. AGent: New Theses in Performance Research. Tectum.

Laclau, Ernesto and Chantal Mouffe. 1985. *Hegemony and Socialist Strategy*. Verso.

Leezenberg, Michiel. 2021. *Foucault*. Series *Elementaire Deeltjes* no. 74. Uitgeverij Athenaeum—Polak & Van Gennep.

Longhofer, Wesley, and Daniel Winchester, eds. 2023. *Social Theory Re-Wired: New Connections to Classical and Contemporary Perspectives*. Third edition. Routledge. https://www.routledgesoc.com/profile/michel-foucault

McKenzie, Jon. 2001. *Perform or Else: From Discipline to Performance*. Routledge.

Said, Edward. 1978. *Orientalism*. Random House.

Şeyben, Burcu Yasemin. 2021. *Struggle and Survival under Authoritarianism in Turkey : Theatre under Threat*. Lexington Books.

Taylor, Diana. 2003. *The Archive and the Repertoire: Performing Cultural Memory in the Americas*. Duke University Press.

9. Creating Art Ecologies through Contextual Analysis

Liesbeth Groot Nibbelink

Summary

This chapter introduces the method of contextual analysis and describes how working with contextual analysis, either discursively or in practice, produces art ecologies. In a contextual analysis, performances or performative events are examined comparatively, with the help of a theoretical concept, and in connection to a larger field of practice. At its core, contextual analysis is concerned with drawing out relations between performances and/or other artworks—through comparing topics, styles or artistic strategies—while exploring how these artworks jointly address and examine wider societal phenomena or developments within a cultural or artistic field. In that act, these intersections produce art ecologies, understood here as supportive, open-ended networks with many spheres of influence, in which artworks and performances enter into dialogue with one another. This method is first demonstrated by comparing the body politics in stage works of Marcelo Evelin, Marlene Monteiro Freitas and Ho Rui An, pivoting around the concept of 'politics of perception' to organise the analysis, and then extended to the identification of 'mycelium thinking' across artistic research, fashion and anthropology.

Introduction

When you are a regular visitor of theatre or dance, or any other artform, it may strike you that at times, artists show a shared interest in topics that have an active relation with societal themes, often connected to a sense of cultural moment, to what happens currently in the world around us. In such emerging, shared interests, artworks—whether they are performances, installations, sculpture, media art, cinema, music concerts or other—operate as the barometers or weather glasses of their time. At other times, artworks show a shared curiosity in artistic tools and strategies. You might notice, for instance, a repeated appearance of robots on stage, or the emergence of 'frames', peepholes or proscenium stage elements in a black box theatre, which might invite a further comparison of their use and meaning. To account for this 'trendwatchery' role of art, I propose a method termed 'contextual analysis' in which artworks are examined in relation to each other and to the themes and topics they bring to the forefront. This method grew out of teaching the MA course on Contemporary Performance: Mapping the Field at Utrecht University, in which my students and I explore emerging themes in contemporary theatre, dance and dramaturgy. This chapter introduces that method of contextual analysis and describes how working with contextual analysis, either discursively or in practice, produces art ecologies.

Contextual analysis can be seen as a form of field research, as performances or performative events are studied in relation to each other and within a larger field of practice. At its core, contextual analysis is concerned with drawing out relations between performances and/or other artworks—through comparing topics, styles or artistic strategies—while exploring how these artworks jointly address and examine wider societal phenomena or developments within a cultural or artistic field. The term 'contextual analysis' is used not only because performances or artworks are situated within a larger context but foremost because in creating connections and relations *between* artworks, they become *each other's* context. In that act, these intersections produce art ecologies, understood here as supportive, open-ended networks with many spheres of influence, in which artworks and performances enter into dialogue with one another.

Contextual analysis is not only carried out by theatre and dance theorists, but is also used by programmers, curators, dramaturgs and other arts professionals. The comparative approach immanent in contextual analysis can be recognised in a variety of professional contexts, for instance, in an opening speech at a theatre festival, in which the artistic director outlines societal or artistic themes in the festival programme, or in an introduction text in a catalogue, where a curator frames the works presented in an exhibition. Those speeches and texts draw out relations between performances and/or other artworks, by comparing themes, artistic choices, or dramaturgical strategies, and by relating these connections to wider societal phenomena such as actual political debates, environmental or economic issues, the impact of social media and digital culture, social or ethical matters and so on. As such, contextual analysis can also inform art criticism, for instance, in identifying artistic developments. A concrete example is an overview essay in a 2024 Dutch newspaper, in which an art critic signals the trend of cross-casting in recent Dutch Shakespeare adaptations—male characters played by female and/or BIPOC performers, in this case—as a strategy to confront the misogynistic dynamics in many Shakespeare plays (Janssen 2024). We might look at such texts—written, spoken or otherwise—as curatorial texts, in that they present and discuss artworks in relation or in a series, while distilling a meaning or argument from this relationality or seriality, and providing an interpretative framework for these connections. Different than (many) curatorial texts though, an academically informed contextual analysis creates art ecologies through concept-driven comparative analysis.

The term 'art ecologies' is used here to call attention to how contextual analysis produces supportive, nourishing networks in and around art, by means of a careful mapping and unpacking of artwork relations. Ecology, in this approach, does not so much refer to nature or the natural environment, but to the idea that everything is connected. This relational ontology is inspired by Timothy Morton's *The Ecological Thought* (2010) and Carl Lavery's *Performance and Ecology: What Can Theatre Do?* (2018). "Nothing exists by itself", observes Morton (2010, 15). Life in all its variety always exists as and within networks of interconnections—networks that can be chaotic or messy and which Morton therefore qualifies as "meshworks" (15). Etymologically, the word 'eco' refers to 'home' or 'house'. Art ecologies, subsequently, help to situate performances in meaningful and supportive networks of connections, and demonstrate how artworks always perform and operate within larger processes of experience and meaning making. By bringing artworks together, and by reading them through one another and in connection to a certain shared theme or topic, these works start to 'speak': they reflect on a theme, they offer a variety of perspectives, they may challenge or complement each another. Put differently, they enter into debate with one another, and become 'discursive objects'. Rather than merely being the object of analysis, such responsive, 'serialised' performances or artworks emerge as forms of thinking themselves, an approach that is also put forward in the book *Thinking Through Theatre and Performance* (Bleeker et al., 2019).[1]

Context | Situating contextual analysis

There are no academic texts available that describe contextual analysis precisely in the way it is presented in this chapter, but there are many debates and discourses that affiliate with this approach. Contextual analysis bears resemblances to dramaturgical analysis, in its attention to context; to curatorial analysis, in the way it frames artworks within a series; and to discourse analysis, in the enquiry of how artworks participate in (societal) debates. It differs from these methods in the explicit focus on the fields or networks that are constituted through comparison and in mutual dialogue—implying a reliance on relational ontology—and in the argument that these relations produce art ecologies. Closely related to this is the method's affirmative approach to its research objects.

Let's unpack some of these terms a bit more. To start with, contextual analysis can be seen as a form of field research. It positions artworks within fields of practice and within societal debates, yet it also regards artwork-relations as constitutive of those fields. This mutual reading of performances, artworks and their environment is grounded in the

---

1   This understanding of research objects as objects to think with is close to Mieke Bal's notion of 'theoretical objects' (Bal 2002). I prefer the term 'discursive objects', since contextual analysis does not focus on how artworks produce concepts, but on how they enter into debate with one another and with a wider societal context.

idea of relational ontology, which fully adopts the 'Mortonian' view that nothing exists by itself. From this relational point of view, performances or artworks are seen not as isolated, static affairs but as processual events, in which a variety of actors produce the event, interactively. Artworks, consequently, exist in and as networks. This art-in/as-network perspective is typical for various forms of field research, including contextual analysis, although some approaches conceptualise these networks in a more systematic and hence less open-ended manner than is suggested in this chapter. A classic within field theory, for instance, is that of the French sociologist Pierre Bourdieu, who identified the cultural field as an arena of the production, circulation, appropriation and exchange of goods, services, knowledge or status. Fields are seen as structured spaces that are organised through the accumulation and distribution of capital—economic but also social and cultural—in which various actors struggle and compete over the unequal distribution of capital (Van Maanen 2009, 45–47).

Whether called field or network, and despite my preference for network rather than field, it is good to bear in mind that no single field can ever be clearly delineated. A field exists only due to the field actors that are identified within it—and as long as these actors keep open the coordinates of the field. The term 'actor' here is used in the broadest sense of the term, inspired by Bruno Latour's widely adopted Actor-Network Theory (ANT), as an agent or organism that can be identified in a field and that has agency i.e. a capacity to have impact on that field, however limited (Latour 2005, 9–12).

To foreground the network within the field, I will briefly discuss two examples of art-in/as-network approaches to give an impression of how network dynamics may look. The first one is Thomas Postlewait's approach to theatre historiography i.e. the study of writing and doing theatre history. Postlewait argues that theatre historians construct rather than describe performance events, through identifying and selecting a series of actors that are deemed constitutive of the theatre event, by which they also produce an argument about the event and its situated context. Within this context, he distinguishes four categories: possible worlds, agents, reception and artistic heritage (2009, 10–19). The 'agents' category lists all the actors involved in the event, either prominent or subtly active: makers, writers, producers, facilitators, sources of inspiration. Hypothetically, this can include non-human actors as well. Next, 'reception' describes how the event has been received, reviewed and experienced, by the general public, specific audiences or professional critics. 'Artistic heritage' positions the event in relation to existing artistic conventions or genres, to examine how the event repeats, resists, re-uses, challenges or changes those conventions. The 'possible worlds' category, finally, allows for exploring how agents, societal events and circumstances are made present within the work, or how the work responds to these. These four categories are of course not so strictly divided in practice. In fact, they precisely help to show that historical events are always cumulative events, a sum of many factors of influence, with fluid temporal barriers.

A second example of art-in/as-network thinking focuses on the artist rather than the artwork and is derived from Pascal Gielen's useful analysis of artistic biotopes and their role in (art) educational institutions (2013). A healthy artistic biotope, for Gielen, shows a balance between four domains in which artists and art students operate: the domestic space, the communal space (the space of peers), the market and the civil domain (2013, 63). The domestic space is the artist's intimate space of personal development, where there is room for learning through experimentation, such as tinkering with things without a goal or trying out ideas in a jam session. The communal space is where work (in-progress) is presented to and discussed with peers, in a cooperative and safe environment such as the academy classroom or the rehearsal space. When the work becomes more public, it enters the civil space, a discursive realm where it is reviewed and perhaps criticised among professionals and wider audiences (similar to Postlewait's 'reception' category). The market space is the space where artworks are sold and commissioned, where artists need to "trade in [their] creativity for money" (62), a complex dynamic of supply and demand, matters of taste, changing trends, power structures, tensions between autonomy and dependency and more (which also calls Bourdieu's 'arena' to mind).[2]

---

2   Pascal Gielen also uses the idea of art-in-networks for institutional analysis, in *Kunst in Netwerken* [Art in Networks] (2003), where he examines selection processes in dance and arts organisations, using field theories of Pierre Bourdieu and elements of actor-network theory (ANT).

Although Postlewait and Gielen tend to focus on one event at the time, whereas contextual analysis always targets relations between multiple artworks, these examples help to show how field research examines and challenges the notion of 'field'—by asking what constitutes a field, what agents are active in this field or remain unseen and what might be their function. The more porous the field, the more often it is conceptualised as an open-ended network rather than as a delineated entity. An often-used model for this open network is the 'rhizome', conceptualised by Gilles Deleuze and Félix Guattari (2004). The rhizome is a root system, radically non-hierarchical, with many entry and exit points and without a clearly identifiable centre. Another, closely related figure of thought is the assemblage. An assemblage is also deeply rhizomatic yet highlights a network's temporal qualities and diversity of encounters. Deleuze and Guattari regard the assemblage as a multiplicity, an emergent, ever-increasing structure of interconnections: "A multiplicity cannot increase in number without changing in nature" (2004, 9). Assemblages emerge through encounters of human and more-than human actors and relations, which is vividly demonstrated in Jane Bennett's *Vibrant Matter: A Political Ecology of Things* (2010), where assemblages are understood as "ad hoc groupings of diverse elements, of vibrant materials of all sorts" (2010, 23). They are "living, throbbing confederations" of bodies and affects (23), and due to how they resonate and act upon one another, form "swarms of affiliates" (31). These are useful terms to keep in mind when mapping out connections in a contextual analysis.

"Swarms of affiliates" come into existence through association and affiliation. This focus on what is shared puts forward a final key concept in contextual analysis, which is affirmativity. Contextual analysis opts for an affirmative approach to its research objects, which means that rather than criticising the object (which often relies on pointing out a form of lack), objects are scrutinised for their potentiality: what kind of connections do they invite, what associations do they bring about? Contextual analysis thus focuses on the artwork's generative potential, by composing connections and creating resonances between artworks and their environment (cf. Goodman 2018). Contextual analysis is geared towards an interpretation of relations, and ultimately, presenting a specific argument about these relations. Therefore, this chain of associations, although endless in principle is limited in practice. Bennett observes that assemblages often have uneven topographies, as some crossings of affects and bodies generate more traffic than others (2010, 24). Translated to contextual analysis, the more trafficked the path—that is, the more prominent the connection shared between the artworks under discussion—the stronger the argument will be.

A final issue that needs to be mentioned here is the notion of 'context' itself. Some art scholars strongly reject the emphasis on context, when it is used to explain the work from the 'outside', rather than allowing the artwork to speak for itself. Context then, when seen as a hegemonic explanatory device, overshadows the work. Such a perspective resonates in a remark by Alan Read, in *Theatre, Intimacy and Engagement: The Last Human Venue* (2008): "There is little point in putting theatre in a wider context when it already shows the complexity of that context within its own acts" (43). Although Read refers here to a distinction he wishes to make between art and politics, his remark is helpful to remind us that a contextual analysis is not something that is applied *to* an artwork or performance, which suggests that a work and its context are two separate things, but instead is something that is active *within* a work, and as such can be brought to the fore by attentive observation and analysis.

How to | Contextual analysis at work

As briefly indicated above, contextual analysis creates art ecologies through concept-driven comparative analysis. Such an analysis can be understood as a map or an assemblage which:

- draws relations between artworks, with a focus on themes, genres or artistic conventions, or dramaturgical strategies;
- exposes and examines connections with wider societal contexts;
- relies on a comparative analysis between artworks, and in relation to wider contexts;
- uses one or more theoretical concepts as a guiding principle in the analysis.

Each component is shortly elaborated. Artwork relations, firstly, can be a lot of different things. Given the scope of this book, the emphasis here is on theatre and dance performances, performative installations or other performative events, but artwork relations can also involve fine arts, film, photography, fashion, social media, architecture and more. The artworks may enter into relation with one another because they share a theme or address a pressing societal issue (e.g. climate change, precarity, decolonisation), or because they use or challenge genre conventions (e.g. exploring elements of slapstick, horror, urban dance, burlesque), or specific ways of telling the story (e.g. use of irony, genre-bending, puppetry, use of digital technologies and so on). The notion of 'dramaturgical strategy' is used here as an umbrella term for compositional strategies or modes of storytelling, how these strategies address and position audiences or spectators and how the themes and issues that result from these strategies may connect to the 'world' at large (see Chapter 2, 'Dramaturgical Analysis: A Relational Approach').

This 'world at large' is a stepping-stone for considering the societal context, the second point of attention, which is used here as an overarching term for a range of ways in which performances address the world(s) we live in today—similar to the 'possible worlds' category in Postlewait's historiographic approach discussed above. How do these artworks explore and approach the societal matters at hand? Do they present a critical examination of them, or propose to look at it from various viewpoints? Do they treat the topic discursively, exploring arguments around the topic, or do they seek to explore the issue in a more experiential way?

Comparative analysis, thirdly, entails a search for similarities, differences or resonances, by looking for related or contrasting viewpoints on the subject matter, or for various ways a shared idea, strategy or genre is put into practice, and so on. This comparative approach ideally is also reflected in the form of reporting on the outcome of the analysis, either in writing or otherwise—meaning that the artworks are discussed together rather than one after the other. Lastly, contextual analysis works with one or more theoretical concepts that function as piloting devices in the analysis, which orients one's argumentation. Such a concept is related to the identified themes, strategies or social context and helps to further unpack these themes and issues. Concepts can also help to identify a set of questions that are addressed in and by artwork relations. For other suggestions of putting concepts to work, see Chapter 1, 'Concept-Based Analysis'.

To start this multi-layered adventure, it is useful to create a rough mapping of the selected artworks, initially drawing out as many connections and associations as possible, looking at themes, strategies, societal relations, artistic innovations and so on. It can be helpful to do some background research on these artworks (e.g. reading/watching interviews with the maker(s) or reviews of earlier works), or to collaborate with others in a collective mapping, to put yourself on track of other themes than those expected. Change tactics, regularly: if the focus is mainly on the societal context, try looking at artistic conventions instead, and the same the other way around. Deleuze and Guattari again provide some inspiration here, as they see maps as rhizomes themselves:

> A rhizome is a map and not a tracing. [...] What distinguishes the map from the tracing is that it is entirely orientated toward an experimentation in contact with the real [...] It fosters connections between fields [...] The map is open and connectable in all of its dimensions; it is detachable, reversible, susceptible to constant modification. It can be torn, reversed, adapted to any kind of mounting, reworked by an individual, group, or social formation [...] A map has multiple entryways, as opposed to the tracing, which always comes back 'to the same'. The map has to do with performance, whereas the tracing always involves an alleged 'competence' (Deleuze and Guattari 2004, 12–13).

Maps have to do with performance: it is the researcher who forges the connections. Or as one my students wrote, while reflecting on the method in a research journal: "Mapping supports free association [...] and reinforces the fact that it is us who have to establish the connections between things, and the quality and the depth of the connection are what counts. It creates an awareness of the multiple dimensions and the complexity of things and situates thinking as a very creative act".[3]

Following this initial phase of experimental browsing and gathering 'in the wild', it is useful to proceed with inventorying which bodies and affects on the map produce "the most trafficked paths", to repeat

---

3 I have used the method of contextual analysis in various courses and class assignments in the MA programme Contemporary Theatre, Dance and Dramaturgy at Utrecht University.

Bennett. Which of these paths will enable you to connect these works in a meaningful, dramaturgical way? Which paths clearly point at societal relations? This helps to eliminate smaller, undoubtedly meaningful but less prominent connections. While using this method in class, I have seen students creating their own map legend, adding symbols to indicate similarities and differences, theme-wise or otherwise. Often, the inventory of interesting or meaningful pathways already suggests useful concepts, such as 'time ecology', 'queering hope' or 'citationality'. Otherwise, such paths can be traced further towards theoretical concepts that are already familiar, which may sharpen your perspective and help to organise your argument. The goal is not to instrumentalise performances in order to justify a theoretical perspective, but to put this framework 'to work' so it helps in identifying and exploring key characteristics in a work. Setting works in a comparative theoretical perspective is at the same time a consideration of the complexity which makes each work more than an example, whereby different aspects yield a more nuanced illustration of an argument.

Demonstration | Resilient bodies and their politics of perception

To demonstrate the method, I present a condensed version of an earlier essay on the body politics of Marcelo Evelin, Marlene Monteiro Freitas and Ho Rui An, where I used the concept of 'politics of perception' to organise the analysis (Groot Nibbelink 2021). A contextual analysis often relies on a shared theme. This example, however, brings together artworks on the basis of a shared dramaturgical strategy. So, while at first sight these works do not have much in common, they share the strategy of working with 'counter-bodies' that resist specific hegemonic systems of signification, namely neoliberalism (Evelin), rationalism (Monteiro Freitas) and colonialism (Ho Rui An), respectively. These counter-bodies invite us to look critically at these hegemonic systems, and the concept of 'politics of perception' helps to describe and examine how this is done.

Slowly moving towards the front of the stage, nine dancers line up in a row close to the audience. It is the opening scene of *Dança Doente* (2017), created by Marcelo Evelin/Demolition Incorporada (Brazil). The dancers' bodies seem strained and tense, there is a sense of anticipation of things to come. Yet nothing comes. Nothing happens. Or so it seems. While pulsating music fills the theatre space, the dancers stand still, the audience is silent and quietly waits. Then, after quite a while, one dancer moves her arm a little. Another dancer shifts the weight of his body. Other bodies seem to move marginally as well. An arm crawls upwards, a leg briefly escapes control, a torso trembles. Through these minimal tremors, vibrations and spasms the performance unfolds, mostly without significant changes in dynamics, slowing down even more towards the end, when the performers (including the light and sound engineer) walk downstage to leave the stage one by one, in an extremely quiet pace.

Dança Doente is a dance performance without stylised or explicitly choreographed movements, without the type of movements we tend to call 'dance'. All dancers are professionally trained, yet there are no overt demonstrations of technical virtuosity. What we see, instead, are bodies that seem resilient to performing 'well': in *Dança Doente*, meaning 'sick dance', we look at 'inoperative' bodies, bodies that refuse to produce 'dance' and live up to expectations.[4] This refusal to function 'properly' questions how we look at bodies on stage, what we expect from dancers' bodies and those of our own and how we treat 'unproductive' bodies in daily life. Put differently, a performance like *Dança Doente* broaches a 'politics of perception' in its critical exploration of perceptual habits and ensuing horizons of expectation. By presenting us with vulnerable bodies instead of 'productive' ones, in a dance performance that refuses to 'deliver' dance, the performance implicitly asks what bodies we predominantly get to see in a market-driven neoliberal and media-saturated society, with its dominant health and sports culture; which bodies are seen as 'common' or successful and which as deviant.

This bond of perception and politics is precisely at the heart of Jacques Rancière's concept of the 'distribution of the sensible'. In *The Politics of Aesthetics* (2004), he argues that our perception and therefore our conception of the world is first and foremost a product of a certain division of what is visible or audible, and therefore, of what is thought, done and imagined (12). The concept helps to investigate what is present

---

4   This strategy is close to those described by Konstantina Georgelou, André Lepecki and others, see Groot Nibbelink (2021, 39).

in the world and what is made imperceptible; to seek the exclusions within the inclusions, to focus on what is ignored, misrepresented or even removed from consciousness. Rearranging or redistributing the sensible, then, can be understood as a politics of perception: a critical surveying and re-framing of what we think we know, of rendering perceptible how we perceive and what strategies make us see what we think we see.

The perceptual politics of refusing to 'perform well' also governs Marlene Monteiro Freitas' *Bacchae—Prelude to a Purge* (2017), although in a rather different way. Freitas is known for being inspired by elements that deviate from well-organised everyday life, such as the carnivalesque, madness, dream logic or play. In *Bacchae*, we see thirteen performers and musicians in a disorderly confusion of events, balancing, in the words of Freitas, "as funambulists over the wire of intensity".[5] Through an amalgam of loosely connected scenes, the (musical) mayhem on stage conjures up loose associations with Euripides' *Bacchae*, where Dionysian desire is pitted against Apollonian reason and discipline. On the one hand we get an impression of a festive, noisy, playful and particularly energetic party or bacchanal, while on the other this energy is explicitly suppressed, the outburst withheld, in scenes that loosely refer to an average day at the office. We see distorted versions of driving a car, cycling, typing, sitting behind a desk and the occasional boredom, (social) competition and (sexual) frustration at the workplace. This distortion is caused by the strained and staccato movement style through which all scenes are delivered. Both performers and musicians move like animated figures from a comic book yet with extreme tension in their gestures and movements. With some exceptions, it seems they are constantly stuttering, physically. *Bacchae's* redistribution of the sensible primarily resides in the impossibility of grasping the performance entirely. Rancière has described this as heterology, referring to instances in which "the meaningful fabric of the sensible is disturbed: a spectacle does not fit within the sensible framework defined by a network of meanings" (2004, 63). Freitas' cartoonesque figures disrupt the logic of rational meaning-making. Instead, these bodies elicit a sense of free-floating energy which generates a feeling of unbound freedom,

---

5 See Marlene Freitas' page on Key Performance, at http://www.keyperformance.se/?page_id=448

an 'anything goes' one may know from experiences of flow or when absorbed in play. *Bacchae* distinctively speaks to the sensitive body rather than the decoding mind.

Vulnerability and sensitivity appear again differently in *Solar: A Meltdown* (2014), by the Singapore-based artist Ho Rui An. *Solar* is an ingenious lecture-performance on Western representations of colonialism, in which Ho provides a resourceful counter-reading of pictures, films and musicals that are set somewhere in 'tropic countries'. It starts with a dissection of an exhibition in the (former) Tropenmuseum in Amsterdam which shows a scene of the anthropologist Charles LeRoux 'at work', photographing pygmies in Papua New Guinea.[6] In a light-humoured tone, Ho Rui An invites us to look closely at this extraordinary scene. While pointing to the sweaty back of the white colonialist, he subtly enquires how often we see a colonial officer as a labouring body, suffering under the merciless sun, meanwhile suggesting that this sweat can also be read as an index of the museum's anxiety towards its colonial past. From hereon he embarks upon presenting a visual history of 'colonial sweat', in which he replaces the dominant idea of the calm and controlled Western colonialist, dressed in stainless white, with that of a labouring, perspiring, suffering and occasionally delirious white body, melting away under the merciless tropical sun. Ho Rui An thus redistributes the sensible by replacing stories of colonial adventure and heroism with those of feebleness and agony, creating a pictorial counter-narrative. *Solar: A Meltdown* disturbs what Rancière terms the 'police', a system of organisation or 'law' that establishes a sensible order and privileged positions (Rockhill in Rancière 2004, 3). 'Politics', instead, interrupts that particular distribution of the sensible by bringing in other stories, stemming from suppressed and marginal positions. Such political subjectivation re-aligns the "perceptual coordinates of the community, thereby modifying the very aesthetico-political field of possibility" (2004, 3).

Although necessarily limited, this brief demonstration intends to show how a politics of perception is at work in these three performances, and how such a concept helps in establishing connections between

---

6   In 2023, the museum's name was changed to World Museum, also due to a merging with three other Dutch museums that sought to account for their colonial past.

them. This comparative analysis exposes bodies as powerful tools for challenging dominant narratives in society, foregrounding lived experience rather than ideal images. Fragile in *Dança Doente*, frantic in *Bacchae*, it seems as if these bodies reach out to us from an other-than-daily consciousness. *Dança Doente* may evoke the kind of outer-worldness that illness or extreme fatigue can create. *Bacchae* swings back and forth between coded action and profuse cacophony, replacing the linear structure of conventional tragedy with a free-floating dream logic instead. *Solar* uses the imagery of feeble, transpiring bodies to dissect colonial narratives. All three works, however different their agendas, make way for vulnerable bodies rather than 'successful' ones. They redistribute the sensible through 'irresponsible' play and by persevering weakness, via bodies that are driven by (sexual) desire. In *Dança Doente*, there is one moment in which the chain of inaction is interrupted, in a fierce, sexually charged duet between a younger and older male dancer. Although different than in Ho Rui An's case, this duet is equally an act of political subjectivation, of making space for bodies we do not often get to see on stage. Political subjectivation is an ongoing theme in *Solar: A Meltdown*, where Ho introduces, with a great sense of wit, the colonial wife next to the imperial ruler, who comes to the rescue by never sweating at all, and the 'punkawala', the servant who manually operates the fan that is to provide fresh air and solace to the sweaty imperial back. Ho's dissection of both colonial women and the punkawala is full of ambiguity as he portrays them as both heroically tasked with being in the centre of what he names a 'fanned planetary interior' and being confined to the colonial house. By rendering them key figures in the story, *Solar* resets the perceptual coordinates of commonality and disrupts traditional hierarchies of knowledge.

In *Aisthesis*, Rancière refers to art encounters and theatre scenes as "little optical machine[s]" that show us thought; they are concepts at work that allow us to think (2011, xi). Not only images or 'optical machines' make us think. Bodies do this as well. Whether controlled or uncontrolled, sweaty, soft or shivering, these bodies instigate a redistribution of the sensible, they generate a sensitivity for our corporeal existence and posit physicality and vulnerability at the heart of commonality.

Expanding the method | Mycelium thinking in-between disciplines

As indicated earlier, contextual analysis is not limited to theatre, dance or performance but can create art ecologies across disciplinary borders. To illustrate this, I present a second example, slightly more 'conventional' as I focus now on a shared theme rather than an artistic strategy, where I briefly look into the emerging interest in mushrooms, fungi knowledge and mycelium teachings across a variety of domains, namely artistic research (Hirvanen), fashion (Bruggeman and Toussaint) and anthropology (Lowenhaupt Tsing). I explore how each of these makers/researchers derive inspiration from ways that fungi grow and operate. Here, the organising concept is close to the thematics of the works discussed, as I will use the notion of *mycelium thinking*—a form of thought that is modelled on the way that fungi create symbiotic, nourishing and restorative networks—to organise the analysis.

In a blog post by the National Forest Foundation (US), with the telling title "Underground Networking: The Amazing Connections Beneath Your Feet", it is concisely explained that mushrooms are the visible 'fruit' of the fungus, while the majority of the fungal organism lives underground, in the soil interwoven with tree roots, forming a vast network of 'mycelium' that consists of innumerable tiny 'threads' that intermingle with tree roots (Holewinski, n.d.). In her book *Let's Become Fungal! Mycelium Teachings and the Arts* (2023), artist and activist Yasmine Ostendorf-Rodríguez describes mycelium as "the thread-like network of the fungus", which consists of hyphae, "self-learning membranes" that facilitate the transfer of water, carbon, nitrogen and other minerals (6). Mycelium is (often) mycorrhizal, as these membranes are interfaces for the creation of symbiotic relationships that not only allow for the exchange of water or nutrients but also of information between different species. She also stresses that there are many variations between fungi: "Fungi do not like to be boxed" (6). Echoing this latter remark is Daniëlle Bruggeman and Lianne Toussaint's observation, referring to Merlin Sheldrake's *Entangled Life: How Fungi Make Our World, Change Our Minds and Shape Our Futures* (2020), that "fungi can be seen as odes to other ways of being, as they assume dozens of different sexes, transform nonlife into life and force us to question where one organism stops and another begins" (2023, 193).[7]

Such symbiotic relations manifest in art and research as well. The artistic research project *Mycoscores/Choreospores* by Maija Hirvanen (2023), for instance, is an artistic tool for exploring the relations between fungi and human movement. It consists of a small box holding thirty-one cards and an accompanying booklet. Each card presents a score: a verb that provides an instruction for action or movement and that can inspire dancing in groups or creating movement patterns together. Each score describes a (movement) process that playfully addresses both fungi life as well as human activity, such as connecting, decomposing, fruiting, growing, healing, rooting, signalling, synchronising or wandering—verbs that are equally components of mycelium thinking. The scores can be combined as well, which would create an even more complex web of connections, just like a mycelium network. Some scores call upon the underground existence of mycelium, a presence felt rather than seen. They address, for instance, the dynamics between the visible and the invisible, or how individuality exists only as part of several collectives, or how processes of decomposition and decay are at the same time a renewal of matter, which refers to the restorative, mycorrhizal qualities of fungi networks.

This restorative potential reverberates in two other fungi-inspired practices I would like to discuss here, expanding this art ecology to the realms of fashion design and anthropology, respectively. Fungi and other bio-based materials increasingly inspire fashion design, as a counterweight to the extractive polluting processes of fast fashion industries. While Hirvanen emphasises the qualities of reciprocity and responsiveness in moving together, this second example explores how such qualities can inform sustainable design. In their essay "Becoming-with: On Textile Companions and Fungi Friends" (2023), Bruggeman and Toussaint describe the work of fashion designer Aniela Hoitink who creates garments based on bio-fabrication, by growing liquid mycelium cultures which are directly modelled on the human body, eliminating the need for cutting or sewing. The process is one of growing textile directly in

---

7   These non-binary qualities have also inspired queer artists: see Ostendorf-Rodríguez (2023) or Nina Scott's project *Be More Mushroom* (2022–2023), a children's cabaret-musical on queer identity.

3D form rather than harvesting and processing materials in an extractive manner. Mycelium thinking here focuses on the role of symbiosis in the design process. Inspired by Donna Haraway's concept of 'becoming-with', which precisely refers to the intimate entanglement of human and more-than-human matter, the authors use the term 'designing-with' to describe how garments and textile can grow from the direct exchange between humans and their bio-textile companions (190).

Restoration is also a key theme in anthropologist Anna Lowenhaupt Tsing's *The Mushroom at the End of the World: On the Possibility of Life in Capitalist Ruins* (2015), in which she traces the fortunes and whereabouts of the matsutake mushroom and its myriad ways of producing transformative encounters. She describes the rich life of matsutake, how it pops up across various timescales and geographies, how it grows on ruins, forges unexpected alliances and hybrid cultural practices that ensure its survival and result from matsutake's survivalist *modus vivendi*. These intermingling processes are catalysed by what Tsing calls "contaminated diversity" (2015, 29) by which she refers to how matsutake (and other fungi) infiltrate other systems; although that sounds somewhat aggressive, this initiates processes of healing and nurturing. Fungi thus spill over to other domains, to create something new that is fruitful and (re)generative. What makes the book so compelling is that this idea of contaminated diversity is not only a key topic in the book but also becomes a stylistic figure for how Tsing organises the chapters in the book: each chapter is a kaleidoscopic twist to the topic, tracing the lives and whereabouts of foragers and traders from several indigenous communities across the Asian-American diaspora, following matsutake from Cambodia and Laos to the pine forests of Oregon (US), to mushroom markets hidden deeply in the forest, to restorative processes in the soil, to gifting practices in Japan, to global infrastructure and much more. Matsutake weaves the chapters together just like a mycelium.

These three examples of mycelium thinking, however varied in terms of genre or discipline, share a genuine concern for the state of our planet and the future of life; they address a social context that has grown out of diasporic movements, migration patterns, the survival of both nature and cultural habits and they cherish interdependency networks as response to ecological disaster. They show how fungi inspire an attitude of resilience, across 'capitalist ruins', to recall Tsing, to meet the challenges of our time.

Mycelium thinking could as well be a model for contextual analysis as a method. Working with contextual analysis is a complex affair, as it is not only about analysing works of art, but also about creating connections. 'Making' a contextual analysis is to compose a puzzle which is as complex as a mycelium, integrating artworks in comparison, putting a theoretical concept to work while attending to societal context. Yet hopefully the analysis establishes some mycorrhizal relations, in that the connections come to fruition and nourish and inspire one another.

Suggestions for further reading

The idea of putting (art)works in dialogue with one another has affinities with the idea of 'diffractive reading', that is, the idea of reading works 'through' one another. Diffraction is a term used in (quantum) physics and described by Karen Barad, in *Meeting the Universe Half-Way* (2007). Iris van der Tuin (2011) demonstrates how diffraction becomes a model for reading literary and philosophical texts through one another. For a concise introduction to the method of diffractive reading, see Geerts and Van der Tuin (2021).

The idea of generative affirmativity is shared by many scholars that are inspired by Deleuze and Guattari, such as Rosi Braidotti, Brian Massumi and other exponents of New Materialist thinking. For a useful elaboration on affirmativity directly related to ecology and the arts, see Goodman, in *Gathering Ecologies: Thinking Beyond Interactivity* (2018).

References

Bal, Mieke. 2002. *Travelling Concepts in the Humanities: A Rough Guide*. University of Toronto Press.

Barad, Karen. 2007. *Meeting the Universe Half-way: Quantum Physics and the Entanglement of Matter and Meaning.* Duke University Press. https://doi.org/10.2307/j.ctv12101zq

Bennett, Jane. 2010. *Vibrant Matter: A Political Ecology of Things.* Duke University Press. https://doi.org/10.2307/j.ctv111jh6w

Bleeker, Maaike, Adrian Kear, Joe Kelleher and Heike Roms, eds. 2019. *Thinking Through Theatre and Performance.* Bloomsbury.

Bruggeman, Daniëlle and Lianne Toussaint. 2023. "Becoming-*with*: On Textile Companions and Fungi Friends." In *Materials of Culture: Approaches to Materials in Cultural Studies*, edited by Liedeke Plate, László Munteán and Airin Farahmand, 189–96. Transcript Verlag. https://doi.org/10.1515/9783839466971-021

Deleuze, Gilles and Félix Guattari. 2004. *A Thousand Plateaus: Capitalism and Schizophrenia*, translated by Brian Massumi. Continuum.

Freitas, Marlene. n.d. "Key Performance." Key Performance. http://www.keyperformance.se/?page_id=448

Geerts, Evelien and Iris van der Tuin. 2021. "Diffraction & Reading Diffractively." *Matter: Journal of New Materialist Research* 1 (2): 173–77. https://doi.org/10.1344/jnmr.v2i1.33380

Gielen, Pascal. 2013. "Artistic Praxis and the Neoliberalization of the Educational Space." *The Journal of Aesthetic Education* 47 (1): 58–71. https://doi.org/10.5406/jaesteduc.47.1.0058

Gielen, Pascal. 2003. *Kunst in Netwerken. Artistieke Selecties in de Hedendaagse Dans en de Beeldende Kunst* [Art in Networks: Artistic selection processes in contemporary dance and the arts]. Lannoo.

Goodman, Andrew. 2018. *Gathering Ecologies: Thinking Beyond Interactivity.* Open Humanities Press.

Groot Nibbelink, Liesbeth. 2021. "Soft Shivers, Sweaty Politics: Dramaturgy, Politics of Perception and the Pensive Body". In *Rancière and Performance*, edited by Colette Conroy and Nic Fryer, 39–55. Rowman & Littlefield.

Holewinski, Britt. n.d. "Underground Networking: The Amazing Connections Beneath Your Feet." https://www.nationalforests.org/blog/underground-mycorrhizal-network

Janssen, Sander. 2024. "De vrouwen van Shakespeare krijgen na 400 jaar de diepgang die ze verdienen." *De Volkskrant*, 28 February 2024.

Hirvanen, Maija. 2023. *Mycoscores/Choreospores*. Friends of Physical Contemporary Art & DAS Publishing/DAS Research.

Latour, Bruno. 2005. *Reassembling the Social: An Introduction to Actor-Network-Theory.* Oxford University Press.

Lavery, Carl. 2018. *Performance and Ecology: What Can Theatre Do?* Routledge. https://doi.org/10.4324/9781315149172

Maanen, Hans van. 2009. *How to Study Art Worlds: On the Societal Functioning of Aesthetic Values.* Amsterdam University Press.

Morton, Timothy. 2010. *The Ecological Thought.* Harvard University Press. https://doi.org/10.2307/j.ctvjhzskj

Postlewait, Thomas. 2009. *The Cambridge Introduction to Theatre Historiography.* Cambridge University Press.

Rancière, Jacques. [2000] 2004. *The Politics of Aesthetics, translated and introduced by Gabriel Rockhill.* Continuum.

Rancière, Jacques. [2011] 2013. *Aisthesis: Scenes from the Aesthetic Regime of Art*, translated by Zakir Paul. Verso.

Read, Alan. 2008. *Theatre, Intimacy and Engagement: The Last Human Venue.* Palgrave Macmillan. https://doi.org/10.1057/9780230273863

Tsing, Anna Lowenhaupt. 2015. *The Mushroom at the End of the World: On the Possibility of Life in Capitalist Ruins.* Princeton University Press. https://doi.org/10.2307/j.ctvc77bcc

Tuin, Iris van der. 2011. "A Different Starting Point, a Different Metaphysics: Reading Bergson and Barad Diffractively." *Hypatia* 26 (1): 22–42. https://doi.org/10.1111/j.1527-2001.2010.01114.x

10. Cultural Materialism and the Politics of Performance

Dick Zijp

Summary

Cultural materialism is a theoretical approach rooted in the work of Raymond Williams and the unapologetically left-wing academic and educational project of British cultural studies. It conceptualises culture as a site of social and political struggle and active meaning-making. This chapter argues that cultural materialism, although retaining a 'residual' status in contemporary theatre and performance studies, has renewed significance and urgency in a cultural moment marked by resurgent right-wing politics and the enduring grip of neoliberal capitalism. Cultural materialism urges us to examine the socio-material conditions under which artworks are produced, and to analyse how they reinforce or challenge social hierarchies and power relations. The author begins by positioning cultural materialism against some of the dominant approaches in the field, highlighting its potential to reinvigorate activist energies in performance scholarship and to reimagine theatre as a space for social and political change. Following a discussion of key concepts—including the distinction between emergent, residual and dominant cultures, as well as structure of feeling—the chapter demonstrates this method through an analysis of the work of Dutch comedian Theo Maassen and scenographer/theatre maker Dries Verhoeven, using a cultural materialist lens to reveal the shifting political and ideological implications of their work.

Introduction

This chapter proposes cultural materialism as a helpful theoretical approach to theatre and performance. Cultural materialism was developed by Raymond Williams (1921–1988), a Welsh literary scholar, social theorist and Marxist cultural critic. His early books are among the "formative texts" (Hall 2019, 49) of British cultural studies, the unapologetically left-wing academic and educational project developed by the Centre for Contemporary Cultural Studies (CCCS) at the University of Birmingham in the post-war period. While this chapter primarily engages with Williams's own work, I use the term 'cultural materialism' to refer more broadly to this tradition of British cultural studies, which has become associated with scholars such as Stuart Hall, Paul Gilroy and Angela McRobbie.

Cultural materialism contributes to a critical understanding of the political and ideological implications and effects of culture. It urges us to investigate the material (social, political, economic, technological) conditions under which an artistic work is produced and to examine how this work bears the imprint of these conditions. Importantly, however, it is a 'cultural' materialism, meaning that it understands culture as a site of social and political struggle, as well as active meaning-making. Cultural materialism does not, therefore, seek to reduce artworks to their material conditions of production. Rather, it enables a more dialectical understanding of the relationship between art and society, aiming to analyse how artworks reinforce, question or challenge social hierarchies and relationships of power. In this way, cultural materialism differs from more orthodox forms of Marxism (more on this below).

Borrowing one of Williams's own terms, theatre scholar Janelle Reinelt argued that cultural materialism holds a "residual" status in contemporary theatre and performance studies (2015, 235). This observation was made in 2015, but it still rings true. While available as an academic resource and quoted in textbooks (e.g. Balme 2008, 87–89; Taylor and Symonds 2017, 61–75), it occupies a marginal position in theatre and performance scholarship.

One of the central claims of this chapter is that cultural materialism has renewed significance and urgency in a cultural moment marked by the global rise of the far right and the enduring grip of neoliberal capitalism. Moreover, it aligns with the emerging desire among Western theatre and performance scholars (as well as theatre practitioners) to explore the potential of theatre and performance to act as collective imaginaries for social and political change (Reinelt 2015; 2021; Shalson 2017; Tomlin 2019). As I will demonstrate, this recent interest in the cultural politics of theatre and performance follows a period during which political activism in the theatre was often met with suspicion.

While cultural materialism is compatible with various approaches to theatre and performance, such as audience and reception research or ethnography, this chapter primarily focuses on how cultural materialism provides tools for the analysis of theatre performances. A helpful way to distinguish cultural materialism from existing models of performance analysis might be as follows: whereas theatre and performance scholars tend to concentrate on the social and political context of a work insofar as it references the world outside the theatre, cultural materialism also attends to the socio-material conditions of the work—conditions which may or may not be explicitly addressed by the performance itself. This does not imply that cultural materialism and other modes of performance analysis are mutually exclusive. On the contrary, I argue that cultural materialism can be productively combined with, and enriched by, existing models, in particular those that place greater emphasis on dramaturgical structure and audience address (See Chapter 2, 'Dramaturgical Analysis: A Relational Approach' and Chapter 3, 'Spectatorship Analysis'). The two case studies discussed in this chapter attest to this.

Context | Why cultural materialism, why now?

Before further positioning cultural materialism within the field of theatre and performance studies, it is helpful to briefly outline Williams's biography and consider how his work contributed to the formation of media and cultural studies as academic fields in the post-war period. Williams was born on 31 August 1921, the son of a railway worker. As a working-class child, it was by no means self-evident that he would receive a university education, but he won a scholarship and was able to pursue a BA in English at Cambridge. During his studies, he joined the Communist Party, which he later left. After the Second World War, he completed his degree and went on to write his first academic books, which addressed the rise of the British working class in the nineteenth century. In 1974, Williams was appointed Professor of Drama at Cambridge.

Although Williams was never formally affiliated with the Birmingham Centre for Contemporary Cultural Studies, he exerted a major influence on both the Centre and the broader academic project of cultural studies. He made two key contributions. The first was his introduction of a sociological definition of culture into the traditional humanities. Since the nineteenth century, the boundaries between 'high' and 'low' culture had been firmly established and defended within humanities departments. Culture was defined, in this context, as "the best that has been thought and written" (Williams 1980, 57) and the artistic and literary canon was regarded as a reservoir of cultural values to which all should aspire.

In *The Long Revolution* (originally published in 1961), Williams observes that the study of culture in the humanities was traditionally grounded either in an "ideal" notion of culture (culture as a source of universal moral truth) or a "documentary" one (culture as a form of historical analysis that situates intellectual and imaginative work within a longer artistic and literary tradition). To these, he added a third approach: a "social" definition of culture, which expands the field to include the popular arts and the study of everyday cultural practices and institutions (1980, 57–58). Williams famously asserted that any theory of culture must be based on "the study of relationships between elements in a whole way of life" (1980, 63).

Second, although Williams was a Marxist thinker, he challenged orthodox forms of Marxist theory, in which art and culture are regarded as mere reflections of the interests of the dominant class. Such a determinist view, he argued, reduces culture to an expression of social and economic relationships and fails to acknowledge the agency of dominated and marginalised groups themselves (Williams 2020). In its place, Williams proposed an understanding of culture as the site of social and political struggle. This conception of culture laid the groundwork for British cultural studies and was further developed in the work of the Black, British-Jamaican cultural theorist Stuart Hall (1932–2014), among others.

How do these interventions relate to the field of theatre and performance studies? First, Williams's definition of culture as "a whole way of life" resonates with, and has contributed to, the 'broad spectrum' approach advanced by the founders of performance studies (Schechner 2006). However, Williams's work also serves as a useful reminder that a broad understanding of performance should encompass not only everyday forms of social interaction and behaviour, but also popular theatre, which continues to be understudied and undervalued (Savran 2004; Zijp 2023).

Williams's second contribution, his definition of culture as a site of social and political struggle, may help to reinvigorate activist political energies in theatre and performance studies. Since the late twentieth and early twenty-first century, there has been a growing sense in Western theatre and performance studies that the modernist ideal of a 'political theatre' is outmoded and that theatre is not a suitable place for collective forms of resistance. Many scholars have questioned the model of political efficacy implicit in the work of modernist theatre reformers such as Bertolt Brecht and Augusto Boal, who envisioned a theatre with an explicit and activist political message. This critique has been accompanied by a shift of focus from 'political theatre' to a 'politics of theatre' (Kelleher 2009), which locates politics at the level of the individual spectator (e.g. Lehmann 2007) and privileges affective, temporary forms of resistance over what Scott Sharp et al. have—somewhat disparagingly—termed a "politics of project" (2013, 118).

A good example is provided by the work of Andy Lavender (2016). In a book that, as its title suggests, focuses on "theatres of engagement" in the twenty-first century, Lavender is less concerned with political commitment and the role of theatre in inspiring collective forms of organisation and resistance (as might be expected from a cultural studies perspective). Instead, he uses the term 'engagement' to emphasise the personal and affective involvement of individual spectators, which he observes in the intimate settings of immersive theatre performances.

Lavender's research is inspired by the French philosopher Jacques Rancière, whose work is widely embraced in theatre and performance studies (e.g. Fryer and Conroy 2021). Rancière's ideas resonate with the aforementioned shift from political theatre to a theatre of politics. As Reinelt and Liz Tomlin have noted, Rancière's emphasis on the emancipation of the autonomous spectator may unwittingly reproduce the rampant individualism at the core of neoliberal capitalism. Furthermore, Rancière's notion of 'dissensus' and the temporary disordering of the prevailing 'distribution of the sensible' may hinder the collective organisation and coalition-building necessary for social change (Reinelt 2015; 2021; Tomlin 2019).

In recent years, some theatre and performance scholars have emphasised the need to move beyond individualist models of theatrical politics, as evidenced by the work of Reinelt and Tomlin cited above. This shift is also reflected in *The Routledge Companion to Theatre and Politics*, which selects 'message' as one of its organising terms and engages seriously with the potential impact of political theatre (Eckersall and Grehan 2019).

Some thinkers have been critical of British cultural studies and the work of Williams. Most importantly, cultural studies approaches have been criticised for reducing art and culture to mere expressions of historical and social 'context', a category often viewed as unhelpfully abstract, deterministic and reductive (e.g. Felski 2015; for a compelling refutation of this criticism, see Ladegaard and Nielsen 2019; Robbins 2019, 30–35). As demonstrated in this section, cultural materialism actually responds to such reductive forms of Marxism by understanding culture as a site of struggle and active meaning-making. Interestingly, while 'context' has often been used as a shorthand for the type of research represented by Williams's work, particularly within American cultural studies (e.g. Grossberg 2013), Williams himself rarely uses the notion of context in his writings, instead insisting on "the study of relationships between elements in a whole way of life" (1980, 63). Cultural materialism, to put it concisely, does not present an analysis of 'context', but of 'relationships', and is more concrete and less abstract than some critics have suggested. This makes cultural materialism especially well-suited to the analysis of theatre and performance.

A similar criticism of cultural materialism has been levelled by New Materialist critics, who argue that older, Marxist forms of materialism are overly abstract and totalising. While a more detailed analysis of the relationship between old and new materialisms falls outside the scope of this chapter, Williams's work arguably prefigures New Materialist strands of thought in intriguing ways (Hands 2015). Williams's conception of culture is grounded in a nuanced understanding of the entanglements of matter and meaning as well as the insight that we must study actual relationships rather than presupposing any abstract notion of culture or society (a line of thought that resonates with the later work of Bruno Latour; see Latour 2005).

Moreover, from a cultural materialist perspective, a potential risk posed by the recent surge in New Materialist and post-humanist approaches in theatre and performance studies is that by radically de-centring the human, these approaches may inadvertently obscure the importance of studying and resisting existing social hierarchies and relationships of power within human societies (DeFazio 2012; Lettow 2017). In the current cultural moment, marked by resurgent right-wing politics, neoliberal capitalism and climate catastrophe, cultural materialism serves as a timely reminder to keep studying theatre and performance in terms of their material conditions and political implications and effects. In the next sections, I will introduce some key concepts from Williams's work to demonstrate their usefulness for the analysis of theatre and performance.

How to | Keywords

This section's title is a nod to one of William's most well-known (and still frequently cited) books, *Keywords* (1983), which offers a lexicon of key terms for thinking about culture and society. The book reflects Williams's interest in terms rooted in everyday language and cultural practices. However, Williams also introduced several new concepts for the analysis of culture. I will discuss two of them here.

The two definitions of culture discussed above—culture as a whole way of life and culture as a site of struggle—correspond to different stages of Williams's intellectual development and career. In his early work, Williams sought to expand traditional, elitist understandings of culture, introducing the concept of structure of feeling as a means of addressing their limitations. In *The Long Revolution*, Williams argues that while defining culture as a 'whole way of life' aims to encompass the totality of cultural meanings and practices within a given society, this definition does not fully account for how culture is embodied and experienced by those who live it. The term 'structure of feeling' is meant to express this affective dimension of a culture, without losing sight of the idea of culture as a totality. As Williams explains: "[Structure of feeling] is as firm and definite as 'structure' suggests, yet it operates in the most delicate and least tangible parts of our activity" (1980, 64).

The concept of structure of feeling underscores the central role of art in Williams's understanding and analysis of culture. Williams contends that the structure of feeling is most fully expressed in the artworks of a given period, albeit often in implicit and unconscious ways. Moreover, the concept can be seen as anticipating contemporary theories of affect (Reinelt 2015) and aligns with the emphasis on embodied knowledge found in theatre and performance studies. Diana Taylor's distinction between archive and repertoire, for instance, strongly resonates with Williams's understanding of culture in terms of a dominant structure of feeling (Taylor 2013).

In the early 1970s, Williams's work became more explicitly activist and more influenced by Marxist thought. In one of his most influential essays from this period, "Base and Superstructure in Marxist Cultural Theory" (1973), he questions reductionist forms of Marxism, in which art and culture are treated as mere reflections of material conditions. In this text, Williams introduces a useful distinction between dominant, emergent and residual cultures.

The dominant culture is "the central, effective and dominant system of meanings and values, which are not merely abstract but which are organized and lived" (Williams 2020, 43). Here, again, Williams emphasises the embodied and affective dimensions of culture. Borrowing a term from the Italian Marxist thinker Antonio Gramsci (1891–1937), Williams uses the concept of hegemony to theorise how the dominant culture utilises everyday interactions, discourses and practices to manufacture consent. A good example of a seemingly innocuous cultural form that may reproduce existing power relationships is street naming, which reflects a culture's choices about its national heroes and, implicitly, about those deemed unworthy of this status.

Residual culture refers to the idea that "some experiences, meanings and values, which cannot be verified or cannot be expressed in terms of the dominant culture, are nevertheless lived and practised on the residue […] of some previous social formation" (2020, 45). Residual cultures are alternative forms of culture in that they do not directly challenge or resist the dominant culture, but exist alongside it as alternative modes of living and meaning-making. For instance, although religion is no longer the dominant system of meaning in many Western societies, residual elements remain present in everyday life—such as churches, which continue to be regarded as important cultural monuments.

There are also forms of culture that not only seek to articulate an alternative to the dominant culture but openly oppose it. Williams refers to such anti-hegemonic cultural forces as 'emergent'. Emergent cultures are continually at risk, however, of being co-opted and neutralised by the dominant culture. A good example is the mass production of T-shirts bearing the image of the guerilla warrior Ché Guevara (1928–1967), a communist icon whose symbolism has been appropriated by capitalist consumer culture, thereby stripping it of its radical potential.

A final and significant point is that, because Williams's work is grounded in an understanding of the importance of historical and cultural change, cultural materialism seeks to trace broader cultural transformations across extended periods of time. We might ask how the structure of feeling of a particular historical culture differs from our own, or how the relationships among emergent, residual and dominant cultures evolve over time. As the following sections will demonstrate, studying a culture and its artists over an extended period is an important characteristic of a cultural materialist approach.

Demonstration | From *emergent* to *dominant*: the 'ironic transgression' of Theo Maassen

In this section, I demonstrate the value of a cultural materialist framework for analysing theatre and performance by examining how a specific cultural form—comedy—has, in recent years, emerged as a site of social and political struggle. My case study focuses on the provocative Dutch comedian Theo Maassen (b. 1966). While space does not permit the analysis of specific scenes or jokes from Maassen's work (but see: Zijp 2023, 70–79), I aim to show how cultural materialism provides concrete tools for analysing the relationship between a performance and broader social and cultural formations. In doing so, it complements existing models of dramaturgical and performance analysis.

Theo Maassen is a popular and critically acclaimed Dutch comedian who experienced his breakthrough in the late 1990s. He continues to perform regularly, with his tours consistently selling out. Although Maassen was trained in the stand-up comedy circuit, his work also belongs to the Dutch cabaret tradition, which predates the introduction of the American/British stand-up comedy format to the Netherlands in the early 1990s. Dutch cabaret is a popular form of comedy that is generally considered more theatrical than stand-up, often incorporating not only joke-telling but also sketches and song. Moreover, cabaret tends to be less minimalist than stand-up in terms of setting and costume. Finally, Dutch cabaret performances typically revolve around a central theme or storyline, in contrast to the loosely connected jokes and anecdotes characteristic of many stand-up routines.

An analysis of Maassen's work in terms of its dramaturgical construction and mode of audience address reveals his consistent use of irony. I have elsewhere described his comedic style in terms of "ironic transgression" (2023, 70). Maassen's humour is consciously transgressive and desecrating: many of his jokes are openly sexist or racist, thereby crossing moral and social boundaries. Maassen gets away with these jokes largely because of his ironic tone. Here, I use the term irony to refer to a type of humour that deliberately creates ambiguity about the maker's intentions (Hutcheon 1995). Maassen's irony arises from the tension between his sympathetic stage persona and his trenchant jokes. He presents himself as the quintessential good guy, troubled in his personal life and uncertain how to navigate an immoral world, thereby mitigating the shock effect of his jokes. Beneath his concealed aggression, he appears to be something of a 'softie'. One of his early shows is aptly entitled *Ruwe pit* (Rough on the inside, 1998), a play on the Dutch expression 'ruwe bolster, blanke pit', meaning rough on the outside but with a gentle nature.

While an analysis of Maassen's work in terms of its aesthetics and mode of audience address might suggest that his comedy is elusive and open-ended, it does little to explain why the reception of his work has shifted in recent years. Maassen has generally been praised for his transgressive humour, but his show *Situatie gewijzigd* (Situation altered, 2019) attracted significant criticism for its perceived lack of irony and for being seriously sexist and racist (e.g. Berkeljon 2019). Whereas Maassen framed the show as "an uncomfortable but hilarious monologue about the rise and fall of the white male" (ANP 2018) and presented an explicit critique of 'political correctness'—making his tone more politicised than in earlier work—his comedy style remained largely unchanged.

Here, a cultural materialist approach helps to demonstrate that the meanings and interpretations of Maassen's work are inherently linked to its material conditions of production. The social and political conditions of Maassen's comedy have changed significantly over the past decades. When I show clips of Maassen's early work (or that of other Dutch comedians from the 1990s) to my students, I struggle to convey the sense of liberation that many progressively minded people once experienced in these transgressive jokes. This is because these jokes bring us closer to the structure of feeling of the period, which is difficult to grasp for the current cohort of students, as they generally lack personal memories of the 1990s. Nevertheless, we can attempt to approach the structure of feeling by exploring the relationships between comedy and the wider culture, e.g. by analysing reviews of the work, media interviews with the artist, or reading historical and sociological work about the period and the culture in which the work was produced.

To understand this underlying shift in the structure of feeling, we must first consider some broader social and political changes. In Western liberal societies, the dominant culture of the 1990s was "post-political" (Mouffe 2005). It was the decade following the fall of the Berlin Wall in 1989, when many felt that the global political tensions between capitalism and communism had finally been resolved, and that a liberal consensus politics offered the best way forward. It was also a time when a postmodern sensibility dominated the arts. In Dutch cabaret, both tendencies were reflected in an emerging aesthetic of transgression. While transgressive humour in the Netherlands dates back to the progressive countercultures of the 1960s, in which Dutch comedians played an active role (Zijp 2023), in the early 1990s, a more nihilistic, amoral form of transgression emerged through the work of young comedians such as Hans Teeuwen (b. 1967), Theo Maassen, De Vliegende Panters and Waardenberg en de Jong, among others. Their comedy was not explicitly political, but rather sought to break with the political cabaret of previous generations, which many viewed as overly moralistic and preachy. This postmodern crossing of boundaries for its own sake appeared to promise liberation from the political and ideological fault lines that had defined the preceding decades.

In recent decades, the post-political climate of the 1990s has been succeeded by an era of "hyperpolitics" (Jäger 2022), marked by the re-emergence of political conflict in the public sphere. Humour has played a key role in this process of "repoliticisation" (Nieuwenhuis and Zijp 2022, 343), which has been driven by wider social, political and technological changes. The rise of social media has enabled marginalised groups—such as women, people of colour and queer communities—to raise their voices online. This has inspired new forms of global activism, exemplified by successful hashtags such as #metoo and #BlackLivesMatter. These movements have increasingly 'called out' comedians and politicians for their use of sexist, racist, homophobic and transphobic humour (Zijp 2022).

At the same time, we have witnessed the emergence of an alt-right meme culture (Pérez 2022), alongside the rise of populist and far-right political leaders such as Donald Trump, Boris Johnson and Geert Wilders, who have decisively broken with the liberal consensus politics of the 1990s. These leaders have employed aggressive humour to attract voters and ridicule political opponents (Basu 2024), thereby reappropriating transgressive forms of humour that were traditionally associated with progressive comedians and political movements (Zijp 2023; cf. Nagle 2017).

All of these changes have made the use of transgressive humour increasingly risky, and the irony of transgressive jokes less self-evident. In the 1990s, transgressive humour was experienced by many as emergent, radical and avant-garde due to its nihilistic transgression which offered a sense of liberation from an oppressive Cold War politics. However, by the 2010s and early 2020s, this humour began to resonate —in often uncanny ways—with right-wing populist sentiments and worldviews, thereby becoming an expression of the dominant culture. In hindsight, one could argue that the ironic transgression of the 1990s was always already an expression of the dominant culture, and that what has shifted is primarily a heightened awareness—at least within more progressive circles—of the serious political implications and effects of humour (Nieuwenhuis and Zijp 2022). This underscores that the seemingly clear-cut distinction between dominant, residual and emergent cultures does not straightforwardly map onto social reality, which is typically complex, messy and structured by competing interests and intersecting domains of struggle.

Expanding the method | Dries Verhoeven's *Brothers exalt thee to freedom* (2021)

While cultural materialism and the broader project of British cultural studies have traditionally been associated with the study of popular culture, their scope can be productively expanded to include the study of experimental art and performance. A cultural materialist approach offers fresh perspectives on such artistic practices. This will be illustrated through a brief discussion of the work of the Dutch scenographer and theatre director Dries Verhoeven (b. 1976). Verhoeven is not a traditional theatre maker; his performances often take the form of performative installations that require active spectator participation (Groot Nibbelink 2019; Studio Dries Verhoeven 2020). Originally trained as a scenographer, Verhoeven excels in spatial design. The dramaturgical setup of his performances is carefully conceived, and his works almost function like machines (Bleeker 2020).

In contrast to the comedy of Maassen, the experimental performances of Verhoeven have received substantial attention in theatre and performance studies. Existing scholarship tends to focus on the dramaturgical choices made by the artist, and how these invite particular audience responses (e.g. Bleeker and Germano 2014; Bleeker 2019; Groot Nibbelink 2019; Lavender 2016). A cultural materialist approach complements these perspectives by combining this valuable focus on dramaturgy and spectatorship with an analysis of the material conditions shaping Verhoeven's work over recent decades, as well as the shifting political and ideological implications of this work.

From the outset of his career, Verhoeven has explored the potential of community-building in an increasingly individualised society. In his early work, he did so by creating intimate and playful encounters. This work belonged to an artistic movement formerly known as 'ervaringstheater' (literally: 'experiential theatre'), a form of immersive theatre that fostered gentle, intimate experiences, lifting spectators out of the everyday without providing overt social or political critique.

Over the past decade, Verhoeven's work has continued to explore the tension between individual and collective, while becoming more openly politicised and disruptive (van Heuven 2019). Verhoeven's recent work both reflects a broader shift in the structure of feeling—a new climate of political activism—and acts as a clever artistic response to it. Additionally, his work signals a renewed interest among theatre makers and performance scholars in the politics of labour (e.g. Georgelou 2019; Ridout 2013; Schmidt 2019).

A good example is the performative installation *Brothers exalt thee to freedom* (2021), which addresses labour migration in the context of capitalist precarisation and the robotisation of labour. Presented during the 2021 edition of the SPRING Festival, the work placed a group of Bulgarian workers inside a glass box on the main stage of Utrecht's City Theatre. These workers/actors performed for 8 hours a day, singing the Dutch labour song 'Broeders verheft u ter vrijheid' (Brothers exalt thee to freedom, 1938). Behind them, robots lifted and moved baskets in a choreographed simulation of warehouse labour. The workers/singers were compensated according to the Dutch collective labour agreement for Theatre and Dance. They received a five-minute break every thirty minutes, mirroring the work schedule of Amazon employees. Spectators were free to visit the performance for as long as they wished. Additionally, they were invited to visit an exhibition in The Hague, which showcased the actual living quarters of the migrant workers involved in the production.[1]

From a Rancièrian perspective, Verhoeven's installation can be understood as a disruption of the given 'distribution of the sensible' by rendering visible Bulgarian migrant workers who are typically invisible to a Dutch middle-class audience attending an experimental arts festival. In addition, following Nicholas Ridout, one could argue that Verhoeven mobilises the critical potential of theatre as a space where productive labour (carried out by actors as part of a service economy) and consumption (by audiences attending a performance during their leisure time) unfold simultaneously, thereby raising awareness of social relations under neoliberal capitalism (2006; 2013).

---

1   I visited the installation twice: on 23 May 2021, during the SPRING Festival in Utrecht, and a second time on 23 May 2024, in Frascati, Amsterdam, during the exhibition *WORK WORK WORK* (curated by Dries Verhoeven).

However, from a cultural materialist perspective, it is worth questioning to what extent Verhoeven succeeds in challenging and resisting the dominant culture. The dramaturgical logic of the installation is ironic and provocative. Verhoeven himself has described this logic as the "outsourcing" of protest to wage labourers (Verhoeven and van Elderen 2021). While this can be interpreted as a clever critique of a neoliberal capitalist logic through "subversive affirmation" (Arns and Sasse 2006; cf. Merx and Groot Nibbelink 2022), i.e. the critical mimesis of the material conditions of capitalist labour, it simultaneously functions as an ironic gesture, suggesting that Verhoeven himself is complicit in the capitalist economy and unable (or unwilling) to escape it or to transcend it through socially engaged art.

The audience is made complicit in the neoliberal logic that the installation parodies. The performers are seated on chairs, facing the audience, while singing for 8 hours (except for brief breaks), thereby making us uncomfortably aware of how exhausting that must be. While calling for a revolution through the lyrics of the song, these performers are trapped inside a glass box, and we are separated from them through the glass, unable to intervene. Moreover, the performers are placed on a traditional proscenium arch stage which does not allow for active participation or resistance by the spectators either. Finally, the Bulgarian performers sing an old labour song in a language that they do not even speak, raising the question of whether traditional vocabularies of protest have now become obsolete.

The installation thereby seems to gesture towards the impossibility of collective organisation and resistance under neoliberal capitalism. If that is indeed the case, what kind of political work does this performance do? Does it inspire critical awareness? Or does it instead reassure audiences by playing into a dominant mode of individualised and ironic spectatorship (Tomlin 2019)? These are some of the questions that a cultural materialist approach might prompt us to ask about this performance—questions that, it should be noted, are not easy to answer. The performance cleverly shifts between moments when the singers are spotlighted and their voices drown out the mechanical sounds of robots in the background, and moments when the lights inside the glass box are darkened and the voices of the workers are no longer amplified, emphasising the robot sounds. The performance thus remains ambiguous, leaving us with the question of which force will prove stronger: technological capitalism, or workers' protests against it.

Suggestions for further reading

Williams introduces his sociological definition of culture and discusses how it relates to traditional humanities scholarship in "The Analysis of Culture", the second chapter of *The Long Revolution* (1961). In this chapter, he also explains the term structure of feeling. In the article "Base and Superstructure in Marxist Cultural Theory" (1973), Williams argues against orthodox Marxist models of base and superstructure and introduces the concept of hegemony. He also explains the distinction between dominant, emergent and residual culture. In theatre and performance studies, Reinelt (2015) has written about the continuing relevance of Williams's legacy to our field and compared his work with that of Rancière. Tomlin (2019) provides an insightful account of contemporary political theatre, seeking to integrate older strands of Marxist theory from the cultural studies tradition with the thinking of Rancière. Ric Knowles (2004) offers a book-length introduction to cultural materialism as a methodological approach within theatre and performance studies, with particular attention to its intersection with semiotics.

References

ANP. 2018. "Theo Maassen eindigt tiende theatertour in Carré." *Het Parool*, September 17 2018.

Arns, Inke and Sylvia Sasse. 2006. "Subversive Affirmation: On Mimesis as a Strategy of Resistance." In *East Art Map: Contemporary Art and Eastern Europe*, edited by IRWIN, 444–55. MIT Press.

Balme, Christopher. 2008. *The Cambridge Introduction to Theatre Studies*. Cambridge University Press. https://doi.org/10.1017/CBO9780511817021

Basu, Sammy. 2024. "'Laughing at Us': Humour, Humiliation, and Trump's Public." *European Journal of Humour Research* 12 (1): 15–40. https://doi.org/10.7592/EJHR.2024.12.1.833

Berkeljon, Sara. 2019. "Sunny Bergman en Theo Maassen in gesprek over mannelijkheid: Dat begint heel gezellig…" *De Volkskrant*, April 4 2019. https://www.volkskrant.nl/mensen/

sunny-bergman-en-theo-maassen-in-gesprek-over-mannelijkheid-dat-begint-heel-gezellig~b27568d6/

Bleeker, Maaike. 2019. "What Do Performances Do to Spectators?" In *Thinking Through Theatre and Performance*, edited by Maaike Bleeker et al., 33–46. Bloomsbury.

Bleeker, Maaike. 2020. "Machines to Get Thought Moving." In *In Doubt*, edited by Studio Dries Verhoeven, 136–38. Kerber.

Bleeker, Maaike and Isis Germano. 2014. "Perceiving and Believing: An Enactive Approach to Spectatorship." *Theatre Journal* 66 (3): 363–83. https://doi.org/10.1353/tj.2014.0073

DeFazio, Kimberly. 2012. "Machine-Thinking and the Romance of Posthumanism." *The Red Critique* 14. http://redcritique.org/WinterSpring2012/machinethinkingandtheromanceofposthumanism.htm

Eckersall, Peter and Helena Grehan, eds. 2019. *The Routledge Companion to Theatre and Politics*. Routledge. https://doi.org/10.4324/9780203731055

Felski, Rita. 2015. *The Limits of Critique*. University of Chicago Press. https://doi.org/10.7208/chicago/9780226294179.001.0001

Fryer, Nic and Colette Conroy, eds. 2021. *Rancière and Performance*. Rowman & Littlefield. https://doi.org/10.5771/9781538146583

Georgelou, Konstantina. 2019. "'100-Days House': Blackout as Political Action." In *The Routledge Companion to Theatre and Politics*, edited by Peter Eckersall and Helena Grehan, 189–92. Routledge.

Groot Nibbelink, Liesbeth. 2019. *Nomadic Theatre: Mobilizing Theory and Practice on the European Stage*. Bloomsbury.

Grossberg, Lawrence. 2013. "Theorising Context." In *Spatial Politics: Essays for Doreen Massey*, edited by Doreen Massey and Joe Painter, 32–43. John Wiley. https://doi.org/10.1002/9781118278857

Hall, Stuart. 2019. "Cultural Studies: Two Paradigms [1980]." In *Stuart Hall: Foundations of Cultural Studies: Essential Essays*, vol. 1, edited by David Morley, 47–70. Duke University Press. https://doi.org/10.1215/9781478002413

Hands, Joss. 2015. "From Cultural to New Materialism and Back: The Enduring Legacy of Raymond Williams." *Culture, Theory and Critique* 56 (2): 133–48, https://doi.org/10.1080/14735784.2014.931782

Hutcheon, Linda. 1995. *Irony's Edge: The Theory and Politics of Irony*. Routledge.

Jäger, Anton. 2022. "From Post-Politics to Hyperpolitics." *Jacobin*, February 14 2022. https://jacobin.com/2022/02/from-post-politics-to-hyper-politics

Kelleher, Joe. 2009. *Theatre and Politics*. Bloomsbury.

Knowles, Ric. 2004. *Reading the Material Theatre*. Cambridge University Press.

Ladegaard, Jakob and Jakob Gaardbo Nielsen. 2019. "Introduction: The Question of Context." In *Context in Literary and Cultural Studies,* edited by Jakob Ladegaard and Jakob Gaardbo Nielsen, 1–14. UCL Press. https://doi.org/10.14324/111.9781787356245

Latour, Bruno. 2005. *Reassembling the Social: An Introduction to Actor-Network Theory.* Oxford University Press. https://doi.org/10.1093/oso/9780199256044.001.0001

Lavender, Andy. 2016. *Performance in the Twenty-First Century: Theatres of Engagement.* Routledge. https://doi.org/10.4324/9780203128176

Lehmann, Hans Thies. 2007. *Postdramatic Theatre.* Routledge.

Lettow, Susanne. 2017. "Turning the Turn: New Materialism, Historical Materialism and Critical Theory." *Thesis Eleven* 140 (1): 106–21. https://doi.org/10.1177/0725513616683853

Merx, Sigrid and Liesbeth Groot Nibbelink. 2022. "Subversive Affirmation." In *Powertools: Artistic Strategies for Social Change,* edited by Isis Germano et al. ArtEZ Platform for Research Intervention in the Arts. https://studiumgenerale.artez.nl/publication/powertools/subversive+affirmation/

Mouffe, Chantal. 2005. *On the Political.* Routledge. https://doi.org/10.4324/9780203870112

Nagle, Angela. 2017. *Kill All Normies: Online Culture Wars from 4Chan and Tumblr to Trump and the Alt-Right.* Zero Books.

Nieuwenhuis, Ivo and Dick Zijp. 2022. "The Politics and Aesthetics of Humour in an Age of Comic Controversy." *European Journal of Cultural Studies* 25 (3): 341–54. https://doi.org/10.1177/13675494221084118

Pérez, Raúl. 2022. *The Souls of White Jokes: How Racist Humor Fuels White Supremacy.* Stanford University Press.

Reinelt, Janelle. 2015. "'What I Came to Say': Raymond Williams, the Sociology of Culture and the Politics of (Performance) Scholarship." *Theatre Research International* 40 (3): 235–49. https://doi.org/10.1017/S0307883315000334

Reinelt, Janelle. 2021. "Resisting Rancière." In *Rancière and Performance,* edited by Nic Fryer and Colette Conroy, 171–94. Rowman & Littlefield.

Ridout, Nicholas. 2006. *Stage Fright, Animals, and Other Theatrical Problems.* Cambridge University Press. https://doi.org/10.1017/CBO9780511617669

Ridout, Nicholas. 2013. *Passionate Amateurs: Theatre, Communism, and Love.* University of Michigan Press. https://doi.org/10.3998/mpub.4537117

Robbins, Bruce. 2019. "Cosmopolitanism and the Historical/Contextual Paradigm." In *Context in Literary and Cultural Studies,* edited by Jakob Ladegaard and Jakob Gaardbo Nielsen, 17–36. UCL Press.

Savran, David. 2004. "Toward a Historiography of the Popular." *Theatre Survey* 45 (2): 211–17. https://doi.org/10.1017/S004055740400016X

Schechner, Richard. 2006. *Performance Studies: An Introduction.* Routledge.

Shalson, Lara. 2017. *Theatre and Protest.* Bloomsbury.

Sharp, Scott, John-David Dewsbury and Maria Hynes. 2014. "The Minute Interventions of Stewart Lee: The Affirmative Conditions of Possibility in Comedy, Repetition and Affect." *Performance Research* 19 (2): 116–25. https://doi.org/10.1080/13528165.2014.928527

Schmidt, Theron. 2019. "How Does Theatre Think through Work?" In *Thinking Through Theatre and Performance,* edited by Maaike Bleeker et al., 158–70. Bloomsbury.

Studio Dries Verhoeven, ed. 2020. *In Doubt.* Kerber.

Taylor, Diana. 2003. *The Archive and the Repertoire: Performing Cultural Memories in the Americas.* Duke University Press. https://doi.org/10.1215/9780822385318

Taylor, Millie and Dominic Symonds. 2017. *Studying Musical Theatre: Theatre and Practice.* Bloomsbury.

Tomlin, Liz. 2019. *Political Dramaturgies and Theatre Spectatorship: Provocations for Change.* Bloomsbury.

van Heuven, Robbert. 2019. "Dries Verhoeven: Interview with Robbert van Heuven." In *The Twenty-First Century Performance Reader,* edited by Teresa Brayshaw, Anna Fenemore and Noel Witts, 565–73. Taylor & Francis.

Verhoeven, Dries, and Wouter van Elderen, directors. *The Recruitment.* 2021. 69 min. https://driesverhoeven.com/en/project/broeders-verheft-u-ter-vrijheid/

Williams, Raymond. 1980 [1961]. *The Long Revolution.* Penguin.

Williams, Raymond. 1983. *Keywords: A Vocabulary of Culture and Society.* Oxford University Press.

Williams, Raymond. 2020 [1973]. "Base and Superstructure in Marxist Cultural Theory." In *Culture and Materialism: Selected Essays,* 35–55. Verso.

Zijp, Dick. 2022. "Is Crossing Boundaries Always Liberating?" In *Powertools: Artistic Strategies for Social Change,* edited by Isis Germano et al. ArtEZ Platform for Research Intervention in the Arts. https://studiumgenerale.artez.nl/publication/powertools/is+crossing+boundaries+always+liberating/

Zijp, Dick. 2023. *Comedians without a Cause: The Politics and Aesthetics of Humour in Dutch Cabaret (1966–2020).* PhD diss., Utrecht University.

11. Tracing Histories: An Archaeological Approach

Evelyn Wan

Summary

This chapter addresses the act of tracing as an archaeological approach, to establish a 'history of the present' while reading a piece of artwork or performance. Tracing is the act of finding out how something has come to be, conceptually and materially. From its raw materials to its conditions of possibility to its conceptual lines of flight, tracing allows the contours of the cultural artefact under analysis to emerge. A contemporary artwork often poses and reflects upon an issue for the present time, which could be traced back historically to present a longer view of its contextualisation, in order to show historical continuations as well as contemporary permutations. Offering a genealogy of a concept or of an object, for instance, could help shed light on how to read the artwork at present. Foucauldian discussions of the archaeology of knowledge emphasises the epistemic conditions of possibility for a particular discourse. This chapter offers two examples of tracing: Singaporean dance artist Choy Ka Fai's *Postcolonial Spirits* and Congolese visual artist Sammi Baloji's *'802. That is where, as you heard, the elephant danced the malinga. The place where they now grow flowers.'*

Introduction

Tracing is a verb, an act of doing. Tracing is the act of finding out how something has come to be, conceptually and materially. From its raw materials to its conditions of possibility to its conceptual lines of flight, tracing allows the contours of the cultural artefact under analysis to emerge.

The focus on 'tracing' in the chapter is inspired by Celia Lury et al.'s *Routledge Handbook of Interdisciplinary Research Methods* in which all methods proposed end with -ings. The *Handbook*'s editors explain that this is to "identify the potential of interdisciplinary methods to compose problems as interruptions of the (historical) present" (Lury 2018, 3). The gerund form emphasises a becoming, a state of things which are unfolding in time, that forms an "activation of the present" (Lury 2018, 3).

What does it mean to activate the present in the archaeological approach? All artefacts come with their own histories, a story of their genesis and development, materially and conceptually. Artefacts are situated in time and space, shaped by those who make and present them. But these works also always carry with them particular histories—a performer's body and their history of training; a screen projection that carries with it the history of moving images; a sculptural object made from raw materials collected somewhere; the oeuvre of a maker... underneath every piece of performance or artwork is a set of potential histories to be traced and understood. The act of tracing highlights the unfolding nature of knowledge production that is activated by the research gesture in the present—when does the tracing begin and when does it end? There is no one 'correct' way to capture these potential histories, but the act of tracing brings particular historical concerns to the fore. In the words of Michael Shanks in *Theatre/Archaeology*, this act of excavating the past "entertains no final and definitive account of the past as it was, but fosters multivocal and multiple accounts" (Pearson and Shanks 2001, XVII).

The archaeological approach here is grounded in Michel Foucault's archaeology of knowledge and genealogy, which emphasises the epistemic conditions of possibility for a particular discourse, and is inspired by the development of theatre/archaeology in theatre studies and media archaeology in media studies. *Theatre/Archaeology* (2001), co-written by archaeologist Shanks and theatre scholar Mike Pearson, blends performance theory with archaeological practice to show how theatre reanimates histories through re-enacting, reconstructing, or creatively interpreting historical events. The archaeological touch emphasises attention to material pasts, specifically through objects, locales and landscapes in site-specific performance. In turn, media archaeology is an interdisciplinary field that investigates the historical and cultural significance of media artifacts and technologies. It focuses on forgotten or overlooked technologies and practices in the past in order to examine how contemporary media technologies take on and expand upon features from earlier inventions. Media archaeologists study the materiality of media, as well as trace the social, political, and economic contexts in which technologies were developed and deployed (Parikka 2012). Tracing as a method is also grounded in new materialist thought. As with the focus of media archaeology on the materiality of technological objects, new materialism invites us to attend to the materiality of things and the agency of objects, also known as "thing-power" (Bennett 2010). In recognising the agency of materials, one investigates what materials do methodologically, politically, and affectively (Coleman 2020), rather than simply looking at the discursive or symbolic meaning of objects. Such tracing of materials opens up an account of material histories that may be non-human-centric. The discussion below will address archaeology, genealogy, and new materialist methodologies that inform the act of tracing.

Context

The archaeological approach turns towards history, but what does it mean to engage with history outside the discipline of history, and in the discipline of theatre and performance studies? In more classical views of history, the task of the historian is to describe historical facts and narrate them through particular explanations of how and why certain events took place. Historians "conceptualize, describe, contextualize, explain, and interpret events and circumstances of the past" (Little 2020), and base their findings on evidence discovered through collection of historical data, e.g. through archival research and oral accounts. Indeed a canonical approach to theatre history maps and traces the development of theatre in time and space, and presents the evolution of the practice from oral, ritual, and shamanic performance to global, intercultural, hybrid forms of performance practices (Nellhaus et al. 2024). Theatre historians conduct research into historical performances, not only of works themselves but sometimes also the institutions that presented them, to shed light on both production and institutional histories. These works can highlight specific communities, such as queer performances or grassroot practices, so as to bring underrepresented voices into the spotlight as a critical intervention. Theatre and performance can also function as a transmission medium for cultural memory and practices, by turning to embodied archives (Taylor 2003, as a canonical example). Theatre's emphasis on the sensorium also means attending to archives of sound, music, visual design, movement, gesture, affect, etc. that go beyond written historical documents.

The mixed methods approach espoused by theatre and performance studies (Davis and Rae 2024) maintains an openness to approaching history, that is informed by other disciplinary methodologies. Here, the archaeological approach suggests another way of engaging with the past, where firstly, the foremost concern lies in the present, and secondly, where material histories of objects may take precedence over human histories. One can be invested in historical context even when firmly situated in the present, when approaching contemporary artworks and productions. As Walter Benjamin states in "On the Concept of History", "[h]istory is the object of a construction whose place is formed not in homogenous and empty time, but in that which is fulfilled by the here-and-now [*Jetztzeit*]" (1940, 395). *Jetztzeit*, translated as 'here-and-now', emphasises the recomposition of past events in the contemporary moment. Historian Dilip Menon explains the quotation as the moment "'when one reaches back to the past in a time of urgency to see the exigencies of the present clearly" (2022, 8). The point is to reach back to reconstruct what the present means. Hence, the archaeological approach is not chiefly concerned with learning about or studying the past, but rather with using the past to understand the present.

This way of looking at history is akin to Foucauldian paradigms of archaeology and genealogy. Archaeology and genealogy address the way Foucault approaches history as a means to understand and critique the contemporary world. Foucault understands the "archaeology of knowledge" in *The Order of Things* (2005) as a way to uncover the underlying structures and rules that shape the production of knowledge within a given historical period or discourse. Knowledge is not a linear progression of truths, but rather a complex network of discourses, power relations, and social practices that is built up over time. By studying these networks of discourses and power, one could understand the rules and logics of power and control that shape our lives.

Applying an archaeological approach to cultural fields such as theatre, performance, and media studies reveals how specific practices have evolved in response to the contexts and circumstances that have shaped their development. Media archaeology, as an application of this philosophical perspective, focuses on a non-linear, fragmented understanding of how technology develops over time. Rather than offering a linear history of media progress, the field provides alternative histories by highlighting forgotten or overlooked media technologies that may be obsolete, discarded, or only ever imagined and never have come to fruition. This methodology has been applied to theatre and performance studies most prominently in the volume *Media Archaeology and Intermedial Theatre: Deep Time of the Theatre* (2019) edited by Nele Wynants. The book offers insight into the long-standing relationship between technology and live performance and demonstrates how evolving technologies have continuously altered the aesthetics and dynamics of theatre. From magic lantern slides to digital screens, stage scenery to social media, the contributions in the book address the materiality of these technologies and traces the genealogy of intermedial performances. Theatre history "reflects the history of science, technology, and media" (Wynants 2019, 1) and opens up the possibilities of tracing particular lines of flight between historical and contemporary media.

Carrying out archaeological research requires active tracing of historical objects. In media archaeology, this might involve entering archives, museums, consulting books, brochures, design prototypes, blueprints, or other historical sources. Through a historical lens, one could trace the way certain discourses or objects have come to be. This act of tracing compiles a genealogy, a series of interconnected moments that continue to shape the present reality. By tracing the development and evolution of historical objects and juxtaposing them with the present, genealogy opens up the analysis of historical processes, events, and practices.

In media archaeology, Jussi Parikka emphasises that such genealogies provide "alternative presents and pasts—and futures" (2012, 12–13), as the juxtaposition of older technologies and contemporary ones opens up new ways of understanding the present. Indeed, Foucault's genealogical approach is often used to challenge dominant narratives and traditional historical accounts, and to reveal the ways in which power operates and shapes society. Its critical use can give space to marginalised voices and experiences that may have been excluded in history, e.g. through "a genealogy of alternatives" (2011, 18), a term stemming from queer studies coined by Jack Halberstam. Halberstam uses the notion of alternative histories to open up critical understandings of contemporary phenomena, and proposes that researchers compile their own archives that challenge disciplinarity and dominant understandings. I highlight here the example of postcolonial and decolonial writings (such as Stoler 2016; Ghosh 2021; Haiven 2022) that make use of tracing to show historical continuities in power domination and oppression, and to present how colonial histories still matter to the urgencies of our current world. As such, tracing genealogies can allow researchers to be sensitive to oppressed voices by delineating the discursive conditions under which such exclusions took place.

The field of new materialism addresses, for instance, the long-standing exclusion of non-human agencies in critical discourses.[1] The emphasis on the material is also a key aspect of media archaeology. By incorporating tenets of new materialism and media archaeology in this chapter, I wish to highlight the possibility of also tracing non-human or post-human histories that are intertwined with human ones. Theatre scholars, for instance, have long been fascinated by the material dimension of performance. In *Theatre/Archaeology* (Pearson and Shanks 2001), archaeology is not limited to the Foucauldian archaeological, but attends to physical archaeological fieldwork, such as through "space and place (site, locale, field)" and "architecture (monument, enclosure, ruin)" (Pearson and Shanks 2001, 1). Set in the context of site-specific performance making, the book attends to memories, stories, and places, and traces how performances perform the past by re-enacting, reconstructing, or interpreting history and archaeological finds. Tracing human acts as well as non-human

---

1   It must be acknowledged, however, that new materialism itself has been criticised for not recognising indigenous perspectives of animism, which has always recognised the agency of things. See Todd 2016.

sediments, landscapes, and heritage, the work exemplifies the archaeological as a viable methodology in the theatre field.

How to

Attending to histories requires tracing. Tracing is a core act that is inherently tied to the research process. As researchers we often trace the histories of concepts and ideas in academic debates and discourses. Here, I am specifically interested in directing attention to this aspect of research in relation to historical and material contexts. By understanding the historical context in which a particular artwork or performance is created or to which it responds, researchers can gain insight into the authorial intentions and situate the various artistic choices made in the production. Studying the history of particular artistic techniques, or methods of making can also provide valuable insight into the evolution of forms, styles, and techniques over time.

Tracing histories can itself be a key methodology that directly adopts the archaeological approach, or it can be used as a supplementary lens in textual analysis of artworks that attends to historical contexts. Offering a genealogy of a concept or of an object, for instance, could help shed light on how to read the artwork at present. For instance, contemporary British-Palestinian installation artist Mona Hatoum often manipulates particular raw materials to achieve specific affects. Barbed wire, steel mesh, steel grid, concrete—how does Hatoum evoke tension, vulnerability, and unease through various artworks using these materials? If we trace the presence of these materials from the installation room to zones of armed conflict, where bombed buildings stand in ruin with exposed steel and concrete rubble, what might be said about the politics of displacement and exile in Hatoum's works? How might tracing the artist's personal histories, as a Palestinian exile born in Lebanon, and knowledge of the ongoing conflicts in the region open up ways of reading her art?

Turning our attention to the act of tracing in composition, such an analysis points to the contingency of knowledge production in relation to the 'histories' selected by the researcher. One could equally produce a valid research project that focuses not on the political meanings of Hatoum's art, but, for instance, on tracing where her artworks are shown and acquired, or the grants and commissions she has received, in order to look at the production histories of Hatoum's oeuvre. This inquiry will instead shed light on the curatorial histories, art market dynamics, and networks of power and discourse that Hatoum's works are inscribed within, and attend more to the discursive dimensions of tracing.

The act of tracing, in particular, can be aligned with 'follow-the-object' methods espoused by new materialism. Rebecca Coleman (2020) attributes the 'follow-the-object' approach to the work of anthropologist Arjun Appadurai, who writes "we have to follow the things themselves, for their meanings are inscribed in their forms, their uses, their trajectories" (Appadurai 1986, 5). In the example above, we could find different meanings attached to following the raw materials of the artworks compared to following their material trajectory as they are displayed at different museums and galleries in the world. But in both cases, the act of tracing provides ways of situating Hatoum's works in context. Many lines of histories can be traced in any given project, and they have to be defined and justified by the researcher through the aims of the research.

The act of tracing can end in the discovery of particular objects of interest. How do the historical objects you have found invite new ways of reading your contemporary case? Juxtaposing past and present, old and new, enables researchers to examine the continuity, intensification, or disruption of specific discourses. The upcoming example in the 'Demonstration' section juxtaposes ethnographic film-making and motion capture technology presented in a theatre performance. I trace the history of ethnographic film-making in my research process to question whether extractive impulses of colonial ethnographic film-making are still present in contemporary motion capture. In the 'Expanding the method' section, I trace the histories connected to the title of an art installation in order to effect an overall reading of the piece.

Tracing is a verb, an act of doing. Tracing is the act of finding out how something has come to be, conceptually and materially. Every single piece of artwork offers myriad potentialities of tracing. Both analyses below sidestep the more obvious ways of approaching the works—analysing the dancing in a dance performance, or analysing the objects in an installation. You might rightly wonder, why is it

11. Tracing Histories: An Archaeological Approach 237

particularly important that I opt to trace other histories in these performances? As discussed above, there is no definitive account of history to be traced through these artworks, but an openness to evoke layers of history in understanding the here and now. You will notice that in both cases, I use the method of tracing to expose colonial histories of technology and material extraction. This is because what we choose to trace results in particular forms of knowledge production in academic research. What knowledges are you bringing to the fore by emphasising particular histories? Whose histories are worth discussing? Are there silenced voices which ought to be amplified? Do not forget: your act of tracing plays a role in constructing future archaeologies of knowledge.

Demonstration

In the examples below, I will demonstrate various acts of tracing I have conducted in my research projects. As mentioned above, the first example involves a restaging of a traditional Javanese dance and is presented in juxtaposition with contemporary motion capture technology in Choy Ka Fai's *Postcolonial Spirits* (2021). The project is part of Choy's longer-term research, *Cosmic Wander* (2020–2024), on the intersection between dance, the supernatural, and shamanism in Siberia, Taiwan, Vietnam, Singapore, and Indonesia. Choy himself is tracing and building genealogies through the work, presenting the history and evolution of shamanism as counterparts of contemporary dance practice. Based on these genealogies, Choy creates multimedia performances using various technologies such as VR and motion capture.

Choy's *Postcolonial Spirits* (2021) restages an Indonesian dance created to mock Dutch soldiers during the colonial era, called Dolaklak. Traditionally, the dancers eventually become possessed and may collapse in the middle of the performance. In Choy's restaging, an Indonesian dancer, Andri Kurniawan, performs online via internet livestreaming for a European stage, together with a Dutch dancer, Vincent Riebeek, live in the flesh. Kurniawan's movement goes from projection to motion capture and eventually turns into an avatar that multiplies on the projected screen, haunting the European stage visibly as a spectre of colonial history.[2]

The discussion below focuses on the specific tracing of the screen technologies used in this intermedial dance performance. The performance makes use of two technologies that are juxtaposed against one another—the older technology of ethnographic filmmaking, and the newer technology of motion capture. This invites a media-archaeological comparison, as the performance suggests that these two technologies can be examined together, and therefore reveals insights into how we might think about motion capture *through* the earlier technology of ethnographic film. Here, I am interested in teasing out coloniality, the knowledge system of colonialism that is mediated by technology, rather than simply focusing on the historical context of Dutch colonisation in Indonesia, which the performance itself also critiques. How is the technology of presentation also implicated in the system of colonialism that the performance seeks to comment on?

Choy's performance *Postcolonial Spirits* (2021) opens with a dual-screen presentation of traditional Indonesian dance rituals. The ethnographic film *Trance and Dance in Bali* (1951) shot by Margaret Mead and Gregory Bateson in 1930s is juxtaposed with Choy's contemporary research 'A Century of Trance in Java'. Intertitles appear in the beginning of both videos, explaining the folk traditions of trance. Across both the Balinese and Javanese cases, spirits would enter the dancing bodies, which enable them to perform supernatural acts without hurting themselves. As Choy's contemporary subjects dance in Java in full colour on the other side of the screen, Mead's voice continues to narrate the happenings in the black and white footage to provide anthropological description and commentary on the ritualistic *Kris* dance. The footage in both cases is largely synchronised to show similar scenes of witches in masks dancing, followed by women dancing, and an incense and smoke ritual. Dancers across both films then enter trance states and are carried off by fellow performers.

---

2   The full version of this analysis is forthcoming in *The Routledge Companion to Performance & Technology*, edited by Norah Zuniga Shaw and Maaike Bleeker, under the title 'Performing Telepresence: Technology and Coloniality in Choy Ka Fai's *Postcolonial Spirits* (2021)'.

To situate the work, my act of tracing began with studying Mead and Bateson's oeuvre, and I looked through visual archives of their ethnographic journeys. I read about the historical reception of Mead and Bateson in anthropology. The Mead and Bateson film featured in the performance was seen as one of the pioneering examples of visual anthropology, which recorded the colonial gaze of the camera on Balinese subjects dancing and entering trance states. Mead and Bateson's work has long been critiqued as a colonialist ethnographic gaze, where labouring Balinese bodies dance forever in the anthropological records, as representatives of their culture frozen in time.

How might a researcher understand the incorporation of Mead and Bateson's film in a dance performance staged in the 2020s, when, in a later scene, *Postcolonial Spirits* turns to the motion capture of the Javanese dance? Using the media-archaeological approach here sheds light on the historical continuity and rupture between the two recording technologies featured in the performance. I began to entertain the idea that Choy, by juxtaposing his contemporary artistic research and dance archive with Mead and Bateson, might be exposing the colonialist practices of investigating trance and shamanism through recording technology.

Choy is fascinated with motion capture technology and the potentiality of capturing the act of trance, and by extension, the possessing spirit, in the 1s and 0s of digital code: "the motion capture was really this very naive idea: what if I could motion capture a person in trance? Maybe it's possessed by a god or a deity. Does it mean that I could capture the presence or the spiritual presence of gods?" (Choy in conversation with the author 2023; transcript edited for clarity). Choy's contemporary interest in capturing trance performances—in the form of documentary and motion capture—resembles colonialist ways of recording the culture of others. The technologies involved carry particular histories and politics, which are revealed through the act of tracing.

Motion capture in the performance results in the rendering of traditional dance and trance as animation. In the scene of interest, Dutch dancer Riebeek is dressed in the traditional Dolalak costume, while Kurniawan appears as an animated avatar against a black background, dancing together with him. Kurniawan's soldier avatar splits at first into two drumming soldiers. Then, more marching band soldiers with darkened facial features appear, and the image of a colonial statue of J. B. van Heutsz (1851–1924) emerges. Van Heutsz was a celebrated hero in The Netherlands in his time, as former governor of Aceh. He was credited as the one who brought islands outside of Java under Dutch authority. Kurniawan's soldier avatars multiply around him and march around this statue, seemingly haunting van Heutsz. The scene closes with the avatars becoming more unnatural and mannequin-like, spinning in a circle and eventually dispersing like discarded dolls.

Juxtaposing the two technologies shows the common thread of ordering and programming bodies in different ways. In Mead and Bateson's work, the order of the trance performance is maintained through Mead's matter-of-fact narrative voice that codifies the action into a historical entry in the anthropological archive. In Choy, the beliefs, rituals, and spirituality of Javanese Dolalak culture become a malleable animation. Motion capture turns the dancing body's labour into abstract data that is programmable, and can be subsumed by animation. This process of animating in fact suggests strong control on the part of the creator, in ways that resemble the ordering of trance performance by Mead's narration.

To further unpack these technological histories, I trace histories of animation to understand the relationship between animation technology and control. A cursory study of the history of animation reaps the observation of primitivism in early animation, "which has long considered dance to be central to the technological process of extracting and circulating an ancient, pre-rational energy" (Warren-Crow 2017, 27). From animals to native Others, so-called primitivised beings are made to dance on screen through hyperanimation and spectacularisation of their bodies. One might argue then that Choy's animation of Kurniawan's avatar exoticises the Indonesian dancer, and forces his digital avatar to perform trance states in a primitive manner. Rather than showing trance through his corporeal body, the audience only sees a representation, through animation designed by Choy.

By tracing the history of ethnographic film-making and animation as antecedents to motion capture, these media histories enable a deeper understanding and contextualisation of how motion capture is activated in this dance performance, and showcases the problematic entanglements between control, coloniality, and different forms of recording technology. Thinking and tracing with media archaeology here opens up the possibility of interpreting other layers of the dance performance, in addition to the context of Dutch-Indonesian colonial histories featured there.

Expanding the method

Aside from analysing performances, the tracing of histories can also take place materially in studying artworks. The second example is an art installation, Sammi Baloji's *'802. That is where, as you heard, the elephant danced the malinga. The place where they now grow flowers.'* ('*802.*' hereafter.) This piece was acquired in 2020 by Tate Modern's Africa Acquisitions Committee and was installed in the museum in London between 2021 and 2023. The work comments on copper mining and trade in Congo and its position in the global materials market in the aftermath of colonialism. Reading the installation involves tracing the various physical materials used and the literary references in the title, in order to uncover the various layers of meanings the piece rests upon.[3] Below I discuss how I traced the title of the piece to a book on minor histories of Elisabethville, the colonial name for Lubumbashi under Belgian rule—how does knowing this reference provide a narrative of the installation and connect the various objects in the room together?

802. is an installation that takes the space of an entire room, and is made to resemble a European salon. The installation is centred around the mining and circulation of copper, as it is central to Congolese economy and political conflicts. In the middle of the room are shiny golden mortar shells displayed as planters, with living plants indigenous to central Africa's Copperbelt.[4] On one wall, a series of 32 black and white photographs feature scarified body parts, predominantly the torsos of naked individuals. Echoing this motif of scarring patterns are

---

[3] The full version of this analysis will appear in my chapter in the forthcoming *SAGE Handbook on Digital Labour*, edited by Ergin Bulut, Julie Chen, Rafael Grohmann, and Kylie Jarrett, entitled 'Mining for Digital Culture: Dispossessed lives through the lens of art'.

[4] Copperbelt refers to a mining region in Zambia and the Democratic Republic of the Congo (DRC), which is one of the ten most polluted areas worldwide, mainly due to mineral mining for phone and car batteries.

two octagonal copper ceiling plates hung on an adjacent wall. Eight prints of red wallpaper, again with similar patterns, are placed opposite the photographs.

My wish to contextualise the analysis through the title was simple—the line struck me as odd. Indeed the title of the installation combines fragments translated into English from the book *Le Vocabulaire d'Elisabethville: Une histoire d'Elisabethville de ses origins* (1965), written by André Yav. In the process of analysis, I decided to read the translated version of the whole book,[5] in order to understand why the artist makes such a strong reference to it. While contextual information offered by Tate Modern led me to the book, the museum did not provide a full interpretation of exactly why certain extracts were featured in the title.

The tracing began with the reference to Elisabethville. The book refers to Elisabethville as "copper capital city" (Yav 1965, VII), showing its importance in the copper trade. Elisabethville turns out to be the colonial name of Lubumbashi, which was the capital of the mining region of Katanga. Understanding the contextual history of Elisabethville/Lubumbashi was then paramount in recognising the Congo-Belgium colonial link the artist wishes to emphasise, as well as the subject of copper mining and trade.

The first part of the title, *'802.'*, is a reference to rail company Compagnie du chemin de fer du bas-Congo au Katanga. The railway was mainly built to transport mined minerals towards ports. 802, specifically, is the model number of a locomotive that carried Kenyan men in World War I in the region. In the book, the author laments the participation of Africans in "the war of the Whites", "the foreigners who domesticated us in slavery" (Yav 1965 XXXVIII, 2). Prompted by this section of the book, I continued to read about the conscription of Africans during WWI in that part of the world to see how the installation responds to this part of history. In my view, this reference to war and colonialism is

---

5   The book, written originally in a local variety of Swahili, has been translated to standardised Shaba Swahili and subsequently into English, in a project spearheaded by German anthropologist Johannes Fabian, with the assistance of Kalundi Mango, administrator at the Ethnological Museum of Lubumbashi. The book is an account of historical events and stories told by domestic servants in Elisabethville from 1843 to 1965, giving detailed accounts from the vantage point of the locals as more and more Europeans arrived, and changed the way they lived and laboured.

reflected in the use of mortar shells in the installation, now repurposed into banal vases, as a reminder of militia activity in the area. Through the mortar shell vases and the reference to 802, Baloji points to how the transportation of copper led to the creation of the railway and how this further implicates the region in other violent colonial histories.

The rest of the title, where *'the elephant danced the malinga'*, is mentioned in Section X of the book. As the book gives historical accounts of actual events, which are at times exaggerated, I also fact-checked the travelling troupe in question by looking up Belgian circuses that toured Congo at the time. Through archival brochures, I found that it described the travelling troupe of Circus De Jonghe from Belgium in Elisabethville. The malinga refers to ballroom dancing in the European style in Swahili. The final line in the title turns to *'The place where they now grow flowers'* and is not a line related to the book. Instead this connects to the plants grown in the installation, native succulents to the Copperbelt that are commonly sold in Europe as houseplants.

Recognising the historical traces that have taken place, I am now confident in proposing that these two lines refer to the cultural crossings between Europe and Africa—European dancing travelled to Congo, while Congolese plants entered European living rooms. This emphasises the web of objects, materials, and cultural practices that bind Congo to its former coloniser.

While one can quite easily read the meaning of the art installation through its aesthetics and various ways of presenting 'copper' visually, exploring this via the title adds a much stronger sense of the work's sensitivity to its historical context, and reveals the necessity of reading the artist's commentary via Belgian-Congo colonial exploitations. The book itself takes the reader into the heart of the colonial experience through the local eye, and provides a different entry point into the objects used in the art installation.

Suggestions for further reading

Some great examples of book-length postcolonial research projects that uses tracing histories, or an archaeological approach, as a central methodology include Ann Laura Stoler's *Duress: Imperial Durabilities in Our Times* (2016), Amitav Ghosh's works, e.g. *The Nutmeg's Curse*

(2021), and Max Haiven's *Palm Oil: The Grease of Empire* (2022). Within performance studies, Pearson and Michael Shanks' *Theatre/Archaeology* (2001) best captures the act of tracing as it unfolds. Aside from written sources, which often inform historical accounts, consult Diana Taylor's *The Archive and The Repertoire* (2003) to think about how to trace through oral histories and embodied histories, and how performance studies broadens ways of working with history. The works of Saidiya Hartman, and her method of critical fabulation, may also be helpful in addressing histories that can no longer be traced because of marginalisation and deliberate omissions in the (Western) knowledge archive. In addition, the chapter "Footnotes (Books and Papers Scattered about the Floor)" in Katherine McKittrick's *Dear Science and Other Stories* (2021) offers great insight into citational practice in research as a political act of tracing, gathering, and knowledge making.

References

Appadurai, Arjun. 1986. "Introduction: Commodities and the Politics of Value." In *The Social Life of Things: Commodities in Cultural Perspective*, edited by Arjun Appadurai, 3–63. Cambridge University Press.

Benjamin, Walter. 1940. "On the Concept of History." In *Selected Writings: 1938–1940*, 389–400. Harvard University Press.

Bennett, Jane. 2010. *Vibrant Matter: A Political Ecology of Things*. Duke University Press. https://doi.org/10.1215/9780822391623

Choy, Ka Fai. 2023. Interview on *Postcolonial Spirits* by Evelyn Wan.

Coleman, Rebecca. 2020. *Glitterworlds: The Future Politics of a Ubiquitous Thing*. Goldsmiths Press.

Davis, Tracy C., and Paul Rae, eds. 2024. *The Cambridge Guide to Mixed Methods Research for Theatre and Performance Studies*. Cambridge University Press. https://doi.org/10.1017/9781009294904

Foucault, Michel. 2005. *The Order of Things*. Routledge. https://doi.org/10.4324/9780203996645

Ghosh, Amitav. 2022. *The Nutmeg's Curse: Parables for a Planet in Crisis*. University of Chicago Press.

Haiven, Max. 2022. *Palm Oil: The Grease of Empire*. Pluto Press. https://doi.org/10.2307/j.ctv2g591vr

Halberstam, Jack. 2011. *The Queer Art of Failure*. Duke University Press. https://doi.org/10.2307/j.ctv11sn283

Hartman, Saidiya. 2008. "Venus in Two Acts." *Small Axe* 12 (2): 1–14. https://doi.org/10.2979/sax.2008.-.26.1

Little, Daniel. 2020. "Philosophy of History." In *The Stanford Encyclopedia of Philosophy*, edited by Edward N. Zalta, Winter 2020. Metaphysics Research Lab, Stanford University. https://plato.stanford.edu/archives/win2020/entries/history/

Lury, Celia, Rachel Fensham, Alexandra Heller-Nicholas, Sybille Lammes, Angela Last, Mike Michael, and Emma Uprichard, eds. 2018. *Routledge Handbook of Interdisciplinary Research Methods*. Routledge. https://doi.org/10.4324/9781315714523

McKittrick, Katherine. 2021. *Dear Science and Other Stories*. Duke University Press. https://doi.org/10.2307/j.ctv1c5cs2w

Menon, Dilip M., Nishat Zaidi, Simi Malhotra, and Saarah Jappie. 2022. *Ocean as Method: Thinking with the Maritime*. Taylor & Francis. https://doi.org/10.4324/9781003279754

Nellhaus, Tobin, Daphne Pi-Wei Lei, Tamara Underiner, and Patricia Ybarra, eds. 2024. *Theatre Histories: An Introduction*. Fourth edition. Routledge. https://doi.org/10.4324/9781003185185

Parikka, Jussi. 2012. *What Is Media Archaeology?* John Wiley & Sons.

Pearson, Mike, and Michael Shanks. 2001. *Theatre/Archaeology*. Routledge. https://doi.org/10.4324/9780203995969

Stoler, Ann Laura. 2016. *Duress: Imperial Durabilities in Our Times*. Duke University Press. https://doi.org/10.2307/j.ctv125jn2s

Taylor, Diana. 2003. *The Archive and the Repertoire: Performing Cultural Memory in the Americas*. Duke University Press. https://doi.org/10.2307/j.ctv11smz1k

Todd, Zoe. 2016. "An Indigenous Feminist's Take On The Ontological Turn: 'Ontology' Is Just Another Word For Colonialism." *Journal of Historical Sociology* 29 (1): 4–22. https://doi.org/10.1111/johs.12124

Warren-Crow, Heather. 2017. "Before and After Ghostcatching." *Screen Bodies* 2 (1). https://doi.org/10.3167/screen.2017.020103

Wynants, Nele, ed. 2019. *Media Archaeology and Intermedial Performance: Deep Time of the Theatre*. Springer International Publishing. https://doi.org/10.1007/978-3-319-99576-2

Yav, André. 2001. "Le Vocabulaire d'Elisabethville: Une Histoire d'Elisabethville de Ses Origins". Translated by Johannes Fabian and Kalundi Mango. Archives of Popular Swahili. 2001. http://lpca.socsci.uva.nl/aps/vol4/vocabulaireintro.html.

12. Archival Research Expanded: Bodily Archives and Embodied Fabulation

Lisa Skwirblies

Summary

This chapter expands the methods of traditional archival research, from the textual and iconographic evidence that is its basis to include what Skwirblies calls 'embodied fabulation'. As a concept, embodied fabulation does two things: one, it helps to focus archival research more strongly on embodied practices in the archive, and two, it fosters a critical reflection on the archive which includes understanding the researcher-subjects in their own embodiment. In that way, embodied fabulation helps to advance a series of speculative arguments about what is not always present in the archive, what has been silenced and marginalised in the logic of archival documentability as well as arguments about how these gaps could occur in the first place. Embodied fabulation not only helps us identify and signal where gaps exist in the archive, it also allows us to imagine embodied and performative knowledge—as archival knowledge—*into* these gaps.

Introduction

The relationship between theatre and the archive has long been contested. Theatre performances have been defined by their ephemeral and transitory nature, as that which vanishes, that which resists storage, recording, and documentation (Schneider 2001). Performances are considered to be live and embodied events, and part of their appeal is that they cannot be repeated, reproduced or captured for eternity. As performance historian Tracy C. Davis points out, "[t]he ephemerality of performance, especially performance before our lifetimes, means that any surviving evidence, even a playscript, is but a poor imitation of an actor's labour, let alone the combined efforts of actors, scenographer, orchestra, and stagehands" (Davis 2004, 203). The archive, on the other hand, is commonly understood as an institution that does exactly that: store material remains of the past for eternity, for the purpose of repetition, reproduction, and documentation. It houses written documents, photographs, and artefacts that can be frequented by historians seeking information about the past. Anyone who has visited an archive must have noticed that live performances are not part of the collections in most archives. Unlike art historians, who can visit museum collections multiple times to see the same painting they are writing about, theatre historians are faced with a unique challenge: how can a past theatrical event be reconstructed using the few sources that survive? How can one write about an ephemeral and embodied phenomenon based on material evidence in the form of texts, photographs, or artefacts?

These questions are not merely academic, nor are they new. The ephemera of a performance that no longer exists once it is over has for years challenged our conception of theatre collections as well: how can theatre history be 'preserved'? How can we understand—as completely as possible—how historical theatre was practised in its own time? A milestone for answering these questions and for theatre history itself surfaced around 1900, when the first public theatre collections were established and theatre studies became a separate academic discipline. Under the heading of 'reconstruction', the aim of these collections was to retrieve and resurrect past performances (see Balme and Szymanski-Düll 2020). Theatre archives, such as the *Bijzondere Collecties* at the University of Amsterdam, still store so-called 'remnants' of performances from the past, which primarily include photographs, film and videos, playbills, personal correspondence, textbooks, reviews of the performances, in some cases even costumes and parts of the scenography.[1] Most of

---

[1] This 'preservation' is more challenging than one might suspect, since theatre companies have long led a nomadic existence, in the sense that they were not tied

these remnants—literally leftovers from a performance—are considered to be sources, even though they were never intended to be archived. Other remnants, by contrast, were intentionally established as historical sources intended to transmit knowledge from and about the past, such as theatre-maker's autobiographies, sketches from rehearsal or texts about the performance.

The crux of discussions in theatre history is therefore often about sources. Source criticism is based on a large set of questions that help us to critically understand the material in front of us: What is the exact nature of this source—is it a review or a director's book? a photo of a rehearsal? a dramatic text? From what time and place? Who is the author of this source and to whom was it addressed? From which perspective is it reported? Is the source complete or are parts missing?[2] Why was this source handed down in the first place? For what purpose was a source archived? How does it speak to other sources? What constitutes a source for the history of theatre and performance in the first place? Rather than a complete or definitive interpretation of a source, source analysis is the starting point for writing theatre histories, since, while remnants and documents of theatrical events and structures help bring the past into the present, they also point to what is missing or not documented in the archive. To justify and negotiate the evidence that is missing from an archive, theatre historians must therefore utilise theory and induction, even "fable and fabulation" (Farge 2013, 30), when writing theatre and performance history.

The questions and strategies outlined above largely pertain to material leftovers of performance. In this chapter, though, I want to expand the methods of traditional archival research, from the textual and iconographic evidence that is its basis to include what I call 'embodied fabulation' as well. As a concept, embodied fabulation does two things: one, it helps to focus archival research more strongly on embodied

---

to a fixed building or location. In the Netherlands, this only changed after 1945. For more, see Franzen, Skwirblies & Van der Zalm 2025.

2   Handwritten passages and notes can be illegible, some pages in director's books might be missing, and stage photographs only show what the photographer found interesting. Older sources are often full of period-specific terms, words and symbols that need to be identified and facts that need to be explained. Historical letters, diaries or performances only become comprehensible once the context to which the sources allude has been determined.

practices in the archive and two, it fosters a critical reflection on the archive which includes understanding the researcher-subjects in their own embodiment. In that way, embodied fabulation helps to advance a series of speculative arguments about what is not always present in the archive, what has been silenced and marginalised in the logic of archival documentability as well as arguments about how these gaps could occur in the first place. Embodied fabulation is deeply informed by decades of feminist and decolonial knowledge production that stresses the manifold ways in which bodies produce, store, and transmit knowledge, and the power relations that worked on dismissing embodied practices as forms of knowledge. Embodied fabulation not only helps us identify and signal where gaps exist in the archive, it also allows us to imagine embodied and performative knowledge—as archival knowledge —*into* these gaps.

Context

Until the 1970s, questions of theatre historiography have significantly determined the methodological framework of theatre studies as a discipline. Since the post-positivist[3] turn of the 1970s, though, historical theatre research has cast a critical eye on the evidence-based approach to the archive. Today, the aim of historiographical theatre research is to understand and contextualise past performances, text genres, and stage forms as products of their time rather than to resurrect a complete and authentic image of the past. Instead of a fixed notion, then, this process of understanding and interpreting is ultimately open-ended, with each new generation of researchers setting the process in motion once again.

While an archive is mainly about the past, it is always re-read in light of the present. Historian Michel-Rolph Trouillot calls this

---

3   Post-positivism is a strand of thought that developed in the 1970s as a critique of positivism, a philosophy of science developed in the nineteenth century and that remained dominant thereafter. Often associated with the philosopher Auguste Comte, positivism holds that objective knowledge can be gained through empirical data, experimentation and observation, and that truth can be uncovered through scientific methods. By contrast, post-positivism, often associated with thinkers like Karl Popper and Thomas Kuhn, challenged positivism's claim about the certainty of scientific knowledge. Instead, post-positivists posited that knowledge is never fully certain and that all scientific claims are open to falsification.

re-reading "retrospective significance" and underscores how important our temporal perspectives are for our understanding of the past: "Historical representations—be they books, commercial exhibits or public commemorations—cannot be conceived only as vehicles for the transmission of knowledge. They must establish some relation to that knowledge" (Trouillot 1995, 149). In other words, the meaning or importance of certain historical events lies not in the past itself or in the events themselves, but rather in the significance we retrospectively attribute to it and them from our position in the present.

Trouillot and others have recognised this retrospective significance as being deeply informed by structures of power. In fact, much of today's scholarly interest in the archive pivots around questions of access and the exclusivity of most archives, and stresses the vital cultural power that archives represent and through which they narrate particular versions of the past. In his famous study *Archive Fever* (1996), Jacques Derrida calls attention to "the power and authority of the archive" by reminding us that the content of an archive has always been determined by the choices and selections of its custodians, whom Derrida called the "archons" (1996, 2).[4] Selecting and organising information from the past is also a process of deciding what is being remembered and what is being forgotten: "There is no political power without control over the archive, if not of memory" (1996, 4). Decisions about what is included and what is excluded shape collective memories and cultural histories as well as our epistemologies, or the ways in which we think we know what we know. Trouillot's and Derrida's critique of the archive are important because they make clear that not only is the authority of the archive political, it is first and foremost epistemological. 'Archons' have the power to shape processes of truth-making and influence what counts as knowledge and what does not. Recent discussions on decolonisation, identity, and social justice have critiqued the exclusiveness and 'whiteness' of most official and institutionalised archives. As in the realm of museum and archival

---

4   *Archon* is a term from Ancient Greek and means 'ruler' or 'magistrate'. Archons were responsible for keeping the records, which gave them control over legal and civic memory. Derrida writes: "[...] the meaning of 'archive', its only meaning, comes to it from the Greek *arkheion*: initially a house, a domicile, an address, the residence of the superior magistrates, the *archons*, those who commanded" (Derrida 1996, 2).

collections and their composition, these debates have also prompted a new—and different—look at the realm of theatre.

An example of a project fuelled by these insights is *Vice Versa* in the Netherlands. Initiated in 2012 by *Theater Instituut Nederland*, this research project focused on the shared theatre histories of Suriname, Aruba, Curaçao, and the Netherlands and resulted in a website with 153 written biographies as well as information about specific locations, companies or 'meeting moments'—places where theatre-makers from various corners of the world descended, collaborated, and influenced each other (Franzen et al. 2025). Similar archival initiatives and projects in the Netherlands include the *The Black Archives* and the more recently established theatre and performance platform *The Need for Legacy*. Both are grassroots initiatives that collect disregarded and ignored sources from the Dutch Black communities and the former Dutch colonies in order to rewrite a (white) Dutch history and challenge the existing Dutch theatre canon.[5]

These important critical interventions into how theatre collections are formed resonates with the scholarly debate on how to archive the ephemeral phenomenon of performance. The debates that have taken place in our field since the 1990s have shown that the ontological questions about the ephemeral nature of performance are deeply entangled with questions of decolonising the Western logic of the archive.

Performance theoretician Peggy Phelan, for instance, claims that performances cannot be saved, recorded, or documented because performance "becomes itself through disappearance" (1993, 146). To Phelan, this ephemeral character of performance is advantageous, because by disappearing it resists reproduction, commodification, and

---

5   As important as it is to create new and alternative archives that attempt to close gaps and reveal silences of the hegemonic archives, this additive modus operandi also has its pitfalls. In responding to the need to decentre hegemonic knowledge productions, other ways of thinking and being are often simply added to the existing epistemologies and canons "without challenging engrained inequalities and epistemic privileges, and without consideration of the intersectionality of race, class, caste, gender, sexuality, ability, and global asymmetries", as theatre scholar Nesreen Hussein rightly points out (Hussein 2022, 3). In other words, the additive approach to decolonisation underlying the approach to inclusion risks enhancing the process of Othering rather than diminishing it, and thus distancing the non-Western cultural production as radically Other.

objectification (1993, 10).⁶ Theatre historian Rebecca Schneider, on the other hand, questions the very ephemerality of performance as defined by Phelan. She points out that the claim that performance is without remains is an understanding of the archive itself and its logic that is informed by a Western idea of documentability linked to texts or objects (Schneider 2001, 137). This logic dismisses other modes of telling or writing history, such as those based on oral storytelling, live recitation, or dance. By operating under this logic, argues Schneider, "we limit ourselves to an understanding of performance predetermined by a cultural habituation to the patrilineal, West-identified (arguably white-cultural) logic of the Archive" (2001, 138). In other words, performance is not in itself ephemeral but within this Western, patrilineal archival logic installed as the archive's ephemeral Other.

Similarly, in her book *The Archive and the Repertoire* (2003) theatre scholar Diana Taylor questions both the power of the archive and the fixity of the performance as record in the archive in the first place. She does so by introducing the concept of the 'repertoire'. While the archive houses objects and artefacts, the repertoire constitutes embodied memory and entails "performances, gestures, orality, movement, dance, singing—in short, all those acts usually thought of as ephemeral, non-producible knowledge" (2003, 20). Taylor shows how the ephemeral and embodied memory of performances persist against the institutional archive. Rather than emphasising a binary opposition of either disappearing or remaining, Taylor's notion of the repertoire bridges the divide by focussing on embodied and performative transmissions of historical knowledge. This concept of the repertoire helps us to revalorise expressive, embodied culture that has not traditionally been included in the Western canon. The repertoire is distinct from the archive because it constitutes "a system of learning, storing and transmitting knowledge" that helps us to "shift our focus from the written to the performatic" (Taylor 2003, 8). The repertoire thus questions the authority and legitimacy of the archive in relation to our epistemologies.

---

6   Troubling the notion of reproduction has had an important influence on feminist theory within performance studies and across academic borders. It this fundamental independence that performance has from technological, economical and linguistic mass reproduction that Phelan sees as giving it its greatest efficacy.

To summarise, Phelan, Schneider, and Taylor all critique—in different ways—the hierarchisation of knowledge derived from the material archive and call for greater focus and emphasis to be placed on the knowledge derived from the embodied repertoire. For Schneider and Taylor, the long-standing focus on the material archive at the expense of the embodied repertoire is rooted in a hierarchy based on a larger, much older, and more persistent hierarchy within Western cultures that values the written more than it does embodied culture.

How to

If the archive is clearly such a problematic concept, how, one might ask, can we still promote archival research as a pertinent methodology for theatre and performance studies? Over the past decade, this question has driven much scholarship across all disciplines and has led to what is known as the 'archival turn'.[7] If dismissing the archive as a tool, medium, and source for our historical research is not an option, how then can we critically engage with it in such a way to challenge or even remove its power and its (Western) logic of documentability?

Anthropologist Ann Laura Stoler suggests that instead of mining the archive for historical data, we should shift to highlighting the archival practices that determine what makes its way into the archive in the first place. This shift means attending to the peculiar form and context of the archive rather than mining the content of the archive alone. Stoler describes this shift as a moving from "archive-as-source" to "archive-as-subject" (2009, 44). Her "ethnography of the archive" (2010, 215) allows us to question the archive itself: to ask how it works, what strategies it uses to document and categorise, and which of its tactics determine inclusion and exclusion. Stoler encourages us to pay attention to the use and repetition of words in the archival files and, importantly, to what was not said and what was crossed out or added in the margins (2010,

---

7 Art historian Sara Callahan argues that "this broader turn to the archive was deeply embedded in the poststructuralist, feminist, and postcolonial methodology that is sometimes described as a 'hermeneutics of suspicion': critical practices that aim to expose gaps, omissions, and unpronounced knowledge structures by reading texts 'against the grain'" (Callahan 2024, 74).

216)—a way of reading the archive both "against the grain" as well as "along its grain" (2010, 216).

Stoler's research interest is the colonial archive, but her 'archive-as-subject' approach can be applied to other archives as well. It is useful for a broad range of historical work because it challenges the idea of a coherent and univocal archive as well as a coherent and univocal past. As Michel Foucault would say, the archives do not necessarily tell the truth but tell of the truth—that is, they can expose how that truth is told, and by whom (Foucault 1977, 13). Whereas we cannot decipher 'the' truth about the past, we can decipher the elements of reality that appear in the "mode of speech" and in the relationships of power in which the individuals uttering these words are embedded (Farge 2013, 34). As Foucault would put it, meaning is produced by this mode of speech, by the sparse words that appear in a given historical time.

Because these methods of interpreting the archive against its grain encourage us to pay attention to what is not said, they provide historians with greater freedom to interpret and extrapolate. Historian Arlette Farge, for instance, in her book *The Allure of the Archive* (2013), calls our attention to the "fable and fabulation" contained in the archive (Farge 2013, 30). Along with power and truth claims, Farge contends that the archive always contains as well "the ability for someone to transform everything into fantasy, to write one's own story or to turn one's own life into fiction" (Farge 2013, 34). In other words, history and fiction are always already part of the same coin.

Historian Saidiya Hartman goes even one step further to argue for using a method of "critical fabulation" to approach the archive, since this method makes it possible to negotiate the aforementioned constitutive limits of the archive (Hartman 2008). Hartman developed this method to critically engage with the history of slavery and to address her ethical hesitations about reproducing the violence of the archive in unearthing some of the stories of the enslaved. She describes her method of critical fabulation as follows:

> By advancing a series of speculative arguments and exploiting the capacities of the subjunctive (a grammatical mood that expresses doubts, wishes, and possibilities), in fashioning a narrative, which is based upon archival research, and by that, I mean a critical reading of the archive that mimes the

figurative dimensions of history, I intended both to tell an impossible story and to amplify the impossibility of telling. (Hartman 2008, 11)

Hartman's method makes it possible to tell the histories of those who do not appear in the official archives of the history of the transatlantic slave trade. It is important that she does not assume that one can fill these gaps and provide closure. Rather than claiming that critical fabulation can do so, Hartman's method exposes the narrative restraint inherent in these archives and at the same time underscores the historiographic difficulties of carrying out archival research, especially on marginalised and oppressed individuals whose histories were not considered worthy of being included in the archives.

Critical fabulation is thus a method that both reveals the gaps in traditional archives, which tend to reflect only the perspectives of those in power, such as colonial authorities and slaveholders, and gives historians a way of engaging with these problematic archives in spite of such gaps. This method allows historians to imagine "what cannot be verified through the archive" (Hartman 2008, 11), and to use reasoned interpolation to plausibly speculate on the feelings and perspectives of enslaved individuals. Recognising that these voices and stories have been distorted or excluded from these archives, critical fabulation fuses historical research and creative narrative by combining historical facts with speculative storytelling. The strength of this method is in its refusal to make definitive claims and it is opening the possibility for the 'what if' in historical research, for imagining what might have been. This method restores agency and complexity to enslaved individuals who, without it, would otherwise be excluded based on decisions made by those in power when the archive was created.

Stoler's, Farge's, and Hartman's epistemological engagements are rooted in the 'literary turn', and their engagement with the archive is largely based on textual sources. Moving away from this textual evidence to embodiment in archives of violence (colonialism, imperialism, slavery) is a way of connecting narrative creation to bodily experiences and embodied practices instead. I argue that this method—what I call embodied fabulation—allows historians to focus greater attention on embodied practices in the archival evidence. Embodied fabulation informs archival research methodology by opening up the possibility for historians to engage in performative and ephemeral practices in and through our bodies, which currently materialise as gaps and silences in the archive. Theories of embodiment generally argue that in the process of meaning-making—and thus the processes of knowledge production as well —the mind and body are inseparable. These theories emphasise that the body's materiality, its experiences of gender, race, age, disability etc. influences how meaning is created. Recognising the body and its role in these processes adds an entirely new set of questions to those that exist to critically engage with sources in historical research: to what extent do these experiences resist the homogenising and universalising impulse of the archive? How can we use embodied fabulation as a lens to look for ways of knowing and doing that produce body-grounded histories of individuals and communities? In what ways does such a focus help us to confront the omissions of embodied and ephemeral practices in the archive that shape our understandings of the past and of the present?

Employing embodied fabulation in archival research also calls on researchers to more critically reflect on our own embodiment and positionality and how we engage with the archival research process, challenging us to question our traditional positioning as allegedly nonhistorical observer. As an historian, I am part of the practice of developing epistemologies; I am an agent in the process and practices by which pastness is authenticated and organised into a field of knowledge. In questioning myself and my positionality, I ask to what degree my insights are informed by my own embodiment as a white German historian, especially in an archive of violence such as those of empire and colonialism. How does my geopolitical, cultural, and epistemic context influence what to me constitutes legible evidence in the archive? What role does my habitus play in mediating the sources I am engaging with?

Embodied fabulation thus conforms to and deviates from the lineage of close reading in Formalism and New Criticism, which claims to be able to speak on behalf of a self-referential aesthetic object (Davis et al. 2024, 232). Instead, the "closeness" of embodied fabulation "brings insight into different subjectivities and awareness of how authorship of various kind intervenes and occludes as well as reveals meanings" (2024, 232). Whether it is cultural kinship or cultural difference, epistemic closeness or epistemic distance, as academics in the archive we face different obstacles in engaging with our sources. Embodied fabulation asks us to do both: to be strategically close so that we can understand the evidence in front of us and to remain critically distant so that we avoid absorption or ventriloquism.

There are three compelling examples of theatre and performance historians working with methods akin to what I here call embodied fabulation: dance scholar Melissa Blanco Borelli, for instances, deliberately intervenes with her research on the *mulata* body in the modernist opposition between the corporeal and the linguistic: "By locating knowledge outside of its historically normative space of language and text, even disturbing past assertions of 'embodied textuality', the lived materiality of an acting body mobilises the historical and cultural codes where it sits and, in this case, dances" (2014, 75). Sound and performance scholar meLê yamomo similarly combines what has traditionally been opposed, asking questions such as, "if subalterns are absent from the written archives and text-based 'history', would they be present in sound?" (yamomo, cit. in Davis et al. 2024, 221). For yamomo, listening to colonial recordings is a method of listening to how the subalterns performed their agency and to argue for understanding this process of listening as deeply embodied: "the archive is not just the object, but it requires another embodied archive to reside there for these things to interact, for the understanding to transpire" (yamomo, cit. in Davis et al. 2024, 230). This approach can even involve doing archival research through the body, in what dance scholar Prarthana Purkayastha calls "kinaesthetic approximation" (Davis et al. 2024, 226). In her research on Indian nautch dancers in human exhibitions in nineteenth-century London, Purkayastha rehearses the gestures and postures she found in the rare iconographical evidence of the dancers in the archive, such illustrated sketches, to better understand how the dancers might have felt and moved: "when faced with archival silences: working out through the body, and through *my* body at times, the possibilities that the historical figures I've been encountering in the archive mobilises" (Purkayastha, cit. in Davis et al. 2024, 218). Her method of using the body to activate what is hidden in the archive has not found its way into mainstream academia yet, but the past years have seen greater interest in incorporating embodied methods into more traditional archival research, as well as artists engaging with the archive and especially engaging their bodies *as* archives, as I will show later in this chapter.

Demonstration

In my own archival research in the German colonial archives, I looked for instances of embodied fabulation asking myself how a focus on bodies and modes of embodiment in these archives of violence (colonialism, imperialism, slavery) can help to counter extractivist modes of doing archival research as well as help to highlight histories of resistance that do not necessarily appear in writing and are thus often occluded from colonial history. Embodied fabulation is thus an invitation, both to do critical research in the archive as well as to critically reflect about the archive. Using this method, I show how the colonial archive works and how ephemeral narratives were turned into archival objects through the colonial archival processes of 'ordering' and 'comprehension'. Applying this method also shows that these colonial orders and categories were less stable than has been assumed, and reveals many fractures in the imperial knowledge-production process.

One specific instance of what this method reveals comes from my research on representations of the colonial genocide of the Herero and Nama committed by German colonial troupes at the beginning of the twentieth century. Between 1904 and 1908, the German colonial military had waged a war against the people of the Herero and Nama in Germany's former settler colony 'German South-West Africa', today's Namibia. The German empire's genocidal warfare had not only reduced the number of the Herero society by 80 percent but also deprived them of their land and their cattle and thus disrupted their entire cultural, social, and political fabric. The war is today acknowledged by many historians as "the first genocide of the twentieth century" (Zimmerer 2023, 29). In the aftermath of the war and the genocide, Herero culture and society was rejuvenated through the formation of the *oturupa,* a social network that is still active and of great importance to the Herero community today.

The *oturupa* were organised in the form of military regiments, and as anthropologist Larissa Förster explains, these regiments were a foundation upon which the Herero community restored itself after the genocidal war: "since many of the older traditional leaders of Herero society had either been killed in the war, executed by the German colonial administration, or had fled into exile, it was left to the younger Herero to create new social structures and institutions that could take the place of those that had been weakened or destroyed" (Förster 2008, 180). In the words of the late Herero oral historian Alexander Kaputu, the movement "grew up to be a very huge and important welfare organization among the Ovaherero people" (Alexander Kaputu, interview by Lisa Skwirblies, Windhoek, 15 February 2019), which can be understood as a form for resisting the Germans' attempt to eradicate the Herero as a people.

There is no written evidence of the *oturupa* practices that is not mediated by the imperial archive. Interestingly much of this mediated evidence describes the practice of the *oturupa* with concepts taken from the realm of the theatre: playing, imitating, staging. For instance, German missionary Johann Jakob Irle, based in the district of Okahandja in, what is today, Namibia, noticed in the beginning of the twentieth century "a spirit of rebellion among the youth" of the Herero (Irle 1906, 299). This manifested in what he described as young Herero men, who "drilled, swore, drank excessively and aped the German soldiers" (1906, 299). The latter behaviour, the mimicking of German soldiers, led him to coin these young Herero men 'Truppenspieler' (literally 'troop players' from which later the word *oturupa* emerged). While the German colonial administration dismissed the movement of the *oturupa* simply as "child's play",[8] the colonial administration of the South African Union, which took over the administration of South-West Africa after the First World War, labelled them as "theatre-play" and "performance".[9] The archival categories thus shifted over time and the imperial anxiety about the potential impact of these performative practices even increased

---

8   SWAA A50/59, Vol. 2, Magistrate of S.W. Africa, Annual Report: Native Affairs, 1928. "There is no doubt that these people are indulging, by fits and starts, in military exercises, probably like children playing at soldiers." The Germans interpreted the appropriation of their own military uniforms and military marching practices by the Herero as the latter's deep admiration for the German colonial military (instead of practices of resistance).

9   SWAA A 50/59, Vol. 1, Military Magistrate Gobabis to Secretary for the Protectorate, 18 August 1919.

over the years. In 1935, for example, the *oturupa* were prohibited from wearing uniforms during their marching and drilling practices and their uniforms were checked for swastikas[10] because they were suspected of being "pro-German".[11] This suggests that the colonial administration feared that wearing these uniforms could do exactly that: transform them into German soldiers.

The imperial anxiety is testimony to the power and agency that the imperialists ascribed to these modes of embodied fabulation, the power to enact (and keep alive) collective memory through embodied cultural performances in order to envision (and manifest) a collective future. Reading the colonial files with the grain of the archive, as Stoler suggests, reveals the *oturupa*'s strategies of negotiating the colonial everyday and the aftermath of the genocidal war through the embodied practice of marching and drilling, which, as I argue, are instances of embodied fabulation, of 'writing' their own history otherwise. What I noticed in the imperial archive is that the colonial administrators and colonial chroniclers had trouble making sense of the embodied practices of the *oturupa*. To some extent, these embodied practices of resistance by the colonised local population remained opaque to the imperial eye, only legible to them as play, make-believe, or imitation.

Whereas I have demonstrated how a focus on embodied practices in the colonial archives can help to unearth a history of resistance by the colonised that is otherwise not visible or legible in the archival documents, the ignorance of the colonial administrators is also an example of embodied fabulation in itself, but one that is trying to hide its embodiedness. Performing the position of a 'neutral' and 'universal' observer, the accounts of the colonisers need to be read as part of a larger imperial strategy during the long nineteenth century that created an invisible observer position, which allowed the Europeans to observe the Africans in order to comment on their physiology and action. By discrediting the invisible-observer assumption and instead highlighting

---

10 SWAA A50/59, Vol. 1, Letter of Deputy Commissioner of Windhoek, 3 July 1940. In fact, a prohibition of uniforms for 'natives' had already been installed by the German colonial government in 1905 but had not been obeyed by the African population.
11 SWAA A 50/59, Vol. 2, Letter from L Trollore, Addl. Native Commissioner, 14 February 1938.

the cracks in these supposedly neutral and unified observer positions, embodied fabulation allows one to discover and write a narrative that counters the unified colonial discourse that the imperial archive tries to perform.

The instances of colonial administrators and chroniclers doubting how to define and 'archive' the embodied practices by the *oturupa* are testimony to a struggle to maintain a colonial order that does not allow for instances of not knowing and of a lack of clarity. It moreover shows how much the imperial archival logic was based on the fixed idea that the cultural expressions of the indigenous population are by definition static (tradition) and incapable of holding and producing knowledge, and how little this was true in the colonial everyday. In other words, it reveals that what wants to appear as a consensus (colonial discourse), masks in fact a history of conflicts, silences, and (embodied) confusions.

These revelations resulting from embodied fabulation echo the warnings of Gayatri Spivak, who cautioned us not to fall into the trap of assuming that one can recover the subjectivities of the subaltern from the imperial archives (Spivak 1999, 146). When engaging with the colonial archives, she urges us not to attempt to recover, add, or fill in the gaps with obliterated voices, but instead to pay attention to "the fabrication of representations of historical reality" in archival production (Spivak 1985, 271). In other words, she calls on us to remain aware of the fact that the representation of the historical to a certain extent always entails fiction and fabulation. We will not find the lost voices of the colonised that will allow us to fill the gaps that the "epistemic fracture of imperialism" has caused (Spivak 1999, 146) because of the archival process itself, which, as a form of alteration, mediation, and production over-codes the materials that enter it and fundamentally transform it, "rendering it a product of the Archival Impulse" (Highmore 2006, 88). For these reasons, the 'voices' of the Hereros in the imperial archive remain inaccessible to us. However, the *oturupa*'s reappearances in the colonial archive by repeatedly nurturing and evading the archival attempts of taxonomies, decipherability, and translatability, challenged the logic by which they were (mis)filed in the first place.

Expanding the method

The 'archival turn' also encompassed a growing number of artists using bodies and embodiment as a tool to engage with the archive. One example of this expanded methodology is the performance project *Motus Mori* by German choreographer Katja Heitman. Her project, I argue, activates the concept of embodied fabulation by doing performance historiography (rather than representing it) through performance.

A long-term project that started in 2019, *Motus Mori* has since then investigated the possibility of archiving human movement through human movement. Travelling to different cities and collecting movements of local residents, the archive *Motus Mori* and its ten or so dancer-archivists interview volunteer 'movement-donors' about their daily lives and interests in movement. It archives everyday movements, ranging from cracking one's knuckles to pacing due to insomnia to making a duck-face when taking a selfie to twirling one's thumbs when bored. These analogue, ephemeral, unconscious routines, distinctive manners of moving, expressions of pain and ecstasy, old age, or absent-minded habits, are inventoried and the record is stored in the muscle memory of the dancer-archivists.

From time to time, the *Motus Mori Archive* is opened for the public in the form of participatory performances or exhibitions. These exhibitions, titled *Motus Mori Museum*, are five-hour live installations in museum spaces in which the dancer-archivists stage the movements they have been collecting for the museum audience. In the *Motus Mori Requiem*, the archive is opened up by having an audience perform the movements themselves. The audience receives instructions via headphones to make them aware of their own body positions as well as the movements stored in the *Motus Mori Archive*. The audience is given detailed descriptions that instruct them how to embody some of the donated movements and give them information about the donors—who possess a wide range of different gender identities, ages, physical abilities, and cultural backgrounds. Theatre audiences get to know the donors through their daily movements and through their highly diverse movement repertoires.

The audience in *Motus Mori Requiem* are thus not only spectators, but participants as well, invited to use their own bodies to perform the movements stored in the *Motus Mori* archive. In a way, the audience become archivists themselves, since the archive of *Motus Mori* only exists if it is (re-)embodied. Even more, the audience's bodies become the archive, a space in which the movement repertoire is not only stored but actualised and thus also transmitted. As dance scholar André Lepecki suggest, thinking of bodies as archives means exploring how embodied actions, gestures, and movements can serve as sites of knowledge production and knowledge storage (Lepecki 2010). Echoing Taylor's concept of the 'repertoire', he suggests that the body acts as a kind of repository of practices and histories that are preserved through physical experience rather than in written or visual form. Instead of simply acting as an alternative archive, 'the body as archive' redefines what is understood by 'archiving' in the first place: By engaging the audience in the performance of the archive, *Motus Mori* employs embodied fabulation as a methodology to store and transmit human movement and highlights the potential of the body to function as an archive.

A notable feature of *Motus Mori* is the presence of affective historiographies, or what Katja Heitmann calls 'kinetic empathy'.[12] Theatre scholar Annika Hilger describes kinetic empathy as follows: by physically engaging with movements of others, one has to make "space within oneself", and to allow for forming "a plural community through difference" (Hilger 2024). Performing the movements yourself as a visitor-researcher can thus lead to a heightened (embodied) empathy, as both Hilger and Heitmann suggest, in which a sense of difference is experienced in the discrepancy that appears at times when performing the movements from the *Motus Mori* archive. This discrepancy highlights the transformational character of the archive, as the person who actualises the movement from the archive will always add something new to the archived movement. In the discrepancy between our re-performance and the movement described, we also experience the different forms of expertise and experience of the movement donors, whether this stems from different abilities, training, or habits.

---

12   See https://www.katjaheitmann.com/work/motus-mori-corpus/

Suggestions for further reading

A variety of scholars have pondered on the question of the archive, especially in relation to alternative ways of doing historiography from within and against the archive. See, for instance, Ariella Aïsha Azoulay's book *Potential History. Unlearning Imperialism* (2019), in which she encourages us to think of history as something that is not closed off but that holds a radical potential for living differently in the future. In her book *Listening to Images* (2017), Tina M. Campt suggests that we engage with archives of images not through our gaze but by listening closely to them and thus attuning ourselves to other senses and other affects that register with these photographs. Alana Kumbier proposes a queer approach to archival research in *Ephemeral Material: Queering the Archive* (2014), which goes beyond collections with LGBTQI content and challenges established archival principles and practices through queer explanatory frameworks.

References

Azoulay, Ariella Aïsha. 2019. *Potential History. Unlearning Imperialism.* Verso.

Balme, Christopher, and Berenika Szymanski-Düll. 2020. *Methoden der Theaterwissenschaft*. Narr Francke.

Borelli, Melissa. 2014. "Hip Work. Undoing the Tragic *Mulata*". In *Black Performance Theory*, edited by Thomas F. DeFrantz and Anita Gonzales, 63–87. Duke University Press. https://doi.org/10.1515/9780822377016

Callahan, Sara. 2024. "When the Dust Has Settled: What Was the Archival Turn, and Is It Still Turning?" *Art Journal* 83 (1): 74–88. https://doi.org/10.1080/00043249.2024.2317690

Campt, Tina M. 2017. *Listening to Images*. Duke University Press. https://doi.org/10.1215/9780822373582

Davis, Tracy C. 2004. "The Context Problem." *Theatre Survey* 45 (2): 203–09. https://doi.org/10.1017/S0040557404000158

Davis, Tracy C., and Paul Rae, eds. 2024. *The Cambridge Guide to Mixed Methods Research for Theatre and Performance Studies*. Cambridge University Press. https://doi.org/10.1017/9781009294904.001

Derrida, Jacques. 1996. *Archive Fever. A Freudian Impression*. University of Chicago Press.

Farge, Arlette. *The Allure of the Archives*. 2013. Yale University Press.

Foucault, Michel. 2002 (1969). *Archaeology of Knowledge*. Routledge.

Foucault, Michel. 1977. "La vie des hommes infâmes." *Cahiers du chemin* 29: 12–29.

Förster, Larissa. 2008. "From 'General Field Marshal' to 'Miss Genocide': The Reworking of Traumatic Experiences among Herero-Speaking Namibians." *Journal of Material Culture* 13: 175–94.

Franzen, Ricarda; Skwirblies, Lisa, and Rob van der Zalm. 2025. "Hoe verzamel je theater?" In *Theater Verzamelen. (On)grijpbaar erfgoed*, edited by Hans van Keulen et.al., 14–27. Wboeks/Allard Pierson.

Hartman, Saidiya. 2008. "Venus in Two Acts." *small axe* 26: 1–14. https://doi.org/10.1215/-12-2-1

Highmore, Ben 2006. *Michel de Certeau: Analysing Culture*. Continuum.

Hilger, Annika. 2024. *Re/membering Bodies. How knowledge is transmitted through movement in performance*. MA thesis, University of Amsterdam (unpublished).

Hussein, Nesreen N. 2022. "Decolonisation and Performance Studies: Questions from the Border." *Global Performance Studies* 5 (1–2). https://doi.org/10.33303/gpsv5n1-2a114.performancephilosophy.org+3

Irle, Johann Jakob. 1906. *Die Herero. Ein Beitrag zur Landes-, Volks-, und Missionskunde*. Bertelsmann.

Kumbier, Alana. 2014. *Ephemeral Material: Queering the Archive*. Litwin Books.

Lepecki, André. 2010. "The Body as Archive: Will to Re-Enact and the Afterlives of Dance." *Dance Research Journal* 42 (2): 28–48. https://doi.org/10.1017/S0149767700001029

Phelan, Peggy. 1993. *Unmarked. The Politics of Performance*. Routledge.

Purkayastha, Prarthana. 2024. "Methodologies Dialogue: Archives and Embodiments." In *The Cambridge Guide to Mixed Methods Research for Theatre and Performance* Studies, edited by Tracy C. Davis and Paul Rae, 217–36. Cambridge University Press. https://doi.org/10.1017/9781009294904.015

Schneider, Rebecca. 2001. "Archives: Performance Remains." *Performance Research* 6: 100–08.

Skwirblies, Lisa. 2021. "Colonial Theatricality." In *The Oxford Handbook of Politics and Performance*, edited by Milija Gluhovic et.al, 27–43. Oxford University Press. https://doi.org/10.1093/oxfordhb/9780190863456.001.0001

Spivak, Gayatri Chakravorty. 1985. "The Rani of Simur: An Essay in Reading the Archives." *History and Theory* 24: 247–72. https://doi.org/10.2307/2505169

Spivak, Gayatri Chakravorty. 1999. *A Critique of Postcolonial Reason. Toward a History of the Vanishing Present.* Harvard University Press. https://doi.org/10.2307/j.ctvjsf541

Stoler, Ann Laura. 2009. *Along the Archival Grain. Epistemic Anxieties and Colonial Common Sense.* Princeton University Press.

Stoler, Ann Laura. 2010. "Archival Dis-Ease: Thinking through Colonial Ontologies." *Communication and Critical/Cultural Studies* 7: 215–19. https://doi.org/10.1080/14791421003775741

Taylor, Diana. 2003. *The Archive and the Repertoire: Performing cultural memory in the Americas.* Duke University Press. https://doi.org/10.1215/9780822385318

Trouillot, Michel-Rolph.1995. *Silencing the Past. Power and the Production of History.* Beacon Press.

Yamomo, meLê. 2024. "Methodologies Dialogue: Archives and Embodiments." In *The Cambridge Guide to Mixed Methods Research for Theatre and Performance Studies*, edited by Tracy C. Davis and Paul Rae, 217–36. Cambridge University Press. https://doi.org/10.1017/9781009294904.015

Zimmerer, Jürgen. 2023. *From Auschwitz to Windhoek? Reflections on the Relationship between Colonialism and National Socialism.* De Gruyter Oldenbourg.

III

SITUATED KNOWLEDGES

13. Intersectionality

Anika Marschall

Summary

This chapter explores the methodological challenges and possibilities of applying intersectionality to the analysis of contemporary performance. It revisits Kimberlé Crenshaw's foundational work in legal studies and critical race theory, particularly her focus on the structural discrimination faced by women of colour in the US legal system. The chapter reflects on how her contributions have influenced broader discussions of social identity, power, and exclusion, while also cautioning against the appropriation and dilution of intersectionality in Western European humanities contexts. Emphasising its relevance for theatre and performance studies, the chapter underscores intersectionality's analytical value in confronting structural omissions related to race, identity, and representation. Drawing on feminist and critical race theorists such as Mari J. Matsuda and Anna Carastathis, it outlines practical strategies—including self-positioning, contextual analysis, and 'asking the other question'—for integrating intersectionality into performance methodologies. The chapter concludes with an application of this approach to a performance analysis of *Being Pink Ain't Easy* by Joana Tischkau, highlighting how intersectionality can help interrogate institutional aesthetics and the dynamics of power in performance production and reception.

Introduction

This chapter introduces intersectionality as a critical approach to analyse contemporary theatre performances. Intersectionality's central premise is that social identity frameworks such as race, class, gender, sexuality, dis/ability, age, religion are not mutually exclusive, but they intersect and constitute each other. Intersectionality helps us analyse how and why certain identity factors seem to be more significant than others within a specific context and what broader cultural values are at stake. Intersectionality allows for a nuanced appreciation of the ways in which different combinations of identity categories are simultaneously at work or at issue in performances and other cultural events, images and creative productions, conditions of political and social life, and understandings of the self. Intersectionality attends to the way multiple structures of power are entangled through "interlocking oppressions" (Combahee River Collective 1982 [1977], 13), rather than how different categories merely add to one privileged category. Intersectionality attends to the specificity of how subjects are socially positioned—including, importantly, the analyst's own positionality as well as how spectators are addressed in performances.

Over the last decades, there has been a heightened awareness and discourse around race in particular and its intersections with other social identity markers in a variety of arts and humanities fields. This discussion has also been specific to theatre and performance studies, with many professional academic organisations as well as universities organising panels and debates on the issue. The Theatre and Performance Research Association, for example, published a manifesto in 2023 that commits members to "practise intersectionality to decentre scholarly practices and to amplify underrepresented voices" (TaPRA 2023). As white, heterosexual, cis-female, able-bodied theatre and performance researcher and teacher, who was taught in the Global European North, I regularly deal with the concept of intersectionality and its implications for theatre production, pedagogy, and critical analysis in classrooms. Yet, there is a gap in the existing research and literature that speaks specifically to a theatre studies readership on intersectional issues. In aiming to start filling this gap, this chapter offers a starting point for charting an intersectional methodology that can contribute to a more complex discussion of how intersecting identities have a bearing on performance analysis and spectatorial reception.

While intersectionality indeed emphasises the simultaneity and interdependence of various identity categories, foundational scholars such as Kimberlé Williams Crenshaw (1989; 1991) and Patricia Hill Collins (2000) developed the concept specifically to address how race is often neglected in analyses that focus primarily on gender or other axes. In the early 1990s, Crenshaw introduced intersectionality in the field of critical legal studies to critique the ways in which Black women in the US, in particular, have been discriminated against by the US legal system. In "Demarginalizing the Intersection of Race and Sex: A Black Feminist Critique of Antidiscrimination Doctrine, Feminist Theory and Antiracist Politics", Crenshaw refers to contradicting class suits: firstly, she refers to two Black women who were refused to act as a class representative on behalf of all Black employees in a case of racial discrimination against their employer Travernol in 1976. In addition to this first suit, Crenshaw refers to a second one, in which five Black women were denied their case against a seniority policy by General Motors that targeted Black women exclusively, because the court ruled that they could not 'combine' the claims of race and sex discrimination, and must either bring a racial discrimination suit or a sex discrimination suit only. Twenty years later, when calling for a field of intersectionality studies, Crenshaw summarises the US legal system's perilous lack of recognising and acknowledging the particular positionality Black women hold:

> both too similar to Black men and white women to represent themselves and too different to represent either Blacks or women as a whole. Although Black male and white female narratives were understood to be fully inclusive and universal, Black female narratives were rendered partial, unrecognizable, something apart from standard claims of race discrimination or gender discrimination (Cho, Crenshaw and McCull 2013, 790–91).

Through the image of a traffic intersection, Crenshaw illustrates the particular situatedness of Black women and the possible number of ways they can experience discrimination:

> Consider an analogy to traffic in an intersection, coming and going in all four directions. Discrimination, like traffic through an intersection, may flow in one direction, and it may flow in another. If an accident happens

in an intersection, it can be caused by cars travelling from any number of directions and, sometimes, from all of them. Similarly, if a Black woman is harmed because she is in the intersection, her injury could result from sex discrimination or race discrimination (1989, 140).

In a later extension of the argument, Crenshaw clarifies that she does not mean that the experience of Black women can only be explained through the frameworks of race and gender, but that other social identity frameworks are often as critical (2013). Intersectionality may provide the means for dealing with other marginalisations as well. For example, an intersectional practice can focus on how certain social identity factors can also be a means for "relating across differences" as Audre Lorde put it (1984, 123), e.g. imagine a coalition between straight and gay people of colour that could serve as basis for a critique of churches and other cultural institutions that reproduce heterosexism.

While this chapter shows that an intersectional method enables inquiry across multiple categories of identity and experience, it is important to acknowledge that these categories do not always operate in purely compounding or additive ways. Identity positions can be both complementary and contradictory—within individuals and between them. Moreover, the foundational premises of intersectionality, grounded in US legal and sociopolitical contexts, may not resonate or translate in the same way across global or local settings (Banerjee and Ghosh 2018).

Hill Collins and Sirma Bilge pinpoint that intersectionality is a way of "understanding and analysing the complexity of the world, in people, and in human experiences", and a way to acknowledge how "the events and conditions of political and social life and the self can seldom be understood as shaped by one factor […]. [I]ntersectionality as an analytic lens highlights the multiple nature of individual identities and how varying combinations of class, gender, race, sexuality and citizenship categories differentially position each individual" (2016, 11; 16). It is important to emphasise both the utility and the limitations of intersectionality as a frame for thinking about identity: while it may narrow certain aspects of complexity and bracket or disregard them (human psychology, relationalities, materialities etc.), it remains a useful means to critique power structures and address—if not take up action to redress—social inequality. Applied to performance and theatre, intersectionality offers a way to think not only of individual cultural 'texts' or performances as objects of analysis, but also of production structures, seasonal programming, ensemble systems, cultural policies, genre histories, aesthetic norms, and white dominance in the discipline of 'performance studies'—i.e. through dominant theories, texts, languages, authors, artists, and practices.

Context

Priscilla Slater, Breonna Taylor, Atatiana Koquice Jefferson, Crystal Danielle Ragland, Pamela Shantay Turner, Nina Adams, Latasha Nicole Walton, Brittany Danielle McLean, Angel Viola Decarlo, April Webster, Tameka Lashay Simpson, LaJuana Phillips, Dereshia Blackwell, Cynthia Fields, LaShanda Anderson, Shukri Ali Said, DeCynthia Clements, Crystalline Barnes, Geraldine Townsend, Sandy Guardiola, India N. Nelson, Charleena Lyles, Jonie Block, Alteria Woods, Morgan London Rankins, Deborah Danner, Korryn Gaines, Jessica Williams, Deresha Armstrong, Laronda Sweatt, India M. Beaty, Kisha Michael, Sahlah Ridgeway, Gynnya McMillen, Bettie Jones, Barbara Dawson, Marquesha McMillan, India Kager, Redel Jones, Raynette Turner, Ralkina Jones, Joyce Curnell, Kindra Chapman, Sandra Bland, Nuwnah Laroche, Sheneque Proctor, Iretha Lilly, Latandra Ellington, Yvette Smith, Michelle Cusseaux, Tracy A. Wade, Aura Rosser, Ariel Levy, Angela Beatrice Randolph, Dawn Cameron, Shonda Mikelson, Kyam Livingston, Renisha McBride, Miriam Carey, Angelique Styles, Angel Chiwengo, Kayla Moore, Amber Nashay Carter, Darnesha Harris, Shelly Frey, Malissa Williams, Erica Collins, Alesia Thomas, Shantel Davis, Sharmel Edwards, Rekia Boyd, Shereese Francis, Jameela Barnette, Catawaba Howard, Brenda Williams, Derrinesha Clay, Shelley Amos, Cheryl Blount-Burton, Carolyn Moran-Hernandez, Latricka Sloan, Aiyana Mo'Nay Stanley Jones, Ahjah Dixon, Sarah Riggins, Katherine Hysaw, Barbara Stewart, Duanna Johnson, Tarika Wilson, Kathryn Johnston, Alberta Spruill, Kendra James, Nizah Morris, LaTanya Haggerty, Margaret Mitchell, Tyisha Miller, Danette Daniels, Frankie Ann Perkins, Sonji Taylor, Eleanor Bumpurs

Dear reader, I kindly ask you, I urge you to go back to the paragraph above and read it carefully, name for name. Take time to acknowledge each one of the Black women and girls named above.

They were between seven and 93 years old.

They lived in the US between the 1980s and 2010s.

All of them were killed by the police.

These Black women and girls are acknowledged also by the social movement #SayHerName which was launched in 2014 by the Center for Intersectionality and Social Policy Studies and the African American Policy Forum. The #SayHerName movement commemorates these women's and girls' lives and supports their families. The movement uplifts their stories and educates on anti-Black racism and the perilous police violence that targets and victimises Black women and girls.

With this in-text intervention, I seek to make tangible that the context of intersectionality is rooted in anti-racism and social justice campaigns, and that to use intersectionality as analytic approach requires us to be particularly cautious about the ways it can be coopted and whitewashed. In doing so, this chapter section engages with multiple registers of violence—ranging from the tragic immediacy of state-sanctioned killings to the slower, often invisible forms of institutional and symbolic violence enacted in spaces such as universities or cultural institutions. While these forms are not equivalent in impact or severity, they can be understood as part of a continuum of racialised power relations. The aim here is not to conflate, but to gesture towards structural relations between different forms of harm, and how intersectional analysis can hold space for both distinction and connection. While theatres and universities are not sites of physical violence in the same way as fatal police encounters, they can nonetheless reproduce forms of structural and symbolic violence—manifested through epistemic exclusion, racialised surveillance, or the erasure of certain bodies and voices. These forms are not equivalent in intensity or impact, but they are connected through broader systems of racialised power. Thus, we need to stay wary and clear about how intersectionality can be appropriated in often exclusively white academic knowledge production, and thus lose its power to reckon with perilous conditions of living under white supremacy.

Intersectionality has been used in gender studies, social sciences, and legal studies, and has gained more and more traction in the arts and humanities. While intersectionality is moving through the institution of the university, it does not remain unaffected and untouched by the university's white-dominated power dynamics and epistemological habits. For example, in the open letter White Colleague Listen!* addressed to UK theatre, dance, and performance studies in August 2020, a collective of Black and Global Majority colleagues and students are clear about the ways in which racism continues to be perpetuated as epistemic erasure and appropriation in our field, in particular when it comes to the appropriation and mis-use of intersectionality:

> To validate the erasures, colleagues co-opt African American legal studies scholar Kimberlé Crenshaw's coinage of the term intersectionality and claim that the absence of race from discussions is compensated by the presence of discussions around gender, sexuality, class and disability. This is a fundamental misuse of Crenshaw's concept of intersectionality which recognises the compounded impact of these different structures of oppression on the lived experience of racialised peoples, thus placing race and racism at its heart. Kalwant Bhopal provides further examples of how the misuse of intersectionality manifests across UK Higher Education. (Revolution or Nothing, 2020)

In the arts and humanities, our critical analyses can attend to how stories are performed and staged and how different stories and modes of storytelling are pervaded by power. Who decides whose stories are being told and how? Storytelling is, in the cultural and institutional context of this very volume and its wider field, dominated by white Eurocentric approaches to knowledge and knowledge production. Similarly, the way the context and 'story' of intersectionality is told, by whom, and in what ways, is pervaded by whiteness and Eurocentrism. Certain stories are being continuously told and become engendered at the cost of other stories and other storytellers, e.g. through the repetition of white-dominated curricula, epistemologies, and pedagogy (see also Bala 2017, Arora 2021).

To get the context or "the history of intersectionality straight" is one such story, but one that is neither possible nor desirable, according to the sociologists Sirma Bilge and Hill Collins (2016, 63–88). In a similar critique, the gender studies scholar Jennifer C. Nash (2019) reflects on how Black feminist scholars have long laboured for intersectionality to be taken seriously as analytic approach in the university while insisting on its long roots in art and activism, before it is now widely being circulated, appropriated, and commodified in university work.

She critically maps the institutional history of intersectionality and the dangers of contextualising intersectionality through debates on "who coined the term, who is its inaugural scholar" (2019, 39), and whose terrain it "originally" was. The longing to "retell intersectionality's history in an ostensibly accurate way" (2019, 40) through a single story is a symptom of epistemological habits and logics dominated by whiteness and Eurocentrism, that do little to "disrupt the logic of 'coinage'" (2019, 42) or the desire to make property of knowledge.

Nash speaks of the paradoxes Black women's bodies navigate while doing university work, i.e. that "simply naming structures [e.g. authority, hierarchy, ownership, territoriality] fails to do justice to how they move against (and inside of) [their] bodies" (2019, 30). This is an important point to be attentive to when using intersectionality as analytic: to do intersectionality justice, it requires wary institutional labour (e.g. speaking truth to those power dynamics dominating university research, epistemologies, and research designs), and it requires wary emotional and political labour (e.g. making effort and space for having profound encounters with the lived experiences and social positions other than one's own—encounters that may undo you). Intersectionality offers an analytic that invites us to attend to the ways in which Black women—whose perspectives have often been marginalised in both mainstream and feminist scholarship—generate critical insights into the operations of power and injustice. This does not suggest that all Black women's perspectives are uniform or universally representative, but rather that centring their historically situated knowledge can reveal overlooked dimensions of structural inequality and epistemic exclusion. Therefore, we need to stay vigilant in using intersectionality as a way to critically counter the different degrees of violence that white supremacy inflicts, asking of performances, performance curricula, and of ourselves as analysts to take an active part in catering to people with lived experiences of intersectional discrimination.

How to

The following section is concerned with the questions of how to apply intersectionality then as method in critical analyses, and importantly, how such critical analyses must respect that "intersectionality is inextricably linked to an analysis of power" (Cho, Crenshaw, McCall 2013, 797) and social justice. To merely apply intersectionality to analyse how different aspects of identity might overlap leads it away from the concerns of how cultural meaning-making can produce perilous consequences, i.e. exclusion, discrimination, and violence. To counter this simplification, I emphasise the importance of gaining knowledge, nuanced vocabulary, and critical concepts to rigorously engage and deal with contemporary debates in the field of structural discrimination, identity politics and culture.

To explain how intersectionality can act as a methodological tool for critical analyses, I refer first to Anna Carastathis's close reading of Crenshaw's work on intersectionality (Carastathis 2014). She argues for a politicised and historicised understanding of intersectionality, which by now has become a well-travelled concept. Such a politicised and historicised understanding of intersectionality as rooted in social justice movements and Black feminisms can disorient habits of essentialism and categorial purity.

There are arguably four main analytic benefits to intersectionality as a research methodology or theoretical framework: simultaneity, complexity, irreducibility, and inclusivity (Carastathis 2014, 307).

1. Intersectionality captures the idea that multiple factors of social identity are active at the same time in a given situation and people might experience them simultaneously. To apply Carastathis's example to my own, highly privileged, situatedness: I am not simply white on Mondays, a cis woman on Tuesdays and hold German citizenship on Wednesdays. I am white, a cis woman and hold German citizenship on all days of the week. Yet, in certain situations, some of the identity categories I share are highlighted more than others, i.e. that I am a heterosexual cis woman might be more relevant in situations where I search for a (gendered) bathroom or teach queer theory in a hetero- and cis-dominated culture. I am more aware of my German citizenship when booking travel or voting during elections, or when I research and produce knowledge on questions of theatre and migration.

2. Intersectionality accounts for the complexity of frameworks of social identity without reducing them to one explanatory

ontologically privileged category, i.e. it can help us to explore how multiple social groups might share certain relations and analytic categories, and how we might examine the differences present within one social group.

3. A third benefit of intersectionality is irreducibility. That means, an intersectional approach refuses an analysis that reduces culturally produced meaning to a single phenomenon or factor.

4. Finally, in regard to the benefits of inclusivity, intersectionality can act as a corrective to the assumptions of whiteness, heteronormativity, elitism, ableism, hegemonic feminist theory, and other essentialisms, that can operate as unmarked and unnamed cultural defaults. Intersectionality can help us become more attentive towards "deeply ingrained cognitive and representational exclusions" (Carastathis 2014, 309) and 'blind spots' in our analyses.

In practice, these benefits mean pragmatically that when studying a certain situation or cultural phenomenon, we might still have to take the first step to isolate certain categories and ask about the impact of structural inequalities on a subject separately, before asking about their simultaneous workings. Carastathis argues that intersectionality thus "may function less as a research method and more as a heuristic to interpret results of quantitative or qualitative research" (2014, 308). Rather than a method, intersectionality requires the researcher to make a methodological commitment to look for potential biases and to avoid (re)producing monistic categories.

In practice, intersectionality requires us to position ourselves. As the performance scholar Steve Greer has taught me, when undertaking performance analyses, rather than presuming a neutral or objective viewing position, consider how your specific social location (your identity, your thinking, your experiences, your previous study) shapes or influences you in specific ways (Greer 2019). This does not mean a mere listing of all the facets of your identity ('I identify as white, heterosexual, cis-female, able-bodied, middle-class German citizen'). Instead, we each need to consider how these aspects inform the ways we are moved by a particular performance or theatre production, why we each might empathise with certain characters rather than others, why we each understand certain parts of a story immediately as important (having seen or experienced them in our own lives) in comparison to the aspects that we need to have explained to us (Greer 2019). Tools such as the Social Identity Wheel (Bogert, Linders and Sanches 2019) can help in understanding and identifying in what ways our social positioning biases our epistemologies, and our selection of research methods and objects. Intersectional performance analyses must become attentive towards aesthetic conventions and performance form, and how they work together to create, reinforce, or even counter cultural and social norms. Asking about an artist's background and the values, assumptions, and perspectives represented in the artist's particular style of performance and stage language(s) used helps to give intersectional performance analyses shape. To do so, we can choose to critically unpack the emphases or intentions articulated by an artist in the statements they have made about their work (in interviews, in publicity, in programmes, and other media). And/or, we might want to locate the theatre performance we are scrutinising in a broader field of cultural production, i.e. within a given genre, within a particular tradition of practice, in relation to works with similar styles or conventions, or works made in a particular country or cultural context.

In practice, to commit methodologically to intersectionality means to become aware of potential biases in our analyses. This means, for example, to "ask the other question", as Mari J. Matsuda has suggested equally for critical legal analyses:

> The way I try to understand the interconnection of all forms of subordination is through a method I call 'ask the other question.' When I see something that looks racist, I ask, 'Where is the patriarchy in this?' When I see something that looks sexist, I ask 'where is the heterosexism in this?' When I see something that looks homophobic, I ask 'Where are the class interests in this?' (1991, 1189).

This procedure seems simple, but is very useful to complicate our thinking about power relations and investigating how people, authors, artists resist or accommodate power through certain stories, modes of storytelling or cultural images and phenomena. Through asking the other question, researchers actively search for axes of power that are less obvious or visible than the ones you see and work through immediately with respect to a given phenomenon or image at hand. We might still have to take the first step to analyse what are the obvious and visible workings of power and structural inequality in the given case study, before asking the other question about our potential oversights and the invisible(ised) workings of power and structural inequality that might simultaneously be at play. When analysing a theatre performance that is representing masculinity, we might ask about the body of the performer and their bodily abilities. Or, when we are analysing a theatre performance that is representing disability, we might ask about gender and sexuality. How do these representational strategies work together? Importantly, committing methodologically to intersectionality does not mean that every category and axis is always already equally important; we still need to critically judge which aspects of a given theatre performance are salient to ask about. Intersectionality does not provide a blueprint that fits all and every analysis, and we still might emphasise what elements are foregrounded in a given theatre performance.

Demonstration

In the following demonstration, I will apply an intersectional approach to an, albeit brief and limited, performance analysis of *Being Pink Ain't Easy* by the Black German choreographer and dance artist Joana Tischkau. *Being Pink Ain't Easy* is a solo which is about white fragility, queerness, (hyper-)masculinity, and the cultural appropriation and commodification of Black aesthetics and creative expression. Tischkau developed the performance as part of the After Europe festival at the Sophiensaele in Berlin in 2019, and, put succinctly, the performance is 'showing doing' (Schechner 2014, 4) the performative de/construction of race, gender and sexuality. The following analysis is structured along four sets of questions: first, 'what is the performance about?', second, 'what else is the performance about?', third, 'how do I position myself in relation to the performance?', and fourth, 'what are the axes of power that are less obvious or visible?'.

What is the performance primarily about? What can be seen and experienced at first glance? Initially, the performance is most obviously about masculinity and centres the white, cis-male solo performer Rudi Natterer. The stage backdrop and floor are coloured in soft purple;

the performer's stage space is surrounded by three rectangular frames which guide the spectator's gaze towards a central vanishing point. It looks like this scaffolding symbolises the confinement of a small room. It looks also like spectators are invited to a photoshoot set or similar. This scenography indexes the way images are technically constructed from a particular angle, as well as the way images are culturally constructed in showing and revealing certain objects, subjects, and points that viewers are looking from. In the middle of this scaffolding we see the solo performer reclining on a pink pouffe, atop a plush blanket, which later turns out to be a fur coat. His pose mirrors that of Michelangelo's *The Creation of Adam*; he attaches his weight onto his right elbow and gently raises his other arm, pointing towards, in this very scene, an invisible god. Rather than being naked like Adam, the performer wears a white, almost translucent durag, a soft pink oversized basketball jersey, pants, and knee pads, with the print "Being Pink 7" on the jersey on his chest. The performer proudly carries long, fat silver chains and flashy rings, and he wears pink Nikes and white tennis socks. He has a tear tattooed below his left eye, and another tattoo on his left arm. He looks like a hip-hop artist or enthusiast. This opening image creates a stark aesthetic contrast that defines the overall dramaturgy of the performance: references to canonical white Western art history, i.e. Michelangelo's famous depiction of Adam, contrasted with hip-hop culture and the dominating colour pink as symbol of femininity and homosexuality.

While the performer does not move during the first few minutes, the stage lighting smoothly transitions the set's colour and overall tone from purple to light blue, yellow and back to light blue and purple, and finally white, with an additional spot lighting the performer from above. It feels as though the dramaturgy is still looking for the 'right' colour or tone. These opening visuals thus invite the spectators to become self-aware of their mode of looking; how they perceive colours and colour contrasts and what feelings, associations, and affects a certain colour scheme might create. The beginning of the action is then marked by the sound of a classic old mobile phone ringtone going off—situating the scene as somewhat anachronistic. The ringtone repeats and the performer, while holding his reclined posture, slowly turns his head. With a stern facial expression and severe look at the audience, he sighs and shows that the phone call bothers him, that it interrupts him from doing something important, interrupts him from the serious and contemplative emulation of the infamous Adam fresco (causing many to chuckle in the audience). He reveals a flip phone in his hand, which he answers. We hear a hushed male voice whisper slowly "Hey big boy, what up?", and the performer immediately snaps his mobile closed. In slow motion, he smoothly places his body into a new posture, holding it for a couple of breaths. The new posture mimics Rodin's *Thinker*. The performer continues to move slowly into other postures, mimicking other classical statues that could be placed in a Western art history repertoire. Spectators see, but might not be able to make out and clearly identify the plethora of references here. At times, other postures suggest references to a different cultural repertoire of images altogether—pop-cultural images of hip-hop artists perhaps, when the performer flexes his muscles, opens his mouth in a way that suggests he is always ready to talk back, transitioning his gaze from stern to provocative, from erotic to sadness and suffering. The way he performs masculinity changes accordingly: from homoeroticism; to the romantic image of a melancholic artist suffering in solitude and contemplating his art-historical lineage; to embodying masculine strength, coolness, and 'street swag.' In certain moments, the audience laughs at him, at other moments, the audience remains quiet—moving, arguably, from believing in the authenticity of how the performer embodies certain images, to responding to the way his performance might fail in embodying other images in an authentic, believable way. This dramaturgical juxtaposition of contrasting cultural images reveals to the spectator how the repertoire itself becomes performative, something being embodied, repeated, known over time, and recognised. Specifically, it explores how only people within a particular social identity framework are able to embody, repeat, know over time, and recognise such a particular repertoire. Repertoire here refers both to a Western art history repertoire, and to a contemporary repertoire of how 'maleness' is culturally represented.

What else is the performance about? How does the performance unfold complexity, simultaneity, and irreducibility? What can be seen and experienced at second, third, fourth glance? Rather than only being about masculinity, the performance is about masculinity and its intersection with the social identity frameworks of whiteness, sexuality, class, and age. The performance's aesthetics respond to a specific cultural image in the early 2000s, when internationally acclaimed hip-hop artists such as Kanye West, Jay-Z, and Cam'Rom began to wear pink polo shirts, fur coats, and golden jewellery, rings, chains, armbands etc.; clothing and accessories that used to be culturally coded as feminine. With the performance, Tischkau asks 'Why don't we associate these images as homosexual? Why were these new cultural images not sexually marginalised, as others were so frequently and quickly?' Through its particular dramaturgy of slowness and minimalism, which I will detail below, the performance investigates how this change in appearance did little to alter the cultural stereotype of Black men, due, presumably, to the way they are racialised as hyper-masculine, rather than only masculine; i.e. 'hyper' in the sense that their masculinity seems to be seen as something that can rarely be touched. On the flipside, bodies read as white male seem to be able to claim almost any cultural space and make themselves appear as performing a more feminine or androgynous figure.

The performance's title, *Being Pink Ain't Easy*, in combination with the scenography make it apparent that this performance engages with 'pink' in some form. To some spectators, this might be a clear metaphor for 'whiteness' and more particularly, the issue of "white fragility" (DiAngelo 2011), the felt vulnerability that white people experience, express, and perform in response to "racial stress", that is psychophysiological discomfort in situations where race is at issue. To other spectators, perhaps predominantly white spectators who have not engaged with race and their own racial identity (before), the metaphorical colour pink might have little to do with whiteness, but might be loaded with questions around gender and sexuality. Pink, of course, also is culturally coded as 'feminine' and 'homosexual' and adds to moments in which the performer's movements and sexual signification becomes queer.

The performer slowly, almost unnoticeably, switches between stern and erotic looks, introducing moments of homoeroticism, in connection to the intimate whispers on the phone we overhear in the audience. Most striking is the constant slow motion of his movements. This slowing down, paired with the lack of narration, offers spectators time and a position from which they can objectify the performer's body and scrutinise every twitching muscle, every inch of skin and drop of sweat, and each costume detail. More importantly, the slowness and dramaturgical minimalism (there is no other feature in the mise-en-scène, no further storytelling, no monologue or dialogue, no other voices) prompt spectators after a while to look for other forms of re/signification, creating new and different cognitive associations, imagining different images and affects. It prompts spectators to think or feel for 'what else is there', to contemplate and turn inward and self-reflect—or to turn towards to their (changing) relation to the performer and his embodiment, asking, perhaps, when and how are genuine moments of 'make believe' created, in which the white cis-male performer's body seems to 'authentically' represent and embody a Black hip-hop artist? In continuing this analysis, we might ask what the spectator does indeed see and experience when the performer fails to do so, and what is at stake in terms of cultural values and aesthetic norms?

How to position myself in relation to the performance? What are the performance's underlying aesthetic conventions and norms and how do they relate to my role in producing knowledge about it? My experience of the performance is predominantly influenced by my own positionality as white theatre academic who is, in particular, interested in critical whiteness and critical race theory. As my colleague Ann-Christine Simke has poignantly formulated for another performance analysis, "this seems a banal observation to make, especially in the field of performance analysis where a phenomenological approach that takes into account one's prior knowledge and experience seems to emphasise exactly that" (2021). However, the category whiteness still remains unmarked and invisible in many analyses and modes of looking in the theatre (and in the German theatre context at large; see also Marschall/Simke/Sharifi/Skwirblies 2023). It is this unmarked position of white subjectivity that creates a hypervisibility of Black bodies on stage as objects, while, at the same time, it negates their subjectivity. In the performance *Being Pink Ain't Easy*, however, the body that is being staged and objectified for the spectator's gaze is a white cis-male body, and the subject that is directing and choreographing this body is a Black woman, attempting to question—if not inverting—these subject/object positions in the momentary time and space of the theatre production. This deconstruction of whiteness might not be visible to all spectators at the same time; it requires is the spectators to unlearn the assumption that whiteness is universal.

How to ask the other question? What are the axes of power that are less obvious or visible? How empowering or oppressive is the performance in regard to identity factors such as gender, race, sexuality, class, caste, dis/ability, age, physical appearance and religion? If in this case, I see a performance that looks like it is addressing masculinity and is about patriarchal gender relations, I could further ask and continue to analyse, 'Where is the heterosexism in this?' 'Where is the racism in this?' 'Where are the class interests in this?' 'Where is the nationalism in this?' 'Where is the ableism in this?' 'Where is the ageism in this?'. I could pay particular attention to the image of the healthy, trained, muscular male body and what it 'shows does' on stage, what values and norms are reproduced or interrupted. I could pay particular attention to classism and the hybridising or clashing of aesthetic genres, in this case hip-hop, classical art, and theatre performance. I could also pay attention to the art of solo performance and question the claiming of space. I could further position myself in regard to the particular generation that the performance addresses.

Expanding the method

State-of-the-art research suggests that, despite Black and Global-Majority-led activism and subsequent institutional efforts, majority-white national theatre industries in Europe fail to demonstrate significant progress in achieving racial equality in their working structures as well as racial literacy in their predominantly white audiences (Simke/Marschall/Sharifi/Skwirblies 2023, Sharifi/Skwirblies 2022, Arora 2021, Snyder-Young 2020, Warner/Liepsch/Pees 2018, Bala 2017). However, a small but increasing number of dramaturges in their programming work take up the challenge to produce inclusive creative spaces with respect to race and other identities, and a small but increasing number of theatres, production platforms, and performance festivals echo mission statements such as the following by the Helsinki-based art institution UrbanApa:

> UrbanApa is an anti-racist and feminist community whose conception of art is diverse and inclusive. Artists working on our platforms come from various backgrounds and their art is diverse both in its aesthetics and ways of doing. However, we acknowledge that curating is never neutral. The curators' personal histories, encounters and experiences always affect their choices. (UrbanApa nd)

As a striking example, UrbanApa under the artistic direction of the Black Finnish performance-maker Sonya Lindfors organises performances, workshops, festivals, art incubators, and site-specific works, focussing on undoing implicit biases across the performing arts industries which create barriers to an inclusive, equitable, intersectional experience for artists and audiences alike.

With an eye to ongoing institutional transformations in the theatre and performing arts industries, we can expand this method from analysing a singular performance event to analysing production conditions, curatorial strategies, and institutional dramaturgy, i.e. from analysing what we are seeing performed and represented on stage to analysing a theatre institution's mission statement, policies, marketing strategies, and governance. Such an institutionally focused analysis might discuss what it means for an institution's artistic profile to actively put forward the idea of intersectionality and what relationships between a theatre institution and its audiences are implied therein (see also Marschall and Simke, forthcoming).

The US-American anthropologist, playwright, and dramaturge Dorinne Kondo has theorised that "race-making" takes place backstage in the creative process and through economic forces, institutional hierarchies, hiring practices, ideologies of artistic transcendence, and aesthetic form (2018, 29). Following Kondo, we can analyse how intersectional "race-making" takes place backstage through observing and mapping production conditions and rehearsal processes, as well as dramaturgical programming and the shaping of artistic profiles through institutional dramaturgy. How do theatre institutions understand the meanings of 'race', 'anti-racism', and 'intersectional theatre practice'? What strategies do they apply to build racial literacy among their personnel and audiences? What efforts do they take to centre Black and Global Majority staff, practices, and aesthetic forms? In what ways are they working with specific action plans and deliverables? How do they sustain their anti-racist work as a structural and long-term process? What artists are selected or self-selecting to submit to particular festivals, i.e. who is readily able to create and disseminate their work like that? What stylistic trends are happening in the vast theatre and performance scene, and whose select voices are privileged within those trends?

Suggestions for further reading

For readers interested in learning from Crenshaw about conducting intersectional analyses of contemporary political moments and policies in the US, I recommend listening to her podcast *Intersectionality Matters!* (2018).

For readers interested in storytelling and intersectionality, I recommend reading the novel *Identitti* (2022) by the cultural studies scholar Mithu Sanyal, which she has also adapted as script for the stage.

For readers interested in body-centred approaches to undoing the workings of racism on our perception, I recommend working with Resmaa Menakem's book *My Grandmother's Hands: Racialised Trauma and the Pathway to Mending Our Hearts and Bodies* (2017), in which he directly addresses different readerships, readers of colour, readers of colour working in the police force, white readers, and white readers working in the police force.

For readers interested in performance analyses that combine critical race theory and audience research methodologies, I highly recommend Dani Snyder-Young's research monograph *Privileged Spectatorship: Theatrical Interventions in White Supremacy* (2020).

For readers looking for cultural analyses that focus on critical race theory and cultural industry perspectives, including audience engagement policies and strategies, I highly recommend Anamik Saha's research monograph *Race and The Cultural Industries* (2017).

For white readers wanting and needing 'to start doing the work', I recommend Peggy McIntosh's short provocation "White Privilege: Unpacking the Invisible Knapsack" (1989) and the complementary performance lecture by Thomas DeFrantz/Slippage "White Privilege" (2018), as well as Gloria Wekker's groundbreaking monograph *White Innocence: Paradoxes of Colonialism and Race* (2016).

References

Arora, Swati. 2021. "A manifesto to decentre theatre and performance studies." *Studies in Theatre and Performance* 41 (1): 12–20. https://doi.org/10.1080/14682761.2021.1881730

Bala, Sruti. 2017. "Decolonising Theatre and Performance Studies. Tales from the Classroom." *Tijdschrift voor Genderstudies* 20 (3): 333–45. https://doi.org/10.5117/TVGN2017.3.BALA

Banerjee, Supurna, and Nandini Ghosh. 2018. "Introduction. Debating Intersectionalities: Challenges for a Methodological Framework." *South Asia Multidisciplinary Academic Journal*. http://journals.openedition.org/samaj/4745

Bogert, Kathrine van den, Elke Linders, and Nicole Sanches. 2019. "Toolbox Diversity in Education." Utrecht University. https://xerte.uu.nl/play.php?template_id=1127#page2

Carastathis, Anna. 2014. "The Concept of Intersectionality in Feminist Theory." *Philosophy Compass* 9 (5): 304–14. https://doi.org/10.1111/phc3.12129

Cho, Sumi, Kimberlé Williams Crenshaw, and Leslie McCall. 2013. "Toward a Field of Intersectionality Studies: Theory, Applications, and Praxis." *Signs: Journal of Women in Culture and Society* 38 (4): 785–810. https://doi.org/10.1086/669608

Combahee River Collective. 1982 [1977]. "A Black Feminist Statement." In *All the Women are White, All the Blacks are Men, But Some of Us Are Brave*, edited by Gloria Hull, Patricia Scott and Barbara Smith, 13–22. The Feminist Press.

Conquergood, Dwight. 2002. "Performance Studies: Interventions and Radical Research." *TDR/The Drama Review* 46 (2): 145–56.

Crenshaw, Kimberlé. 1989. "Demarginalizing the Intersection of Race and Sex: A Black Feminist Critique of Antidiscrimination Doctrine, Feminist Theory and Antiracist Politics." *University of Chicago Legal Forum* 1989, no.1, Article 8: 139–67. https://scholarship.law.columbia.edu/faculty_scholarship/3007/

Crenshaw, Kimberlé. 1991. "Mapping the Margins: Intersectionality, Identity Politics, and Violence against Women of Color." *Stanford Law Review* 43 (6): 1241–99. https://doi.org/10.2307/1229039

Crenshaw, Kimberlé. 2018–. *Intersectionality Matters!,* podcast, https://www.aapf.org/intersectionality-matters

DeFrantz, Thomas F./Slippage. 2018. "White Privilege" [lecture performance] *Theater* 48 (3): 23–37, https://doi.org/10.1215/01610775-7084669

Greer, Steve. 2019. "Intersectionality as Critical Practice." Lecture, Gilmorehill Theatre, University of Glasgow.

Hill Collins, Patricia, and Sirma Bilge. 2016. *Intersectionality*. Wiley.

Hill Collins, Patricia. 2000. *Black Feminist Thought: Knowledge, Consciousness, and the Politics of Empowerment*. Routledge.

Kondo, Dorinne. 2018. *Worldmaking: Race, Performance, and the Work of Creativity*. Duke University Press.

Liepsch, Elisa, Julian Warner, and Matthias Pees, eds. 2018. *Allianzen: Kritische Praxis an weißen Institutionen*. Transcript Verlag.

Lorde, Audre. 1984. *Sister Outsider: Essays and Speeches*. The Crossing Press.

Marschall, Anika, Ann-Christine Simke, Azadeh Sharifi, and Lisa Skwirblies. 2023. "Voicing Our Concerns: Attempts at Decentring German Theatre and Performance Studies." *Global Performance Studies* 5 (1–2): https://gps.psi-web.org/article/view/110

Marschall, Anika, and Ann-Christine Simke. Forthcoming. *Intersectional Theatre Practices*, Cambridge University Press.

Matsuda, Mari J. 1991. "Beside My Sister, Facing the Enemy: Legal Theory Out of Coalition." *Stanford Law Review* 43 (6): 1183–92. https://doi.org/10.2307/1229035

McIntosh, Peggy. 1989. "White Privilege: Unpacking the Invisible Knapsack." *Peace and Freedom Magazine* (July/August): 10–12.

Menakem, Resmaa. 2017. *My Grandmother's Hands: Racialized Trauma and the Pathway to Mending Our Hearts and Bodies*. Penguin.

Nash, Jennifer C.. 2019. *Black Feminism Reimagined: After Intersectionality*. Duke University Press.

Revolution or Nothing. 2020. "White Colleague Listen!* An Open Letter to UK Theatre, Dance and Performance Studies. https://medium.com/@revolutionornothing/white-colleague-listen-2d098d6a4a5d

Saha, Anamik. 2017. *Race and The Cultural Industries*. Polity Press.

Sanyal, Mithu. 2022. *Identitti*. Cossee.

Schechner, Richard. 2014. *Performance Studies: An Introduction*. Routledge.

Simke, Ann-Christine. 2021. "'Words Don't Come Easily': Reflections on Monster Truck's *Sorry* and Race in the German Theatre Landscape." Paper presentation at IFTR, 12 July 2021, Belgrade Serbia.

Snyder-Young, Dani. 2020. *Privileged Spectatorship: Theatrical Interventions in White Supremacy*. Northwestern University Press. https://doi.org/10.2307/j.ctv15vwkdw

UrbanApa. Nd. https://urbanapa.fi/info/

Wekker, Gloria. 2016. *White Innocence: Paradoxes of Colonialism and Race*. Duke University Press. https://doi.org/10.1215/9780822374565

14. Personal Narratives and Social Constructs through Autoethnography in Performance Studies

Wigbertson Julian Isenia

Summary

This chapter combines personal experience and cultural analysis through the method of autoethnography.[1] The author, a Black, non-binary, queer researcher, draws on their fieldwork in Curaçao to examine *Bos di Nos Pueblo*, a 2015 play by Teatro Kadaken. Through a combination of diary entries, observations, interviews, and self-reflection, the chapter explores how issues of sexuality, identity, and belonging are expressed through performance. The author reflects on their own position within the community and recounts moments of closeness and tension, including a public vote on same-sex marriage that highlighted their family's rejection and the resulting emotional distance this created. The chapter concludes by linking these descriptions of autoethnography to other contexts, such as a project in which undocumented migrants

---

1   A note from the editors: We would like to point out to readers that this book also includes another contribution on autoethnography as a method in performance research, titled "Autoethnography in Performance Studies: The Performativity of Queer Parenting." These contributions are different in subject matter, but they do also contain some overlaps, since they deal with the same methodological approach. We recommend reading these as paired contributions.

developed a bilingual theatre piece based on their lived experiences. Using these examples, the chapter shows how autoethnography can connect individual stories to broader social and political issues.

Introduction

Autoethnography is a fundamental method within qualitative research because it uniquely combines two methodologies: autobiography, which pertains to the writer's own life, and ethnography, which involves the scientific observation of cultures and people. It gives the researcher a dual role as both a reflective observer, who critically examines and interprets their own experiences, and an engaged participant, who actively takes part in and influences the cultural contexts being studied. Central to this approach is the use of the 'I' voice, which shifts from impersonal observation to research grounded in the author's personal experiences. This method avoids self-indulgence and allows the reader to gain knowledge through the author's insights, mistakes, and encounters with others. Autoethnography centres the author's cultural experience and shows how rituals, ceremonies, theatre productions, everyday interactions, protests, and sports create meaning through the author's experiences. Autoethnography is not a stand-alone method in my research; I combine it with performance analysis and interviews to enrich my findings. My identity as a Black, non-binary, queer individual is a central aspect that inherently shapes my research perspective. This positionality underscores a fundamental practice in autoethnography: all researchers should explicitly acknowledge their personal background and inherent biases. In this chapter, I leverage my fieldwork in Curaçao, focusing specifically on my interactions with the performance of *Bos di Nos Pueblo* (2016) by Teatro Kadaken to examine the recognition and inclusion of lesbian, gay, bisexual, transgender, and queer (LGBTQ) sexual rights and identities on the island.

Drawing on my experiences, I can address gaps in research about queer Caribbean people and gain insights that outsiders might not access. As an 'insider', I have access to information and interviews that would otherwise be inaccessible. This role allows a deeper understanding of customs, aided by pre-existing cultural and linguistic knowledge (Hayano 1979). While this stance foregrounds subjectivity in ethnographic work, it carries significant responsibility in gathering and interpreting information. Additionally, although I belong to the community, I acknowledge that I may not fully identify with every subgroup, and I embrace this productive tension in my research rather than suspending it.

Through a detailed account of my engagement with *Bos di Nos Pueblo*, this chapter underscores the potential of autoethnography as both a methodology and social inquiry. My approach is grounded in ethical commitments specific to autoethnography, including reflexively navigating my dual role as an insider and researcher, thoughtfully determining how much of my personal experience to disclose, and inviting community members to review and comment on my interpretations. I also attend to emotional care by acknowledging the personal risks of deep self-examination and remain sensitive to cultural nuances when representing shared experiences. By weaving these practices into every stage of the research, I demonstrate how autoethnography can be both rigorous and respectful of the community it explores. By applying this method to the study of theatre in Curaçao, I aim to examine how autoethnography can serve as a powerful tool for bridging the gap between individual lived experiences and collective cultural practices.

Context

Historically, the term 'autoethnography' has been applied in four overlapping contexts: a first-person account by a non-academic societal member; an ethnography of one's own culture by either academics or non-academics; an ethnography that incorporates significant autobiographical elements of the author; and a narrative with the researcher as the subject (Reed-Danahay 1997).

Through a detailed study of the Dani people in Irian Jaya, Karl G. Heider first applied the term 'autoethnography' in 1975 to describe a method in which local schoolchildren voiced their own daily activities, thereby providing an insider's perspective on cultural practice. This approach to autoethnography therefore aligns with the initial definition outlined above. Heider's study chose to address a simple question: 'What do people do?' His method involved compiling responses from

60 Dani schoolchildren and documenting 106 verbs reflective of their daily activities. It offered a glimpse into the Dani way of life by valuing mundane practices over sensational or conflict-driven aspects, and thus presenting a fuller representation of their existence. This method is crucial because it provides an insider's perspective on important or customary activities, which may differ from external assumptions.

Autoethnography, rooted in anthropology, prompts us to question our stereotypes of anthropology's early stages, including proto-anthropology and evolutionism, a Darwinian theory that ranks cultures from savagery to civilisation. In these formative years, anthropologists aimed to understand 'the other' by studying different societies and developing theories on the basis of their observations. However, this observational process was inherently unequal, with some findings inadvertently supporting colonial logic. Knowledge became a tool for conquest and subjugation and was used to exploit, manage, and "civilize" populations domestically and in the colonies (Pels and Salemink, 2000).

Building on critiques that emerged in the early twentieth century, Karl G. Heider's 1975 autoethnographic study of the Dani people marked a decisive break from the long-standing evolutionary paradigm. In those formative years, anthropologists sought to understand 'the other' through detached observation, yet their findings often served colonial agendas by casting such societies as inherently inferior.

This historical context highlights anthropology's contentious history and diverse debates, including questions about who writes or conducts research, the nature of knowledge, methods of acquisition, and the study's subjects. Traditional fieldwork, defined as the process of observing and collecting data about people over an extended period, often positions researchers as detached, objective outsiders who never reflect on their role. In response to these debates, anthropology has shifted towards a more inclusive approach, embracing diverse voices and experimental writing forms such as autobiography (Clifford and Marcus 1986; Behar and Gordon 1995; Ellis and Bochner 1996).

However, Heider's ethnographic approach is now relatively standardized and is absorbed into broader ethnographic fieldwork practices. Autoethnography differs by foregrounding the researcher's own cultural experience or by weaving substantial autobiographical elements into the ethnographic account. Autoethnography is not defined by a single research method or theory; instead, it is a comprehensive approach that shapes all aspects of fieldwork. These aspects of fieldwork include preparation, planning, site selection, data collection, analysis, interpretation, and dissemination.

Autoethnography combines autobiographical and ethnographic elements and grants the author a dual role: simultaneously engaging as a participant within the culture and as an observer analysing it. Autoethnography stands apart from autobiography, which typically recounts an individual's life story, centred on personal milestones and obstacles, mostly devoid of cultural or social analysis. In contrast, ethnography is a disciplined anthropological approach focused on the observational study of cultures over an extended period, with ethnographers typically acting as external observers of customs. By merging the introspection of autobiography with the analytical scope of ethnography, it delivers a comprehensive contextualized account. Autoethnography adds introspection to traditional research, blurring the line between researcher and subject. This approach encourages a more engaged stance. By using the 'I' voice, autoethnography moves away from the detached, objective stance of traditional ethnography.

Autoethnography has attracted a range of criticisms, some of which are well-founded and others less so. Critics rightly warn against self-indulgence, narcissism, and ethical pitfalls when personal narratives risk exploiting relationships or compromising confidentiality (Atkinson 2006; Sparkes 2000). Less warranted objections include claims that first-person writing lacks scientific rigour, that its findings cannot be generalised beyond the individual, that its non-replicability renders it unreliable, and that it breaches the necessary detachment of academic inquiry.

Autoethnography embeds personal narrative within systematic analysis, linking individual experience to broader sociocultural frameworks. It aims for analytical transferability rather than statistical generalisation, and ensures reliability through transparent methods, reflexive journals, thick descriptions (a detailed, context-rich account of behaviour), and clear analytic steps. Far from abandoning ethical standards, it governs self-disclosure with informed consent, anonymisation, and boundary-setting, thus maintaining both scholarly integrity and respectful engagement with participants. It is crucial to remain vigilant against the risk of self-indulgence. Peer review during publication and peer-to-peer discussions are essential to maintain rigor and balance in autoethnographic work.

Finally, I demonstrate how anthropology and performance studies approaches to autoethnography complement rather than conflict with each other. Anthropology has played a crucial role in developing the theoretical tools needed for autoethnographic work in performance studies. Anthropologists such as Dwight Conquergood and Victor Turner were instrumental in this development. Conquergood's integration of ethnographic methods with performance theory introduced the idea that culture is something people do, not just possess (1985; 1986). This performative turn allows for the study of individuals and their actions as performers and cultural performances. Turner's reframing of ethnography as a performance further expanded this approach (1986). He argued that ethnographers actively participate in the rituals and social interactions they study, paving the way for a more reflexive, self-aware practice.

This shift enabled autoethnography to foreground researchers' perspectives, as seen in the work of artist Michael Sakamoto and cultural studies scholar John Freeman. Sakamoto uses autoethnography to explore his performances, blending his Japanese heritage with his American upbringing and connecting with his cultural past through self-analysis (2022). Similarly, Freeman emphasized the importance of reflexivity and challenged the notion of a single authoritative voice (2015). This means that the way a person interprets their life story is influenced by a larger, shared sense of time and experience that exists beyond just the individual. In other words, while each person has a unique perspective, this perspective is shaped by broader, collective experiences and histories.

How to

Unlike other practice-based or ethnographic methods in performance studies, autoethnography foregrounds the researcher's own story as a site of analysis. It documents performances external to the self and interrogates how the act of 'performing' one's life, through a reflexive narrative, generates analytical insights. Although autoethnography does not adhere to a singular methodology, several essential aspects and considerations are crucial. Before beginning the study, the researcher should choose a topic, formulate a clear research question, and articulate the aims and relevance of the study. With these foundational elements in place, the first step is to explore a mix of qualitative methodologies to build a robust methodological framework. These methodologies could include journaling (keeping a daily journal throughout the fieldwork process), participant observation (immersing oneself in the community being studied, observing and participating in daily activities), and in-depth interviews (open-ended, conversational interviews with participants).

A literature review is conducted to identify key authors, understand the differences between these methodologies, and find research similar to yours in terms of topic, geography, experience level, or allocated time. This review will help you choose the best methods for your study and create an effective research design. Secondly, choose a study site or phenomenon that offers rich insights and personal interests.

Next, when you are in the field, embracing dual roles as both an observer and participant is crucial to capture detailed experiences and reflect on your role in the context. Focus on documenting personal experiences that stand out as significant, puzzling, or transformative, even if their full importance is not immediately apparent (Johnson 2021). This documentation is vital for later analysis and helps connect one's personal experiences to broader cultural contexts. By doing so, you will see individual stories as part of larger systems of power, revealing the political dimensions within personal narratives.

Fourthly, it is vital to reflect on your background and positionality during your fieldwork to understand the perspective you bring to your research, acknowledging biases and leveraging your skills to enrich your approach. Engage in systematic introspection and reflexivity to examine how your background influences your research and analysis. It is crucial to document your identities and others. Publicly declaring privilege can serve as a form of absolution that reifies hierarchies by centring, for example, whiteness, redeeming guilt and covertly asserting authority, thus underlining the need for reparative scholarship (Gani and Khan, 2024). This approach commences with recognising the complex nature of individual identities and understanding how race, gender, class, and sexuality, among other factors, shape experiences (Johnson 2021). These identities should not merely be listed but instead reflected upon to discern how the intersection of these identities influences your interactions with interlocutors and, consequently, your fieldwork. For example, by reflecting on moments of confusion, clarity, joy, and discomfort, researchers show readers how they arrived at insights and how specific interactions shaped their fieldwork.

Fifthly, ethical integrity should be ensured by prioritising consent, anonymity, and the careful handling of information, always considering the impact of your research. Ethical considerations are crucial in all forms of autoethnography, with a focus on respecting the autonomy, dignity, and privacy of everyone involved. This ethical approach should guide how you document and share your research journey, encouraging ongoing dialogue and reflection. Crafting effective autoethnography involves producing work that exemplifies high standards and demonstrating a deep understanding of autoethnographic practices that others can learn from or emulate (Salvo 2021). Additionally, good autoethnography should engage with and address injustices, acting as a form of storytelling that inspires change or raises awareness.

Sixthly, writing should be treated as a recursive process of inquiry and presentation, involving continuous reflection and revising to deepen analysis. Seventhly, ground your study in relevant scholarly works to add depth and situate your narrative within theoretical frameworks, while integrating your work into academic dialogues through a focused literature review and positioning your narrative within broader debates to address gaps. Consider how each theoretical framework aligns with your research objectives, aims, and questions.

Eighthly, share your findings with academic and broader audiences, articulating the significance of your work even for those unfamiliar with autoethnography. This is a formality, a responsibility, and a commitment that comes with conducting autoethnographic research. Sharing your findings can be accomplished through various means. Typically, academic findings are shared via conferences and academic publications. For junior researchers and Master's students, consider submitting to graduate-level journals with your supervisor's approval. Throughout the writing process, you can share your work with colleagues in peer groups and with your supervisor during meetings. It is beneficial to have a clear sense of your main observations, arguments, and conclusions, even if they are not perfect or are still half-baked, during these peer group meetings so that you can work them out together. Reviewing your 'raw' data together might be beneficial if you encounter difficulties. Be mindful that this process can consume a significant amount of meeting time, so reserve it for addressing particularly challenging issues.

Demonstration

This segment of autoethnography stems from my fieldwork in Curaçao, where I attended the performance of *Bos di Nos Pueblo* by Teatro Kadaken approximately eight times in 2016 and 2017. My repeated visits were motivated by a fictional segment of the performance in which, after a brief discussion, the audience voted on the legalisation of same-sex marriage, an issue that was not under consideration at that time. However, in 2024, the Dutch Supreme Court ruled that Curaçao, Aruba, and Sint Maarten must allow same-sex marriage. This ruling aligns Curaçao with other Dutch Caribbean islands such as Bonaire, St. Eustatius, and Saba, where same-sex marriage has been legal since 2012, because they are Dutch municipalities and follow Dutch laws. Same-sex marriage was thus not legal in Curaçao in 2016, and the discourse surrounding same-sex marriage gained momentum, especially since Bonaire, Saba, and Sint Eustatius legalized same-sex marriage. This discussion proved crucial to my PhD research on sexual citizenship, highlighting how LGBTQ individuals claim rights through cultural practices and revealing which rights remain denied to them. I chose this example for this chapter despite its imperfections and my own mistakes, hoping it will serve as a valuable learning model for the reader.

For the first step, the methodological framework, I chose archival research to connect contemporary events with historical events and to relate them to my experiences growing up on the island. Building on archive autoethnography (Escalante et al. 2025), walking dramaturg (Garcia 2018), and performative autoethnography (Radwan & Kariotis 2025), I adopted a reflexive, narrative-driven method that treats personal experience, by journaling (Hertoghs et al. 2024), observation, and interviews, as primary data rather than privileging staged events. I frame *Bos di Nos Pueblo* as both performance and rights-claiming. A focused keyword search ('autoethnography' × 'performance studies'; 'sexual citizenship' × 'Caribbean') yielded multiple results, from which I selected the most relevant. For the second step, a site of study or phenomenon, as a Black, non-binary, queer person from Curaçao, is chosen, and discussions about the LGBTQ community resonate with me on a personal level. Thus, when, during fieldwork, I encounter the all-too-common assertion, 'I have nothing against homosexuals, as long as they stay away from children'—a conflation of homosexuality with paedophilia—it becomes my task to explore my astonishment and hurt and to understand the 'other side.' I question what motivates someone to hold and express such a belief, and I contextualize both my response and that of others.

Other aspects of my life also proved relevant during my research. My relocation from Curaçao to the Netherlands, which occurred over 15 years ago, significantly influenced my perspective. It is also vital to acknowledge that I grew up in a middle-class environment. Returning as a PhD student only highlighted my middle-class background further, positioning me as a 'respected' individual approaching the topic of homosexuality with a so-called objective perspective. This position facilitated my research, granting me easier access at times due to my status as a respected PhD student, sometimes because of my Afro-Curaçaoan background, and at other times because I was part of the LGBTQ community. At other times, a white straight American female friend and colleague would gain access to information that I could not, likely because she was perceived as an outsider. This perception may have made it easier for individuals to share information anonymously or because they were not seen as having so-called insider bias. During fieldwork, I embraced dual roles as both an observer and participant (step 3), documenting significant moments.

Bos di Nos Pueblo is a production that explores the island's political culture, and the challenge young people face in balancing passive observation of party politics with developing their viewpoints. Following its premiere, the play was performed in secondary schools, accompanied by an educational program. It challenges the audience to express their thoughts, preferences, and beliefs, and to contemplate the changes they would make if they were politicians for a day. Through interactive engagement with the actors, the audience forms a new political party, *Bos di Nos Pueblo* (BDNP, The Voice of Our People), reflecting on difficult choices between reality and ideals, rules and freedom, and the tension between self-interest and the common good. The play features Christopher Barrow, Donovan Benett, Norma Cova, and Albert Schoobaar, with the script by Schoobaar and the direction by Silvia Andringa. Het Fonds Podiumkunsten, Stichting Doen, and the Prins Bernhard Cultuurfonds Caribisch Nederland supported the production.

Teatro Kadaken, under Albert Schoobaar's artistic direction, uses theatre to discuss complex themes in an accessible manner, encouraging young people and adults to engage with everyday dilemmas. The play, which premiered in November 2015, was performed in community centres and secondary schools, tackling the island's political culture and young people's political engagement through a narrative section, participatory segments, and a chorus alternating throughout the performance. It focuses on the populist politician Lucius Gomes Sr. and his party, Kòrsou Uni Emansipá (Curaçao United Emancipated), and humorously plays with the acronym 'KUE' for its double meaning in Papiamentu, the creole language of the island: it means 'to grab power', and it is also a vulgar expression with another meaning.

I first encountered this performance at a public show in Punda, the city centre of Curaçao. Despite the area's usual evening quietness, Casa Moderna, a temporary art space, was lively. While attending a meeting with my family, who reside in Curaçao, I was particularly interested in the pre-vote discussion on same-sex marriage. During the presentation, viewers collaborate to establish a new party platform for BDNP in response to or in alignment with the more conservative KUE. Topics vary, including the legalisation of soft drugs and lowering the voting age. These party positions are determined after a brief discussion, allowing viewers to present their arguments for or against each issue. A vote is subsequently conducted, and the option that receives the most votes secures its place in the party program.

Unexpectedly, my father and sister voted against same-sex marriage legalisation, provoking my astonishment and discomfort. My father and sister offered an uneasy laugh as they raised their hands, with my sister also shrugging her shoulders. I had never discussed this specific moment—the performance and the way they voted—with them afterward, likely because I had never openly shared it with anyone before. In this instance, my experience and autoethnography could have been effectively complemented by interviews to better and more accurately illustrate their perspectives. Interestingly, when I asked my sister about this moment nearly eight years later, an event that was vivid in my memory, she could not recall it. However, she mentioned that, given the opportunity today, she would vote in favour of same-sex marriage. This reflection over time, a crucial aspect of ethnography, also reveals how perspectives can change, both for my sister and myself.

This experience led me to view the performance several more times in various school settings, observing diverse student reactions. I observed the theatrical performance at a secondary school during the other seven instances. An unexpected yet significant issue was the dilapidated state of the gymnasium where the event occurred. The 2011 census revealed that the average monthly gross household income in that neighbourhood was below the island's average (3814 ANG versus 5332 ANG), with 11.6 percent of the housing in the area described as being in a poor to deplorable condition. Additionally, the school's proximity downwind from the local oil refinery necessitated frequent closure due to overpowering odours.

Moreover, 26.5 percent of households in the neighbourhood reported experiencing discomfort from air pollution in 2011—nearly double the island-wide average of 14.5 percent. This discrepancy starkly contrasted with the middle-class environment of the school I had attended, underlining the socioeconomic disparities encountered in my fieldwork. Be mindful, as self-indulgence is a potential risk here. While I continuously reflect on my background and positionality (step 4), I do so to clarify the context of my fieldwork and to ensure that readers understand the differences between myself as a researcher and my interlocutors, as well as the perspective from which I am writing.

In these sessions, the question of legalising same-sex marriage in Curaçao was revisited, with students often using graphic language to express their disapproval. Sexual metaphors were prevalent; for example, the saying 'a sword does not fit with another sword' implied the belief that compatibility requires opposites, echoing the concept of yin and yang or a man and a woman. The most common argument against same-sex marriage stemmed from biblical interpretation, suggesting that God created a man and a woman for each other, immutable and complementary. This argument underscores the conflation of sexuality and gender in the discourse, where a homosexual man is perceived as effeminate, and the roles of men and women are seen as fixed and divinely ordained.

A particularly distressing incident occurred during a discussion when a teacher singled out a timid, quiet schoolkid of ten who slouched and looked down. The teacher asked provocatively if this student would like to comment, insinuating his homosexuality by calling him 'mariku' (a derogatory term comparable to 'faggot'). My heart sank as the student stiffened, and neighbouring schoolchildren erupted in laughter, including from the teacher, unnoticed by other faculty members and performers. This moment could have been an opportunity to expand the scope of autoethnography by incorporating my own experiences as a queer person from Curaçao, combining my reaction (or lack thereof) and a subsequent conversation with the teacher. However, any potential discussion with the student was foreclosed by ethical considerations, as obtaining consent from the parents of a minor for research purposes was not feasible (step 5).

If I expand this autoethnography, I might explore the bystander effect further—the phenomenon where individuals freeze or refrain from acting upon witnessing harassment, an attack, or, in this case, bullying. Alternatively, I might examine how others behave within a classroom environment or during publicly accessible evening events, especially when they are part of a minority or hold minority viewpoints. Finally, I examined how the dynamics between the pupils and this teacher unfold in the classroom over an extended period beyond this single incident, which is characteristic of ethnographic research. Writing was a recursive process involving continuous reflection and revision to deepen my analysis and enhance the clarity of my narrative (step 6). I selected one or a combination of these focal points as my starting point and then proceed with steps 7 and 8.

In step 7, I positioned Curaçao as a bridge between North American/ European sexual-citizenship models and Caribbean LGBTQ scholarship, treating *Bos di Nos Pueblo* as a live rehearsal of rights-claiming and filling the empirical void on postcolonial theatre as sexual-citizenship practice.

In step 8, I convened peer-review loops, and the polished chapter appeared in this edited volume.

Expanding the method

In *Decolonizing Ethnography*, the authors Carolina Alonso Bejarano, Mirian A. Mijangos García, Daniel M. Goldstein, and Lucia López Juárez proposed an approach to social science research, especially with marginalized communities (Bejarano et al. 2019). Their research began in August 2011 with Bejarano and Goldstein's involvement at a New Jersey migrant worker centre, emphasising community engagement and volunteerism. The inclusion of Mijangos García and López Juárez, two immigrant workers from Latin America, in 2013 transformed the research into a collaborative project where autoethnography and activism became inseparable.

The authors gathered insights and embarked on a mission of empowerment by immersing themselves in the undocumented immigrant community. They informed participants of their legal rights and guided them to defend these rights in various contexts. Importantly, as indicated, two of the researchers were community members. This approach was a deliberate effort to address the challenges faced by individuals, who are often relegated to the shadows of society owing to their undocumented status. This approach expanded autoethnography by integrating the creation and performance of a play with a strong social justice component. The method employed created a bilingual play, *Sin Papeles, Sin Miedo* (Undocumented, Unafraid), following an autoethnographic study, documenting the challenges faced by undocumented individuals.

Fieldnotes acted as records of observations and were integrated as evocative narratives aimed at a wider audience. Through storytelling and song, these narratives sought to educate people about their rights, organise communities, and underscore the shared humanity of undocumented individuals. The authors also combined their observations with songwriting. This creative output was a strategic move to extend their research's impact beyond academic circles, engaging the public in a dialogue about the political and social issues immigrant workers face.

Suggestions for further reading

For a more extensive overview of the relationship between performance and autoethnography, see Norman Kent Denzin's *Performance Autoethnography: Critical Pedagogy and the Politics of Culture* (2003). The book provides a guide to performance autoethnography, covering its foundations, methods, and ethical considerations. For works that employ performance autoethnography in marginalized contexts, see Santhosh Chandrashekar (2017) for a decolonial perspective; Shelby Swafford (2022) for a feminist perspective; Julie-Ann Scott-Pollock, Frank Trimble, and Evan Scott-Pollock (2022) for a disability perspective; and Tony Adams and Stacy Holman Jones (2011) for queer perspectives.

References

Adams, Tony, and Stacy Holman Jones. 2011. "Telling Stories: Reflexivity, Queer Theory, and Autoethnography." *Cultural Studies ↔ Critical Methodologies* 11 (2): 108–16. https://doi.org/10.1177/1532708611401329

Atkinson, Paul. 2006. "Rescuing Autoethnography." *Journal of Contemporary Ethnography* 35 (4): 400–04. https://doi.org/10.1177/0891241606286980

Behar, Ruth, and Deborah Gordon, eds. 1995. *Women Writing Culture*. University of California Press. https://doi.org/10.1525/9780520916814

Bejarano, Carolina Alonso, Lucia López Juárez, Mirian A. Mijangos García, and Daniel M. Goldstein. 2019. *Decolonizing Ethnography: Undocumented Immigrants and New Directions in Social Science*. Duke University Press. https://doi.org/10.1215/9781478004547

Chandrashekar, Santhosh. 2017. "Not a Metaphor: Immigrant of Color Autoethnography as a Decolonial Move." *Cultural Studies ↔ Critical Methodologies* 18 (1): 72–79. https://doi.org/10.1177/1532708617728953

Clifford, James, and George E. Marcus, eds. 1986. *Writing Culture: The Poetics and Politics of Ethnography*. University of California Press.

Conquergood, Dwight. 1985. "Performing as a Moral Act: Ethical Dimensions of the Ethnography of Performance." *Literature and Performance* 5 (2): 1–13. https://doi.org/10.1080/10462938509391578

Conquergood, Dwight. 1986. "Performing Cultures: Ethnography, Epistemology, and Ethics." In *Miteinander sprechen und handeln: Festschrift für Hellmut Geissner*, edited by Hellmut Geissner and Edith Slembek, 55–66. Scriptor.

Denzin, Norman K. 2003. *Performance Autoethnography: Critical Pedagogy and the Politics of Culture*. Routledge.

Ellis, Carolyn, and Arthur Bochner, eds. 1996. *Composing Ethnography: Alternative Forms of Qualitative Writing*. Rowman Altamira.

Escalante, A, Brunton, JE, Nichols, AM & Kaell, H. 2025. ,Autoethnography of an archive in process', *Holotipus*, vol. VI, no. 1, pp. 1–7. https://doi.org/10.5281/zenodo.15023925

Freeman, John. 2015. *Remaking Memory: Autoethnography, Memoir and the Ethics of Self*. Libri Publishing Limited.

Gani, Jasmine K., and Rabea M. Khan. 2024. "Positionality Statements as a Function of Coloniality: Interrogating Reflexive Methodologies." *International Studies Quarterly* 68 (2): sqae038. https://doi.org/10.1093/isq/sqae038

Garcia, Giselle G. 2018. "The Walking Dramaturg: An Autoethnographic Methodology for Performance Documentation." *Proceedings from the Document Academy* 5 (1). https://doi.org/10.35492/docam/5/1/5

Hayano, David. 1979. "Auto-Ethnography: Paradigms, Problems, and Prospects." *Human Organization* 38 (1): 99–104. https://doi.org/10.17730/humo.38.1.u761n5601t4g318v

Hertoghs, Maja, Wigbertson Julian Isenia, Willemijn Krebbekx, and Rahil Roodsaz. 2024. "Recalcitrance and Feminist Pedagogy: Autoethnographic Reflections on Anti-Gender Mobilisations at the University." *Tijdschrift voor Genderstudies* 27 (2/3): 132–50.

Johnson, Amber. 2021. "How Intersectional Autoethnography Saved My Life: A Plea for Intersectional Inquiry." In *Handbook of Autoethnography*, edited by Tony E. Adams, Stacy Holman Jones, and Carolyn Ellis, 147–53. Routledge. https://doi.org/10.4324/9780429431760-15

Pels, Peter, and Oscar Salemink, eds. 2000. *Colonial Subjects: Essays on the Practical History of Anthropology*. University of Michigan Press.

Radwan, Jon, and Angela Kariotis. 2025. "Right Out the Gate: A Performative Auto-Ethnography on Race, Place, and Faith." *Religions* 16 (3): 281. https://doi.org/10.3390/rel16030281

Reed-Danahay, Deborah, ed. 1997. *Auto/ethnography: Rewriting the Self and the Social*. Routledge.

Sakamoto, Michael. 2022. *An Empty Room: Imagining Butoh and the Social Body in Crisis*. Wesleyan University Press.

Salvo, James. 2021. "Thinking Through Rejection: Reflections on Writing and Publishing Autoethnography." In *Handbook of Autoethnography*, edited by Tony E. Adams, Stacy Holman Jones, and Carolyn Ellis, 241–48. Routledge.

Scott-Pollock, Julie-Ann, Frank P. Trimble, and Evan Scott-Pollock. 2022. "Managing the Able-Bodied Gaze: The Complicated, Risky Decision to Perform Disabled Identity in Autoethnographic Performance." *Liminalities* 18 (2): 1–20.

Swafford, Shelby. 2022. "Embodying/Writing/Performing 'Women's Work': Pleasurable Tensions and Double Binds of Feminist Performative Autoethnography." *Text and Performance Quarterly* 42 (1): 1–16. https://doi.org/10.1080/10462937.2021.1993318

Turner, Victor. 1986. *The Anthropology of Performance*. PAJ Publications.

15. Autoethnography in Performance Studies: The Performativity of Queer Parenting

Fabiola Camuti and Annemijn van der Schaar

Summary

This chapter contributes to the discourse on methodologies in performance studies by examining autoethnography, highlighting its core elements, challenges, and applications.[1] This method involves reflexive engagement with personal experiences and ethnographic self-exploration within a socio-cultural context, blending the roles of researcher and subject to uncover insights into personal narratives. The study builds on the work of Carolyn Ellis, Arthur Bochner, Stacy Holman Jones, Heewon Chang, and Tony E. Adams. The chapter includes a case study titled 'Who's the real mother: the performativity of queer parenting'. Performativity, in this context, refers to how actions and behaviours shape and reveal identities and social roles. This case study provides insights into the practical application of the method and the use of a theoretical lens to analyse personal experiences. It

---

[1] A note from the editors: We would like to point out to readers that this book also includes another contribution on autoethnography as a method in performance research, titled "Personal Narratives and Social Constructs through Autoethnography in Performance Studies." These contributions are different in subject matter, but they do also contain some overlaps, since they deal with the same methodological approach. We recommend to read these as paired contributions.

demonstrates how identity construction, societal expectations, and role negotiations are embedded in queer parenting. Additionally, the chapter discusses a participatory theatre project with formerly incarcerated individuals, showcasing the versatility of autoethnography in diverse and interdisciplinary research settings. By integrating theoretical foundations, case studies, and practical examples, this chapter enhances understanding of autoethnography and its ability to reveal the intricate nature of lived experiences.

Introduction

This chapter embarks on a journey into the methodological landscape of autoethnography, a dynamic approach increasingly embraced across various disciplines, including but not limited to theatre, dance, and performance studies. As scholars and practitioners seek nuanced, critical, and conscious ways to engage with complex questions, autoethnography emerges as a powerful tool, offering a blend of reflexivity, subjectivity, and ethnographic inquiry (Adams, Ellis, and Holman Jones 2022). Autoethnography, at its essence, is a methodological approach that intertwines personal narrative with ethnographic exploration, inviting researchers to delve into the depths of their own lived experiences within broader socio-cultural contexts. It blurs the traditional boundaries between researcher and subject, positioning the researcher as both the instrument and the interpreter of their own narrative. In this way, it directly challenges the norms of traditional research practices and knowledge production and dissemination. This method not only enriches scholarly inquiry but also offers a means of amplifying marginalised voices and revealing the intricacies of human experience.

In recent years, autoethnography has gained traction across diverse disciplines, owing its flexibility and adaptability to various research paradigms. It is particularly suitable for inter- and transdisciplinary approaches, where complex questions demand multifaceted perspectives and methodologies.

Throughout this chapter, we illustrate the practical application of autoethnography through an ongoing project serving as our case study: 'Who's the real mother? The performativity of queer parenting.' In this ongoing study, we embark on an autoethnographic exploration of the complexities surrounding the experience of becoming two mothers within a queer family structure. We work with autoethnography as research method and employ the notion of performativity as a theoretical lens to analyse our journey.

The concept of performativity, often associated with gender studies and linguistic philosophy, posits that actions not only reflect existing norms and values but also actively create and reinforce them through repetition and societal acceptance. In this context, performativity refers to the idea that individuals 'perform' their identities, roles, and beliefs in ways that contribute to the continuous construction and reinforcement of social norms and structures. Performativity in gender and feminist studies refers to the concept that gender is a social construct that is continually performed and reinforced through actions, behaviours, and language, rather than being a fixed or inherent quality (Butler 1990; Parker and Sedgewick 1996).

By immersing ourselves in the lived experiences of queer parenthood, we unravel the layers of identity negotiation, societal expectations, and familial dynamics inherent in this unique context. By examining our experiences through the concept of performativity, we aim to show how queer parenting navigates a delicate balance. It both reinforces societal norms and challenges them, creating new possibilities by performing different kinds of acts.

Furthermore, this chapter wants to offer the possibility of expanding the method of autoethnography by examining its potential within community-based theatre projects. We explore how autoethnography can serve as a methodological anchor for collaborative artistic endeavours, particularly those involving marginalised communities. By presenting examples stemming from a participatory theatre experience with formerly incarcerated individuals, we demonstrate how autoethnography can foster meaningful engagement, empowerment, and transformation. By centering the voices and narratives of participants and by including the researchers as part of the whole process, autoethnography amplifies the agency of marginalised communities, fosters a process of experience articulation rather than representation, and enriches the artistic process with authenticity (Camuti 2022).

In weaving together theoretical foundations, practical insights, and experiential narratives, this chapter contributes to the ongoing dialogue on autoethnography in performance studies. By contextualising it, elucidating its core principles, showcasing its application in diverse contexts, and envisioning its potential in interdisciplinary research, we aim to foster a deeper understanding of autoethnography's capacity to unveil the performative essence of lived experiences. Through this exploration, we invite scholars, practitioners, and artists alike to embrace autoethnography as a transformative methodological tool, capable of navigating the complex balance between subjectivity, empathy, rigor, and creativity.

Context

Understanding the roots and underpinnings of autoethnography requires exploring its historical development and its response to broader philosophical shifts within research paradigms and society. The origins of autoethnography date back to the 1970s, when anthropologist Karl Heider (1975) introduced the term to describe a type of cultural study where insiders provide accounts of their own culture (Adams, Holman Jones, and Ellis 2015, 16). In the 1980s, fields such as sociology, anthropology, and communication began to embrace personal narrative and reflexivity in research. This marked a significant shift away from the traditional objectivity paradigm, recognising the inseparable relationship between researcher and research subject (Adams, Holman Jones, and Ellis 2015, 16). Strongly inspired by postmodernism—a philosophical movement characterised by scepticism towards traditional notions of truth, objectivity, and knowledge—scholars began advocating for relativism and rejecting absolutism (Basharat and Shaukat 2019). Scholars started to grapple with the limitations of traditional research methodologies, prompting critical introspection into the ontological, epistemological, and axiological limitations of conventional research methodologies (Ellis and Bochner 2000).[2] As a result, a new approach emerged, with autoethnography offering a compelling alternative that embraces subjectivity, emotionality, and the rich complexities of human experience. By the end of the decade, autoethnography was

---

2   Ontology refers to the study into the nature of reality and our understanding of it; epistemology examines the nature and acquisition of knowledge; while axiology focuses on the study of values.

being used to explore the relationship between introspective, personally engaged selves and cultural phenomena (Adams, Holman Jones, and Ellis 2015, 16), also integrating a range of creative arts genres, such as autobiography, fiction, poetry, and performance arts, to present findings and democratise scholarship (Lapadat 2017). This rise in autoethnography as a methodology has both contributed to and resulted from the reform of qualitative inquiry (Denzin and Lincoln 2005).

In the following paragraphs, we highlight some of the defining characteristics of this reform and how they differ from traditional research methods. Our focus is on key changes: autoethnography prioritises subjectivity, proximity, diversity, and reflexivity over the traditional emphasis on objectivity, distance, and neutrality (Adams, Holman Jones, and Ellis 2015).

Firstly, subjectivity in autoethnography acknowledges that researchers' biases and perspectives shape their work, recognising that personal experiences influence the research process (Ellis and Bochner 2000). Unlike traditional research, which aims for an objective and neutral stance, autoethnography posits that true objectivity is unattainable, as researchers' identities and backgrounds inevitably influence their interpretations, methodologies, and conclusions (Ellis, Adams, and Bochner 2011). Autoethnography assumes research is inherently subjective.

Secondly, proximity in autoethnography emphasises the close relationship between researchers and their subjects. While traditional methods often strive for distance to maintain neutrality, autoethnography values personal involvement and engagement, arguing that such proximity allows for a deeper, more nuanced understanding of cultural phenomena.

Thirdly, diversity is central to autoethnography. Traditional research has often centred on perspectives rooted in norms associated with whiteness, maleness, heterosexuality, affluence, Christianity, and able-bodiedness. Autoethnography challenges this by valuing the perspectives of marginalised groups, including a wider range of worldviews, values, and beliefs (Adams, Holman Jones, and Ellis 2015). By embracing diverse perspectives based on race, gender, sexuality, age, dis/ability, socio-economic status, education, and religion, autoethnography offers a more inclusive and nuanced understanding of human phenomena.

Finally, reflexivity is crucial in autoethnography. Reflexivity involves researchers continually examining their own positionality, biases, and assumptions throughout the research process (Ellis, Adams, and Bochner 2011). Traditional methods often prioritise an impersonal stance for neutrality, whereas autoethnographers actively question their beliefs and privileges to understand how these shape their interpretations. Reflexivity ensures that researchers integrate self-awareness into their work, acknowledging their influence on the research.

As part of our overview of the methodology's context, it is also important to address key criticisms. As both a form of ethnography and autobiographical research, autoethnography faces substantial critique. When evaluated within the framework of ethnography, it is often criticised for perceived deficiencies in rigor, objectivity, and theoretical and analytical robustness. Concerns regarding subjectivity, lack of objectivity, and challenges related to generalisability, representativeness, validity, and reliability of data and interpretations are prevalent (Chang 2022; Ellis 2009; Ellis, Adams, and Bochner 2011; Lapadat 2017). Critics also characterise autoethnography as overly emotional, aesthetic, and therapeutic (Chang 2022; Ellis 2009; Ellis, Adams, and Bochner 2011). Emphasis on personal experiences is sometimes seen as biased, excessively subjective, self-indulgent, and narcissistic (Anderson 2006; Ellis, Adams, and Bochner 2011; Johnson-Bailey 2021; Lapadat 2017). From an autobiographical standpoint, autoethnography faces criticism for prioritising scientific legitimacy over artistic creativity and being inadequately aesthetic, despite its goal of bridging the art-science divide by integrating both elements (Ellis, Adams, and Bochner 2011). The autoethnographic approach, drawing on creative arts genres for scientific research (Lapadat 2017), challenges the 'science-art binary'— the idea that scientific methods are valued for their objectivity, rigor, and generalisability, while artistic methods are appreciated for their creativity, emotional depth, and subjective insight, making them seemingly incompatible. The emphasis on subjectivity, diversity, and reflexivity in autoethnography seeks to move beyond this binary. Additionally, there are discussions around the need for transparency and accountability in autoethnographic research, highlighting the necessity for clear and comprehensive documentation to uphold credibility and ethical integrity (Lapadat 2017). In the subsequent section of this chapter, we explore quality criteria that autoethnographers utilise to address these criticisms.

How to

To unpack how to work with autoethnography as a method, it is first essential to define its three core components: auto, ethno, and graphy (Adams, Ellis, and Holman Jones 2022, 3–5).

Auto: Self-reflection and reflexivity

The 'auto' component emphasises self-reflection and autobiographical content. This process includes employing significant artifacts and memory work to investigate the intersection of personal histories and cultural contexts. It is through articulating their positionality that researchers reveal how their social, cultural, and personal contexts influence their interpretations.

Ethno: Connecting self and social

The 'ethno' element links the self to the social world. Autoethnographers critically explore how personal experiences are intertwined with cultural norms and expectations. By combining rigorous self-reflection with a broader cultural and social analysis, researchers identify and examine the intersections between individual lives and broader societal structures.

Graphy: Representation and description

The 'graphy' component involves describing and representing cultural experiences. This includes various narrative forms and writing styles, such as poetry and creative writing, to convey personal experiences. The aim is to create rich, evocative accounts that resonate with both personal and cultural significance.

So, how do we collect, analyse, and write autoethnography?

Autoethnography starts with picking a research focus, which is a crucial step. Many autoethnographies dive into personal and emotional topics. These might include family relationships, health issues, or experiences with trauma, allowing for a deep and authentic exploration. The power of autoethnography lies in its emotional engagement. Personal topics are effective because researchers have direct access to their own experiences. The key is to not just tell personal stories but also to analyse and interpret them within their cultural and social contexts (Chang 2008, 49–54).

- Tip: Choose personally meaningful topics. Be ready to explore memories and details deeply and connect these to the wider sociocultural environment. This ensures that the research is insightful and turns personal experiences into valuable academic work.

Once you have established a focus and understand why this is relevant, you can move to the data collection phase. Autoethnography involves collecting various forms of data, such as drawings of significant places, inventories of people and artifacts, event chronicles, personal journals, field notes, letters, and photographs. Self-observation, both introspective and interactive, is crucial.

When working with autoethnography, be prepared to gather a large amount of material. If your research is based on personal memories of past events, you will likely write, draw, and collect photos or videos from that time. If your research is ongoing, you will create an archive of newly generated material. This phase can be tricky. How do you know which materials to select? How do you avoid becoming overwhelmed?

- Tips: When researching the past, start by making a timeline of the main events you plan to study. Sketch out the highlights you need to focus on. From there, select existing material (like photos and letters) or create new material based on memory recollection. For ongoing autoethnographic processes, use field journals. Include tags such as date, location, and people. Add a visual tag for photos of specific moments.

Since autoethnographic research often involves personal memories, it is possible to consider using interviews to supplement data. Interviews can offer external perspectives and validate, enhance, or question internal data. Ellis (2004) discusses various interview formats.

- Tip: You might interview people directly involved in relevant events or ask a fellow researcher to interview you to discuss a specific topic.

Due to potential researcher-participant involvement, face-to-face interviews might be challenging and could hinder open exchanges, making alternative narratives like emails, surveys, or questionnaires preferable (Chang 2008, 104–06).

Data analysis and interpretation

Data analysis in autoethnography intertwines with data collection. During data collection, researchers continually evaluate experiences against their research focus, a process that helps shape and refine the analysis criteria (Chang 2008, 131). The following guidelines provide a framework outlining steps involved in autoethnographic data analysis.

1. Identify themes and apply codes: review the collected material multiple times and annotate it with 'themes' or 'codes'. These codes and themes help systematically organise and categorise your data. Be aware that you will frequently revise and refine these codes. That is all part of the process. Coding can be done in many ways, for example based on the emotions recalled or experienced by someone (emotion coding), based on the basic topic of a part of the data (descriptive coding), based on quotes of participants (in vivo coding).[3]

2. Recognise patterns: notice any patterns in behaviours, thoughts, or events. Patterns might reveal deeper insights into the cultural and social contexts you are studying.

3. Connect with others and with contexts: relate your personal experiences to broader social contexts and other people's experiences. This step helps you understand how individual experiences reflect larger societal patterns.

4. Relate data to theory: theoretical concepts and theories are relevant and important within autoethnography. We

---

[3] See, for more information on the coding process, Saldaña, Johnny. 2016. *The Coding Manual for Qualitative Researchers*. Thousand Oaks: Sage.

advise (and challenge) you to combine the processes of personal narrativisation with theoretical exploration, as they complement and deepen one another. Your research topic has likely been explored before, and engaging with theories and concepts from scholars who have studies similar issues can significantly enhance your process.

5. Iterate and refine: as you delve deeper into your data, new themes or patterns may emerge, requiring you to adjust your focus and analysis methods. Refining and rephrasing themes, patterns, and theoretical connections to ensure they accurately capture the essence of your findings is a crucial aspect of the research process.

Data management

Data management encompasses the systematic organisation, storage, and governance of data to ensure its accuracy, accessibility, and security throughout its lifecycle. In autoethnography, this process connects data collection with analysis and interpretation, forming a dynamic process (Chang 2008, 122). This process often involves multiple iterative cycles, where you reassess and adjust your management approach based on the data analysis. Here is a practical approach to managing your data effectively:

1. Organise and classify your data: Chang (2008, 116–19) suggests a systematic process for organising and refining your data. Start by classifying your data in various ways:
    a. Time-Related: when was the data collected or when did the event occur?
    b. Person-Related: who provided the data? Who was involved?
    c. Object-Related: what type of data are you using (e.g. drawings, photos, interviews)?
    d. Spatial-Related: where did the event happen or where was the data collected?

2. Refine your data: focus your data collection by trimming redundant and less important data and expanding on the relevant and significant data (Chang 2008, 119). This step helps uncover any gaps in your data and guides you on what further data you might need to collect or how to interpret the existing data.
3. Represent your findings: in the final phase, represent your experiences, reflections, and socio-cultural contexts graphically. This could involve creating charts, diagrams, or other visual aids that help illustrate your findings clearly.

Writing styles

Autoethnographic writing can take various forms. Chang (2008, 2022) identifies five distinct writing styles. Additionally, we have introduced a sixth option, commonly used for more embodied dissemination strategies:

1. Imaginative-Creative: incorporates poetry and performative dialogues, departing from traditional scholarly discourse.
2. Confessional-Emotive: personal and emotional, seeking direct interaction with the reader.
3. Descriptive-Realistic: provides rich, vivid details of experiences.
4. Analytical-Interpretative: engages with academic discourse, incorporating conceptual literature for socio-critical analysis.
5. Critical-Provocative: aims to provoke criticism and advocate for transformation through personal accounts.
6. Filmic-Intersubjective: expands the concept of writing to a more visual form. Here mainly photos, audio, and video recordings are used, advocating for alternative and more embodied knowledge dissemination strategies.

There are no strict rules regarding the blending of these styles, allowing for creative and flexible representations in autoethnography.

Finally, it is important to note that autoethnography can be carried out either individually or collaboratively, and this choice significantly influences each phase described earlier. In collaborative autoethnography, it is essential to clearly define roles and agree upon the processes for data collection, management, and interpretation.

Evaluation and ethics

Autoethnographic research requires careful consideration of evaluation criteria and ethical principles. Unlike traditional research, autoethnography does not adhere to standard measures of reliability, generalisability, and validity (Ellis, Adams, and Bochner 2011). Attempting to delineate a definitive set of criteria can seem futile, as they are inherently influenced by political dynamics and power structures (Adams, Holman Jones, and Ellis 2015; Sparkes 2022). However, here is how you can navigate these aspects by following some practical tips:

1. From reliability to credibility: ensure your writing is authentic and believable. This means being honest about your experiences and reflecting on them deeply (Guba and Lincoln, 1989).

2. From validity to verisimilitude: focus on making your narrative coherent and immersive. Your story should engage readers and help them understand your perspective.

3. From generalisability to relatability and relevance: consider how your experiences might resonate with others. The goal is for readers to see connections between your narrative and broader cultural contexts (Ellis, Adams, and Bochner 2011).

Ethical awareness is also crucial in autoethnography. Ethical considerations integral to autoethnography encompass the delicate balance between personal narratives and methodological rigor, navigating ethical dilemmas in disclosure, power dynamics, and safeguarding participant privacy. Here are key guidelines:

1. Mitigate harm: always consider the potential impact of your writing on yourself and others involved.

2. Informed consent: make sure you have permission from anyone you write about and keep them informed throughout your research.

3. Ongoing consent: continuously check in with participants to ensure they are comfortable with your representations of their stories.
4. Reflect on biases: be aware of your own biases and positionality. Reflect on how your background influences your writing (Lapadat 2017).
5. Member checks: share your work with participants to confirm accuracy and representation (Adams 2008; Tullis 2022).
6. Respectful representation: write about yourself and others with respect, acknowledging the lasting impact of your published work.

By following these tips and maintaining a reflective and ethical approach, you can ensure that your autoethnographic research is both rigorous and respectful.

Demonstration | Who's the real mother: the performativity of queer parenting

Fabiola: I was working on my laptop in the living room when she called me. She always does at the end of her therapy sessions. This time after seeing her new therapist. 'How was it?'—I asked. 'Ok, I think'—she replied. She did not seem really convinced, so I asked one more time, 'but how did it go?' 'I'm not sure there was a real click.' She said they talked about her family, about us. And at some point, she got asked a question and was not sure how to read into that. 'Wie is de echte moeder?' Who is the real mother? The therapist asked referring to Enea, our kid. I actually was quite sure about how to read into that. I was pissed, annoyed, and sad. And guilty. That is how I felt. Because this was the cold reality shower that reminded me of the impossibility to escape the look of people on our family. That difference that society pushes and will keep on pushing onto us. One is the real mother. The other is not. Then she said the therapist mentioned something about a father figure, about Freud (of course). I was too furious to know exactly the words she used. 'I'm sorry'—I remember saying.

Annemijn: There I was, sitting in front of yet another therapist. We discussed Enea. A subject both easy and vulnerable. Easy because he feels like the most self-evident part of my life. Vulnerable due to my fear of making mistakes and proving myself as the non-biological mother.

'Who's the real mother?' Though familiar, the question stung deeply. Feeling neither safe nor comfortable, I answered, 'My wife, Fabi, carried him'. The follow-up question 'Do you have a father figure for him?' unsettled and confused me. In a flurry of thoughts, I rationalised my fear, wondering if I'd missed any studies on this matter. I felt so unsafe I just wanted the conversation to stop, while being annoyed with my compliance in her narrative. I even nodded along as she referenced Freud and the importance of the father figure for every child, telling me to find one for our son. Right after the session, I called Fabi in a confused state, knowing this conversation was far from over.

The paragraphs above provide brief, summarised accounts in our own words, highlighting a pivotal moment in our autoethnographic case study: the trigger that initiated our research journey on performativity in becoming two mothers. It was an aha-moment, revealing how we constantly enact our queer performativity in society and continuously navigate our interactions with the world, others, and even with Enea. This process profoundly impacts us and our relationships. The short demonstration in this chapter offers a glimpse into our ongoing autoethnography, aiming to answer the research question: how do queer mothers experience and respond to rhetorical messages that reinforce heteronormativity in parenting?

We use the concept of 'performativity'—referring to how individuals and groups enact actions or behaviours that actively shape and construct social reality, encompassing aspects of identity and power dynamics—as our theoretical lens to analyse our direct experiences and responses.

For our study, we employ an unmediated co-constructed narrative approach (Ellis 2004, 75), which facilitates individual reflection followed by collaborative synthesis. As our research is ongoing and we continue to collect data, we present a portion of our autoethnography alongside current data, recognising that it will evolve. We blend confessional-emotive and analytical-interpretative writing styles. After initiating this demonstration with examples from our individual reflections, we now present a collaboratively constructed narrative and analysis based on another shared experience.

Co-constructed narrative

In line at the airport, excitement and anxiety mixed as we prepared for our first family trip. Enea, our 10-month-old son, was nestled against Fabiola's chest in the baby carrier. But our joy turned to tension when the officer asked, 'Who is the baby's mother?' Initially relieved to see a woman conducting the check, Fabiola calmly responded, 'We both are', as Ann's stress grew. 'Yes, I understand, but who is the mother?' Ann pointed out Enea's passport, insisting it shouldn't matter since Enea and Fabiola share the same last name. It did matter and we had to explain the legal construction of our family and show the adoption papers.[4] Fabi was trying to sooth an upset Enea, while her stomach tightened with familiar unease with the fact that affirming her own maternal status implicitly invalidated Ann's role. Fabiola reluctantly showed the officer Enea's birth certificate and adoption papers, feeling detached from her actions. Ann felt the sting of justifying her motherhood, facing questions on her legitimacy. She was angered and considered refusing but feared the officer's power and consequences. It felt unjust, her bond reduced to paperwork, humiliated by the validation needed. Not wanting to cause a scene, we complied without further questions.

Finally passing the checkpoint, hand in hand, the incident left us shaken. We knew such challenges would arise, but the emotional toll was nonetheless significant. Ann harboured lingering anger, not just towards the officer but the systemic issues. Constantly proving her motherhood was painful, a reminder of queer parenting's complexities. Luckily, we have each other.

---

4   In The Netherlands, where we live and where Enea was born, same-sex couples can legally be registered as parents through a simple declaration at the city hall. However, adoption provides stronger legal standing than registration alone. Following our lawyer's advice, we decided that Annemijn should adopt Enea. Initially, Enea was registered with only one parent, listing Fabiola as the single mother on the birth certificate. After the legally required waiting period, the adoption was confirmed, and the city hall issued a new birth certificate listing both parents, granting us full parental rights. Fabiola is Italian, giving Enea dual nationality and passports. Despite presenting the adoption papers issued by a Dutch courthouse, Italy still does not recognise Annemijn as a parent. Officials have refused to do so, and Enea is officially registered in Italy as only Fabiola's child. The adoption procedure and the legal complications with Italy are integral parts of our ongoing study.

Analysis

Judith Butler (1988) introduced the idea of performativity in their work, emphasising that gender identity is constructed through repeated performances that adhere to societal norms and expectations. This perspective challenges traditional notions of gender as a binary and stable category, highlighting the fluid and dynamic nature of gender expression (Butler 1990). Moving also beyond gender, performativity entails examining how individuals and groups enact and embody social roles, norms, and expectations in their daily interactions, thus shaping and reinforcing social structures and hierarchies.

What Butler writes about gender can to some extent be applied to parenting. In our interpretation, parenting, much like gender in Butler's words, "is thus a construction that regularly conceals its genesis" (Butler 1990, 273). In other words, parenting, in the way we read it and live through it, is closely linked to gender, inasmuch as it is constructed through the regular enactment of performative acts and repetitions of norms. This creates a uniformity that strongly shapes the binary conception of masculinity/femininity and the related father/mother roles.

In our narrative, the airport interaction exemplifies these dynamics. The officer's insistence on identifying "the baby's mother" highlights the societal expectation of a singular, identifiable mother, a role traditionally performed by the primary caregiver. Fabiola's response, "We both are", challenges this expectation by presenting a dual-motherhood scenario, which deviates from conventional norms. However, the officer's follow-up question underscores the strength of traditional norms, compelling us to re-enact these norms to some degree.

Queer parenting, as Lara McKenzie (2022) notes, involves redefining traditional notions of motherhood and fatherhood, embracing diverse performances that transcend conventional gender norms. Our need to present adoption papers and explain our family structure underscores the gap between legal recognition and societal acceptance. This bureaucratic requirement enforces a normative framework where non-traditional families must justify their legitimacy, indirectly reiterating traditional binary roles.

The emotional toll described in our narrative, with Fabiola's discomfort and Annemijn's anger, reflects the societal pressure to conform to traditional parenting norms. The performative act of showing legal documents both reaffirms and challenges the heteronormative structure—reaffirming by complying with the demand for proof yet challenging by asserting a non-traditional family structure within that proof.

Our experience at the airport encapsulates broader societal dynamics, where explaining and validating our family structure becomes an unconscious performance aimed at achieving acceptance and belonging within a heteronormative society. This act of seeking to belong, while reinforcing the norms we aim to challenge, can also be seen as a performative act in itself. Furthermore, each assertion of dual motherhood is a subversive act that not only resists existing norms but also represents a gradual reshaping of societal expectations around gender and parenting. Thus, the performance of our family identity contributes to the broader process of societal transformation, challenging and redefining traditional narratives in the process.

Expanding the method

Above, we presented an example of a study that utilised autoethnography from its inception. Now, I [Fabiola] will illustrate how autoethnography can be integrated into an existing project, drawing on my own experience in a participatory theatre project with formerly incarcerated people. Initially, autoethnography was not part of our study design but proved beneficial in addressing criticalities during the research.

For many years, I have worked as a theatre maker in various participatory theatre projects, from schools to hospitals, engaging with different communities. However, things changed when I undertook a project as both an artist and researcher. At a challenging juncture, I had to acknowledge my dual role and my own position within the work rather than solely focusing on 'studying the other'.

Context

Between 2013 and 2016, I participated in research projects funded by Sapienza University of Rome, fostering collaboration between the humanities and natural sciences. My former department, the Department of Art History and Performing Arts, partnered with the Department of Physiology and Pharmacology "Vittorio Erspamer" to explore the concept of "Theatre as Enriched Environment".[5] This initiative aimed to engage individuals who were formerly incarcerated or on probation through theatre-based methodologies in their post-release environments. Our project involved interdisciplinary collaboration with social scientists from the University of Pisa and experienced theatre professionals with over a decade of experience in Rome's Rebibbia prison. Our research focused on demonstrating how theatre practices could enrich and improve the quality of life for formerly incarcerated individuals. The artistic practice centred on a theatre laboratory designed to build a performance, involving participants in an intensive creative process. The final performance, staged in various theatres, including Teatro Argentina in Rome, showcased the participants' work, blending personal narratives with theatrical expression.

The trigger moment

Initially, our theoretical goals were aligned, but methodological and epistemological differences posed challenges. Despite prison theatre's global recognition for its artistic and social impact (McAvinchey 2011), our physiology colleagues needed quantitative data to measure its benefits. We devised an evaluation protocol that included both quantitative and qualitative approaches: observational activities documented through

---

5   Environmental enrichment refers to social, mental, and physical stimulation that positively affects brain plasticity and function. The human brain can modify neural connections and functions with specific stimulation. Theatre practices, with their enhanced social interactions and sensory inputs, can increase brain plasticity and cognitive performance. Due to its embodied nature, theatre fosters social interactions through physical and mental stimulation, potentially enriching impoverished environments and improving participants' quality of life (Van Praag. Kempermann, and Gage 2000; Sale 2016).

reports and diaries, high-resolution electroencephalography (EEG) to assess emotional responses, and standardised psychological tests (PGWBI and MMSE).

With the groundwork laid, the project could finally begin. Fully immersed in its development—participating, recording sessions, and keeping diaries to compile a comprehensive report—I nearly overlooked the evaluation protocol of our research project. When I explained the procedure to the participants, they not only refused to perform any tests but also confused the EEG with electroshock therapy. They felt we intended to subject them to experimentation, compromising the mutual trust built through theatrical exercises and improvisations. This perception risked reducing them back to inmates and us to researchers exploiting them.

To preserve trust and address concerns, we consulted with the project leader and theatre director, deciding to abandon the quantitative evaluation protocol and adopt an ethnographic approach. This approach focused on observation, including diaries, interviews, and recordings, aligning more closely with the participatory nature of the theatre project. Typically, an observer is seen as someone detached from the activity, perhaps sitting quietly in a corner, a role common in ethnographic work. However, during our days at Teatro Abarico in Rome's San Lorenzo neighbourhood, it became clear to me that remaining 'outside' the activity was impossible. In this kind of theatrical intervention, the dichotomy of 'us' and 'you' dissolves immediately. In a complex web of relationships—participants, facilitators, professional actors, directors, students, and researchers—we all slowly and subtly became part of a world yet to be discovered. Each day, as sessions began, everyone entered the room ready to embrace a role that was never isolated but always part of the collective. This collective involvement broke down the 'us' and 'them' divide, leaving only a unified 'we' (Camuli 2020).

Personal sub-study and autoethnography

I then began a parallel study to investigate the role of the artist-researcher in the project, focusing on the necessary considerations and ethical implications of researching a practice in which I was deeply involved. This blurring of roles underscored the specificity of autoethnography.

Unlike an external observer who documents from a distance, my personal involvement, narratives, and positionality were too integral to ignore.

I critically reflected on my position, the roles of other researchers, and the participants, addressing their direct and indirect involvement in the project. In addition to my diaries and logbooks, I started working backwards to retrace the project's timeline, from the initial idea to the final performance. This process involved coding events and meetings, noting who was present and the locations. I found that until the theatre laboratory began, the participants were never involved in decision-making meetings. The theatre director herself missed the first two meetings, which involved only university researchers discussing possible activities. I was the only constant attendee, navigating the balance between scientific rigor as a 'researcher' and practical theatre needs as an 'artist.' I also included conversations with participants about their perception of my role. Initially, they did not see me as part of the research team but as an artist/facilitator. This changed when I introduced the evaluation protocol, making them view me solely as a researcher who would analyse them, alienating me from the theatre community. However, this perception shifted again when I began sharing my notes, doubts, and role considerations directly with them. They started to feel included once more and gradually reintegrated me into 'their' group.

Autoethnography allowed me to critically reflect on the complex role of artist-researchers, particularly in relation to their own practices, and the risks of appropriation and saviourism when working with marginalised communities. During the analysis phase of my study, I focused on literature evaluating the impact and social benefits of socially engaged art. Engaging with critical perspectives on the neoliberal implications of assessing art projects solely for their social benefits helped me scrutinise our actions as a research team. This reflection gave me the confidence to approach future artistic research projects more thoughtfully and to learn from past mistakes. To conclude, I present the three A's from my personal study findings, which I now adhere to in these contexts (Camuti 2022):

- Accessibility: questioning our roles as artist-researchers involves considering how we make ourselves accessible. What knowledge do we offer, from which perspective, and how do we use it in our practice? Participatory practices are inherently situated and cannot be reduced to strict academic analysis. They thrive on the encounter between the facilitator's skills and the participants' unknown reactions and lives, requiring a holistic perspective.

- Agency: participants' agency must be considered at every step—from the project's genesis to its implementation, presentation, and evaluation. Stripping participants of their agency and ownership creates a gap that cannot be filled by our account alone and can jeopardise the project's completion. Involving participants in important decisions, like evaluation methods, ensures they reclaim their agency and gain ownership within the process.

- Articulation: the risk for artist-researchers is to become spokespersons for communities they do not belong to, reproducing patriarchal and colonial dynamics. Instead, we should engage in politics of articulation paired with solidarity practices, prioritising collective over individual experiences and accepting the possibility of failure. This approach allows for contingent and friction-generating processes, ensuring everyone gets a voice. Art and collective creation can be powerful tools for narrating individual and collective stories through co-created exhibitions, happenings, or performances.

Suggestions for further reading

Carolyn Ellis' *The Autoethnographic I: A Methodological Novel about Autoethnography* (2004) seamlessly integrates comprehensive methodological explanations with the personal narratives of the founding mother of autoethnography in modern times, ensuring an engaging and informative read. Kathryn Church's *Forbidden Narratives: Critical Autobiography as Social Science* (1995) is an inspiring example of how autoethnography disrupted professional discourse decades ago. The author describes the shift and overlap of the many different roles she embodies and what this means for the narrative you tell and the narratives that are heard. In *The Handbook of Autoethnography* (second edition) (2022) edited by Adams, Holman Jones, and Ellis, the authors present not only a comprehensive examination of autoethnography as a research methodology, but also present different forms and application of the method in several disciplines. Moreover, the book offers a section on 'failing' that can be very interesting to see how to learn from mistakes. Chang's *Autoethnography as Method* (2008) is a thorough and well-written guide to the understanding and practical use of autoethnography. The author gives clear tools to work with when approaching autoethnography and suggests useful exercises that can be directly applied to conduct autoethnographic research. Norman Kent Denzin's *Performance Autoethnography: Critical Pedagogies and the Politics of Culture* offers a direct link to performance and to the performative. The author not only addresses different performance models by connecting them to autoethnographic analysis, but does so by directly using performance text as writing form.

References

Adams, Tony E. 2008. "A Review of Narrative Ethics." *Qualitative Inquiry* 14 (2) (March): 175–94. https://doi.org/10.1177/1077800407304

Adams, Tony E., Carolyn Ellis, and Stacy Holman Jones. 2022. *Handbook of Autoethnography*. Routledge. https://doi.org/10.4324/9780429431760

Adams, Tony E., Stacy Holman Jones, and Carolyn Ellis. 2015. *Autoethnography: Understanding Qualitative Research*. Oxford University Press. https://doi.org/10.1002/capr.12111

Anderson, Leon. 2006. "Analytic Autoethnography." *Journal of Contemporary Ethnography* 35 (4): 373–95. https://doi.org/10.1177/08912416052804

Basharat, Tahira, and Muhammad Awais Shaukat. 2019. "A Critical Analysis of Some Ideals of Postmodernism in Various Fields of Knowledge and Morality." *Journal of Islamic Thought and Civilization* 9 (2): 112–26. https://doi.org/10.32350/jitc

Butler, Judith. 1988. "Performative Acts and Gender Constitution: An Essay in Phenomenology and Feminist Theory." *Theatre Journal* 40 (4): 519–31. https://doi.org/10.2307/3207893

Butler, Judith. 1990. *Gender Trouble: Feminism and the Subversion of Identity*. Routledge.

Camuti, Fabiola. 2020 "Performative Approaches to the Cultural Policy Field." In *Situated Knowing, Epistemic Perspectives on Performance*, edited by Ewa Bal and Mateusz Chaberski, 104–17. Routledge. https://doi.org/10.4324/9780367809584-8

Camuti, Fabiola. 2022. "Critical Tactics in Participatory Art." In *Powertools for Young Artists: Artistic Strategies for Equality*, edited by Isis Freitas Vale Germano, Fabiola Camuti, Els Cornelis, Catelijne de Muijnck and Aude Mgba. APRIA Platform.

Chang, Heewon. 2008. *Autoethnography as Method*. Routledge. https://doi.org/10.4324/9781315433370

Chang, Heewon. 2022. "Individual and Collaborative Autoethnography for Social Science Research." In *Handbook of Autoethnography*, edited by Tony E. Adams, Carolyn Ellis and Stacy Holman Jones, 53–66. Routledge. https://doi.org/10.4324/9780429431760-6

Church, Kathryn. 1995. *Forbidden Narratives: Critical Autobiography as Social Science*. Routledge.

Denzin, Norman Kent, and Yvonna Sessions Lincoln. 2005. "Preface." In *The SAGE Handbook of Qualitative Research*, edited by Norman K. Denzin and Y.S. Lincoln, IX–XIX. Sage.

Ellis, Carolyn. 2004. *The Ethnographic I: A Methodological Novel about Autoethnography*. AltaMira Press.

Ellis, Carolyn, and Arthur P. Bochner. 2000. "Autoethnography, Personal Narrative, Reflexivity: Researcher as Subject." In *Handbook of Qualitative Research*, edited by Norman Kent Denzin and Yvonna Sessions Lincoln, 733–68. Sage.

Ellis, Carolyn, Tony E. Adams, and Arthur P. Bochner. 2011. "Autoethnography: An Overview." *Historical Social Research* 36 (4): 273–90. https://doi.org/10.12759/hsr.36.2011.4.273-290

Guba, Egon G., and Yvonna S. Lincoln. 1989. *Fourth Generation Evaluation*. Sage Publications.

Johnson-Bailey, Juanita. 2021. "A Scholarly Journey to Autoethnography: A Way to Understand, Survive and Resist." In *Handbook of Research Methods on Gender and Management*, edited by Valerie Stead, Carole Elliot, and Sharon Mavin, 10–24. Edward Elgar Publishing. https://doi.org/10.4337/9781788977937.00008

Lapadat, Judith C. 2017. "Ethics in Autoethnography and Collaborative Autoethnography." *Qualitative Inquiry* 23 (8): 589–603. https://doi.org/10.1177/1077800417704462

McAvinchey, Caoimhe. 2011. *Theatre & Prison*. Palgrave Macmillan.

McKenzie, Lara. 2022. "Parenthood: Beyond Maternity and Paternity." *Feminist Anthropology* 3 (2): 299–306, https://doi.org/10.1002/fea2.12105

Parker, Andrew, and Eve Kosofsky Sedgwick, eds. 1996. *Performativity and Performance*. Routledge. https://doi.org/10.4324/9780203699928

Saldaña, Johnny. 2016. *The Coding Manual for Qualitative Researchers*. Sage Publications.

Sale, Alessandro, ed. 2016. *Environmental Experience and Plasticity of the Developing Brain*. Wiley Blackwell.

Sparkes, Andrew. 2022. "When Judgment Calls: Making Sense of Criteria for Evaluating Different Forms of Autoethnography." In *Handbook of Autoethnography*, edited by Tony E. Adams, Carolyn Ellis, and Stacy Holman Jones, 263–76. Routledge. https://doi.org/10.4324/9780429431760-25

Tullis, Jillian A. 2022. "Self and Others: Ethics in Autoethnographic Research." In *Handbook of Autoethnography*, edited by Tony E. Adams, Carolyn Ellis, and Stacy Holman Jones, 101–13. Routledge. https://doi.org/10.4324/9780429431760-10

Van Praag, Henriette, Gerd Kempermann, and Fred H. Gage. 2000. "Neural Consequences of Environmental Enrichment." *Nature Reviews Neuroscience* 1 (3): 191–98. https://doi.org/10.1038/35044558

IV

EMBEDDED AND PROCESS-BASED APPROACHES

16. Practice-led Research: Transversal Ways of Sensing/Knowing

Konstantina Georgelou

Summary

What are possible research methods in performance that move transversally between the classroom, the studio, and public space? This chapter discusses practice-led research, focusing on transversal ways of knowing and sensing that swerve through artistic, social, and theoretical spaces. Doing research by means of affective, embodied, and politicised methods is approached in this chapter through the conceptual frameworks of 'fugitive knowledge' (Moten and Harney; Akomolafe), 'practice-as-research' (Melrose; Nelson), 'performative research' (Haseman), 'attending laterally' (Georgelou and Protopapa), and 'decolonial pedagogy' (Vázquez). To illustrate this method, the chapter first discusses Dramaturgy at Work, a three-year collaborative research project on dramaturgy, which is then followed by a shorter reflection on an interdisciplinary bachelor course on Engaged Citizenship designed and developed with colleagues. Both examples emphasise the entwined interpersonal, politicised, and artistic methods practiced and transmitted in practice-led research. These methods can lead to interventionist and affective ways of doing research, the chapter argues, fostering social imagination and embedded action in performance and beyond.

Introduction

What are possible research methods in performance that move transversally between the classroom, the studio, and public space? This question motivates the methodological quest discussed in this chapter. It is worth explaining that I write from the experience of starting my academic life as a student in a rather conservative academic climate in Athens, Greece, in the early 2000s, while also working with a dance company and being socio-politically engaged. The resonances and shared intensities—but also forced divisions—between these three zones were very present then. It was assumed that academic knowledge, creative processes, and citizenship are linked thematically but kept apart methodologically. To sketch this more anecdotally, imagine going to a philosophy class at the university in the morning, then joining a protest, and after that going to the dance studio. In the philosophy class we listen to a lecture on ethics, in the protest we shout against unjust working conditions, and in the studio we practice moving together like a flock of birds. None of them refers to each other. But in all these instances, practices of togetherness, dissensus, conflict, solidarity, and trust are evoked by ways of attending, listening, voicing, and moving as a group. And while in each space these practices are differently expressed, they have been inseparable in my learning experience. Practice-led research in performance can be approached, I propose, as a way of listening to the resonances and questioning such divisions, and of figuring out how to move through them.

Practice-led is a term used to describe the kind of research that happens through practical engagement, which means in multimodal and dynamic ways of doing. Performance scholar Robin Nelson (2021) explains this by specifically pointing to the incorporation of 'know-how' (embodied knowledge), 'know-what' (critical reflection), and 'know-that' (propositional discourse). Herewith I additionally point to practice-led research as transversal; a kind of research that passes through theoretical, artistic, sociopolitical, and affective spaces of probing and acting. Transversality refers to a movement that resists separation. It can be represented as a diagonal that cuts through both horizontal and vertical lines, defying compartmentalised modes of organization. Philosopher Félix Guattari (2015) conceptualised transversality to critique institutionalised psychiatric practices of his time in the 1970s, proposing collective forms of psychotherapy (through, for instance, a reciprocal relationship between the therapist and the patient). Transversal ways of knowing and sensing in the context of practice-led research involve swerving through spaces—such as the studio, the classroom and public space—in reciprocal and non-hierarchical ways too.

This approach aligns with philosopher and activist Bayo Akomolafe's understanding of 'fugitive knowledge' (2022), a concept that emphasises the corporeality and politicality of knowledge. The concept of fugitivity comes from Black studies, and theorists Fred Moten and Stefano Harney discuss it in their book *The Undercommons: Fugitive Planning and Black Study* (2013). As Jack Halberstam explains in the prologue of the book, "fugitivity is being separate from settling. [...] It is a being in motion that has learned [...] that there are spaces and modalities that exist separate from the logical, logistical, the housed and the positioned" (Moten and Harney 2015, 11). Fugitivity is hence a way of moving that is improvisational, affective, and modulating, instead of linear, quantifiable and fixed. It is crucial to add that in Black studies the concept of fugitivity specifically speaks to racialised experiences and to modes of sociality of racialised people. In his approach to fugitivity, Akomolafe (2022) refers in a podcast to embodied ways of knowing how to be in that motion, which he explains as "navigating the world by becoming lost". Fugitivity thus also relates to instability, disorientation, and moving with no clear sense of direction. Transversality is approached here through the lens of fugitivity, admitting perplexity and volatility in the research process.

Practice-led research methods are invaluable for doing research transversally and from within embodied and affective aspects of performance. To demonstrate this proposition, I discuss the collaborative research project on dramaturgical practice called Dramaturgy at Work that I pursued with artists-researchers Efrosini Protopapa and Danae Theodoridou (2014–2017). To further expand on practice-led methods, the course Engaged Citizenship: Media, Performance, Activism is thereafter discussed, showing how a transversal approach can be relevant to an undergraduate course and thus indirectly responding to the experiences described at the outset of this text.

The field of performance entails ways of sense-making that are embodied, affective, political, and poetic. Hence, following a practice-led methodology means that these aspects of sense-making are not only discussed or written about in performance research. They shall rather be embedded in the research process and put into practice. To contextualise practice-led research from that perspective, I specifically allude to 'practice (as) research' (Nelson, 2021) and 'performative research' (Haseman, 2006).

Context | Situating practice-led methods

The discussion around the academic relevance of practice-led research dates back to the beginning of the 21st century in the performing arts. It was especially prominent in the UK, where performance scholars Susan Melrose and Robin Nelson have played a major role in advocating for performance practice to be recognised as part of academic knowledge. With their work, they greatly influenced the emergence of practice-based PhDs in dance and performance in the UK and beyond.[1] Melrose's influential work specifically aimed to interrogate why artists would not qualify as 'experts' in the knowledge-politics of the performing arts in the academic context.[2] And, in his turn, Nelson proposed the term 'practice as research' (PaR)—which was later more commonly referred to as 'practice research'—refusing the separation between theory and practice and siding with research "in its concern with values and orientation to action" (2021, 19). Nelson linked practice to the notion of 'praxis', which refers to action, alluding to critical pedagogue Paulo Freire whose pedagogical aim was to create conditions for structural transformation. In a similar spirit, Augusto Boal's uses of theatre practices to transform society are mentioned as influential in the context of PaR's development in Brazil (Nelson 2021, 177). Praxis in this sense connects not only to reasoning and reflection in speaking and in writing,

---

1   This has also raised a lot of critical and justified concerns, since a new economy of 'practice-based PhDs' was created in the universities and where, as a result, practical research was also standardised when looking at the modes and forms it takes. For a critical consideration of this economy see Paschal and Protopapa (2023).

2   See especially Melrose's writings in 'Confessions of an Uneasy Expert Spectator' (2007).

which are the most common practices in academic research, but also to play, experience, action, embodying, and crafting (2021, 20). It entails trying out (in practice), documenting the process, contextualizing the influences, and conceptualizing relevant frameworks (2021, 40). Practice research then also suggests a degree of defamiliarization with the academic methods one is used to in terms of research (i.e. analysis, academic writing, argumentation). Imagination, pleasure, repetition, editing, and presenting are mentioned by Nelson as ways of knowing otherwise (2021, 43). Echoing Nelson, *Practice Research* (Bulley and Şahin 2021) consists of two reports that study what practice research is and how it can be shared. The authors argue at the outset of these reports that practice research is relevant across all research disciplines and that "in practice research, forms of intuitive, embodied, tacit, imaginative, affective and sensory ways of knowing can be conveyed" (2021, 1).

Even though the debate on practice research most often leads to arguments regarding research in the art fields, or discussions about the difficulty of assessing practice-based PhDs in the arts, or how practice-led research can happen across disciplines,[3] here I'd like to consider more carefully its relevance in how performance, as an academic field, is researched. Nelson has pointed to how performance studies has been an "all-inclusive category" and cautions that a generic term such as "practice" risks furthering this vagueness (Nelson 2021, 20). To avoid that, practice should be pinned down more precisely without being solely determined by professionalism and academic standards.[4] The invitation is thus to consider practice, 'doing', as the research activity as well as the outcome of research, similarly to what scholar Brad Haseman has named "performative research" (2006). Like Melrose and Nelson, Haseman has been influential in the developments in practice-led research. In his "Manifesto for Performative Research" (2006) he underscored the performativity of any kind of research and thus specifically sought to move beyond art education by proposing performative research as a new paradigm for research, sitting next to quantitative and qualitative modes. In the same article, he identifies two

---

3   Nelson's book (2021) includes all these directions.
4   Nelson follows Ben Spatz in making this point, explaining that the latter advocates practice "as the more radical proposition", and therefore proposes a "new rigour of method quite different from professional definitions and standards" (2021, 20).

methods in applying performative research across disciplines: trialling and prototyping. These two are not unpacked in his text but they echo methods that are more familiar to performance, such as rehearsing, trying out, scoring, and sketching.

A number of practice-led research methodologies can be found online in the *Journal of Artistic Research* (JAR) as well as in academic research that happens across the humanities and social sciences. It is worthwhile to indicatively mention, however, a few examples whose interwoven collective, political, and artistic methodology has been inspiring for me and resonate with the focus of this chapter. One of them is TkH, the 'Walking Theory' platform, which began in 2000 in Belgrade, Serbia, and for ten years put emphasis on theory as (social) practice that can be interventionist, performative, and even indistinguishable from artistic practice. TkH was an independent non-funded body consisting of artists and theorists who organised workshops, lectures, publications, and performances, and interfered with cultural policies and academic protocols (Djordjev and Vujanovic 2011). In a similar vein, 6Months 1Location (2008) was a project initiated by seventeen dance artists in France, who spent six months together, exchanging and re-inventing conditions of work, research and education. Later they published methods that they use in their practices, online and in a book, creating an open source platform for ways of working in choreography (Ingvartsen 2009). SenseLab, a laboratory with artists, researchers, dancers, and writers, founded by philosopher and artist Erin Manning in Montreal, Canada, was also place of encounter and exchange, in this case around creative practice and thinking about aesthetic and political interventions (SenseLab nd.). Lastly, a far more interdisciplinary research group, which connects to this chapter's section on expanding practice-led methods, is the Forensic Architecture research agency based in London, UK: a team that consists of artists, lawyers, scientists, architects, and journalists who investigate states and corporate entities (such as police, military, governments etc.) for human rights violations. Forensic Architecture reconstructs incidents of violence through rigorous spatial analysis and digital modelling, to trace state or corporate accountability (Forensic Architecture, nd.).

Against this backdrop of discourse and practice, one would expect that practice-led research is fundamental to the academic field of performance studies, a forerunner in studying performativity and embodied action. And yet, there has been only little room and resources dedicated to properly developing methods of practice-led research within the curricula.[5]

How to | Attending laterally

In light of the debates on practice-led research and the notion of transversality as proposed in the introduction, doing performance research suggests attending to research laterally.[6] Attending laterally, sideways, instead of linearly and directly, makes possible decentring, incidentalness, inconsistency, and opacity in knowledge, echoing Akomolafe's take on fugitivity. It suggests moving sideways with research. In Western academia, research is mostly expected to be progressive, to go in depth, to be innovative and quantifiable, and laterality is often associated with thinking creatively and 'out of the box' in order to arrive at a new product. In this proposition however, attending laterally suggests an emergent process-based approach that resists being quantifiable as well as following the 'out of the box' thinking models. Non-linear, improvisatory, expansive, fugitive, and very likely disruptive to structures of academic standards, such research cannot be fully predicted or defined in advance.

To attend laterally in practice-led research, these prompts can be useful:

- Circulate for as long as possible around something particular (e.g. a question, a thought, an observation, a concern, an

---

5   Over the last couple of years there has been more attention paid to the 'social impact' of universities (see Netherlands, UK, Nordic countries), which paves the way for more practice-led approaches to research. This demand has already been introduced in the domain of art practice for the last decade, as social impact is one of the criteria for public funding. Indicatively, see Sofia Lindström et al. (2022). While these developments open the way for more practice-led learning (especially in community work), the risk of instrumentalising and standardising education through the institutional demand for social impact has to be taken into account. For more insight, look at the work of Claire Bishop (2012), as well as Sruti Bala's critical discussion on theatre's social impact (2019).

6   This proposition connects to the research that I have pursued with Efrosini Protopapa since 2020, entitled 'Moving Laterally as a Dramaturgical Practice', https://www.atd.ahk.nl/das-research/whats-on/open-calls/moving-laterally-as-a-dramaturgical-practice/

intuition) in any way you want, alone or with others, without trying to improve, clarify, or fix things.

- Notice how distraction is a constitutive part of this process.
- Let distractions move you to other spaces (e.g. physical, mental, imaginary) and observe what this does to what was particular at first.
- Document the movement of displacement (e.g. through journaling, audio/video recording, story-telling, photography, movement practice etc.). Let the documentation be messy.
- Remember who/what else you are with in this research, and notice what/who comes (in) your way and what/whom you might get in the way of.
- Include in your documentation unforeseen (power) structures that you identify (with) and in which you might become implicated during this process.
- Find a way to share with others (i.e. peers, teachers, friends) this nonlinear process of moving, with the help of your documentation material/practice. This can take a form that better reflects the experience that you have had: for instance, it can be a game, an exercise, a presentation, a sound recording, a piece of writing, etc.
- Listen carefully to the questions and experiences that will arise.
- Decide how and from which 'particular' point to continue and re-engage with this process. Attend to the swerves and patterns that will occur in the process and decide if, when and how to follow them.
- The end of this process will have to come. Notice and decide what shapes it might take or shift into in order to possibly share the material and outcomes of your research process with a larger public.

Demonstration | Practice-led research on dramaturgy

My two collaborators, Efrosini Protopapa and Danae Theodoridou, and I initiated the three-year research project 'Dramaturgy At Work' because of a shared enquiry: how to research dramaturgy as a practice and through practice with each other. The durational and collaborative aspects of this project make it a worthwhile and also challenging case to apprehend. The demonstration here is largely drawn from material from our project's website, which is also part of the documentation process, and from our co-edited book *The Practice of Dramaturgy: Working on Actions in Performance* (2017), where a more detailed account of the research can be found.

As a method of researching dramaturgical practice through practice, we improvised a bottom-up series of practical workshops, gatherings, and exchanges with students, artists, theorists, and dramaturges across different European cities and in diverse types of institutions (universities, festivals, art schools, a squat) and geopolitical realities (west and south of Europe, the Balkans, and the UK). How long it would take and how this project would 'end' was not predicted or decided as we began. During the process we developed themes, workshop exercises, and encounters that allowed us to engage with our questions by transversing between poetic, theoretical, institutional, and political contexts with others. In a series of two- or three-day workshops with participants followed by public roundtable discussions with guests, dramaturgical practice was explored from several perspectives. In hindsight, it can be said that, in this project, four entangled practice-led research trajectories were present, and I refer to them all here: the research project on dramaturgy as a whole, the workshops and roundtable discussions, our practice of collaboration, and the co-editing of the book.

At the outset of the research, our attention was on 'what is present' in the field of dramaturgy in Europe, visible and invisible to us, as we were interested in current dramaturgical forms, methods, aesthetics, and structures in choreography and performance. We thus began with the large question: what kinds of dramaturgies are present? We started by doing a workshop in the then-freshly-occupied Embros Theatre in Athens (2012), in an energizing and activist environment with choreographers and dramaturges who were at that moment collectively generating dramaturgies by ways of self-instituting. Our question was relevant to the Doctoral School of Arts at Ghent University too, where we were invited afterwards to give a workshop to researchers in performance and dramaturgy who were highly skilled in conceptualizing dramaturgical tendencies. These two first phases of our research enriched our understanding of how dramaturgical practice and theorisation are codependent on the institutional and sociopolitical contexts in which they emerge, and confirmed our hypothesis that there is often a disconnect between the theory (discursive literature) and the practice (in an artistic process) of dramaturgy.

Other perspectives from which we researched dramaturgical practice included: feedback, critical and creative response, dramaturgy as the creation of actions in artistic work, and the relation of dramaturgy to institutional critique and to the production of social imaginings. Each perspective derived from the previous experiences and outcomes, and was not predetermined in the research. The workshops that we designed each time were task-oriented, with scores[7] and directives that we devised together, seeking to generate spaces for peer-exchange. The first day focused on 'what is already there'. Participants were given a framework through which to reflect on the relationship between their diverse practices and dramaturgy. We asked them to prepare a self-interview (written, audio, or video) where they articulate and respond to their own questions on dramaturgy before the workshop. The workshop then started by sharing the interviews with each other. On some occasions, we jointly made 'dramaturgical portraits' for everyone's project on the first day, by listening or viewing what each participant is working on and by learning about the conditions in which they live and work. Part of this exercise was to then offer 'gifts' to each other, which could take the form of a question, a 'wrong' instruction, a constraint, a distraction. We named those 'gifts' to signal a generous attitude in working towards one another's processes.

---

7   A score in the performing arts refers to a set of guidelines or tasks that creates conditions for generating actions and movement. It is used widely in dance improvisation and in devised theatre practices to avoid repeating prescribed actions and movement (taught or shown, for instance, by the choreographer or the director). For a concise description, see Chernetich and Franco (2024).

On the second and third day, the participants' dramaturgical ways of working were further researched through peer exchange that was triggered with different kinds of scores and exercises. Distraction, close listening, collaboration, and interference were vital operations in this exchange. These are some examples of the exercises we used:

'Invent a metaphor that characterises the way you work and describe it for two minutes to the other people in your group. They will then pose questions aiming to detect working modes, strategies, infrastructures, concerns, and challenges in how you work.'

'Set up an experiment that will help you "test" an aspect of your project with others. This can take any form and can happen in any location possible to access.'

For another exercise that happens in groups of three, we worked with choreographer Lisa Nelson's *Tuning Scores*,[8] an improvisational composition practice and performance research tool that we translated for the context of this workshop (see Fig. 16.1). The instructions are that: person 1 speaks in detail and without stopping about the artistic/research project they are currently involved in for about 20 minutes. Person 2 calls out the directives from the image below in any order and frequency, with the intention of live-editing the speaking/thinking process of person 1. Person 3 does not speak but makes a score for a performance on the basis of this exchange, using words, drawings, sketches etc.

Exercises of conceptualization, writing, speaking and composition were practiced without blending the diverse practices in the room or forcing collaboration in the sense of 'making with' someone whose materials and tools could be different. The dramaturgical research in the workshops was on practising attentiveness to details, and to decision-making processes through practice-led methods of peer-exchange.

At the same time, we were pursuing this research independently and without funding, while working in different institutions. The workload from our jobs together with this joint research was intense and the distractions were therefore plenty, which made the research even more disorientating.

---

8 A collection of resources about Lisa Nelson's Tuning Scores can be found on the website *Tuning Scores log*: https://tuningscoreslog.wordpress.com/about/

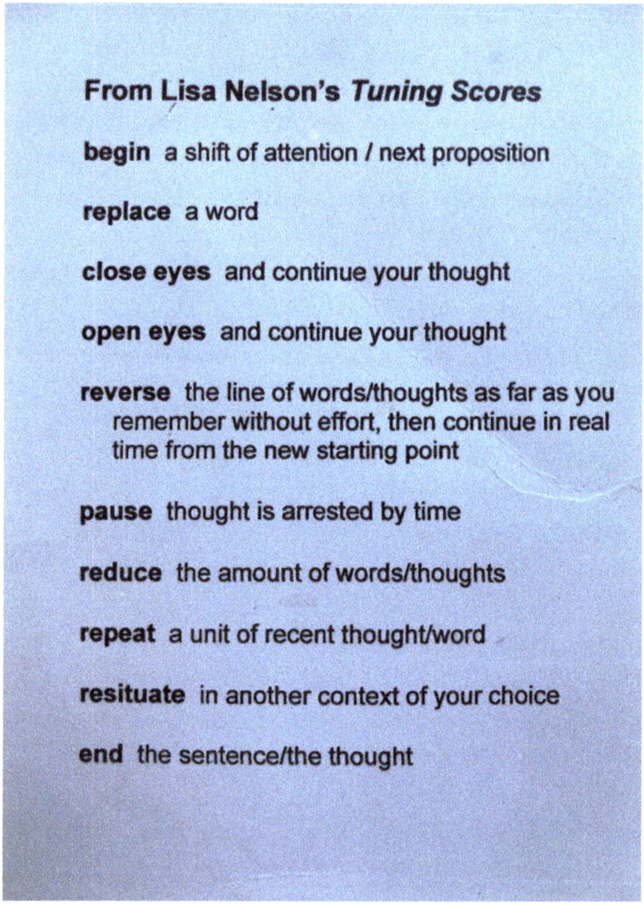

> **From Lisa Nelson's *Tuning Scores***
>
> **begin** a shift of attention / next proposition
>
> **replace** a word
>
> **close eyes** and continue your thought
>
> **open eyes** and continue your thought
>
> **reverse** the line of words/thoughts as far as you remember without effort, then continue in real time from the new starting point
>
> **pause** thought is arrested by time
>
> **reduce** the amount of words/thoughts
>
> **repeat** a unit of recent thought/word
>
> **resituate** in another context of your choice
>
> **end** the sentence/the thought

Fig. 16.1 An example of the cards used for 'Dramaturgy At Work' with the translated version of Lisa Nelson's *Tuning Scores*. ©Konstantina Georgelou.

Finding a viable way to work together was essential. Before each workshop, we thus revisited individually the documentation material of what had happened (i.e. photos, exercises, footage, notes from discussions that we had gathered and shared with each other) and then came together to exchange our thoughts, impressions, questions, (new) readings, performances, images, imaginings, and other resources, figuring out how to move next. Those meetings were long. Sometimes they happened online, since we live in different countries, and, when possible, in person, at each other's houses, or at cafés, offices, and libraries in the cities where we lived and met. In these encounters, we arrived at the themes for the next workshop, organised the logistics (communication with places and institutions to offer these workshops), devised workshop plans for each occasion, and finally arrived at tailor-made questions to send to the invited guests each time, depending on the themes and on the institutional and sociopolitical contexts we would visit next. In each workshop, we thus prepared and facilitated anew different set-ups that would allow the participants, the guests, and ourselves to delve into practising dramaturgy from the proposed perspective.

Entangled with the research project on dramaturgy was the research process happening between us, and how we worked with each other. The dramaturgy of our collaboration was largely improvisatory and revealed several (power) structures with we were involved or bumping against. For instance, as we explain in the book, although our project had a name, there was no name that referred to us, as a group of researchers working together in the field of performance. Due to this non-institutional formation and despite opportunities that we had come across, we were also not eligible to apply for large funds or European Union projects that usually demand a 'planning ahead' attitude and also often lead to greater visibility. We were, by choice, operating in the shadows of 'big' institutional structures and funding bodies. At the same time, we had affiliations with several institutions that formed part of the project. It was often precisely by attending to our professional contexts and through the complex relations with a variety of organizations as employees or freelance workers, that we managed over the years to support the research projects while exercising relationships simultaneously inside and outside particular systems. In this frame, the dramaturgy of our collaboration was a significant part of our practice-led research, which meant seeking to understand and reveal how the work we did together related to the infrastructures within which we work, and how we make decisions in that respect. This aspect of our collaboration provided another rationale for our suggestion to consider dramaturgy as a practice with political implications, rather than as a service or a toolbox for successful work.

This project lasted for three years, during which we decided to additionally co-author and co-edit a book on dramaturgy. Through this practice-led research we realised that an important skill in the field of dramaturgy is attending to the complex relationships between the 'why', the 'how', and the 'what'—the motivations/questions, methods, and outcomes of a process—while considering the positions from which one is (invited to be) implicated in those. One of the main purposes of this co-authoring was to consider the manifold political articulations of dramaturgical practice. In light of this approach, in the book we conceptualised dramaturgical practice as a catalytic process of working on actions that resembles a chain of reactions, "acting as an initiator that does not seek to necessarily control the process but rather aims at constant shifts and mini-breakdowns" (Georgelou et al. 2017, 67). Thinking through the concept of praxis, we argued that contrary to expectations of coherency that dramaturgy often aims to ensure in an artwork, the "doing" of dramaturgy rather aims to "an opening up of spaces of dissensus, un-sensing, disorientation, and un-knowing that enables space for interference, intervention and imagination" (2017, 77). In addition, we outlined principles of dramaturgy that activate zones of ambiguity in terms of products and outcomes, and that acknowledge polyvocality and plurality in ways of knowing and sensing. With this approach to dramaturgy we echo practice-led methods, pointing to research being about both the 'how-to's' and 'doings' of research.

Expanding the method | Embedding practice-led methods in a course

In 2023 I co-developed the BA course Engaged Citizenship: Media, Performance and Activism with media scholar Nina Köll, social anthropologist Paul Mepschen, and education scholar Tatiana Bruni, at the University College Utrecht. This course introduces students to methods of practice-led research, proposing an interdisciplinary approach. Students learn how to sketch, plan, enact, and document 'micro-actions', which refers to small-scale live or mediated activism that aims to make a problem visible (raise awareness), intervene into an existing structure (intervention), and/or actualise a different kind of gesture that more directly seeks to transform reality (prefigurative action). Practice-led research here refers to an approach to teaching and learning that moves between classroom, rehearsal, and training towards micro-actions and enactments in public space. Aylin Kuryel's recent discussion of Cultural Analysis as a field of research and teaching is useful to mention as an analogy here. She criticises the insistence on "social relevance", which has become a useful bureaucratic and profiling term that "implies a prior knowability of the tenets and needs of a context according to which the (ir)relevance of knowledge and analysis can be measured" (2025, 191) and proposes instead to focus on "public intervention", which "might allow putting the emphasis on being/becoming part of what is engaged with, without assuming a preexisting context" (192). Practice-led methods thus suggest here interference, intervention, and rupture through social imagination and embeddedness. As Kuryel also demonstrates through her own course at the University of Amsterdam, art and performance practices are very helpful to that end because of their focus on process, embodied experience, and transformation of identities. These methods resist categorisation and encourage failure, exceptions, and impossible solutions (Lewis and Hyland 2022). One's involvement in creating performative interventions and micro-actions thus allows analysing in tacit, material, and interpersonal ways and navigating shared feelings of doubt, humour, fear, boredom, fascination, embarrassment, obsession etc.

The assignments that students receive in this course on the one hand focus on close reading and conceptualization (i.e. reading notes, take-home exam), and on the other hand on the ability to translate concepts into praxis, as pointed out by Nelson earlier, with live-action prompts, improvisation scores, and tasks for experimenting with tactical media and culture jamming. On the basis of specific themes on activism and relational and post-national accounts on citizenship, students are for instance asked to make protest signs, to write a manifesto, a poem, or a public apology, to make a photo collage, or to work with props. They share some of the exercises in the classroom, which they then transform into micro-actions for other parts of the university campus (see Figs. 16.2, 16.3) and eventually do micro-actions outside the campus addressing larger publics (see Fig. 16.4).

Fig. 16.2 Micro-actions from the course 'Engaged Citizenship': Sleeping strike in the campus. ©Konstantina Georgelou.

Fig. 16.3 Micro-actions from the course 'Engaged Citizenship': printed quotes from @blackliturgies stuck up in public spaces. ©Konstantina Georgelou.

Fig. 16.4 Micro-actions from the course 'Engaged Citizenship': chalk project on the streets of Utrecht about street harassment. ©Konstantina Georgelou.

The practice-led part of the course helps students develop awareness of their own experience of creating and carrying out these actions in relationship to the kinds of experience and effects these generate to different publics. As indicated in the course manual, this approach is "oriented towards a plural, diverse and open society, earth justice and planetary citizenship" (Köll et al. 2023, unpublished course manual).[9]

---

9   Course manual created by the four above-mentioned initiators and teachers.

And part of this orientation is to explicitly address ethical and political considerations that are integral to the assignment of micro-actions, such as exposure of one's self, emotional states, situatedness, invitation for others to participate, relationality, remembering, trust, reciprocity, kinship, and care. These values connect to Rolando Vázquez's (2020) work on decoloniality and specifically to how he has articulated decolonial pedagogies through practices of positionality, relationality, and re-existence. With positionality, the claim to universal knowledge, academic canons, and normative narratives is critically questioned. "By asking who is speaking, we are moved to ask not for an identity of choice, but for a genealogy, the historical grounds of the enunciation in order to acknowledge and locate its validity" (2020, 170). With relationality, dualisms of subject/object, self/other, and reality/representation are replaced by an ethics of reception, hosting, and listening towards a possibility of plenitude. "[T]he pedagogies of relationality call for the task of building dialogues and opening up towards the worlds of sensing and meaning that have been subjugated, suppressed under the colonial difference" (2020, 172). And with re-existence, an affirmative attitude of pluriversality and a mourning for what has been lost are foregrounded by engaging with histories of colonial subjugation. Pedagogies of re-existence "seek the recovery of the possibility of re-emergence, re-existence, of the coming into world-historical presence for the voices, the bodies, the forms of earthing that have been subjugated or erased in the modern colonial order" (2020, 174). Against this backdrop, the practice-led methods of this course follow a decolonial path of acting in awareness of and in relation to colonial histories and presents.

When working within the decolonial framework of a method, it is important to ask what registers of sensation are addressed, evoked, and experienced. In this specific course, parallel to the form, shape, and outcome of the micro-actions, we place emphasis on the sensory experiences we work with and seek to transmit through research. For instance, we foster practices that relate to sound, touch, and movement and not only text and image, and we are explicit in welcoming opacity and not-knowing. In addition, we encourage a recovering and remembering of dormant knowledges, instead of the production of 'new knowledge', by asking students to engage with memories and testimonials, and offering a lot of examples of Western and non-Western interventions and actions that students can draw from in their micro-actions.

In a similar vein, performance scholar and artist Ben Spatz (2019) makes the call for a decolonial move in performance studies especially through the lens of embodiment and embodied research. According to Spatz, there is a disparity between the methods of performance and decolonial studies in the academic field, and the political underpinnings of the radical methods in artistic research, in the American and European contexts respectively. Spatz writes:

> Artistic research, if it does not engage thoroughly with cultural and performance studies, risks failing to understand its own implicit and potential politics. On the other hand, decolonial thought and writing, if it does not find ways to radicalise at the level of method, risks articulating a critical program without a sufficiently developed program for institutional change. (2019, 23)

Questioning methods from a decolonial perspective has consequences for the typical processes of normativising research in the university. A more radical approach, and some daring to let research processes out of our control, is required for interfering with implicit hierarchies in academia, i.e. mind/body, thinking/sensing, acting/receiving. The corporeality and political nature of knowledge thus depend on resisting academia's tendency to institute its values by stripping away sensory ways of knowing the world

Suggestions for further reading

Stefano Harney and Fred Moten have written about the dangers and challenges with regard to the university's turn towards professionalisation, logistics, policies, and management in relation to resisting practices of social life that can arguably exist within the university (2004, 2020). These publications are connected to their seminal co-authored book *The Undercommons: Fugitive Planning and Black Study* (2013), which provides a theoretical approach to the notion of 'study' as a collective, social and fugitive practice within the black radical tradition.

Bayo Akomolafe's and Erin Manning's online conversation in the context of Sher Doruff's Ways of Knowing course (2023) makes connections between knowledge, knowing, and practice by critically looking at how these are conditioned by whiteness, ableism, and neurotypicality. In their insightful and personal exchange, they discuss how predispositions of whiteness can be destabilised through neurodiverse and transversal embodied ways of knowing.

Robin Nelson's book *Practice as Research in the Arts and Beyond: Principles, Processes, Contexts, Achievements* (2021) is the second edition of his earlier book (2013), with contributions by Nelson and other Western and non-Western authors that offer diverse perspectives on practice as research (PaR). The book provides contextual information on PaR as well as approaches of 'how-to', with a focus that is not exclusive to art practices but stays open to any kind of research that invites entangled modes of knowing and that is not limited to academic writing methods.

In *Vistas of Modernity: Decolonial Aesthesis and the End of the Contemporary* (2020), Vázquez proposes decolonial thought as a way of thinking/feeling relationally. In the "Postface: What does it mean to decolonise?", he dedicates a section on decolonial pedagogies. In this section we are encouraged to position and question aesthetic and academic canons as a way to humble them and to open up more space for other worlds of sensing and meaning that have been erased by modernity.

References

Bala, Sruti. 2019. "What is the impact of theatre and performance?" In *Thinking Through Theatre and Performance*, edited by M. Bleeker, A. Kear, J. Kelleher, and H. Roms, 186–99. Bloomsbury Publishing. https://doi.org/10.5040/9781472579645

Bishop, Claire. 2012. *Artificial Hells: Participatory Art and the Politics of Spectatorship*. Verso.

Bulley, James, and Şahin Özden. 2021. *Practice Research—Report 1: What is practice research? and Report 2: How can practice research be shared?* Practice Research Advisory Group UK (PRAG-UK).

Chernetich, Gaia Clotilde, and Susanne Franco. 2024. "Score." In *Dancing Museums Glossary*, edited by A. Mikou. https://www.dancingmuseums.com/artefacts/score/

Djordjev, Bojan, and Ana Vujanovic. 2011. "TkH Platform—research and education in performing arts through writing, self-education and theoretical performance." *Artea: Research and Scenic Creation*, www.arte-a.

org. https://archivoartea.uclm.es/wp-content/uploads/2019/03/TkH-PlatformVujanovic-Djordjev.pdf

Georgelou, Konstantina, Protopapa, Efrosini, and Danae Theodoridou. 2017. *The Practice of Dramaturgy: Working on Actions in Performance*. Valiz.

Guattari, Félix. 2015. "Transversality". In *Psychoanalysis and Transversality: Texts and Interviews 1955–1971*, translated by Ames Hodges, 102–20. Semiotext(e).

Harney, Stefano, and Fred Moten. 2004. "The University and the Undercommons: Seven Theses." *Social Text* 79 (22: 2): 101–15. https://doi.org/10.1215/01642472-22-2_79-101

Harney, Stefano, and Fred Moten. 2013. *The Undercommons: Fugitive Planning and Black Study*. Minor Compositions.

Harney, Stefano, and Fred Moten. 2020. "The University: Last Words." https://www.academia.edu/43580248/The_university_last_words_by_stefano_harney_and_fred_moten

Haseman, Brad. 2006. "A Manifesto for Performative Research." *Media International Australia* 118 (1): 98–106. https://doi.org/10.1177/1329878X0611800113

Hyland, Peter B., Lewis E. Tyson. 2022. "The Antifascist Politics of Studioing." *Revista Portuguesa de Pedagogia* 56: 1–18. https://doi.org/10.14195/1647-8614_56_21

Ingvartsen, Mette, ed.. 2009. *6 MONTHS 1 LOCATION.* everybodys publications.

Köll, Nina, Paul Mepschen, Tatiana Bruni, and Konstantina Georgelou. 2023. *Course Manual for Engaged Citizenship: Media, Performance and Activism*. Unpublished internal teaching material. University College Utrecht.

Kuryel, Aylin. 2025. "From Social Relevance to Public Intervention: Cultural Analysis in and out of the Classroom." In *The Future of Cultural Analysis: A Critical Inquiry*, edited by Murat Aydemir, Noa Roei, and Aylin Kuryel, 191–208. Amsterdam University Press.

Lindström, Sofia. 2022. "Mapping research on the social impact of the arts: what characterises the field?" *Open Research Europe* 1 (124). https://doi.org/10.12688/openreseurope.14147.2

Melrose, Susan. 2007. "Confessions of an Uneasy Expert Spectator." https://www.sfmelrose.org.uk/

Nelson, Robin. 2021. *Practice as Research in the Arts and Beyond: Principles, Processes, Contexts, Achievements*. Palgrave Macmillan. https://doi.org/10.1007/978-3-030-90542-2

Paschal Paul, and Efrosini Protopapa. 2023. "The Spider and the Crab: Ways of Being with Practice-as-Research." *Dance Research* 41 (2): 181–93. https://doi.org/10.3366/drs.2023.0402

Spatz, Ben. 2019. "Notes for Decolonizing Embodiment." *Journal of Dramatic Theory and Criticism* 33 (2): 9–26. https://doi.org/10.1353/dtc.2019.0001

Vázquez Rolando. 2020. *Vistas of Modernity: Decolonial Aesthesis and the End of the Contemporary*. Mondrian Fund.

Online resources (podcasts, videos, websites):

Akomolafe, Bayo. 2022. "On Coming Alive to Other Senses," online podcast. https://forthewild.world/listen/dr-bayo-akomolafe-on-coming-alive-to-other-senses-300

Akomolafe Bayo, and Erin Manning. 2023. "Ways of Knowing," online video. No longer available online.

Forensic Architecture. https://forensic-architecture.org/

Georgelou, Konstantina, Protopapa, Efrosini, and Danae Theodoridou. 2014. *Dramaturgy at Work*. https://dramaturgyatwork.wordpress.com/

Georgelou, Konstantina, and Efrosini Protopapa. 2022. "Moving Laterally as a Dramaturgical Practice." https://www.atd.ahk.nl/das-research/whats-on/open-calls/moving-laterally-as-a-dramaturgical-practice/

Journal for Artistic Research. https://www.jar-online.net/en/journal-artistic-research

Nelson, Lisa. *Tuning Scores log*. https://tuningscoreslog.wordpress.com/about/

SenseLab. https://senselab.ca/wp2/about/

17. Affective Attunement: Mapping the Invisible

Theron Schmidt

Summary

This chapter describes methods for researchers to attune to the affective dimensions of their social and environmental conditions. These are placed within the context of feminist and decolonial ideas of 'situated knowledge' as opposed to universal knowledge: the view 'from ground level, in the thick of things', as Dwight Conquergood puts it. Sociology and ethnography have also developed methods for critical self-positioning, but the author argues that performance-based practices add to these by introducing embodied and experiential techniques to make apprehensible—that is, literally perceptible—the forces acting upon and through the observing subject. In this chapter, the focus is on the use of creative constructs to displace the intentional and authorial subject in place of an experiencing subject, open to chance influences and attenuated to that is which is preconscious or presubjective. Ant Hampton's *Borderline Invisible* (2023) is discussed as an example of 'performative mapping' that brings to the surface the buried but very much live currents of migration, genocide, and ethnic displacement in the European context. This method is then extended to learning and teaching situations where practicing researchers can develop their affective sensitivities.

Introduction

To perform is to do, to carry out, to enact. So 'performance' carries meanings that range from the very specific sense of performing something that has been rehearsed or is an act of representing something else—the narrow sense of performance studies as the analysis of theatre, dance, or ritual as objects of study—to more general consideration of transformative actions—as in the pervasive understanding of 'performativity' as enacted practices that construct our social realities. Somewhere in between these two points on a spectrum, I focus here on performance as embodied experience, not restricted to the domain of rehearsed and staged actions, and instead considered as an epistemological framework, as a way of encountering and knowing the world. As a performance research methodology, then, I am describing here not a method of researching objects called 'performances', but instead performance as a research method in itself, where the object of inquiry can be taken from a wide range of lived spaces and social relationships. In this way I argue for performance research as a method that is relevant to the humanities and social sciences more broadly.

Specifically, I discuss here methods of attunement to social and environmental situatedness, as experiential techniques to make apprehensible (that is, literally perceptible) the embeddedness of the experiencing subject within affective and politicised vortices of determination. Whereas other disciplines, such as sociology and ethnography, also offer methods for the observation of social forces, I argue that performance-based methods supplement these by incorporating a diverse range of sensitivities (or 'affects'), drawing on embodied experience for a wider range of attenuation, and also using creative constructs to deindividualise these observations. These are methods for investigation, not theoretical analysis, intended to bring into view that which might be unlooked-for, or rendered invisible by power structures at work, within a particular context; and to draw affective connections where they may not be obvious.

Such methods can take many forms, both in the shape of the creative inquiry and the form of the output; in this chapter, I focus on an approach I characterise as 'performative mapping', in which spatial experience is mapped following affective and embodied qualities of encounter, rather than physical or cultural geographies. I describe how such an approach informs British/German artist Ant Hampton's practice of traversing national and cultural borders in order to make visible histories and flows of forced migration that shape our present contexts. His resulting work, *Borderline Visible* (2023), can be considered a research output of such a method—one whose innovative form of a nonlinear book with accompanying audio track immerses the reader/participant in a similarly affective experience. I also present the uses of this method in teaching contexts, outlining pedagogical exercises that are designed to generate modes of encounter that defamiliarise public space. As I describe here, these techniques can be used to expand the field of 'grounded theory' (an existing method within social sciences and other fields) into directions that are more playful, but also more disruptive: not only describing existing relations, but also calling new ones into being.

Context | Situated knowing and unknowing

Performance is not just a subject of knowledge but also a way of knowing, one that offers affinities with quotidian, unofficial, embodied, and otherwise subjugated epistemologies. Michel Foucault ([1976] 1980) describes the totalising effects of explanatory theories, even those that have radical critical intentions, such as Marxism or psychoanalysis, such that they can become "global, *totalitarian theories*" ([1976] 1980, 80). In contrast to these, he describes an "insurrection of subjugated knowledges", those local and specific ways of knowing that, from the perspective of "official" knowledge appear as "unqualified, even directly disqualified knowledges"—for example, in relation to medicine or psychiatry, the knowledge of their condition of the psychiatric patient or person with illness ([1976] 1980, 81–82). Diana Taylor (2003) connects such disqualification of knowledge to contexts of European colonisation and so-called 'discovery', where it is the colonising framework, often taking the form of writing, which displaces and erases lived, body-to-body, and intergenerational practices. She opposes the colonising 'archive', which accumulates texts, maps, photographs, and artefacts separated from their use, with the 'repertoire', which "enacts embodied memory" through "performances, gestures, orality, movement, dance, singing—in short, all those acts usually thought of as ephemeral, nonreproducible knowledge" (2003, 20). Whereas the archive claims permanence and fixity, a knowledge that accrues and sustains power, the repertoire is characterised by transfer, transmission, and transformation: it becomes knowledge in its *doing*, and "people participate in the production and reproduction of knowledge by 'being there', being a part of the transmission" (2003, 20).

Positions such as Foucault's and Taylor's argue for an understanding of the ways in which knowledge is not found but produced, and produced within the context of hierarchies of power and differentiated valuing of life. Similar arguments are put forward in feminist critiques of science, as in those by Donna Haraway (1988) and Sandra Harding (1991). Against the illusion of objective, universal knowledge, which she characterises as "the god trick of seeing everything from nowhere," Haraway argues that *all* knowledge is 'situated knowledge': always rooted in a particular perspective and embedded within a particular social and embodied experience (1988, 581). Feminist standpoint theory, as developed by Harding and others, challenges the supposed 'impartiality' of knowledge, instead emphasising its partiality: partial both in the sense of being incomplete, and embedding a set of personal and/or cultural values. The significance of these critiques is amplified in decolonial scholarship and practice, such as Walter Mignolo's critique of the epistemological imperialism of Western modernity: "Its imperiality consists precisely in hiding its locality, its geo-historical body location, and in assuming to be universal and thus managing the universality to which everyone has to submit" (Mignolo 2011, 80).

Research methodologies that take seriously these provocations from feminist and decolonial thought begin by articulating their own positionality in order to acknowledge the power relations and valued presumptions that are implicit in their standpoints. As Aileen Moreton-Robinson (2013) writes, "Standpoint theory's recognition of partiality and subjectivity brings together the body and knowledge production, which is in contrast to the disembodied epistemological privileging of 'validity' and 'objectivity' within Western patriarchal knowledge production" (2013, 333). But the challenge of such an approach is that this could be seen to demand an even more all-encompassing knowledge: claiming not only one's own knowledge but the knowledge of all intersecting fields of power and displacement within which knowledge is held, as well as the limitations of one's knowledge. As Gillian Rose (1997) puts it, the demands of such an exhaustive self-reflexivity risk being overly presumptuous about the analytical superpowers of the researcher: in attempting such a thorough awareness of the hierarchies and distributions of power, "we may be performing nothing more than a goddess-trick uncomfortably similar to the god-trick" (1997, 311).

Rather than attempting an exhaustive knowing of one's positionality, then, an alternative approach begins from a position of un-knowing, decentring the autonomy of the knowing subject. Here, recent developments in the theorisation of 'affect' have articulated the limitations of the subject as 'master' of knowledge, instead emphasising the ways in which our experience is shaped by affective flows and forces that are outside the capacities of comprehension by the conscious, rational self. As I will describe later in the 'how to' section, it is in this context that performance-based methods can offer ways of working with these invisible and unknowable networks of feeling and sensation, by adopting playful and arbitrary rules that displace individual authority and foreground embodied attunement and responsiveness.

'Affect' is an interdisciplinary concept that draws on and connects fields of cultural studies, performance studies, and literary studies, but also psychology, neurobiology, and social development, where the self is understood not as a fixed entity but fluid and changing, shaped by a sea of sensations that our conscious selves fix into 'meanings' and 'emotions', but which precede and exceed such narrations of the self. In the context of child development, Sylvan Tomkins describes affects as literally preceding the formation of the self, identifying nine primary affects that are hard-coded into our neurological makeup as pre-conscious response circuits, such as distress, excitement, joy, fear, shame, and disgust (Tomkins Institute 2014). As we experience these affects, we identify them as 'feelings', and over time we start to identify them with 'emotions', which we cultivate into feedback loops that we call our personalities, but at their core they are based on autonomic firings of neural pathways.

The neurobiologist David Eagleman (2004) argues even more strongly for the illusory nature of a coherent self, instead describing consciousness as peripheral to the core operations of the brain apparatus. We may think we are making decisions, Eagleman proposes, but actually our decisions arise from complex interactions prior to consciousness: he proposes that intention may be "an illusion arising from *watching yourself* [...] make actions" (2004, 1146). For this reason, philosopher Brian Massumi (1995) argues that "Will and consciousness are *subtractive*. They are *imitative, derived functions* which reduce a complexity too rich to be functionally expressed" (90). Drawing on Massumi and Tompkins, Eric Shouse (2005) helpfully differentiates the affective register from that of the personal: "affect is not a personal feeling," he writes. "Feelings are *personal* and *biographical*, emotions are *social*, and affects are *prepersonal*."

These ideas and observations argue for an understanding of self that exceeds that which is perceptible to the conscious mind. As Eagleman (2011) puts it, "The conscious mind is not at the centre of action in the brain; instead, it is far out on a distant edge, hearing but whispers of activity" (16). Moreover, affect theory argues that these flows of distributions of affective forces exceed the individual body. Theresa Brennan (2004) emphasises the communicability of affect, the way that it flows between so-called individuals and their environments, breaking down the distinction between the two: "the transmission of affect, if only for an instant, alters the biochemistry and neurology of the subject. The 'atmosphere' or the environment literally gets into the individual" (1). In this way, she writes, "There is no secure distinction between the individual and the 'environment'" (6). In these views, the 'body' is not a discrete, individuated entity, but continuous with its surroundings, in an ongoing exchange and flow; and these exchanges are not just mechanistic ('hot', 'cold', 'hungry') but emotional in complex ways that shape our orientation to being in the world ('anxious', 'bored', 'ashamed'). As Sara Ahmed (2004) puts it, "emotions should not be regarded as psychological states, but as social and cultural practices" (9).

Crucially, then, affects and emotions are part of the same hierarchies of power and oppression that value some lives and experiences over others: in these 'affective economies', "affects circulate in uneven ways, becoming attached or sticking to certain bodies more than others," as Rebecca Coleman (2016) summarises. "As such, it becomes important to explore the ways in which affects and relations of movement and stoppage map onto, or indeed remake, sociocultural differences and inequalities" (23). How does one attend to these affective flows and forces, which exceed and precede the conscious self, and are sometimes deliberately invisibilised and naturalised in consort with racialised, gendered, and otherwise minoritised inequities? How does one render them perceptible, so that they enter into the domain of critique? We cannot sit above or outside them, for that 'we' is in some ways produced by them, as one of their effects. So, we begin in the midst of them.

How to | Performative mapping

In both feminist approaches to situated knowledge and theories of affect, the self is understood relationally, "less a coherent agent and more a decentred site of differences," as Rose (1997, 314) puts it. Performance-based practices can foreground experience that is responsive in ways that are not under the control of the experiencing subject. As such, they can generate what performance scholar and ethnographer Dwight Conquergood (2002) characterises as "a view from ground level, in the thick of things" (146). There are a wide range of creative practices developed in many fields of performance, site-responsive art, and socially engaged art which contribute to such situated knowledges. Here, I focus on performative mapping as a special practice of affective attunement.

I borrow the idea of affective attunement from cultural anthropologist Kathleen Stewart, who describes her practice as "attuned to the forms and forces unfolding in scenes and encounters" (2017, 192). Elsewhere she describes this as a process of "atmospheric attunement," where she defines atmosphere as "not an effect of other forces but a lived affect—a capacity to affect and to be affected that pushes a present into a composition, an expressivity, the sense of potentiality and event" (2011, 452). In Stewart's work, this takes the form of a writing practice that develops a heightened attentiveness to the everyday: not an analysis of underlying structures or an explanation via totalising theoretical frameworks, but an attempt to notice and record the fleeting impulses and desires of 'ordinary' experience.

In her collection *Ordinary Affects*, she presents a series of scenes, fragments, and observations, rather than conclusions or analyses, following the hunch that richly describing the complexity of a lived moment will tell us something about what she elsewhere describes as "the matterings, the complex emergent worlds, happening in everyday life" (Stewart 2011, 447). Everyday life, she writes, "is a life lived on the level of surging affects," and what may be dismissed as 'the ordinary' can be treated as "a circuit that's always tuned in to some little something somewhere" (2007, 9; 12). Stewart's ethnographic practice relies on a literary sensibility: writing that is not the documentation of observation, but is itself observational, using auto-ethnographic observation, narrative, and critically informed attentiveness in order to generate a hybrid literary form. As she describes it, her work "tries to slow the quick jump to representational thinking and evaluative critique long enough to find ways of approaching the complex and uncertain objects that fascinate because they literally hit us or exert a pull on us" (Stewart 2007, 4).

But in what follows, I argue that performance—as embodied experience, and as intentional and arbitrary constraints on that experience—can also offer techniques of affective attunement, in ways that help to decentre the primacy of the experiencing subject and bypass the gatekeeping role of intentionality. Rather than search for evidence for theories, affective attunement is a practice of cultivating openness and sensitivity to that which is already there, the affective mesh that is indeed producing our sense of 'us', triggering our pre-conscious desires, fears, attractions, and avoidances. It is about not only noticing what is around us, but trying to notice what it might be that is shaping how and what we notice in the first place, the situatedness of our knowledge, and what remains unnoticed and invisible. These are modes of attention that prioritise the embodied and the visceral over the conceptual and analytical.

In the Euro-American context, site-responsive performance practice often cites the influence of the Situationist International (SI) and its concept of 'psychogeography', defined by Guy Debord ([1955] 2006) as "the study of the precise laws and specific effects of the geographical environment, whether consciously organised or not, on the emotions and behavior of individuals" (8). In addition to the physical topology of the built environment, the SI argued that "cities have psychogeographical contours, with constant currents, fixed points and vortexes that strongly discourage entry into or exit from certain zones" (Debord [1958] 2006, 62). Such an idea prefigures the interdisciplinary concept of affect, but an updated version is articulated by Nigel Thrift (2007): "Cities can be seen as roiling maelstroms of affect. Particular affects like anger, fear, happiness and joy are continually on the boil, rising here, subsiding there, and these affects continually manifest themselves in events which can take place either at a grand scale or simply as a part of continuing everyday life" (171). As a tool for mapping these 'psychogeographical contours', the SI advocated the technique of the *dérive*, or drift, in which the practitioner tries to abandon their conceptual understanding of the city and instead follow affective impulses. As theorists more than practitioners, the implementation of the *dérive* by the SI themselves is relatively unremarkable, but has nevertheless influenced a wide range of contemporary artists and urban activists.[1]

One key form that this psychogeographical technique takes is the use of arbitrary and non-correlational constraints to shape one's experience. In Debord's original treatise, cited above, the example is given of navigating a region of Germany by "blindly following" a map of London, where using the wrong map for the purpose can produce unintended discoveries. Robert MacFarlane suggests an updated version of this exercise, beginning with using a cup to trace a circle over a map of a city:

> Pick up the map, go out into the city, and walk the circle, keeping as close as you can to the curve. Record the experience as you go, in whatever medium you favour: film, photograph, manuscript, tape. Catch the textual run off of the streets; the graffiti, the branded litter, the snatches of conversation. Cut for sign. Log the data-stream. Be alert to the happenstance of metaphors, watch for visual rhymes, coincidences, analogies, family resemblances, the changing moods of the street. (MacFarlane 2005; reproduced in Coverley 2018, 9)

---

1 For a more thorough history of the *dérive*, see Lavery 2018.

Techniques of counter-intuitive maps, disorientations, and 'psychogeographical' attentiveness inform numerous artistic practices that seek to intervene and disrupt the ordinary uses of space. For example, UK-based artist duo Lone Twin undertook site-responsive works through rules that echo MacFarlane's arbitrary circle: in *Totem* (1998), the two artists drew a straight line across the town of Colchester, and attempted to carry a 20-foot (6-metre) telephone pole following this line, negotiating with residents and property owners to pass through their homes and businesses, traversing some distance each day and continuing where they left off the next day (Lone Twin 2001). And in *Spiral* (2007), they again followed a multi-day itinerary, this time following a spiral drawn over the densely populated Barbican Centre in central London. The path required them to take long detours around walls and landscape features in order to resume the smooth line of the spiral; along the way, they accumulated objects and stories, and encountered inhabitants and users of the spaces who became part of the 'performance' (see Fig. 17.1; see also Williams and Lavery 2011, 115–18).

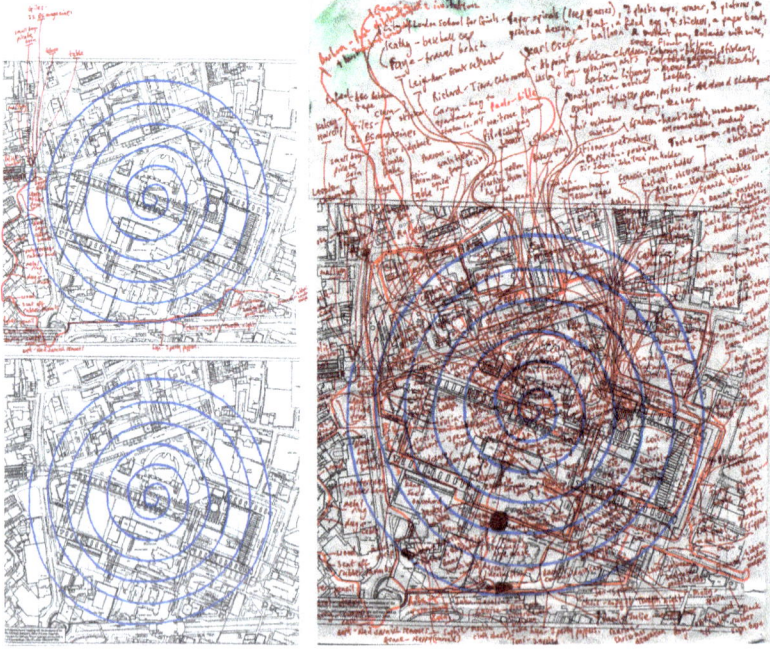

Fig. 17.1 Lone Twin, *Spiral* (2007). Courtesy of the artists.

Other performative mapping techniques are less spatially directive and more suggestive. In their *Mis-Guide to Anywhere*, intended as a guidebook that can be used to defamiliarise the experience of any lived space, artist collective Wrights & Sites (2006) present a compendium of more open-ended scores or instructions: "Go exploring with children—let them choose a special way of traveling"; "Find somewhere to be private in a public space"; "Follow your shadow"; "Fall out of a taxi onto a dark road. Watch it drive away. Set out across country" (83, 64, 4, 26). Such prompts are reminiscent of Fluxus scores, the instructions put forward by a wide range of international artists from the 1960s onwards that varied from the straightforward—"Watch a flower until one of them falls or until all of them fall" (Takehisa Kosugi, "Malika 5" [nd], in Friedman, Smith, and Sawchyn 2002, 74)—to the more open-ended and elegiac— "Take the sound of the stone aging" (Yoko Ono, "Tape Piece I: Stone Piece" [1963], in Friedman, Smith, and Sawchyn 2002, 86). As Josefine Wikström (2021) writes, these scores "provide a structure that intensifies and frames reality—'flux'—into a coherent experience" (19).

The usefulness of rules and constraints, however simple or arbitrary, is that they displace the 'knowing subject' in favour of an experiencing subject. As artist Vito Acconci reflected about his *Following Piece* (1969), in which he followed a randomly selected passerby in the city until they entered private space, "I am almost not an 'I' anymore; I put myself in the service of this scheme" (Linker 1994, 20). And from a queer/disability experience, Petra Kuppers (2022) uses an expanded understanding of *dérive* as a "technique of de-/refamiliarizing oneself with one's environment" (7 note 2). "By orienting toward the environment," Kuppers writes, "a self assembles, and an 'I' emerges, in relation" (14). As techniques for decentring the self, performance practices open space not only for differently situated knowledges but for different ways of knowing: not a methodical search for evidence, but an openness to the 'flux' of experience.

Such techniques also enable artists-as-researchers to 'tune in' to the invisible—or even deliberately invisibilised—force fields of power and subjectification, of memory and erasure, and the accumulation of affective residues that shape and determine our present interactions, often without us even knowing it. A range of such possibilities can be seen in the urban actions of Francis Alÿs, such as *Paradox of Praxis 1 (Sometimes making something leads to nothing)* (1997), in which he pushes a large block of ice through Mexico City until it melts; *Samples II* (2004a), in which he uses a stick to 'play' the myriad railings and fences of central London as if they were a musical instrument; and the more overtly political *The Green Line (Sometimes doing something poetic can become political and sometimes doing something political can become poetic)* (2004b), in which Alÿs walked with a dripping can of green paint (58 litres in total) to make a visible trace of the arbitrary 'Green Line' that divides Jerusalem after the 1949 armistice. The following case study demonstrates a more sustained engagement with the politics of visibility.

Demonstration | *Borderline visible*

Hampton's *Borderline Visible* (2023) centres around a number of literal maps: charting a journey undertaken by the artist from Lausanne, Switzerland, to İzmir, Turkey; the historical diasporic journey of Sephardic Jews following their expulsion from Spain in 1492; and maps of so-called 'pushbacks' (or 'drift-backs') in the Aegean Sea, a euphemism for the practice by European border forces of returning people who attempt oceanic migration to the sea with no provisions and barely serviceable vessels ('inflatable baskets', in the words of one of the migrants interviewed by Hampton).[2] Such a practice is often officially denied by the governments involved, but extensively documented, as in the maps by the interdisciplinary research group Forensic Architecture (2023) which Hampton draws upon. Along the way there are also more localised maps: descriptions of how to find a cemetery for the so-called 'nameless' persons who have died at sea in their attempts to reach Europe, or a GPS pin showing where Hampton is waiting in a rental car to pick up someone he has recently met who is being held indefinitely in a Greek detention centre for those attempting migration.

---

2   Quotations are from the audio component of the work, based on a transcript provided to the author by the artist.

17. Affective Attunement: Mapping the Invisible 371

Fig. 17.2 Forensic Architecture, *Drift-Backs in the Aegean Sea*, 2023. Screen capture from https://aegean.forensic-architecture.org/ ©Forensic Architecture.

But *Borderline Visible* is also an affective map, of the resonances of trauma and violence, of empire and racism, and the invisible but indelible effect they have in shaping this fiction called 'Europe'. As spectators, we engage with Hampton's experience in an unusual form: a book, almost 200 pages, made up of scraps of photographs and text, extracts from archives, and snapshots from trains, which we navigate while simultaneously listening to an audio track of Hampton's voice (at least for those listening in English; other translations exist, too). In the context of an important body of artistic work that shares the stories of those attempting migration, humanising and validating these experiences, I think *Borderline Visible* is significant in working from and through the situatedness of this particular White European, implicated within these structures of privilege and exclusion, and moving with considerable privilege across borders that are impassable by others: "I pay a ticket," Hampton recalls, "show my passport, and with other passengers slip effortlessly from west to east, through a space where other bodies are being regularly thrown into the sea." Despite—or indeed, because of—this privilege, Hampton traces how his identity is nevertheless shaped by these political economies of undervalued lives and the violent fictions of nationhood and empire. One might call it a map of Europe's broken heart.

As Hampton describes in the voiceover track, the precursor to *Borderline Visible* was a performance investigation called *Mouthpiece*, created by Hampton and Rita Pauls. This earlier work offers a good example of the use of arbitrary structure imposed by performative rules: beginning from a field which Google Maps identifies as the centre of Germany, Hampton and Pauls walked to a nearby road, and began randomly hitchhiking, flagging down passing drivers while holding a sign that read *'irgendwohin'*—'anywhere'. Over the course of a week's travels on an itinerary determined by the people who picked them up, they asked these strangers, "What, in your opinion, needs to be said?" The answers to these questions formed the basis of a theatre production, in which the artists memorised and repeated the answers verbatim, reproducing all the accents, pauses, and verbal tics. *Mouthpiece* was motivated by Pauls' heritage as the descendant of Jewish grandparents who fled Germany in the 1930s, and Hampton's process of seeking German citizenship. Hampton tells us that *Borderline Visible* was intended to be a similar process, informed by the other side of Pauls' lineage, who were Sephardic Jews and hence travelled eastwards from Spain to Turkey. But because Pauls had to abandon the project for health reasons, it turned into a different kind of exploration, with Hampton's journey informed by histories of diasporic fugitivity that are not his own, retracing someone else's lineage, and as such, having to find ways to attune himself to the lines of flight that he traverses.

This is nonfiction performance, a form of open-ended cultural inquiry that begins from a set of deterministic rules but is open to chance encounter, attuned to the psychogeography of lived environment, and attentive to the self as more than its conscious processes. Hampton is guided—or mis-guided, to borrow Wrights & Sites' term—by impulses and connections, often unsure of why he has made choices he has made, roughly following the trajectory traced on the European map of migration.

17. Affective Attunement: Mapping the Invisible   373

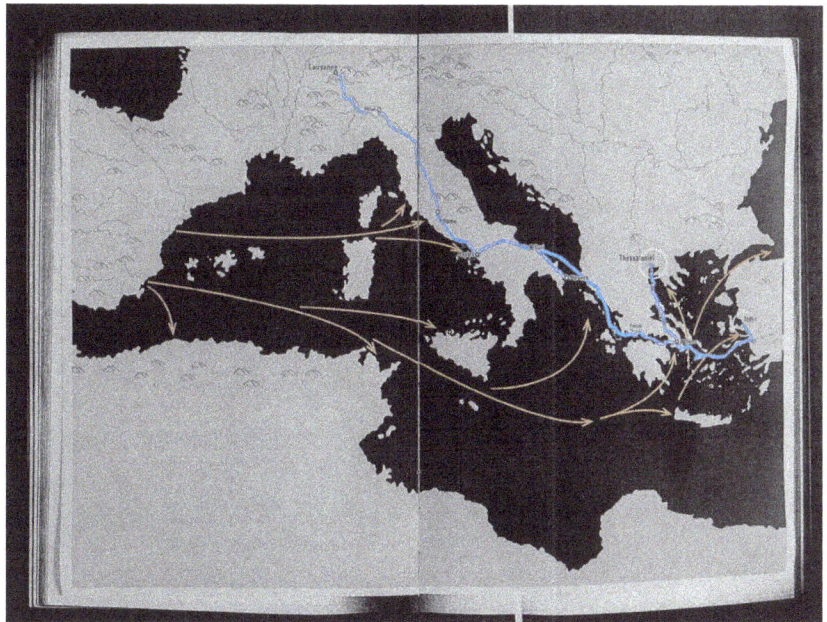

Fig. 17.3 Map detail from Ant Hampton, *Borderline Visible* (2023). Courtesy of the artist.

And his observations are strikingly similar to Stewart's atmospheric attunement: amidst the grand historical arcs that he intersects, there are also the flightpaths of swifts and swallows, the cries of an old woman with Alzheimer's locked indoors by her son who has no other choice, memories of his own half-sister who suffered from Alzheimer's, and his narrative attempt not to explain or theorise these connections but simply to notice them, where "things matter not because of how they are represented but because they have qualities, rhythms, forces, relations, and movements" (Stewart 2011, 445).

In Thessaloniki, he and Pauls (still with him at this point) stand in a cathedral, the floor of which was remade after the second World War with slabs of stone that had previously covered Jewish graves. Now turned over so the unmarked sides are up, the undersides still carry Hebrew writing. Elsewhere in the same city, he records a conversation with a police officer outside a synagogue, who Hampton notices stumbles over saying the word 'Jewish', taking five attempts to get the syllables out. Later in the Karataş area of İzmir where Pauls' Sephardic ancestors lived, and missing his friend who has since departed, Hampton is wandering, hoping for clues and connections that will help him to understand what he is looking for and what he is missing:

> The Jewish story is not mine. I tell myself: that's the point, one good reason for me to continue alone. If only Jewish people were interested in Jewish history, where would we be? Standing there, I remember imagining for a moment people everywhere feeling the absence of Jewish people with the same weight, and in the exact same way, that I miss my friend.

Hampton drifts, *dérive*-like, through these hot and unpopulated streets, feeling multiple layers of history and genealogy. And as distant audience to the narration of the events—not quite readers and not quite spectators—we are also drifting through experience. As we hear him recall his encounters, we are instructed to flip between the pages, sometimes forwards, sometimes backwards, sometimes coming back to the same photograph again and again but from different directions. Sometimes we are asked to close our eyes, to cover the images with our hands, to hold our place with one hand while we flip back to another part of the story (see Fig. 17.4).

Fig. 17.4 Readers interacting with *Borderline Visible* (2023). ©Bernard Kalu (www.bernardkalu.com).

17. Affective Attunement: Mapping the Invisible   375

In this way, *Borderline Visible* is not only made from an open-ended process of affective attunement, but also produces such an experience in the way it stages its encounter for its audience. Affective memory works like this: not a linear narrative, but holding multiple trajectories simultaneously, connecting the feeling of having a beloved family member lose her memory to Alzheimer's, with the cultural compartmentalising of genocide and erasure, with turning one's back to the 'pushbacks' at sea. The form of the reader/listener's experience also decentres the supposed autonomy of the 'knowing subject', who cannot be said to stand apart from their experience but is made (and indeed sometimes *undone*) through it. Where is the vantage point from which one can regard the 1922 massacre of Christians and Armenians in İzmir (then Smyrna)? From the British and US warships that stood passively by in the harbour as those fleeing the burning city drowned? From the negotiations between imperial powers in Lausanne? From the telescope overlooking the harbour, mounted at the top of the Asansör in the Jewish quarter, which was built long before the massacre, and stood there surveying the harbour and its history of atrocities?

Near the end of the book/performance, Hampton describes how he is weeping in the cemetery of hundreds, thousands of numbered wooden stakes that serve to commemorate the so-called 'nameless' who have died at sea. Not on any official map, somehow he has found himself here. Looking through the hills to the harbour, he realises he is probably within eyesight of that same telescope. Remembering that there was a message in braille next to the telescope, he asks, "What should that braille message describe? What are the so-called 'seeing' not seeing?" As a reader, I am flipping between these two pages, one showing the telescope and the braille marker, and the other showing Hampton's pointed finger across the graves to the place where the telescope might be. What is it we can now see? Can we start to see our own situatedness, the way there is no hard and fast distinction between 'their' stories and 'our' stories, between self and environment, between history and the present? This affective network that connects us, this "force field in which people find themselves" (Stewart 2011, 445), is perhaps what is being described by the figure of Hani, whom Hampton meets in the migrant camp in Greece, and whose family was murdered in Sudan. In voice message spoken in Arabic, automatically translated by Google in the soundtrack to *Borderline Visible,* Hani says:

> Don't think, don't think, don't think about water and don't get wet in all life is based on change this planet is built on change everything changes the house other than the house other than the person changes everything changes anything changes the ruler and changes everything say anything in this non-polar planet the water that you drink it big, it will break. Change you are in it.

Expanding the method | Grounded theory

Examples such as *Borderline Visible* demonstrate how performance as a mode of embodied and affective knowing can inform performance practice in the more traditional sense of constructed works of art—both in the research process that generates the work, and in the way that the experience of the work by spectators can foreground their situatedness.[3] But I also argue that performance-based modes of knowing have much to offer to other fields of practice within ethnography and the social sciences. For example, this "view from ground level, in the thick of things," as Conquergood puts it (2002, 146), has some affinities with the method of 'grounded theory', developed within the social sciences and medicine. One parallel is the way in which grounded theory resists 'tacking on' a theory after observation, or selecting data from observation that match a pre-selected theory, and instead "generates conceptual categories or their properties from evidence" that is derived from the lived experiences of those who actually inhabit the context being analysed (Glaser and Strauss [1967] 2004, 23). Whereas some earlier proponents of grounded theory understood themselves as 'discovering' structures of knowing and feeling that are 'out there', independent of the act of observation, more recent practitioners align themselves with the constructivist, situated view of knowledge advocated in the context section of this chapter. "Theory is not discovered," Ylona Chun Tie et al. (2019) write in their recent overview; "rather, theory is constructed by the researcher who views the world through their own particular lens" (3).

---

3   For more detailed discussion of the relationship between spectatorship and situatedness, see Groot Nibbelink and Merx 2021, and Chapter 2 in this volume.

Performance research can learn much from methods of ethnography and grounded theory; however, it also has much to contribute. Firstly, embodied and affective responsiveness can enrich and expand the qualitative act of 'data collection', bringing into consideration not only that which is seen and heard, but also that which is felt or experienced through movement and interaction, through the process of affective attunement described here. But perhaps more importantly, such methods can help to address a fundamental question for grounded theory: if you are not starting with an explanatory theory or a question, then where do you start? Even apparently open-ended forms of data-gathering—observations, interviews, measurements—all presume a set of parameters that are to be measured, subjects who are within the scope of enquiry and those without, and questions that are relevant. But neither is it a satisfactory approach to begin with no method at all and to start with just aimless wandering and observation, as this can reinforce inherited and invisibilised preferences and dispositions toward what is worthy of observation in the first place. I would suggest that this is where the kinds of observational constraints described in the 'How to' section can be useful: they are not 'structureless', which is another way of concealing inherent structures (see Freeman [1970] 2013), but instead are structured redirections of our normal ways of attending to the world.

Taking inspiration from these (and many other) forms of performative mapping, I have developed a set of practical exercises to displace the intentionality of self and activate an open and unpredictable attention to lived environment. In the context of the Utrecht University course The City as Stage, for example, I invite learners to undertake group 'drifts', working within constraints that limit the role of the active choosing 'self'. For example, move through the outdoor environment as a group of 5–6 persons bound together by a circular length of rope wrapped around each person's body, moving without speaking or designating a leader, and instead following the tension in the rope. Or, following the example of Lone Twin's *Spiral*, use a superimposed spiral of the area surrounding the classroom as a guide, entering into spaces where possible, and moving through and around obstacles in order to rejoin the spiral on the other side. Or, inspired by Vito Acconci's *Following Piece* (1969), silently agree upon a stranger whom the group will discreetly follow at a distance, until it is no longer possible to follow them (because they go into a private space, for example)—taking care not to cause discomfort to the person being followed. As described in the 'Context' section above, the intention of these tasks is to displace the intentional subject, opening experience to the accidental and the unlooked-for in everyday life.

A second set of exercises draws implicitly and explicitly on ideas of affective attunement, psychogeographic experimentation, and the use of performance constraints to further deactivate intentionality and to open attentiveness to what might be unnoticed, undervalued, or naturalised (and thereby invisibilised) in our social environments. A first set of instructions, designed to be usable in any context, give prompts that place the practitioner in an unusual site of observation, directing the user away from default patterns of where to look and feel *from*:

- Find a threshold—between indoors and outdoors, on a curb or intersection, at a gate or perimeter.
- Find someone who appears to be on their own or separated from everyone else. Position yourself near them.
- Find a place where no one pauses, where people just keep moving through. Pause there.
- Look for the colour orange. Place yourself near an object of that colour.
- On Google Maps, search for "a". Click "More filters" and select "Sort by: distance". Go to the first location that comes up.
- Get as far away as you can from where you just were, but so you could still see you, if you were still where you were before. Now look at what else you can see from this new location.
- Close your eyes. Pick a sound that you can hear from where you are, other than people speaking. Open your eyes and follow that sound to as close to its source as you can.
- Choose someone passing by and follow them for five minutes, or until they go into a private place. After either of these events, remain where you have stopped.
- Go to a place that you think will be the busiest place near where you are.
- Find somewhere you can be completely alone.

17. Affective Attunement: Mapping the Invisible 379

Having arrived at a location, a further set of instructions are designed to shape the quality and focus of attention with which to engage with this new situation: what to look and feel *for*:

- How do people use, move through, or inhabit this space? Translate what you see into a set of prescriptive rules for behaviour.

  This could be a list of rules for a game, a script for an actor, a choreographic sequence for dancers or a flash-mob, etc.

- What stories does this place hold? How does it hold them? Look closely; listen closely.

  You may eavesdrop to what people are saying, but don't be noticed. You may look at leaflets, advertisements, noticeboards. You may search online for histories. You may make things up.

- Find a place in the middle of what is happening, but where you can stay still without feeling uncomfortable. Set a timer for five minutes and close your eyes. Listen. Feel.

  When the timer goes off, set another timer for five minutes and write continuously, without stopping.

- Who is not welcome here? How would it feel to be them? What would they notice about this place?

  Write a description of what would need to change for this place to be welcoming, without being explicit about who you are imagining: just describe the changes.

- Catalogue the non-human (including non-animal) life that inhabits this place. What timescales do they inhabit?

- Collect four objects. Arrange them in relation to each other.

  Write a caption for each object, as if for a museum display (any genre of museum: science museum, art museum, ethnographic museum, etc.).

- How would you describe the affective atmosphere here? What are the sensations that your body experiences? What is producing those sensations?

  Attend to visual stimulus, sound, smell, temperature, gut responses, memories, associations, etc.

- Write down all the questions you overhear people asking. Write down all the questions you can see that are printed anywhere.
- Imagine you are a tour guide. What would be the significance of this stop on the tour? Write as if you are the guide, introducing this location.
- Find something that you think is in need of care. Describe what this care would look like, as if it is happening now or over time (maybe many years or centuries) as you watch.
- Find a way to make a rhythmical or repetitive sound out of the stuff you find here. Record the sound for a few minutes.

Play back the sound (on a loop) and write in a way that is shaped by the rhythmic sound.

I think of these as examples of what Phillip Vannini (2015) calls "non-representational research methods": they are not oriented toward documenting an empirical reality, but instead understanding observation as *event*: "it is enactment, rupture, and actualisation that engage your attention" (12). Of course, the data produced in this way is highly partial and situated; that is the point. But the intention of these constraints is that they generate attentiveness to more than the merely personal: not on the individual level of "I am feeling this", but rather the affective register of "this feeling-body is registering this." As Shouse (2005) writes in the passage cited above, "affect is not a personal feeling." At this point, other complementary methods could be introduced to help work with and from these affective observations. For example, gender and critical race theory could interrogate the role of affect in maintaining racialised or gendered hierarchies (Ahmed 2004); social science methods or community art practices could broaden the enquiry to wider populations; or historiographical or archival methods could enquire further into the sites and histories being brought into focus. In the example of *Borderline Visible*, Hampton's research methods included not only the constraints of his itinerary and his attentiveness to the affective, but also historicisation, interviews, and gathering testimony.

In my teaching practice, I take inspiration from Linda Knight's practice of "inefficient mapping," which resists "hegemonic cartographic practices" by attending to "different readings of space, life, community, presence, time, and belonging" (Knight 2021, 22). I ask experimenters to produce their own maps in the form of instructional scores for others to follow. This completes a circle, turning affective observation back into a performative constraint, and investing in knowledge not as something found or discovered (and then objectively recorded), but instead as an event to be encountered, and to be encountered differently. For example, one student writes (see Fig. 17.5):

> This is a trace of a route I walked while following a pigeon. You can start by finding a pigeon yourself and turning on an app that would allow you to see the route you've made afterward. From my route, I isolated a few looped patterns that you can see at the top. If you do not have time for pigeon-following, then feel free to use them. Find a space that allows you to perform the loop of your choice—there is no scale, you can make it as big or as small as you want. With your group, start from the same point (perhaps someone was throwing breadcrumbs there?) When you feel ready, start following your pattern. You can take breaks. If you encounter another person, exchange the patterns and start again from that spot. Finish when something else has caught your attention.

Fig. 17.5 Agata Kok, score composed for The City As Stage at Utrecht University (2023). Courtesy of the artist.

And another (see Fig. 17.6) traces lines of interaction and affect, with Fluxus-like open-ended instructions ('learn how to listen', 'cross') interwoven into graphical representations that suggest lines of flight, a trajectory that must be interpreted corporeally, through dancing and rolling through an environment:

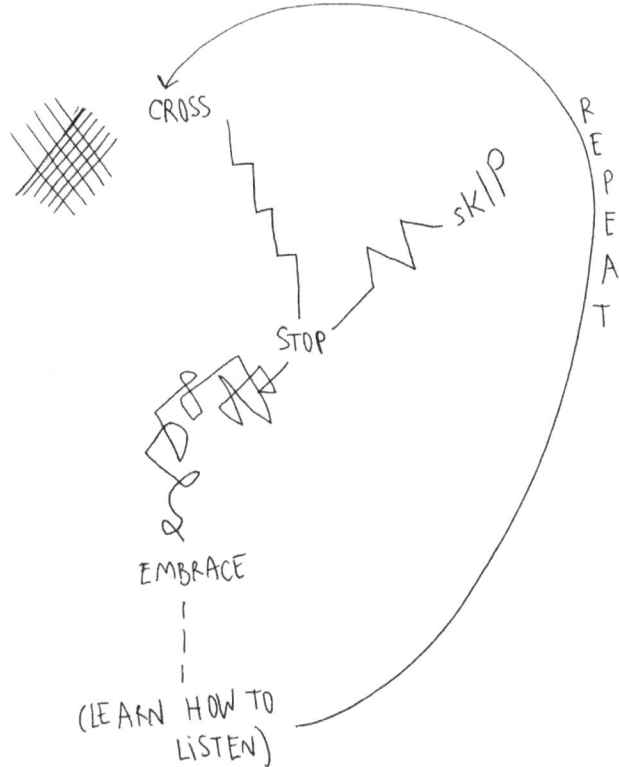

Fig. 17.6 Júlia Pejó Vergara, score composed for The City As Stage at Utrecht University (2023). Courtesy of the artist.

I close with this graphical score that, despite its simplicity, returns us to the three senses of performance with which this chapter opened. As a prepared action, the score frames experience in a way that separates it from 'ordinary' life, introducing intentionality and self-awareness along with interpretative and agential choices. As a way of knowing, it counters top-down surveillance maps of a landscape by instead prescribing an intimate and embodied encounter. The shape this encounter will take will be very different if the score is executed in a populated city centre, or down a hillside of wildflowers and insects, or in a classroom or workplace. And the instructions function performatively, in the sense of generating that which is named through its enaction. That is, they do not represent or describe a relationship between self and environment; instead, they call into being this possibility of affective attunement.

Suggestions for further reading

Conquergood's numerous writings combining ethnographic studies with performance research are collected in the posthumously published volume *Cultural Struggles: Performance, Ethnography, Praxis* (2013). Kathleen Stewart' *Ordinary Affects* (2007) is the best demonstration of what she means by 'atmospheric attunement', collecting vignettes of varying lengths that capture moments of everyday affective flux. For a contextualisation and demonstration of alternative approaches to mapping, see Linda Knight's *Inefficient Mapping: A Protocol for Attuning to Phenomena* (2021—which is also available Open Access.

References

Ahmed, Sara. 2004. *The Cultural Politics of Emotion*. Routledge.

Alÿs, Francis. 1997. *Paradox of Praxis 1 (Sometimes Making Something Leads to Nothing)*. https://francisalys.com/sometimes-making-something-leads-to-nothing/

Alÿs, Francis. 2004a. *Samples II*. https://francisalys.com/samples-2/

Alÿs, Francis. 2004b. *The Green Line (Sometimes Doing Something Poetic Can Become Political and Sometimes Doing Something Political Can Become Poetic)*. https://francisalys.com/the-green-line/

Brennan, Teresa. 2004. *The Transmission of Affect*. Cornell University Press.

Chun Tie, Ylona, Melanie Birks, and Karen Francis. 2019. "Grounded Theory Research: A Design Framework for Novice Researchers." *SAGE Open Medicine* 7 (January). https://doi.org/10.1177/2050312118822927

Coleman, Rebecca. 2016. "Affect." In *Gender: Sources, Perspectives, and Methodologies*, edited by Renée C. Hoogland, 15–26. Macmillan Reference/Gale.

Conquergood, Dwight. 2002. "Performance Studies: Interventions and Radical Research." *TDR/The Drama Review* 46 (2): 145–56. https://doi.org/10.1162/105420402320980550

Conquergood, Dwight. 2013. *Cultural Struggles: Performance, Ethnography, Praxis*. Edited by E. Patrick Johnson. University of Michigan Press.

Coverley, Merlin. 2018. *Psychogeography*. 3rd edn. Oldcastle Books.

Debord, Guy. [1955] 2006. "Introduction to a Critique of Urban Geography." In *Situationist International Anthology*, edited and translated by Ken Knabb, revised and expanded edition, 8–12. Bureau of Public Secrets.

Debord, Guy. [1958] 2006. "Theory of the Dérive." In *Situationist International Anthology*, edited and translated by Ken Knabb, revised and expanded edition, 62–66. Bureau of Public Secrets.

Eagleman, David. 2004. "The Where and When of Intention." *Science* 303 (5661): 1144–46. https://doi.org/10.1126/science.1095331

Eagleman, David. 2011. *Incognito: The Secret Lives of the Brain*. Pantheon.

Forensic Architecture. 2023. *Drift-Backs in the Aegean Sea*. https://aegean.forensic-architecture.org/

Foucault, Michel. [1976] 1980. "Two Lectures." In *Power/Knowledge: Selected Interviews and Other Writings, 1972–1977*, edited by Colin Gordon, translated by Colin Gordon, Leo Marshall, John Mepham, and Kate Soper, 78–108. Pantheon.

Freeman, Jo. [1970] 2013. "The Tyranny of Structurelessness." *WSQ: Women's Studies Quarterly* 41 (3/4): 231–46. https://doi.org/10.1353/wsq.2013.0072

Friedman, Ken, Owen Smith, and Lauren Sawchyn, eds. 2002. *The Fluxus Performance Workbook*. 40th anniversary edn. Performance Research e-publication.

Glaser, Barney G., and Anselm L. Strauss. [1967] 2004. *The Discovery of Grounded Theory: Strategies for Qualitative Research*. Aldine Transaction.

Groot Nibbelink, Liesbeth, and Sigrid Merx. 2021. "Dramaturgical Analysis: A Relational Approach." *FORUM+* 28 (3): 4–16. https://doi.org/10.5117/FORUM2021.3.002.GROO

Hampton, Ant. 2023. *Borderline Visible*. Time Based Editions. https://timebasededitions.com/Product-page

Haraway, Donna. 1988. "Situated Knowledges: The Science Question in Feminism and the Privilege of Partial Perspective." *Feminist Studies* 14 (3): 575–99. https://doi.org/10.2307/3178066

Harding, Sandra. 1991. *Whose Science? Whose Knowledge? Thinking from Women's Lives*. Cornell University Press.

Knight, Linda. 2021. *Inefficient Mapping: A Protocol for Attuning to Phenomena*. punctum books. https://doi.org/10.53288/0336.1.00

Kuppers, Petra. 2022. *Eco Soma: Pain and Joy in Speculative Performance Encounters*. University of Minnesota Press. https://doi.org/10.7302/4171

Lavery, Carl. 2018. "Rethinking the *Dérive*: Drifting and Theatricality in Theatre and Performance Studies." *Performance Research* 23 (7): 1–15. https://doi.org/10.1080/13528165.2018.1557011

Linker, Kate. 1994. *Vito Acconci*. Rizzoli.

Lone Twin. 2001. "Totem." *Performance Research* 6 (3): 13–111. https://doi.org/10.1080/13528165.2001.10871801

MacFarlane, Robert. 2005. "A Road of One's Own: Past and Present Artists of the Randomly Motivated Walk." *Times Literary Supplement*, October 7, 2005.

Massumi, Brian. 1995. "The Autonomy of Affect." *Cultural Critique*, no. 31, 83–109. https://doi.org/10.2307/1354446

Mignolo, Walter D. 2011. *The Darker Side of Western Modernity: Global Futures, Decolonial Options*. Duke University Press.

Moreton-Robinson, Aileen. 2013. "Towards an Australian Indigenous Women's Standpoint Theory: A Methodological Tool." *Australian Feminist Studies* 28 (78): 331–47. https://doi.org/10.1080/08164649.2013.876664

Rose, Gillian. 1997. "Situating Knowledges: Positionality, Reflexivities and Other Tactics." *Progress in Human Geography* 21 (3): 305–20. https://doi.org/10.1191/030913297673302122

Shouse, Eric. 2005. "Feeling, Emotion, Affect." *M/C Journal* 8 (6). https://doi.org/10.5204/mcj.2443

Stewart, Kathleen. 2007. *Ordinary Affects*. Duke University Press.

Stewart, Kathleen. 2011. "Atmospheric Attunements." *Environment and Planning D: Society and Space* 29 (3): 445–53. https://doi.org/10.1068/d9109

Stewart, Kathleen. 2017. "In the World That Affect Proposed." *Cultural Anthropology* 32 (2): 192–98. https://doi.org/10.14506/ca32.2.03

Taylor, Diana. 2003. *The Archive and the Repertoire: Performing Cultural Memory in the Americas*. Duke University Press.

Thrift, Nigel. 2007. *Non-Representational Theory: Space, Politics, Affect*. Routledge.

Tomkins Institute. 2014. "Nine Affects, Present at Birth, Combine with Life Experience to Form Emotion and Personality." https://www.tomkins.org/nine-affects-present-at-birth

Vannini, Phillip. 2015. "Non-Representational Research Methodologies: An Introduction." In *Non-Representational Methodologies: Re-Envisioning Research*, edited by Philip Vannini, 1–18. Routledge.

Wikström, Josefine. 2021. *Practices of Relations in Task-Dance and the Event-Score: A Critique of Performance*. Routledge. https://doi.org/10.4324/9780367809614

Williams, David, and Carl Lavery, eds. 2011. *Good Luck Everybody: Lone Twin—Journeys, Performances, Conversations*. Performance Research Books.

Wrights & Sites. 2006. *A Mis-Guide to Anywhere*. Wrights & Sites.

18. Doing Performance Philosophy: Thinking alongside Performance

Laura Cull Ó Maoilearca

Summary

Performance philosophy is an interdisciplinary field of thought, creative practice, and scholarship concerned with the relationship between performance and philosophy. Emerging since around 2012, performance philosophy can be broadly defined as a performative paradigm of knowledge-making attentive to how thinking performs and performance thinks. This chapter introduces performance philosophy as an experimental practice of 'thinking alongside performance', starting from the premise that performance is itself a mode of thinking with the capacity to expand and transform normative paradigms of what counts as thought. The author highlights how performance philosophy often takes up a non-anthropocentric, relational approach—moving away from the notion of the individual subject of thought towards the sense of thought as constituted by unique assemblages of human and nonhuman materialities in specific eventual contexts. The method is also contextualised as emerging from a nondualist, nonreductive understanding of mind and body, in which the physical world is understood as movement or change and matter is construed as a process of emergence. Three ways of doing performance philosophy are offered: attention-training, letter-writing, and an experimental approach to format. The method is demonstrated with *An [Interrupted] Bestiary*, a performance philosophy project by the author produced through a process of thinking alongside the Chicago-based company *Every house has a door*.

Introduction

Performance philosophy is an interdisciplinary field of thought, creative practice, and scholarship concerned with the relationship between performance and philosophy. Emerging since around 2012, performance philosophy can be broadly defined as a performative paradigm of knowledge-making attentive to how thinking performs and performance thinks. It questions disciplinary distinctions and challenges the persistent hierarchies between ways of knowing as reinforced by the standard formats of academic teaching and research, including by understanding the identity of philosophy itself as performative and the "performative aspects of research" per se (Haarman 2020, 121). Attentiveness to performativity is offered as a method to work against the standardisation of knowledge in research, teaching, and learning, including expanding attention to how knowledge is performed outside academic institutions (Holkenbrink and Seitz 2020, 206).

Performance philosophy as a field is not reducible to a single method; better to say *performance philosophies* plural, some have suggested (Blanco Borelli et al. 2020, 162). And indeed, there are many different approaches and methods that have been proposed as ways of doing performance philosophy, including: dialogue (Zene 2020); theatre-thinking (Garcin-Marrou 2020); play (Koubová 2020); and as a thinking through touch (Woo 2020) wherein performance philosophy is construed "as a means by which two bodies of thought and thinking can touch each other" (2020, 285).[1] Scholars have suggested decolonial ways of doing performance philosophy (Henao-Castro 2020; Blanco Borelli et al. 2020) and explored how it manifests in epistemologies of the global south— suggesting, for instance, "a deep connection between anthropophagy and

---

1   Interested readers can look to "Part III: Methods, techniques, genres and forms" in *The Routledge Companion to Performance Philosophy* edited by myself and Alice Lagaay which introduces further methods emerging from/as performance philosophy.

performance philosophy" (da Costa Dias 2020, 94).[2] Some practitioners use the methods and means of performance to collectively investigate theoretical and/or philosophical questions with interdisciplinary groups (for instance, in the case of *Theater der Versammlung* in Bremen);[3] others invite philosophers "to incorporate artistic practices and methods into their philosophical research" (Böhler and Valerie 2020, 390); and still others expand on artistic research paradigms with the specific notion of performance as embodied philosophy (Cvejić 2015; Katan 2016).

However, within this diversity, performance philosophy as a method has been particularly investigated as an approach seeking to go beyond application in relation to standard approaches in performance analysis and the philosophy of performance (Cull 2012). In performance philosophy, the aim is not to apply a philosophical approach to performance as object or to analyse a case study of performance through a philosophical lens. Performance philosophy hopes to avoid using performance in order to illustrate philosophical ideas, whether from a scholarly or makers' perspective. In this respect, performance philosophy tends to eschew false binaries of 'theory' and 'practice' and the still persistent association of philosophy with abstract theorising.

The methodological issue of 'application' has been a matter of recurring concern and debate within performance philosophy from the outset—echoing a wider discussion in related fields such as film philosophy. It has been a core theme of initial articulations of the field in terms of the distinction between performance philosophy and the philosophy of performance (Cull 2012, 2014; Cull Ó Maoilearca 2018). By 'application', we might mean: a tendency within the philosophy of art or in related fields such as art theory to use the work of art more as a means to illustrate a pre-existing set of ideas, than to generate new ones; to privilege a given idea of philosophical thinking over one of artistic thinking, rather than allowing the arts to expand our understanding of philosophy and of thought, perhaps. When we think of application, we may also think of a rather one-way relationship between philosophy and

---

[2] As Luciana Da Costa Dias discusses, anthropophagy or anthropophagia— understood as a mode of cultural cannibalism—is a term associated with the 1960s Brazilian art movement Tropicália (Da Costa Dias 2020).

[3] For more on the method of *Theater der Versammlung*, see Holkenbrink, Jörg and Anna Seitz (2020) "Daring to transform academic routines: Cultures of knowledge and their performances".

the arts in which a concept is understood to change how we perceive the arts, but in which little attention is paid to the reciprocal capacity of the arts to change how we understand a concept.

In contrast, one way in which the method of performance philosophy has been proposed is as an experimental practice of 'thinking alongside performance', starting from the premise that performance is itself a mode of thinking with the capacity to expand and transform normative paradigms of what counts as thought, including philosophical thought. The core idea of a performance philosophy approach—at least in this interpretation—is that there is no single and fixed method of performance philosophy but that performance philosophy is a performative practice of thought that mutates with or is determined by performance as its 'object'. Performance philosophy attempts to produce thought *from* performance rather than about it: amplifying the logics at work in specific instances of performance by inhabiting and re-enacting them and demonstrating their capacity to generate new epistemologies including through modes of 'creative response' (Goat Island 2009) and 'concept creation' (Deleuze and Guattari 1996).

The notion of performance philosophy as an experimental practice of thinking alongside performance is particularly informed by the non-philosophy of contemporary French thinker François Laruelle. Non-philosophy or non-standard philosophy is not an anti-philosophy nor a call for the negation of philosophy. Rather, the 'non' in non-philosophy is intended to signal the radical extension of philosophy: an extension that entails a mutation or transformation of philosophy by other knowledges—including, potentially, by performance's ways of knowing. Non-philosophy as non-standard aesthetics aims to practice an extension and democratisation of thought by thinking 'alongside' or 'according to' the thought of art itself. For Laruelle, for example, art is "thought circularity" in standard philosophical aesthetics (Laruelle 2011, 142). In contrast he describes the aim of his own non-aesthetics is to think art "outside every vicious circle" (Laruelle 2012, 4), according to a radical extension of art to philosophy: "the moment when thought in its turn becomes a form of art" (2012, 2) and there is "the reciprocal determination of art and philosophy" (2012, 1).

Breaking the circle of the application paradigm is not only necessary from the side of philosophy, but also from the side of the performing arts, given its long-standing pursuit of recognition for itself as a field of knowledge development. 'Think alongside performance' is an important epistemological imperative. It speaks to dance practice, say, as a site of multiple forms of thinking—somatic, choreographic, improvisational, social, theatrical—not only as the object of thought for other disciplines. Thanks in part to the institutional acceptance of artistic research in many national contexts, it is largely uncontroversial to suggest that arts practices are forms of 'thought' and/or ways of 'knowing'.

When we say 'think alongside performance', the 'alongside' is an acknowledgement of and act of resistance to the hierarchical power relations that have historically structured encounters between performance and philosophy. For example, Bojana Cvejić (2015) and others (Kunst 2003; Clark 2011) have been highly critical of the methodological issues in the treatment of dance by European philosophers such as Alain Badiou and Jacques Rancière, where the emphasis tends to be on what philosophy can teach dance rather than the other way around. In contrast, Cvejić calls for a 'dance-philosophy', understood as "a kind of thought which arises within the material practice of dancing" (Cvejić 2015, 18). So, as an international transdisciplinary field of research and practice, performance philosophy is committed to thinking alongside performance. But for this field, the cogent imperative to 'perform thought' is equally important. This speaks to thought as a domain of a plurality of practices—embodied, attentional, emotional, material, nonhuman—not only as the exertion of human intellectual or cognitive capacities, normatively defined.

One context in which this method of performance philosophy as 'thinking alongside' might be used is by performance scholars or philosophers seeking to practice knowledge-production in relation to performance practices in more collaborative, relational, and embodied ways. For example, in the case of the demonstration offered in this chapter, *An [Interrupted] Bestiary,* performance philosophy was practiced and created from a position of embeddedness within a performance project in ways that resonate with dramaturgical practices.[4] 'Thinking alongside'

---

4   Certain approaches to dramaturgy could certainly be considered as performance philosophy (or vice versa) on account of their embeddedness within creative processes of performance making. Among the myriad themes that might be seen as shared across the two fields are the power relations between aesthetic and

involved setting up a parallel process of creative investigation that was both entangled with and independent from the making process of the performance company *Every house has a door*. In this particular instance, it relied on the access, willingness, and trust on the part of the participating artists insofar as I was asking to be included as a collaborator—as a collaborating 'performance philosopher'—in their creative process. It felt possible to take a performance philosophy approach because I already had a long-standing connection to and experience of collaboration with the company involved. However, this is not to say that performance philosophy as a practice of 'thinking alongside' performance could not happen under different circumstances—including in a context where there is no immediate, interpersonal relationship or proximity between performance philosopher and the performance. Likewise, the way I have practiced performance philosophy thus far has been process-oriented rather than production-oriented: I practiced performance philosophy alongside performance companies throughout the research and development, devising, and rehearsal phases, not only through an encounter with a final work. But this is not to say that performance philosophy as a 'thinking alongside' could not be reconceived in different ways according to differing modes of practice. Fundamentally, what matters is the capacity to perform new ways of thinking from within the ecology or universe of a particular performance practice: to be attentive to both i) the specificity of how performance practices might operate as (new) ways of thinking and knowing irreducible to extant philosophical concepts or knowledge frameworks and ii) the material performativity of philosophising (or theorising).

One challenge of performance philosophy as an approach is the concern regarding its own redundancy. In some ways, it seems clear that performance does not 'need' performance philosophy. Certainly, in my own experiments with performance philosophical practice, I have sometimes struggled to articulate to myself what it is that my presence or process adds to what is already there. Performance

---

discursive knowledges and the role of discourse in legitimising the intellectual value of performance. However, perhaps a potential site of distinction, at least in how I am characterising performance philosophy here, is the idea of performance philosophy as a method that generates its own creative outcomes that are both embedded in a performance practice but also able to operate as independent works in their own right.

already performs itself as thinking and as philosophy for those who are open to participating in it as such. Performances or performative research trajectories can already be considered to function as fully fledged manifestations of performance philosophy in their own right, without need of a supplement. This is particularly the case when companies themselves already have a dramaturg—as is the case with my collaborators *Every house has a door* and as Jonas Schnor has also discussed in his work on performance philosophy and/as dramaturgy (Schnor 2022). However, at the same time, I have been repeatedly reassured by the companies themselves that there is a value in this work: to embody the generative potential of performance; to manifest its fertile performativity not as 'explanation' but as more creation. Performance philosophy can make tangible what performance does—including those aspects of its creative processes that might never make it into the public domain—locating formats that offer a better fit with its ways of thinking than standard approaches to documentation or scholarship.

The performance philosopher I have in mind is not someone who philosophises about performance or who makes performances about philosophy.

The performance philosopher is someone who attends to the philosophy that comes from performance, or, to how performance itself does philosophy—including by transforming our very ideas of what philosophy is, who does it, and how.

The performance philosopher attends to performance as a philosophical practice—both in the sense of attending to the philosophy performed by others and to her own philosophy, in the event of its unfolding as performance.

Context

Performance philosophy can be situated in the context of a wide variety of different philosophical and artistic lineages: including the broad-spectrum notion of 'performance' (which extends performance beyond the performing arts to include the performative production of identities, ritual, and other forms of cultural performance) and an expanded notion of 'philosophy' as irreducible to what takes place in Philosophy departments. The field also emerged in dialogue with cogent developments in film and music studies, where there is a long tradition of philosophers and film researchers alike calling for alternatives to the epistemological hierarchy set up by the standard 'philosophy of x' approach and/or the use of philosophy as a mere 'lens' through which to analyse objects rather than a practice in its own right (for film philosophy see John Mullarkey 2008 and Robert Sinnerbrink 2022; for music philosophy see Bowie 2009; Tromans 2023). Philosophically speaking, performance philosophy has had a particularly close relation to European philosophies of difference and immanence, and with non-representational paradigms of aesthetics put forward by thinkers like Gilles Deleuze (Cvejic 2015; Cull 2009) and Laruelle (Ó Maoilearca 2017; Nauha 2016; Cull Ó Maoilearca 2017). But in attending to the embodied and performative nature of thought and philosophy, it has also developed through strong engagements with phenomenology. For instance, in her contribution to the recent *Routledge Companion to Performance Philosophy*, noted dance phenomenologist Maxine Sheets-Johnstone writes:

> It may certainly sound odd to speak of performing a methodology, but producing a phenomenological analysis of experience is in fact a veritable performance: it is definitely not an act or even a series of acts. Like any performance, it requires vigilance, exactitude, perseverance, alertness, dedication, and myriad other qualities, all of which cohere *in an ongoing and wholly interconnected investigative flow* that in this instance is, as indicated, punctuated by discoveries, revelations, wonderings, questionings, rethinkings, elaborations, and so on (Sheets-Johnstone 2020, 196, italics in the original).

In terms of its emphasis on how performance thinks: the context for performance philosophy includes the 'practice as research' and 'artistic research' movement that has been operating within international higher education since the 1980s. This movement starts from the insistence that research done by arts practitioners—including performance makers—needs to be respected by the academy as a valid and valued form of research equal to academic or scientific research. Practice as research shows how artistic and creative practices can function as methods and forms of praxis but also as the outcomes or outputs of research. The overlap of concerns here becomes particularly apparent in the writings of those like Estelle Barrett (2007) who suggests that in artistic research, arts practices are "viewed as the production of knowledge or *philosophy in action*" (Barrett 2007, 13, italics in the original). For some, like Paulo de Assis and Lucia de Erico (2019), it has been important to clarify the distinction between artistic research and philosophy.[5] However, from the point of view of performance philosophy, there is also an interest in how philosophers might indeed engage in artistic research and/or where philosophy might be approached as a mode of practice as research, building on the acknowledged place that practical and embodied methodologies like walking, yoga, and meditation have in the history of global philosophies.

In terms of its emphasis on how thinking (and specifically philosophical thinking) is performed: performance philosophy often takes up a non-anthropocentric, relational approach, moving away from the notion of the individual subject of thought towards the sense of thought as constituted by unique assemblages of human and nonhuman materialities in specific evental contexts. Informed by (so-called) 'new materialism' but also its historical precedents (including 19th-century European process philosophies, and First Nations, Indigenous philosophies), performance philosophy investigates how philosophy materialises in a context that recognises the extension of life to matter and the expansion of thinking to the more-than-human. Building on Foucauldian power-knowledge discourse and Judith Butler's performativity (amongst others), performance philosophy is also part of the wider conversation on disciplinary power dynamics and the relationship of the academy to its 'outside', including in a context of gatekeeping around what counts as proper 'philosophy' and non-philosophy.

The specific performance philosophy approach outlined here departs from some fundamental ontological premises that are not representative of the field as a whole, but only one possible characterisation of its method. It starts from a nondualist, nonreductive understanding of the relation between mind and body, in which the physical world is

---

5   "Artistic research is not to be confused with 'research on the arts', or research on aesthetic matters, or research about the arts […]. Artistic research is not a subdiscipline of musicology, art history or philosophy. It is a specific field of activity where practitioners actively engage with and participate in discursive formations emanating from their concrete artistic practice" (de Assis and de Erico 2018, 12).

understood as movement or change and matter is construed as a process of emergence (Ó Maoilearca 2023, 13). It is fundamentally premised on the radical contingency, singularity, and processuality of any so-called 'object' of research; and the notion that research does not happen in a context where objects exist in 'time' (as container), but are themselves dynamic, temporal entities "unfolding at different speeds" (Khandker 2020, 85). A non-dualist approach to mind and body has methodological consequences insofar as thought (or research) is considered as a material process that is part of, not separate from, the world it seeks to know. As the discourse of performance and performativity have shown us, ideas—including the idea of 'thought' itself—are never 'just ideas', but material forces that get under the skin and make themselves manifest in and as 'restored behaviours', norms that are more or less consciously repeated and resisted albeit in ever differing circumstances (Butler 1988; Schechner 1981). It departs from the premise that the ontological-epistemic question at hand is: how to think alongside the world as change; how to perform the thought of change as a changing thought?

In this context, questions of 'method' are inevitably fraught. For example, my approach here starts with the idea that research is always a situated praxis: a matter of embodied behaviours improvised between differing (human and nonhuman) actors in contexts that are radically singular in their dynamics between the unpredictable and the scripted.[6] This is both the basis of a method; a caution to the notion of method per se; and a methodological question. In this way, the need to continually re-invent and re-enact what performance philosophy might be can present an obstacle to offering any kind of 'how to' guide. Nevertheless—and as I have already experimented with elsewhere—there are performative devices like 'directives', scores, tasks, and prompts that can provide a structured approach for experimentation without determination (an instruction that can be followed without a given approach or outcome being determined in advance). There are also specific performative

---

6   This might seem paradoxical in positing a given or a priori that determines the approach. But the difference of an approach grounded in difference is that this 'given' is not defined but remains indeterminate. To point to situatedness, for example, is to insist on the primacy of context and the impossibility of any universal research or research conducted from a 'view from nowhere'.

techniques for embodying 'encounter': in terms of unlearning or dismantling extant knowledge and habitual ways of knowing/relating; and/or inhabiting openness as a mode of attending or noticing without recognition and judgement. Performance philosophy is not a free-for-all, 'make it up as you go along' without method; but at the same time, it is resistant toward the fixity of 'knowing what we are doing' that standard notions of method can sometimes imply. Not-knowing is not a 'negative' capability or lack, in this instance, so much as an embodied posture that takes some skill to inhabit (Ó Maoilearca 2017, 367). Structured improvisation might become an important potential tool for performance philosophy in this respect, in that, just as improvisation (in dance and music contexts) is understood to be done by highly trained practitioners with heightened embodied expertise, so we might imagine training towards a parallel praxis of improvised theorising.

How to

Performance philosophy is irreducible to a single or general method. Many researchers in the field share a strong desire to protect the "fundamentally open nature of performance philosophy as an approach to thinking and creating that is not, for instance, bound by any agreed body of methods" (Cull Ó Maoilearca and Lagaay 2020, 4). Performance philosophy has marked a space for methodological exchange—where philosophers test out methods from performance and vice versa, including sharing tactics for the kinds of methodological 'unlearning' we might need to go through in order to undo disciplinary habits and experiment with new practices of thinking (ibid., 4). There are no hard and fast rules about how you go about a process of inquiry in order for it to be considered specifically as 'performance philosophy' rather than, for example, philosophically informed performance analysis. If performance philosophy is particularly characterised by an effort to break the circle of application, then the extent to which a given experiment is deemed successful or not may well be a matter for debate.

In turn, as I have introduced, a fundamental principle of a performance philosophy approach is that the method comes from or is shaped by the performance material it relates to. In this respect, it is not possible to describe a step-by-step method of performance philosophy per se, because exactly how you work with this approach will vary depending on the performance practices you are thinking alongside. Emergence, experimentation, and iteration remain a deliberate feature of performance philosophy as a method—wherein performance philosophy is always a mode of methodological investigation as well as a method *of* investigation. This can be daunting from the perspective of the researcher in the sense that it can require a high degree of tolerance for inhabiting a position of not-knowing and perhaps a more flexible attitude to the practicalities of conducting research than other approaches. Practically speaking, for example, an emergent approach to method means that you might not always have the right tools with you for those required by unfolding circumstances; you might retrospectively wish that you had prepared otherwise. But this is where an iterative and durational approach can help: performance philosophy is probably better suited to situations where you have the time to engage in the experimental development of the method itself, rather than to 'one-off' opportunities: to consider performance philosophy as an ongoing aesthetic, ontological, epistemic, and ethical practice that you are cultivating.

However, even though performance philosophy is not entirely amenable to the 'how to', I can outline one possible approach to performance philosophy as a 'thinking alongside performance'. This is based on the example and experience of my own practice in the context of the project *Performance Philosophy and Animals: towards a radical equality* which can be taken up and adapted to other contexts:

1. Selection: select the performance, practice, company, or maker that you are interested in 'thinking alongside'. You may want to think about questions of access, willingness/capacity, and trust. If we consider 'thinking alongside' performance as a form of creative and conceptual intimacy, who are the artists that you have already worked with or who you know might be open to doing this intimate experiment with you? Whose creative process would you be interested in being included in and who might be willing to include you? Which instances of performative thinking are you curious about or dream of inhabiting?

2. Performance [methods] as philosophy: *do as they do, but otherwise— according to an unfaithful mimicry*: Locate the method/s and approaches of the performance, practice, company, or maker that you have selected.

How does performance think in the case of their past works or practices? Which of these methods and approaches could be used in/as scholarship, to generate thinking alongside performance and/or adapted to the skills and techniques that you are bringing with you?

For example, the companies I worked with—the UK-based company Fevered Sleep and the US-based company Every house has a door— use poetic 'directives' as part of their creative method. Directives are prompts given to performers to create performance material, not as instructions that can be followed with pre-determined expectations as to the results, but as a stimulus to their own creative invention that also provides a point of focus or constraint. In my approach to performance philosophy, I explored how a performance method—directives—could be used as a technique to generate philosophical material in writing and image-making.[7] I asked the directors to give me directives during the creative process alongside the directives that they were giving to their performers. In the case of *Every house*, we found ways for me to share the material I had devised in response to the directives (which took the form of writings and collages) with the rest of the company, feeding back into their process. What happens to philosophy or scholarship if it is created with a director and in the context of a process of collaborative devising?

3. Invitation/request: invite the performance, company or maker into the experiment in performance philosophy and/or ask if they would be willing to include you as a performance philosopher in their process or project.[8] This can be a difficult thing to do in itself since, by definition,

---

[7] I chose writing and image-making because of my own history and training in these practices. I trained as a visual artist before I studied philosophy and performance. This is also informed by Every house has a door's approach to the valuing of differences in expertise in practice. That is, I did not choose to produce choreographic material in response to directives because I do not have embodied expertise in choreographic thinking. I do have embodied expertise in visual and material thinking that did not standardly get to express itself in academic contexts. The performance philosophy approach allowed me to make space for this within, alongside and entangled with more textual and theoretical thinking.

[8] Being included in a performance maker's process can mean many different things. "Thinking alongside" does not necessarily mean that you have to be in the same physical space. For example, during my performance philosophy experiment with Every house has a door, we conducted 'remote residencies' where I was working on the project from my home in the UK while company members were working on it in different countries. For us, this was an unplanned way of dealing with

what exactly you are asking of or offering to your partners cannot be laid out in advance. But what you can do is introduce them to the figure of the 'performance philosopher'—the principles of the approach—and offer them an initial indication of your method based on method/s you have located in their practice.

For example, when I approached Fevered Sleep with this request, here is part of what I wrote:

> *I wonder if you might be willing to consider me as part of your "toolbox" for Sheep Pig Goat. I wonder if you can consider me as one more improvising performer to whom you might offer directives.*
>
> *I bring with me a different set of embodied skills, techniques, contextual knowledge and habits to the dancers and vocal performers you work with: various forms of academic and creative writing and speaking, concept, question and argument creation, alongside some residual skills in drawing, photography and other forms of image and object making that I am in the process of recovering from my history of practice as a visual artist.*
>
> *I would like to invite you to experiment with what these skills and embodied techniques might do in the context of this new iteration of Sheep Pig Goat.*
>
> *This experiment can take any form that you like: from asking me a question, to inviting me to try different (writing, thinking, drawing, attending) tasks during the Encounters; to setting me a concrete task to produce a particular form of response to a particular moment. Tasks might take me 5 minutes or 5 hours. They might produce 1 word or 500.*

4. Philosophy as performance: akin to situated knowledge, performance philosophy seeks to be attentive to how thought always emerges from the particular contexts and specific configurations of material bodies. It invites consideration of how philosophy or scholarship operates as an embodied practice and therefore something we might need to warm up and train for in comparable ways to performance.

So, as you begin your practice of thinking alongside performance, identify techniques that help you remain attentive to the performativity of the thinking you are situated in. This might include: bodily warm-up exercises (such as breathwork and touch practices), journaling, and attending to the constitutive effects of the embodied, situated, and relational dimensions of traditional scholarly activities (such as reading and writing). How do nonhuman phenomena such as place, weather,

---

the conditions of the COVID-19 pandemic. However, it could also be a deliberate strategy.

or the time of day, contribute to constituting the thinking that emerges? What practices support you to enter into performance philosophy as a full body practice rather than something merely in the head?

Three ways of doing performance philosophy

Directives for attention-training: performing philosophy as encounter

Elsewhere I have written further about the idea of a praxis of *attention* as a way of performing knowledge as encounter rather than mastery. I have applied this specifically to my work on and with interspecies performance and in terms of thinking about the ethics of knowledge production in relation to nonhuman animals. However, this praxis could be used more widely in relation to other entities and forms of performance; it could also be a site where theoretical praxis might be informed by attentional, sensory, and perceptual techniques that originate in the performing arts and embodied practices, such as somatics.

The performative approach of performance philosophy is informed by the idea of the constitutive nature of encounters that we find in ontologies that assert the primacy of difference (Bergson 1911, Deleuze 1994, Haraway 2008). In this relational model, there is not a researcher and an 'object' of research that precede and create encounters; rather, subjects and objects are created by their encounters, including in the context of research practices. Researchers and their 'objects' create each other through *how* they meet, including how they practice paying attention to each other. In Deleuze and Guattari's philosophy, an encounter is contrasted with an event of recognition; an encounter involves the emergence of new thinking on the basis of an openness to that which eludes extant concepts; an encounter is a becoming of embodied thought with its 'outside' as distinct from our tendency to perceive life through habitual modes of representation and pre-existing ideas (or 'images of thought'). In turn, the ecophilosopher Freya Matthews has proposed approaching knowledge as encounter, rather than mastery, suggesting that "whereas traditional knowledge seeks to break open the mystery of another's nature; encounter leaves that mystery intact" (Matthews 2003, 78).

Practically speaking, a method of encounter can be supported by techniques such as question cards (as used by Fevered Sleep in *Sheep Pig Goat*) which invite a mode of open curiosity rather than any premature practice of recognition or interpretation, which can restrict our capacity to notice the qualities of an unfolding present. Cards read: "What are your questions? What do you notice?". Alternatively, or additionally, a nonhabitual attention can be guided through specific directives for writing that orient attention toward relation and movement. Notably, attention does not give anthropocentric priority to the visual (or to the notion of attention as a spotlight) but refers to a relational, distributed and full-bodied process of heightened sensitivity. For example, here are some of the directives that Fevered Sleep offered me as prompts for the creation of performance philosophy:

Write a word for the atmosphere in the space every time it changes.

Describe or draw the weather in the space (NB. to describe includes to draw).

The space feels very, very full. What is it full of other than 'stuff'? Make a list of all the things that are in the space that are not physical or objects.

Describe all the ways in which each of the animals is looking.

Describe what's happening from the point of view of any of the performers' skin.

In the context of my own interspecies performance philosophy, directives offered help to pay attention. I needed help to attend. I needed help to behave differently so that *these* sheep and cows might appear strange to me. Artist-philosopher, Eva Meijer says: "The question of the animal is always intertwined with the question of what it means to think, and the animal is used to demarcate the human subject" (Meijer 2019, 25). I would like to add: 'The question of the arts is also always intertwined with the question of what it means to think'—amounting to an entanglement of art, thought and animals, both human and nonhuman. The larger research project, of which this version *Sheep Pig Goat* was a part, sought to use performance philosophy to attend to these events of demarcation—of human and nonhuman, of different kinds of knowledge—but also to the question of how to think. But it was less concerned with what it means to think (as a meaning we can define and articulate) and more concerned with how thinking is performed (practiced, embodied, felt, lived, improvised, fumbled toward) in interspecies and interdisciplinary encounters.

Thinking from correspondence: performing philosophy as letter-writing

According to the relational model I have outlined, thought is always already collaborative: never something you do alone, but always something that emerges in and through relation which can be approached as processes of collaboration. I have written about collaborative authorship in the context of performance and philosophy in more detail elsewhere; but, for now, I wanted to include specific reference to the method of letter-writing or correspondence as a mode of performance philosophy. Performing theorising as an act of "thinking through or thinking with or thinking alongside someone else" (Simpson in Maynard et al. 2021, 140)—including through the method of letter writing—is an established practice within Black feminist and Indigenous work, like that of Robyn Maynard and Leanne Betasamosake Simpson. In my own practice, I have used letter-writing as an approach for a range of reasons and according to a range of conditions: including constraint-based writing, simultaneous writing, and experiments with writing at specific times of day and/or under specific bodily conditions (for instance, in a project where the theatre-maker Tess Denman-Cleaver and I wrote letters to each other at dawn and twilight, and after being submerged in water).[9] Letter-writing suits performance philosophy in valuing the interactions between multiple ways of knowing, allowing for the intertwining of the personal and the scholarly; and it re-orients potentially abstract notions of theorising in relation to others or difference towards embodied and practical matters of address towards a particular recipient. Akin to holistic and feminist approaches to art and pedagogy, performance philosophy invites unlearning the persistent academic to exclude and devalue the personal and instead to welcome lived, emotional, and embodied

---

9   This was in the context of the project, *The Sea, Lies Open* (2015) which culminated in a sound installation and series of performative walks for Philosophy on Stage #4 held at the Tanz Quartier in Vienna, Austria. Documentation is available here https://homepage.univie.ac.at/arno.boehler/php/laura-cull-o-maoilearca-tess-denman-cleaver-the-sea-lies-open-draft/

experience as a source of knowledges that can come into dialogue with other ways of knowing.

Performance philosophy as formal experiment

Attend to how the thought needs to be performed; don't limit thinking according to standard formats. As Alice Lagaay and I have noted elsewhere, "one of the methodological principles of performance philosophy is a dramaturgical sensitivity to the relationship between content and form" (Cull Ó Maoilearca and Lagaay 2020, 8). A fundamental aim of performance philosophy is to expand and pluralise the forms in and through which thought is performed with a critical eye to the restrictive nature of the imposition of normative formats in the academy—including the predominance of "the written word in its most habitualised or conventional academic, neutrally voiced linear form" (2020, 8). Premised on the fundamental inseparability of form and content, performance philosophy aligns with other performative paradigms of knowledge-making which insist on the need for a more emergent and flexible approach to the 'outputs' of knowledge, especially in academia. Performance philosophy proposes that the standard academic formats of the paper, lecture, thesis, book, and so forth need to be multiplied by other formats that afford more scope to the enactment of other modalities of thinking: embodied thinking, choreographic thinking, theatrical thinking, musical thinking, and so on. Indeed, it goes as far as to suggest that "each instance of performance philosophy calls for a conscious reflection and establishment of what is the appropriate format in which to present and perform itself" (2020, 9). From a methodological perspective, this means that we need to be attentive to how internalised expectations of standard formats can enter into a creative process of investigation and delimit emergent invention.

Again, the notion of attention is important here: where "attention/attentiveness means precisely countering default, system thinking by dramaturgical, sensory awareness" including an active attention to others which "carries ethical and political consequences" (2020, 10). Indeed, Lagaay suggests that this critical reflection of form can also be considered part of an extension of the concern to *decolonize performance philosophy*. It is understood that every instance of performance philosophy [...] must find and establish its own way of communicating within itself the rules by which it is to be 'read'—as opposed to presuming that every proposal, text or instance of performance philosophy counts towards reaffirming a universalizable standard by which it can be measured (Lagaay in Cull Ó Maoilearca and Lagaay 2020, 10).

This can be a disorienting experience for researchers used to knowing the format of final outputs from the start. For example, I had no idea that the process of thinking alongside *Every house has a door* would result in *An [Interrupted] Bestiary*, only that I knew I wanted to be open to making something that emerged from the method of 'thinking alongside', the form of which—by definition—I could not yet know.

Fig. 18.1 Doing Performance Philosophy: an image of the author during *Sheep Pig Goat* by Fevered Sleep (2020), Surrey. ©Malachy Luckie.

Demonstration

I would like to offer my recent project *An [Interrupted] Bestiary* as a demonstration of performance philosophy. *An [Interrupted] Bestiary* is an expanded publication project that comprises an artist's book, exhibition, and the animated short film, *Done Dying*. *An [Interrupted] Bestiary* was developed through a process of 'thinking alongside' the US-based performance company, *Every house has a door*, during their process of creating the performance *Broken Aquarium* (2019–2022). *Broken Aquarium* is one act of the company's large-scale, multi-year project *The Carnival of the Animals*: a 14-movement work engaging the titles from Camille Saint-Saëns's 1885 musical suite for children, but with a concentration on endangered and extinct underwater creatures. Echoing the mediaeval bestiaries, the artist's book element of *An [Interrupted] Bestiary* is structured as a series of quires and folios with writing and images dedicated to a series of endangered underwater creatures personified by the performers in the company's work: The Eyelash Seaweed, The Lesser Electric Ray, The Red Pencil, and The Devil's Hole Pupfish. Created in the period leading up to and following the death of my father, the outbreak and unfolding of the COVID-19 pandemic, the murder of George Floyd, and the growth of the Black Lives Matter movement, *An [Interrupted] Bestiary* reflects on themes of bewilderment, vulnerability, extinction, and grief, and the complex entanglement of speciesism and racism. The work haunts, ghosts and speculates within the creative process of *Broken Aquarium*—carrying traces of parts of the performance that no longer exist, summoning missing performers, materialising the imaginative work of the spectator, and envisioning future alternative versions that may yet come. Whilst the performers approach their interconnectedness with the underwater creatures through movement and costume, *An [Interrupted] Bestiary* is informed by Alexis Pauline Gumbs' *Undrowned* (2020) and enacts a fluidity of writing from the point of view of nonhuman and human perspectives: *as* Eyelash Seaweed, *as* Lesser Electric Ray, *as* Red Pencil, *as* Devil's Hole Pupfish.

Given the emphasis that performance philosophy places on attending to the ways in which the formats of thinking constitute its contents, it is not something that fits neatly into the standard book format of this publication. As such, in order to encounter the project, I invite you to:

Download the online version of the book:

18. Doing Performance Philosophy: Thinking alongside Performance 407

18.1 Laura Cull Ó Maoilearca, *An [Interrupted] Bestiary* (2022), https://www.academia.edu/104641611/An_Interrupted_Bestiary

Watch the short film:

18.2 Laura Cull Ó Maoilearca, *Bestiary Animation* (2022). Duration: 8.44, https://www.youtube.com/watch?v=WcB9Js2F9SQ

Listen to the podcast:

18.3 Laura Cull Ó Maoilearca, *An [Interrupted] Bestiary: Climate Imaginaries at Sea*, 7 episodes, https://podcasts.apple.com/nl/podcast/an-interrupted-bestiary/id1725621904

Consider An [Interrupted] Bestiary as an act of thinking alongside performance.

Consider An [Interrupted] Bestiary as an experiment in performance philosophy.

This book is and is not part of the performance project,

The Carnival of the Animals by Every house has a door.

It is an expression of contaminated diversity: both distinctive and multiply derivative.

Here lies a bestiary: a compendium of creatures.

But one that has been interrupted.

And interrupted.

And interrupted.

There is a correspondence between the realms of performance and text.

Performers have their textual and visual counterparts.

Consider An [Interrupted] Bestiary as its own work

— but one that lives within the ecology of The Carnival of the Animals.

Expanding the method

The particular framing of performance philosophy in this chapter—as 'thinking alongside performance'—could be taken up by philosophers, art historians and other arts and humanities scholars curious to explore a more practical, embodied and creative approach to engaging with performance than is standard in aesthetics. The emphasis of performance philosophy on the performativity of learning could also be fruitfully taken up in education by those looking for a methodological framework to advance the critique of standardisation (see Holkenbrink and Seitz 2020).

Performance philosophy is always already an interdisciplinary field. Researchers and practitioners engage with it from a wide range of disciplines and from non-academic fields: as independent artists and creatives, scholars, and practitioners from fields such as social justice and care work. That is, performance philosophy as a field and method is not straightforwardly situated within theatre, dance, and performance studies—as the focal disciplines of this book—but emerged as much from philosophy, and other related areas such as critical theory, political science, religion, gender studies, and media theory. From the outset, part of the intention and practice of performance philosophy was to cultivate cross-disciplinary encounters and exchange on the relation between 'performance' and 'philosophy' (openly and plurally construed) for researchers coming from a wide variety of disciplines—including music, English and comparative literature, art history, design—and also from outside academia. At times, this has led to the emergence of sub-strands based on the need for greater disciplinary specificity; for example, authors like Anthony Gritten have considered what might constitute "a specifically musical Performance Philosophy" (Gritten in Cull Ó Maoilearca and Lagaay 2020, 98). But performance philosophy also continues to function as a 'home' for those who seek to work across artistic and academic disciplines and for those seeking to develop a multiform practice combining academic, artistic, and socially situated work.

Suggestions for further reading and listening

The Routledge Companion to Performance Philosophy (2020) provides a substantive introduction to and overview of a wide range of perspectives and approaches to performance philosophy as a field and method. The journal issue *how to think* (2021) edited by Rajni Shah and the author is the first all-podcast volume of the *Performance Philosophy* journal that indicates the emphasis of the field on the methods and formats through which philosophical thinking is performed and offers particular insight into slow conversation as an approach. In *Rehearsals for Living* (2022), Maynard and Leanne Betasamosake Simpson use daily letter-writing to think alongside one another in a way that resonates with the aims of performance philosophy to marry form and content. These letters are not only 'about' themes of regeneration, relationality and reciprocity; they are a regenerative, relational and reciprocal practice. Gumbs' *Undrowned* (2020) was a key influence on *An [Interrupted] Bestiary* and provides a wonderful example of how intersectional, interspecies thinking can be practiced through formal experiment and the alignment of this content, method, and form.

References

de Assis, Paulo and Lucia de Erico, eds. 2019. *Artistic Research: Charting a Field in Expansion*. Rowman and Littlefield. https://journals.sagepub.com/doi/10.1177/0263276415592245

Barrett, Estelle. 2007. "Introduction." In *Practice as Research: Approaches to Creative Arts Enquiry*, edited by Estelle Barrett and Barbara Bolt. I. B. Tauris. https://doi.org/10.1057/9781137282910

Bergson, Henri. 1911. *Creative Evolution*. Translated by Arthur Mitchell. Macmillan. https://doi.org/10.5962/bhl.title.17594

Blanco Borelli, Melissa, Anamaría Tamayo Duque and Cristina Fernandes Rosa. 2020. "Decolonizing performance philosophies." In *The Routledge Companion to Performance Philosophy*, edited by Laura Cull Ó Maoilearca and Alice Lagaay. Routledge. https://doi.org/10.4324/9781003035312

Böhler, Arno and Valerie, Suzanne. 2020. "Philosophy on Stage." In *The Routledge Companion to Performance Philosophy*, edited by Laura Cull Ó Maoilearca and Alice Lagaay. Routledge. https://doi.org/10.4324/9781003035312

Bowie, Andrew. 2009. *Music, Philosophy, and Modernity*. Cambridge: Cambridge University Press. https://doi.org/10.1017/CBO9780511487569

Butler, Judith. 1988. "Performative Acts and Gender Constitution: An Essay in Phenomenology and Feminist Theory." *Theatre Journal* 40 (4): 519–31. https://doi.org/10.2307/3207893

Clark, Jonathan Owen. 2011. "Dance and Subtraction: Notes on Alain Badiou's Inaesthetics." *Dance Research Journal* 43 (2): 50–64. http://dx.doi.org/10.1017/S0149767711000052

Cull Ó Maoilearca, Laura, and Alice Lagaay, eds. 2020. *The Routledge Companion To Performance Philosophy*. Routledge. https://doi.org/10.4324/9781003035312

Cull Ó Maoilearca, Laura, and Alice Lagaay, eds. 2014. *Encounters in Performance Philosophy*. Palgrave Macmillan. https://doi.org/10.1057/9781137462725

Cull Ó Maoilearca, Laura. 2017. "Equalizing Theatre and Philosophy: Laruelle, Badiou, and gestures of authority in the philosophy of theatre." *Performance Philosophy* 3 (3): 730–50. https://doi.org/10.21476/PP.2017.33191

Cull, Laura. 2012. "Performance as Philosophy: Responding to the Problem of 'Application'." *Theatre Research International* 37 (1): 20–27. https://doi.org/10.1017/S0307883311000733

Cull, Laura. 2016. "Since Each of Us Was Several: Collaboration in the Context of the Differential Self." In *Collaboration in Performance Practice*, edited by Noyale Colin and Stefanie Sachsenmeier. Palgrave Macmillan. https://doi.org/10.1057/9781137462466_5

Cull, Laura. 2009. *Deleuze and Performance*. Edinburgh University Press. https://doi.org/10.1515/9780748635054

Cvejić, Bojana. 2015. *Choreographing Problems: Expressive Concepts in Contemporary Dance and Performance*, Performance Philosophy series. Palgrave Macmillan. https://doi.org/10.1057/9781137437396

da Costa Dias, Luciana. 2020. "Performance Philosophy in Latin America: how to perform a Utopia called America?" In *The Routledge Companion to Performance Philosophy*, edited by Laura Cull Ó Maoilearca and Alice Lagaay. Routledge. https://doi.org/10.4324/9781003035312

Deleuze, Gilles. 1994. *Difference and Repetition*. Columbia University Press.

Deleuze, Gilles and Guattari, Félix. 1996. *What is Philosophy?* Columbia University Press.

Garcin-Marrou, Flore. 2020. "Theatre-thinking: philosophy from the stage." In *The Routledge Companion to Performance Philosophy*, edited by Laura Cull Ó Maoilearca and Alice Lagaay. Routledge. https://doi.org/10.4324/9781003035312

Goat Island. 2009. "Creative response". *Goat Island* company website. http://www.goatislandperformance.org/creativeResponse.htm

Gritten, Anthony. 2020. "Diminishing returns: the performativity of musical sound." In *The Routledge Companion to Performance Philosophy*, edited by Laura Cull Ó Maoilearca and Alice Lagaay. Routledge. https://doi.org/10.4324/9781003035312

Gumbs, Alexis Pauline. 2020. *Undrowned: Black Feminist Lessons from Marine Mammals.* AK Press. https://doi.org/10.3898/SOUN.78.01.2021

Haarman, Anke. 2020. "The theatre of research." In *The Routledge Companion to Performance Philosophy*, edited by Laura Cull Ó Maoilearca and Alice Lagaay. Routledge. https://doi.org/10.4324/9781003035312

Henao Castro, Andrés Fabián. 2020. "Whose *Tempest*? Performance philosophy and/as decolonial cacophony." In *The Routledge Companion to Performance Philosophy*, edited by Laura Cull Ó Maoilearca and Alice Lagaay. Routledge. https://doi.org/10.4324/9781003035312

Haraway, Donna. 2008. *When Species Meet*. University of Minnesota Press.

Holkenbrink, Jörg and Anna Seitz. 2020. "Daring to transform academic routines: Cultures of knowledge and their performances." In *The Routledge Companion to Performance Philosophy*, edited by Laura Cull Ó Maoilearca and Alice Lagaay. Routledge. https://doi.org/10.4324/9781003035312

Katan, Einav. 2016. *Embodied Philosophy in Dance*. Palgrave Macmillan. https://doi.org/10.1057/978-1-137-60186-5

Khandker, Wahida. 2020. *Process Metaphysics and Mutative Life: Sketches of Lived Time*. Palgrave Macmillan. https://doi.org/10.1007/978-3-030-43048-1

Koubová, Alice. 2020. "Play in performance philosophy." In *The Routledge Companion to Performance Philosophy*, edited by Laura Cull Ó Maoilearca, and Alice Lagaay. Routledge. https://doi.org/10.4324/9781003035312

Kunst, Bojana. 2003. "Subversion and the Dancing Body: Autonomy on Display." *Performance Research* 8 (2): 61–68. http://dx.doi.org./10.1080/13528165.2003.10871929

Laruelle, François. 2011 *The Concept of Non-Photography*. Translated by Robin Mackay. Urbanomic/Sequence Press.

Laruelle, François. 2012. *From Decision to Heresy: Experiments in Non-Standard Thought*. Edited by Robin Mackay. Urbanomic/Sequence Press.

Matthews, Freya. 2003. *For Love of Matter: A Contemporary Panpsychism*. State University of New York Press. https://doi.org/10.1353/book4707

Meijer, Eva. 2019. *When Animals Speak: Toward an Interspecies Democracy*. New York University Press.

Maynard, Robyn, Simpson, Betasamosake, Leanne. 2022. *Rehearsals for Living*. Haymarket Books.

Maynard, Robyn, Simpson, Betasamosake, Leanne, Voegele, Hannah and Griffin, Christopher. 2021. "Every Day We Must Get Up and Relearn the

World: An Interview with Robyn Maynard and Leanne Betasamosake Simpson." *Interfere* 2: 141–65. https://philarchive.org/archive/MAYEDW-2

Mullarkey, John. 2008. *Refractions of Reality: Philosophy and the Moving Image*. Palgrave Macmillan. https://doi.org/10.1057/9780230582316

Nauha, Tero. 2016. "A thought of performance." *Performance Philosophy* 2 (2): 272–85. https://doi.org/10.21476/PP.2017.2276

Ó Maoilearca, John. 2017. "Laruelle, Immanence, and Performance: What Does Non-Philosophy Do?" *Performance Philosophy* 3 (3): 718–29. https://doi.org/10.21476/PP.2017.33143

Ó Maoilearca, John. 2015. *All Thoughts Are Equal: Laruelle and Nonhuman Philosophy*, University of Minnesota Press. https://doi.org/10.5749/minnesota/9780816697342.001.0001

Ó Maoilearca, John. 2023. *Vestiges of a Philosophy: Matter, the Meta-Spiritual, and the Forgotten Bergson*. Oxford University Press. https://doi.org/10.1093/oso/9780197613917.001.0001

Schechner, Richard. 1981. "Restoration of Behaviour." *Studies in Visual Communication* 7 (3): 2–45.

Schnor, Jonas. 2022. *Microdramaturgy. Between Practice and Event: A Performance Philosophy*, PhD diss., University of Surrey. https://doi.org/10.15126/thesis.900483; https://openresearch.surrey.ac.uk/esploro/outputs/doctoral/Microdramaturgy-Between-Practice-and-Event-A/99683265902346

Shah, Rajni and Cull Ó Maoilearca, Laura. 2021. "how to think." *Performance Philosophy*, 6 (1). https://www.performancephilosophy.org/journal/issue/view/how-to-think

Sheets-Johnstone, Maxine. 2020. "Performing phenomenological methodology." In *The Routledge Companion to Performance Philosophy*, edited by Laura Cull Ó Maoilearca and Alice Lagaay. Routledge. https://doi.org/10.4324/9781003035312-22

Sinnerbrink, Robert. 2022. *New Philosophies of Film: An Introduction to Cinema as a Way of Thinking*. London: Bloomsbury Academic. https://doi.org/10.5040/9781350181960

Street, Anna, Alliot, Julien and Pauker, Magnolia, eds. 2017. *Inter Views in Performance Philosophy*. Palgrave. https://doi.org/10.1057/978-1-349-95192-5

Tromans, Steve. 2023. *Rhythmicity and Deleuze: Practice as Research in the Musical-Philosophical*. Lexington. https://doi.org/10.5040/9781978728714

Woo, Naomi. 2020. "Touch." In *The Routledge Companion to Performance Philosophy*, edited by Laura Cull Ó Maoilearca and Alice Lagaay. Routledge. https://doi.org/10.4324/9781003035312

Zene, Cosimo. 2020. "Performance Philosophy as inter-philosophical dialogue." In *The Routledge Companion to Performance Philosophy*, edited by Laura Cull Ó Maoilearca, and Alice Lagaay. Routledge. https://doi.org/10.4324/9781003035312

19. Hyphenated Thinking in Performance Processes: Thinking through Performance-pedagogical Entanglements with More-than-human Matter

Christel Stalpaert

Summary

Building on new materialist and decolonial writings, performance philosopher Christel Stalpaert coined the term 'hyphenated thinking' in performance studies: the resurgence of knowledge in relationality and across multispecies, interweaving cultures, disciplines, and fields of study (art, science, and activism). She rehearses this epistemology with university students in close collaboration with performance artists. In this contribution she demonstrates a practice of hyphenated thinking through her long-term commitment with Natural Contract Lab and their ephemeral performance process *STILL HERE—An Alliance of Care for the SZenne River* (2023–). In co-creation with scientists, artists, activists, local stakeholders, and participants, the Natural Contract Lab group seeks to trace hydro-(ecological) matters of concern and to fabulate justice to compensate for the harm inflicted by ecocide on the hydro commons. The artistic practices of walking-with, sensory mapping, storying, Agoras, and Guardian Schools activate pluriversal and collaborative modes of knowledge production. Stalpaert describes the particular outcome of the research method of a hyphenated thinking in the university context of the arts department at Ghent university: as a way for unlearning eurocentric and anthropocentric modes of knowledge production.

Introduction

As a performance philosopher, I am inclined to the thought that art works perform philosophy: they activate particular ways of thinking. Laura Cull Ó Maoilearca supports this in her writings on performance *as* philosophy. Encountering "performance *as* thinking", she sidesteps the tendency of merely applying philosophical concepts to performances, as in an illustrative attempt to explain what the performances mean (2014, 15). In this contribution, I consider performances as an open epistemological framework, with artistic practices activating ecological encounters.

Etymologically, the term ecology combines the Greek words 'oikos', meaning house or dwelling place, and 'lógos', meaning reason, or study. Ecology for that matter connects environmental thinking with notions of 'home' and 'belonging'. How is one allowed to be or feel truly at home in their dwelling place, in their 'milieu', so to say, and to develop fully according to their intrinsic capacities? Or, as Vinciane Despret puts it: "Ecology studies the conditions under which those it studies exist [...]. The ecological question is about the needs that have to be respected in the continual creation of an association" (2021, 9). This definition of ecology as generative association is at stake in this chapter.

Over the past decade, I have participated in several performance processes, and I experienced how some of them not only raise ecological topics, but also challenge and transform habitual ways of thinking ecology. Firstly, I was moved into epistemological humbleness. I became acutely aware that there are far more ways of 'knowing' or 'understanding' our being in and moving with the world than the monological and hierarchical science-accustomed format in Western academic knowledge institutions. Practicing a pluriverse throughout a performance process, I encountered performance *as* decolonial philosophy. The pluriverse is an alternative to the violence of universalism underpinning eurocentric, mechanistic-imperialist worldviews—worldviews that can also be found in universities. It relates to the multiplicity of worlds and world-making practices (Escobar 2018 and Yakoub 2024). Secondly, I was moved to explore my entangled becoming *with* the world rather than my being *in* and control *of* the world. I acknowledged my response-abilities in an ecological meshwork of multispecism. A persistent anthropocentric worldview was disrupted as I encountered performance *as* new materialist philosophy.

One could say—in terms borrowed from visual scholar Ariella Aïsha Azoulay—that these performances "unlearn" habitual and "rehearse" alternative modes of knowledge production (2019). When performances rehearse potential histories or differential futures, for example, they are unlearning imperialism, colonialism, and racial and sexist capitalism. When performances rehearse multispecies interconnectedness, they are unlearning human exceptionalism and triumphalism. Rehearsal is not considered here as a preparatory phase in creating a performance, but as an ongoing exercise that becomes inspirational for, and—ultimately—part of life.

In this contribution, I unfold my concept of hyphenated thinking as a way of unlearning eurocentric and anthropocentric modes of knowledge production (Stalpaert 2020). Hyphenated thinking suggests that the production of knowledge is not organised around one privileged subject, culture, or discipline. Philosopher and art theorist Gerald Raunig calls this a relational imparting of knowledge: a "moving along a relationship (or multiple posited relationships) without fixing the production of knowledge in a firm center" (2013, 58). Hyphenated thinking allows for a resurgence of knowledge in relationality, not only of body and mind, but also across multispecies entities, interweaving cultures, disciplines, and fields of study (art, science, and activism). From an ecological perspective, hyphenated thinking acknowledges that there are multiple ways in which the human and more-than-human encounter, interact, entangle, and affect each other.

Hyphenated thinking is not an applicable method; it is foremost an open learning and research attitude, in this case activated by particular art practices. It is an enacted practice and requires other forms of attention and language than our custom. As such, this chapter is not intended as an exhaustive overview of forms of hyphenated thinking to be applied by performance scholars. It rather examines the conditions of a performative zone to allow for a hyphenated thinking to take place.

I will demonstrate a practice of hyphenated thinking through my own engagement in *STILL HERE—An Alliance of Care for the SZenne River* (2023–) initiated by Natural Contract Lab.[1] *STILL HERE* takes place across Wallonia, Brussels and Flanders—from the source of the SZenne in Soignies to its bifurcation at the Zennegat in Mechelen. In co-creation with scientists, artists, activists, local stakeholders, and participants, the Natural Contract Lab group seeks to trace hydro-(ecological) matters of concern and to fabulate justice to compensate for the harm inflicted by ecocide on the hydro commons.[2] I will demonstrate how the artistic practices of walking-with, sensory mapping, storying, Agoras, and Guardian Schools activate pluriversal and collaborative modes of knowledge production. In these enacted practices of hyphenated thinking, the participants are moved into a state of in-betweenness and rehearse networked, situated, and embodied modes of knowledge production.

---

1   The performance project *STILL HERE: An alliance of care for the SZenne River* (2023–2025) is funded by the Flemish Government, Erfgoedcel Mechelen, Zenne Archives of Rijksarchief Brussel (BE), and the European Forum for Restorative Justice (EFRJ). The project facilitates a long-term commitment with Natural Contract Lab and an ephemeral performance process that is produced by HIROS, in co-production with VierNulVier, workspacebrussels, Kanal Centre Pompidou, Sint Lucas Antwerpen School of Arts KdG, and the Research Centre S:PAM (Studies in Performing Arts & Media) at UGent. FWO, the Research Foundation—Flanders has (co-)financed the underlying research of this publication conducted within the context of the Senior Research Project *Confluvial: Towards an art-science-activist worlding activating awareness of (hydro)ecologies* (PI, Christel Stalpaert, G093425N).
2   I would like to sincerely thank Maria Lucia Cruz Correia, Vinny Jones, Lode Vranken, Jef Seghers and Brunilda Pali for their collaborative thinking in the Natural Contract Labs meetings, for reading this text, and for providing valuable feedback.

19. *Hyphenated Thinking in Performance Processes* 417

Fig. 19.1 State of affairs of the area covered by *STILL HERE* (2023–2025), ©Maria Lucia Cruz Correia, 2024.

Of particular interest is also how the 'modus operandi' of these artistic practices can be expanded to the knowledge system of a university infrastructure. Over the past ten years, I have implemented several performance processes in the academic context of the performance studies unit of the arts department at Ghent university, some of them even in the university at large. What happens if we bring the rehearsal space of these performances into the university? Is it possible to infuse a university infrastructure with the potential of performances to speak decolonial and new materialist philosophy? Can art practices transform infrastructures of knowledge? In the final part of this contribution, I will reflect on how the enacted practice of a hyphenated thinking in a performative zone can be expanded within a university infrastructure. In this context, the artistic practice of schooling, as developed in NCL's Guardian School, is given a deeper dimension.

Context | Decoloniality and new materialism

The practice of a hyphenated thinking is interwoven with decolonial and new materialist thinking. Peruvian sociologist and humanist thinker Aníbal Quijano defined the term 'decoloniality' in the late 1960s to criticise the entanglements of histories of (colonial) power, modernity, and Western civilisation and to cultivate practices for undoing epistemic violence in relation to the European colonisation of the Americas. Key figures in this school of thought are Arturo Escobar, Walter Mignolo, and Rolando Vazquez, amongst others. While decolonisation refers to the "political processes of reaching independence from imperial structures" (Vazquez 2023), decoloniality is also an epistemic project. It looks into various academic aspects and seeks to transform eurocentric knowledge systems and infrastructures: the classroom set-up, the teaching methods, the research methodologies, or the exclusive mechanism of the canon.

Despite the noble ideals of educational institutions (at least after World War I)—that is, to grant democratic access to citizens across classes and beyond privileges, to increase literacy and gender equality worldwide—we are still struggling with the persistent relics of a mechanistic-imperialist worldview in the current landscape of infrastructures of knowledge. Epistemic violence is still at work. Western thought considers the compartmentalised, cognitive development of 'common sense' still superior to other forms of knowledge production, such as embodied or intergenerational knowledge. Cognitive knowledge is "passed on from one to another as property, from teacher to pupil in a long chain of tradition, in a hierarchy of generations and a uniform, static order of knowledge. In this order, the various techniques and disciplines are rigidly striated and separated" (Raunig 2013, 56). Moreover, since the 1980s, the focus on progressive rationality and efficiency took on exuberant competitive proportions, which philosopher and art theorist Raunig coined as the "machinic thinking" of "cognitive capitalism" (17).

More than being a mere vehicle for critique or a form of deconstruction, decoloniality involves an engagement with unlearning, undoing, recasting, and transforming eurocentric knowledge formations. Indian writer Amitav Ghosh calls for decolonial practices that disrupt the mechanistic-imperialist worldview, both in ecological and pedagogical terms (2021, 37). For Azoulay (building on Audre Lorde's writings), activating such an epistemological change means disabling the master's tools of white, patriarchal knowledge institutions. She proposes to unlearn imperialism, and to rehearse "'non-qualified' forms of knowledge production" as "one of many" (Azoulay 2019, 385). From his side, Raunig argues for disobedience to the knowledge machine. "We have to develop a risky practice that seeks conflict and transversal exchange beyond the boundaries of traditions and disciplines", he says (2013, 56).

The decolonial critique of eurocentrism resonates with the new materialist critique of anthropocentrism. The plea for pluriverse and collaborative thought, as a response to the recent call for decoloniality, resonates with the new materialist call to de-emphasise human exceptionalism in favour of multispecism. New materialism is a field within contemporary philosophy that is critical of the object-subject divide in modern and humanist traditions. The term was coined by Manuel DeLanda and Rosi Braidotti in the second half of the 1990s. Both were inspired by vitalist poststructuralists Gilles Deleuze and Félix Guattari to abandon the dualist ontology nature-culture, mind-matter, and human-non-human. Philosophers such as Bruno Latour, Karen Barad, Jane Bennett, Vinciane Despret, Donna Haraway, Isabelle Stengers, Arturo Escobar, and Tim Ingold all relate to the diverse strands of new materialist thinking. An attribute they share is to consider matter as an underexplored, dynamic force. They are part of a broader posthuman strand of thought which thinks the entanglement of human and more-than-human matter, and acknowledges the worlding potential of multispecies entanglements.

The term hyphenated thinking is also inspired by new materialist thinker Donna Haraway. In her book *Staying with the Trouble*, she proposes the vital model of "art-science-activist worldings" as a way of "staying with the trouble" (2016, 79; 76). The trouble refers to the ecological crisis that we are experiencing: climate change *is* happening, sea levels *are* rising, and ecosystems *are* collapsing. In order to cope with these disturbing, troubling times, we need to acknowledge our response-abilities in the ecological meshwork. Staying with the trouble is "learning to be truly present" (1) and "getting on together" (10). "The task is to become capable, with each other in all of our bumptious kinds, of response" (1).

An art-science-activist worlding is an example of such a radical interconnectedness in which humans are not separable from non-humans. Haraway focuses on practices instead of representations of social and environmental relations, and she believes in the world-making potential of a particular coalition of art, science, and activism in the struggle for a partial resurgence in this troubled world. This world-making potential is what Haraway considers as worlding.

Worlding is not a representation of the world, but an understanding of the world as a verb. It is a world-making practice, but in a sense that humans are no longer understood as individual subjects that can control, exhaust, and destroy their environment. According to the anthropocentric perspective, nature is but the passive backdrop of our devastating human-centred actions. Worlding is understood here as an autopoietic system: it is an intertwined system that produces and maintains itself, and in which the 'human' is radically enmeshed. In Haraway's non-representational theory of the world, humans are becoming-*with* and attending *to* the world rather than being *in* and in control *of* the world. As such, worlding is an enacted and embodied activity, and hence implies performativity:

> Worlding is informed by our turning of attention to a certain experience, place or encounter and our active engagement with the materiality and context in which events and interactions occur. It is above all an embodied and enacted process—a way of being in the world—consisting of an individual's whole-person act of attending to the world. (Palmer and Hunter 2018)

For Haraway, a narrative frame that understands worlding as such is speculative fabulation. It is a form of science fiction that intertwines art, science, and activism. A worlding is for that matter not a representation, but a practice as artistic understanding, an imagination, and the creation of a world teaming up with science and activism. I consider the performance process of *STILL HERE* as such a worlding practice.

Haraway introduces the term 'art-science-activist worldings' in different ways throughout her book. Most of the time, she doesn't use hyphens. Occasionally, she does (2016, 79). I am particularly drawn to her hyphenated use of the term. For it is precisely in the hyphens that non-conformist modes of knowledge production resurge. A hyphenated thinking for that matter is inspired by the new materialist belief that the world-making potential of art practices lies in fabulating a world-to-come in-between art, science, and activism. However, taking into consideration decolonial urges for unlearning imperialism, colonialism, and racial and sexist capitalism, I consider these hyphens also an opportunity for rehearsing pluriversal, multispecies and collaborative modes of knowledge production. The enacted practice of a hyphenated thinking in *STILL HERE* is a speculative fabulation, a continuous exploration of our radically enmeshed becoming-*with* and attending-*to* a world-to-come.

How to | Hyphenated thinking in performance processes

A hyphenated thinking is an enacted practice, rather than an applicable method. This *How* to-section should therefore not be mistaken for a prescription of how to conduct a hyphenated thinking in performance studies. Rather than enlisting techniques (in the imperative form of a verb), I propose five artistic practices (in the present participle form of a verb[3]) that are accompanied with related, open (research) questions. They are enacted throughout the performance process of *STILL HERE: An Alliance of Care for the SZenne River*. Their worlding potential lies not in representing a 'better' world, nor in setting one goal for an ideal future to come, but in activating a performative zone for a hyphenated thinking-with worldly reconfigurations in-between multispecies, cultures, disciplines, and fields of study.

1. *Constituting an alliance of care*: What does the particular coalition of art, science and activism look like in *STILL HERE*? What kind of collaborative practices are developed in these performance-pedagogical entanglements? And how do we move through the hyphens in-between these fields of knowledge?

2. *Walking-with SZenne River*: How do we think our hydro(ecological) entanglement with SZenne River in *STILL HERE*?

---

[3] The difference in meaning between the infinitive form and the present participle form of a verb is small. However, I prefer the present participle tense, as the -ing form emphasises the 'processual doing' inherent to the verb itself. The to-infinitive puts the emphasis more on the preference for, or the results of, the action.

3. *Sensorial Mapping*: How does STILL HERE call upon other senses than the science-accustomed of distant observation? (How) do they raise ecological awareness and constitute ecological encounters? What kind of sensory exercises are activated? (How) do they acknowledge a not-knowing? How do they activate an unlearning of cartographic mapping devices?

4. *Storying*: How do we express and share our relation with SZenne River as water body? How do we fabulate a common world-to-come?

5. *Agora*: How do we weave individual stories into a Living Bill, as a way to include the rights of SZenne River in the Constitution?

These artistic practices are five opportunities for activating a hyphenated thinking in (hydro-)ecological matters of concern.

Demonstration

Constituting a transdisciplinary alliance and moving through the hyphens in-between fields of knowledge

Natural Contract Lab was initiated by the Ghent-based, Portuguese eco-artist and water-steward Maria Lucia Cruz Correia in 2021. It is a transdisciplinary, ongoing, co-creative Lab that brings together artists, scientists, local stakeholders, and river bodies.[4] The Lab develops an artistic *Protocol of Reciprocal Care* to imagine new forms of environmental justice, and to realign the harm inflicted on the hydro commons. Its multispecies constellation affirms the (usually underexplored) dynamic force of water-as-matter and the entanglement of water bodies and agency. STILL HERE is a case study of NCL and initiated an alliance of care for SZenne River in 2023, practicing a hyphenated thinking in-between art, environmental law, restorative justice, rights of nature,

---

4   NCLs have been initiated with Sijoumi Lake in Tunisia (2021–2023), Tejo River in Portugal (2021–2023), Rhone in Switzerland (2022–2023), and Lieve and Aa in Belgium.

and ecological grief. It includes core NCL team members Correia, Vinny Jones (sensory scenography/dramaturgy), Lode Vranken (design/philosophy), Brunilda Pali (restorative justice), Margarida Mendes (research/sonic guidance), as well as artists and scientists invited for *STILL HERE*, such as Matteo Deblasio (river vessel/clay mediator), Marzia Dalfini (walking-with costumography), Saartje Monden (river guardian pedagogue, and Jef Seghers (environmental lawyer). I am engaged as 'a hyphenated thinker' from performance studies: I take field notes throughout the various events, give dramaturgical advice on walking methodologies, mourning and water rituals, and assist in developing tools for tracing and transferring a repertoire of care for SZenne River. Involved stakeholders are (human and more-than-human) beings that have a direct interest in the hydro-ecology of SZenne River. These range from local inhabitants, such as people who live by the river, and local flora and fauna, to organisations that take care of the river, such as environmental stakeholders monitoring the area, the Walloon organisation Contrat de Rivière Senne, Coordinatie Zenne, Brussels Environment, Natuurpunt Mechelen, and Zenne Garden Collective.

As the roles of the artists, scientists, and stakeholders-cum-activists are well-defined, the implementation of their fields of study in the Lab seems logical. However, the moment they join NCL, they practice a hyphenated thinking in-between the fields of art, science, and activism. Besides their long-term commitment, the network also collaborates on joint articles, performance-lectures, and work demonstrations. The 'wheres' and 'hows' of these collaborations are shaped by the needs that emerge over time, and thinking is constantly refracted by the shared laboratory culture. This transforms the accustomed format of academic knowledge production organised around one privileged centre and hierarchical knowledge transfer.

The diverse range of artists, scientists, and stakeholders cum-activists produces different and sometimes diverging perspectives on the hydro-ecological matters of concern of SZenne River. However, the alliance does not aim to propose one solution to a problem, but to connect the participants in an alliance of care for *SZenne River*. They are activated as river guardians in an ecological community as network, and are engaged in ongoing protocols of care and natural contracts. To put it in Haraway's terms, the alliance is "cultivating conditions for ongoingness" (2016,

38). There is a continuous "making and unmaking" of the performance, with an alliance of collaborators soliciting response, "passing on and receiving" artistic practices, "picking up and dropping" information (3). As such, *STILL HERE* is an artistic practice and an ongoing learning process at the same time. Everyone involved thinks through these performance-pedagogical entanglements.

This means first and foremost acknowledging the human entanglement in SZenne River ecologies and the importance of safeguarding the well-being of its biotopes. To activate this, NCL invites the alliance of care and the broader public for several site-responsive artistic walks along the riverbanks of SZenne River. They propose sensory exercises, and create context-specific gatherings (such as Agoras and Guardian Schools) for storying and weaving together the diverse experiences of relating with the water body of SZenne River.

Thinking through the milieu of the SZenne River landscape and hyphenating with more-than-human matter

Walking-with is a key artistic practice of NCL. Moving 'in situ' along SZenne River urges the participants to hyphenate with the river as a constant walking companion. During these "site-responsive artistic walks" we "become witnessing bodies, giving and receiving care. Walking-with is an act of accountability, a gesture of solidarity, a moment for unlearning and reconciling with the river" (SZenne River website). This walking-with differs from a solitary leisure walk. In the site-responsive artistic walking-with, the NCL group mediates an intersubjective, entangled multispecies relation with the landscape (Stalpaert 2010, 121–34.)

We receive a little booklet at the beginning of each walk, with a map of SZenne River drawn on it, but this is rather an impressive evocation than an accurate cartographic representation. We have to let go of our cartographic reading skills and surrender to an embodied, site-responsive walk. We move along without a plan, and allow ourselves to be 'instructed' along the walking-way, led by the encounters in the ecological meshwork.

19. Hyphenated Thinking in Performance Processes   425

Fig. 19.2 Maria Lucia Cruz Correia, *Booklet with Map for Walking-With SZenne River*, Soignies, April 13, 2024. ©Christel Stalpaert.

During a first *Walking-with SZenne River* in Soignies, Saturday 13 April 2024, we soon leave the marked trajectory of a pathway, and move into the fields, on the lookout for SZenne River's source. This feels like stepping across a threshold. I no longer look at a landscape from the street side, my body is no longer situated in a Google-mappable-landmark. I am immersed in the landscape. There is no pathway to receive or retrieve my walking steps, I am surrounded by the soft rippling of water through the earth's skin.

When we perceive the SZenne river source, in all its percolating surfacing, Correia invites the participants to collect, one by one, a small quantity of water in a clay vessel and to think of our intention for attending the artistic walk, for being here with SZenne River. Its water, collected in the clay vessel, is carried with us during the whole walk, from beginning to end. From now on, SZenne River walks with us too, as a constant walking companion. Its presence makes us move in particular ways. We are careful not to spill the water. We move carefully, slower than usual, more considerate, passing on the vessel to another walking companion when we feel our muscles become tired of carrying the weight of the water. The water demands our careful attention, and activates a site-responsive, embodied mode of knowledge production. While cartographic mapping produces a discourse of ownership *of* the water, the site-responsive artistic walk activates stewardship in the sense of attending *to* the water: we acquire a sense of its omnipresence and develop a responsibility towards it.

Fig. 19.3 Natural Contract Lab, *Walking-With SZenne River*, Soignies, April 13, 2024. ©Christel Stalpaert.

Walking-with SZenne River, I stumble onto very fascinating terrain. When I perceive the continuous stream of water 'in situ' along the walking-way, following its riverbanks, gayfully rippling alongside us, disappearing under houses and paved streets, and re-appearing as a pool of dark depth, my cognitive cartographic knowledge skills are stretched. Cartographic mappings of waterways usually only consider surface water (the water that visibly flows downhill, into the sea), and ownership of water bodies (visualised along lines representing national boundaries). Vast masses of blue indicate main streams and, smaller, tributary branches. A legend explains the symbols and colours used. Looking back and forth at the colourful imprint of SZenne's contours on the booklet, I realise that a topographic name is more than an objective, vast blue space on a map. Its con-fluvial meshwork exceeds any cartographic representation. Its surfacing ground water, for example, is very difficult to display on a map depicting only the surface of our planet. SZenne's source surfaces in multiple locations, percolating the earth's soil. Its hydro-ecological 'milieu' confluences with many other water bodies[5] and interconnects with several terrestrial and marine ecosystems. Its body flows, travels across national boundaries, transforms into ice, rain, and liquid, and merges with other bodies, including us. I am shocked into this recognition while encountering SZenne 'in situ'. I acknowledge what remains unnoticed, invisible, and hidden in cartographic representations. This enacted practice of a hyphenated thinking with more-than-human matter is an encounter with not-knowing. I am unlearning cartography. I am infused with the embodied and situated knowledge of the particular area, which can only be experienced through a walking-with.

Rehearsing a deep sensorial mapping and unlearning conventional cartographic mapping methodologies

Together with the booklet, the participants receive a pencil at the start of the walk. We are invited to map our sensory data, to record our experience as we walk-with SZenne River, and hence to constitute "a

---

5 SZenne River is an indirect tributary of the Scheldt estuary through Dijle River and Rupel River.

moving narrative" (SZenne River website). Some bodies have a magnetic pull on me, some remain silent, invisible to my mind's eye. Others only come to the fore after Vinny Jones' practical, yet poetic propositions that sharpen our senses.

Stretch your eyes completely to the horizon,

the furthest you can.

Try to stay connected to the landscape.

What is present?

What is absent?

Stay in your body while walking.

Through several sensory exercises we are rehearsing an attitude of attentive perception and deep listening. "We become witnessing bodies, giving and receiving care" (SZenne River website).

Towards the end of the site-responsive artistic walk, my notebook contains snatches of conversations, re-occurring words, grief stories that took me by surprise, dried flowers that I picked up when they parted under the weight of my footfalls, and doodles next to meandering thoughts. I observed rhythms of walking, patterns and constellations of walking companions, mood shifts in the group, shifts in dynamics of the waterways, I have photographs taken with my mobile phone, recordings of birds identified with Birdnet... This is more than mere data collection, more than a listing of things seen and heard. My notes reveal how the sensory scores, these practical, yet poetic propositions intensified my response to the landscape as networked environment. The site-responsive artistic walk accounts for a heightened awareness of an ecological entanglement with and the transformational potential of the space encountered.

Reading through my notes again, I can conceptualise it as a hyphenated thinking: a learning through following the actors in the network (Latour), through following the living and the dead from the 'milieu', in observing what holds them together in a generative ecological network (Despret). I allowed these actors to guide me in my understanding of the experience of walking-with SZenne River. And maybe understanding is not the right word here. When anthropologist

Heonik Kwon uses the word understanding, he does so with ontological tact: he respects the enigmatic and accepts that these actors and their particular constellations are not asking for explanation or elucidation.

This anthropological method differs from the 'old-school' anthropological method that has rightly been criticised as a colonial observation tool. Its disembodied, distant, and objectifying gaze constitutes a hierarchical power relation that facilitates imperialist knowledge production (Asad 1973). The deep and pragmatic sensory mapping, on the other hand, recalibrates my observation skills. I can put down the burden of perfection, and find the liberty for shape-shifting in-between senses and perspectives. I do not follow one observational track, and not mine alone. Moving and shape-shifting in-between walking companions, and listening carefully to their manifestations, I discover different vocabularies and diverse languages testifying of their bonding presence or active absence. Walking companions move(d) in mysterious ways and have other and multiple ways of expressing their ways of being and bonding. I learn from these ways as they present themselves, allowing different perspectives to co-exist, and to include the complicities, paradoxes and frictions that come with this deep, but pragmatic sensory mapping.

Storying (hydro-)ecological matters of concern and fabulating our common world-to-come

The site-responsive artistic walk with SZenne River takes a couple of hours, and NCL repeatedly invites us to sit down. We unfold the multifunctional waist tool-holder that we received at the beginning of the walk, and perceive fragments of SZenne River imprinted on it. We use it as a blanket to sit on and join in conversational circles. We exchange water memories, river stories, and grief testimonies. The vessel, carrying our intentions for being there with the river, functions as a talking piece. It is passed on from hand to hand and it is held by those who are testifying of their concerns, sorrows and hopes for SZenne River ecologies. Remembering our water and grief memories and sharing it with our walking companions, we are storying our relation with water. Some stakeholders in the group testify of their fear while measuring the growing pollution of the water, some stakeholders testify of their hope while observing the resurgence of the formerly disappeared yellow iris along the riverbanks, other participants testify of a favourite swimming spot in a river, lost because of development and construction projects. Through these testimonies, the mimetic relation of a cartographic map with reality is revealed as even more deceptive. The bright blue colour on a map might conceal a toxic water environment, or a heavily polluted water basin near an industrial area. A national boundary that represents a territorial claim might conceal imperial activities of water extraction, inflicting harm on the hydrology commons or on indigenous communities. While the map indicates buildings, a covered water body might flow underneath.

The conversational circles reveal a "vexed place", in the sense of a "disturbed place" (Haraway 2016, 133) in the seemingly objective cartographic representations. The individual water and grief memories 'story' these vexed places in several ways: they testify to our complicity in anthropocene violence, but they also speak nearby invisible or nearly extinct bodies, activating ripples of care. Living on the edge of extinction, the wild yellow iris, for example, is storied as an active absence. So are the invisible, covered parts of the river, or the bird species that remain silent, hovering on the edge of extinction.

I am particularly touched by Lode Vranken's grief memory of the loss of the sound of house sparrows. These little, sociable birds used to be a common guest all around the world, but their population has dramatically declined over recent years. Living on the edge of extinction, the house sparrow becomes actively absent through Lode's ecological grief memory, and my vain attempt to locate the bird with my Birdnet App.

Listening to each other's grief testimonies, in a collective mourning circle, we learn that SZenne River is currently under deep ecological transformation. Not through solidified matters of fact, but through shared matters of hydro(ecological) concern, we learn that, for centuries, the river has had an important impact on the development and the design of the city of Brussels. That, on the other hand, the rapid industrialisation, changes in agricultural practices and urban wastewater management, also affected the water body in many ways. The grief memory of a scientist testifies to the degradation of the water quality of the river and the modification of the ecological and hydrologic continuum of the river system by anthropogenic pressures. Water memories of swimming-with the water flow make us realise that when, in times of expansion, a river is made to exchange water fluxes with canals to prevent the city from flooding, aquatic ecosystems and natural tidal flows are disturbed. River stories of local stakeholders tell us that large parts of the river systems were covered for safety and sanitation purposes in Brussels, and our walking-with SZenne River learns us that this is still the case.

Weaving individual grief memories into a Living Bil during Agoras

Our hyphenated thinking does not judge, but it remembers. The rituals of care are archived in our enmeshed bodies. As such, the sensorial mapping and the conversation circles constitute a repertoire—a situated, embodied, and networked archive that continuously feeds the creating of a Living Bill. This Living Bill "serves as a proof of evidence of our relationship with the river and legitimacy as allies through which we can call for its legal recognition in the Belgian constitution" (SZenne River Website). It consists of the very diverse sensory data collected during the walks, and the memories shared. These are woven together into an artistic patchwork during Agoras: gatherings of the participants that are open to the wider public and that seek social activation of water (re-)distribution, (hydro)ecological justice, and reconciliation with the water. The gathering in Agoras builds on the idea that the model of democracy in Classical Athens is articulated through participatory political activities in the public centre of the *agora*. 'Agora' actually means 'place of assembly'. Such an Agora as assembly took place in the SZenne Garden and allowed "moments of exchange between the many river guardians, allies and species. It is a communal moment to weave tools of river governance and care to grow alliances between those we have met along the river" (SZenne River website). Agoras like these resulted, for example, in a partly uncovering of the river in collaboration with the city of Brussels.

Expanding the method | Schooling within the university infrastructure

In autumn 2025, the art practice of STILL HERE—*An Alliance of Care for the SZenne River* was implemented as a twelve-week-long research seminar in the arts department at Ghent university. This meant that the students joined NCL and participated in the ongoing co-creation of the transdisciplinary alliance of care. They contributed to the *Protocol of Reciprocal Care* and rehearsed the enacted practice of a hyphenated thinking in Walks-with SZenne River, sensory mapping, storying, and Agoras.

What happens when the performative zone of *STILL HERE*—its rehearsal space so to speak—is transferred into a university infrastructure? What happens when a hyphenated thinking is practised and enacted in a university? A performative zone does not render the university setting less serious. It becomes the university's autonomous, free space for nonconformist thinking and action. The enacted practice of a hyphenated thinking within a university infrastructure not only functions as a critique or a deconstruction of dominant modes of knowledge production. It activates an epistemological change within the university infrastructure itself.

In this context, the artistic practice of schooling is of particular interest, with NCL's Guardian School as a practical example. These schools activate not a univers(al)ity, but a pluriversality: they introduce alternative forms of critical pedagogy, assert a discourse of decoloniality, and experiment with diverse modes of knowledge production. It is "a place where different forms of knowledge can enter into dialogue without the habitual hierarchies between them, exploring a variety of formats in which to operate, including the performative, the experiential, the discursive and the visual" (Piña 2029, 48; see also Yakoub 2024). Implementing *STILL HERE* in a research seminar setting, means activating pluriversality within the university infrastructure in several ways.

Firstly, implementing artistic practices differs from the usual three-hour format of guest lectures and workshops in an academic university context. The artist, performer, director or choreographer is not invited for a three-hour talk *about* their art practice. They are invited as an artist fellow and teaching companion throughout a whole university course or throughout several workshop sessions within a university setting. The whole performative zone is transmitted to the pedagogical context of the university. This means adopting the artistic practices developed in a performance process as ways of thinking in (and beyond) the classroom.

Secondly, the monological and hierarchical science-accustomed format in universities is disrupted. Every participant deploys a hyphenated thinking in-between performance practice and pedagogical method. The divide between audience, art work, and scholar is no longer tenable, and gives way to a meshworked constellation. Our position as student, teacher, artist, researcher, software developer, activist, spectator, performer... shape-shifts throughout the sessions. Our mindset is recalibrated repeatedly, as our thinking unfolds in a network of interconnectivity.

Thirdly, rather than learning *about* performance processes, applying analytical tools to understand what they mean and how they work, we encounter performance *as* philosophy in (and beyond) the classroom. Rather than watch performances in a theatre venue, read related theoretical and philosophical texts, and conduct a drama or performance analysis from a particular (human) perspective, we experience what artistic practices *do*, in the sense of activating situated, embodied, and networked ways of thinking.

Fourthly, rather than writing a performance analysis with case studies, and submitting a paper that is graded, the students 'produce' fieldnotes, practicing the anthropologist skill of sensory mapping in site-responsive artistic walks. Rather than collecting data in view of an archive, they are constituting an embodied repertoire during conversational circles and Agoras. They rehearse practices for weaving and knotting stories together in a hyphenated thinking. Their entangled thinking-with artists, stakeholders, and other participants (human and more-than-human) transforms the university format of academic writing organised around one privileged centre into a pluriversity, and the hierarchical knowledge transfer into collaborative multispecism.

Fifthly, the implementation of the SZenne River practices allows for a reinvention of knowledge production *outside* the university. The hyphenated thinking here receives an outward dimension. There is a "complicity between the inside and the outside of an institution" (Raunig 2013, 53). The collaboration of the university institution with sustainable organisations, local stakeholders, and the city government generates knowledge that primarily deals with matters of entangled concern in times of ecological crisis.

Why should a university infrastructure be the only valid knowledge institution? And why should the university be thought of—as Heidegger did—as a place where ideas are built from a solid ground or fundament? With Ingold, I wonder:

> What if we were to think of the ground not as a level platform – like the nursery floor – upon which to raise an edifice, but as a permeable zone in which substances welling up from the earth bind with the air and moisture of the atmosphere in the ongoing production of life? (2013)

Along these lines, I wonder: How would a school look if it is knotted rather than block-built? And where would a thinking through weaving and knotting lead us in our world-to-come?

To be continued… for staying with the trouble…

Suggestions for further reading

In *Potential History. Unlearning imperialism* (2019), Azoulay argues that activating an epistemological change means unlearning imperialism. Inspired by philosopher and activist Audre Lorde, she proposes ways to disable the master's tools of white, patriarchal knowledge institutions. In *The Nutmeg's Curse: Parables for a Planet in Crisis* (2021), Ghosh explains how the Western Enlightenment installed a mechanistic-imperialistic worldview that is still operative in infrastructures of knowledge. It advances through expansion, conquest, extraction, and segregation. Drawing on science, art, feminism, and speculative fiction, in *Staying with the Trouble: Making Kin in the Chthulucene* (2016), Donna Haraway invites us to reconfigure our relations, attending to the earth and all its inhabitants. For an analysis of how the Western machine of knowledge transfer is increasingly driven by capitalist valorisation, Raunig's *Factories of Knowledge: Industries of Creativity* (2013) is an insightful source. My article "Performing Arts Activating Climate Change Awareness" (2023) provides another demonstration of hyphenated thinking, now in relation to *Common Dreams—Flotation School*, another performance process initiated by Correia. This survival climate school co-creates and (re)collects strategies for survival in a floating society.

References

Asad, Talal, ed. 1973. *Anthropology & the Colonial Encounter*. Ithaca Press.

Azoulay, Ariella A. 2019. *Potential History. Unlearning Imperialism.* Verso.

Cull Ó Maoilearca, Laura. 2024. "Performance Philosophy—Staging a New Field." In *Encounters in Performance Philosophy*, edited by Laura Cull Ó Maoilearca and Alice Lagaay, 15–38. Palgrave Macmillan. https://doi.org/10.1057/9781137462725_2

Despret, Vinciane. 2021. *Our Grateful Dead: Stories of Those Left Behind*, translated by Stephen Muecke. University of Minnesota Press. https://doi.org/10.5749/j.ctv1w7v24k

Escobar, Arturo. 2018. *Designs for the Pluriverse*. Duke University Press. https://doi.org/10.1215/9780822371816

Ghosh, Amitav. 2021. *The Nutmeg's Curse: Parables for a Planet in Crisis*. The University of Chicago Press.

Haraway, Donna J. 2016. *Staying with the Trouble: Making Kin in the Chthulucene*. Duke University Press. https://doi.org/10.1215/9780822373780

Ingold, Tim. 2013. "Of Blocks and Knots: Architecture as Weaving." *The Architectural Review*. 25 October. https://www.architectural-review.com/essays/of-blocks-and-knots-architecture-as-weaving

Kwon, Heonik. 2008. *Ghosts of War in Vietnam*. Cambridge University Press. https://doi.org/10.1017/CBO9780511807596

Palmer, Helen and Vicky Hunter. 2018. *New Materialism. How Matter Comes To Matter*. 16 March. https://newmaterialism.eu/almanac/w/worlding.html

Piña, Amanda. 2019. "The School of the Jaguar: Rehearsing an ecology of knowledge." In *Endangered Human Movements. Vol. 3: The School of the Jaguar*, edited by Amanda Piña, 47–85. Nadaproductions.

Raunig, Gerald. 2013. *Factories of Knowledge: Industries of Creativity*, translated by Aileen Derieg. MIT Press.

Stalpaert, Christel. 2010. "Intersubjectief wandelen met het landschap. Nomadisch denken in Agnès Varda's *Sans toit ni loi* (1985) en Chantal Akerman's *Les rendez-vous d'Anna* (1978)." In *Anders zichtbaar. Zingeving en humanisering in de beeldcultuur*, edited by Johan Swinnen, 121–34. VUBPress.

Stalpaert, Christel. 2020. "De slagkracht van de verbindingsstreepjes." *Collateral: Online Journal for Cross-cultural Close Reading*, no. 25. (June) Thematic Issue on *Traag Geweld: kan Kunst het Klimaat redden?*, edited by Stef Craps and Mahlu Mertens. https://collateral-journal.com/index.php?collision=traaggeweld

Stalpaert, Christel. 2023. "Performing Arts Activating Climate Change Awareness: Hyphenated Thinking in *Common Dreams—Flotation School* (2018)." *The Drama Review* 36(5): 74–81. (Thematic issue *On Climate Change*). https://doi.org/10.1017/S1054204322000892

SZenne River website. https://naturalcontractlab.com/szenne-river/

Yakoub, Yoachim Ben. 2014. "Breathing out of the University, and into many Schools: Storying abolition as a way of activation." *Performance Research 28* (8): 109–19 (Thematic Issue *On Activation*, edited by Christel Stalpaert and Eylül Fidan Akıncı). https://doi.org/10.1080/13528165.2023.2401251

X. 2023. "Interview with Rolando Vazquez", Utrecht: Utrecht University. 28 September. https://www.uu.nl/en/news/interview-with-dr-rolando-vazquez

Index

03:08:38 States of Emergency 67–68, 70, 72–76, 79, 81
'*802. That is where, as you heard, the elephant danced the malinga. The place where they now grow flowers.*' 229, 241–243. *See also* Baloji, Sammi
ABBA 85, 87, 102–104
  ABBA Voyage 85, 87, 102–104
absorption 28, 71, 82, 258
accessibility 320, 330
Acconci, Vito 369, 377
action 4, 45, 63, 89, 92–93, 99–100, 118, 133, 135–136, 152, 158, 201, 203, 240, 261, 274, 283, 288, 337, 340–341, 343, 350–351, 364, 382, 395, 421, 432
activism 31, 62, 211, 220, 222, 277, 287, 306, 350–351, 413, 415, 420–421, 423
activist 100, 202, 209, 213, 216, 339, 345, 367, 413, 416, 419–420, 423, 433–434
Actor-network theory (ANT) 191–192
Adams, Tony E. 171, 307, 311–312, 314–317, 322–323, 331
Adorno, Theodor 146
Adshead, Janet 109–110, 113, 122
Aeschylus 182
  Persians, The 182
affect 82, 216, 232, 363–365, 367, 380, 382
affective 15, 30, 51, 85, 103, 105, 153, 160, 213, 216, 264, 337–341, 359–361, 363–367, 369, 371, 375–381, 383
affective attunement 15, 359, 365–366, 375, 377–378, 383
affinities 52, 119–120, 205, 361, 376
  broken 119–120

affordance 32, 34, 85, 145, 147–150, 152, 154, 160
African American Policy Forum 276
Agamben, Giorgio 34
age 56, 113, 257, 263, 272, 285, 287, 315
agency 63, 114, 138, 149, 179, 191, 212, 231, 234, 256, 258, 261, 313, 331, 342, 422
Agora 414, 416, 422, 424, 431–433
Aïsha and the Women of Madina 173, 176, 184
Akomolafe, Bayo 337, 339, 343, 355
algorithmic performance 85, 102, 104
Althusser, Louis 148
Alÿs, Francis 370
animation 97, 239–240
annotation 111, 116
anti-Nazi resistance 156
Apollon 57, 59
Apollon Musagète 57
Appadurai, Arjun 236
archaeology 16–17, 34–35, 229–235, 238–239, 241, 243. *See also* media archaeology; theatre archaeology
  of knowledge 229–230, 232
archival knowledge 247, 250
archival research 13, 15, 231, 247, 249, 254–259, 265, 301
archives 5, 9, 111, 119, 141, 216, 232–234, 239–240, 244, 247–265, 301, 318, 361–362, 371, 431, 433
  colonial 259, 261–262
  embodied 232, 258
Artaud, Antonin 88, 158
art ecologies 16, 187–190, 194, 202
articulation 89, 313, 331
artistic biotope 52, 192
artistic research 187, 202–203, 239, 330, 342, 355, 389, 391, 394–395
artist-researcher 329

assemblage 48, 150, 152, 181, 193–194
attending laterally 337, 343
attention 25–27, 37, 44–45, 47–49, 60–63, 67–68, 70, 73, 79, 81, 85, 91, 93, 95, 102–104, 111, 114, 135, 142, 146, 148, 151–153, 170, 174, 178–181, 189–190, 195, 221, 224, 231, 235, 251, 254–256, 262, 287, 343, 345, 366, 377, 379–381, 387–388, 390, 401–402, 404, 416, 420, 426
   active 148, 404
   zone of 148
audience 9, 23, 36, 44–46, 48–49, 51–55, 59, 67–70, 72–82, 86, 89, 96–99, 101–104, 116, 129–130, 133–139, 141, 148–149, 151, 155–159, 171, 177, 179–181, 192, 195, 197–198, 211, 218, 221–223, 240, 263–264, 283–285, 287–289, 300–302, 306, 374–375, 433
   address 44–46, 49, 54, 211, 218
audition 147, 155, 161
auditory imagination 146–147, 151, 157, 161
Austin, J.L. 12
autobiography 16, 155, 294, 296–297, 315
autoethnography 15–16, 293–298, 300–302, 304–307, 311–324, 327, 329–332
   collaborative 322
avatars 33, 87, 97, 102–103, 140, 237, 239–240
Azoulay, Ariella Aïscha 265, 415, 418–419, 434
ΑΦΕ 97

Bacchae—Prelude to a Purge 199
Back to Back Theatre 85–86, 99. *See also small metal objects*
Balanchine, George 57–59, 114
Bala, Sruti 15, 17, 169, 277, 287, 343
Bali 238
Bal, Mieke 21–22, 24–29, 36, 38, 71, 190
Baloji, Sammi 229, 241, 243

Barthes, Roland 31, 113
Bateson, Gregory 238–240
Bausch, Pina 89, 114
Bava, Mario 161
Beck, Alan 147, 151
Behar, Ruth 296
Behrndt, Synne 44, 46, 48, 50
Being Pink Ain't Easy 271, 282, 285–286
Bench, Harmony 113–114, 122
Benjamin, Walter 232
Bennett, Jane 48, 193, 197, 231, 419
Bharatanatyam 89
bias 55–56, 62, 146, 280–281, 288, 294, 299, 302, 315–316, 323
Bilge, Sirma 274, 277
biomechanics 33, 112, 115
Bird Song (2004) 119–120
Black feminisms 279
Black feminists 273, 277, 403
Black studies 339
Bleeker, Maaike 6, 28, 36–38, 46–48, 52, 54, 63, 67, 69, 71, 190, 221, 238
Boal, Augusto 213, 340
Bochner, Arthur 296, 311, 314–316, 322
body 31–33, 35, 48, 58, 62, 86–88, 90–92, 94–95, 97–98, 100–104, 110–111, 114–116, 118, 120–121, 131–132, 139, 171, 175, 179, 181–182, 187, 197–198, 200, 203, 230, 240–241, 257–258, 263–264, 282, 284–287, 289, 342, 355, 361–362, 364, 371, 377, 379–380, 387, 395–397, 401, 415, 422, 424–425, 427–428, 430
   as archive 264
Boot, Fred 155, 159
Borderline Visible 361, 370–376, 380
Bos di Nos Pueblo 293–295, 301–303, 305
Bourdieu, Pierre 191–192
Brahms, Johannes 159
Braidotti, Rosi 94, 205, 419
Brandstetter, Gabriele 86, 105
Brecht, Bertolt 46, 52, 93, 213

Index 441

bricolage 183
broadcasting 153
Broken Aquarium 406. *See also* Every house has a door
Brothers exalt thee to freedom 221–222
Bruggeman, Daniëlle 202–203
Butler, Judith 71, 169, 175–176, 313, 326, 395–396
Butoh 89

cabaret 137, 203, 218–219
Camuti, Fabiola 16, 311, 313, 329–330
Candelario, Rosemary 2–3, 122
canon 212, 231–232, 252–253, 283, 418
Carastathis, Anna 271, 279–280
catharsis 81
Cavalli, Francesco 161
Center for Intersectionality and Social Policy Studies 276
Chang, Heewon 311, 316, 318–321, 332
Chion, Michel 128, 130, 137, 142, 148, 151
choreographic analysis 113–114, 122
choreomusical analysis 112, 114, 118, 122
choreopolicing 95, 101, 103
choreopolitics 95
choreutics 110, 117
Choy, Ka Fai 229, 237–240
Church, Kathryn 331
class 13, 56, 141, 196–197, 211–212, 222, 252, 272–274, 277, 280–281, 285, 287, 299, 302, 304, 338
classroom 1–2, 4, 13, 43–44, 192, 272, 305, 337–339, 351, 377, 383, 418, 432–433
codes 57, 148–149, 153–154, 158–159, 239, 258, 262, 319
coding 319, 330
  descriptive coding 319
  emotion coding 319
cognitive 24, 105, 109, 116, 149–153, 280, 286, 328, 391, 418, 427
cognitive capitalism 418. *See also* Raunig, Gerald

Coleman, Rebecca 231, 236, 364
collaboration 8, 37, 44, 102, 162, 196, 303, 328, 345, 347, 349, 392, 403, 413, 423, 431, 433
colonial 6, 161–162, 200–201, 234, 236–243, 255–256, 258–262, 296, 331, 354, 418, 429
  archives 259, 261–262
  orders 259, 262, 354
colonial order 262, 354
colonisation 141, 238, 243, 261–262, 361, 418
Combahee River Collective 272
complexity 26, 29, 33, 110, 117–118, 120, 138, 194, 196–197, 256, 274, 279, 284, 364, 366
composition 43–46, 49–51, 53, 55, 57–58, 60, 68, 70–71, 86, 118, 127, 131–132, 140, 159, 193, 205, 230, 235, 252, 347, 365, 381–382
compositional units 118
concept 3, 5–6, 10, 14–17, 21–38, 47–48, 69–71, 85, 87, 89–91, 94–97, 103, 105, 112, 125, 129–130, 132–135, 142, 147, 169, 178, 180, 183, 187, 189–190, 193–198, 200–202, 204–205, 209, 215–216, 224, 229, 235, 247, 249, 253–254, 260, 263–264, 272–273, 277, 279, 304, 313, 319–321, 324, 328, 339, 350–351, 363, 366–367, 390, 392, 400–401, 414–415
  travelling concepts 21, 36
concept album 132, 134–135
concept-based analysis 15, 21–22, 24, 27, 29, 31, 196
concert 29, 85, 87, 128, 134, 148, 152, 154
Congo 229, 241–243
Conquergood, Dwight 3–5, 7, 298, 359, 365, 376, 383
consent 145, 153, 216, 297, 300, 305, 322–323
contemporary art 232
contextual analysis 15–17, 30, 187–191, 193–197, 202, 205, 271
Copperbelt 241, 243

credibility 316, 322
Crenshaw, Kimberlé 271, 273–274, 277, 279, 289
critical fabulation 244, 255–256
Cull Ó Maoilearca, Laura 16, 387, 389, 394, 396–397, 404–405, 407–408, 414
cultural analysis 6, 15, 21–24, 27, 38, 71, 293
cultural materialism 14–16, 161, 209–211, 214–215, 217, 221, 224
cultural studies 113, 127, 153, 209–214, 221, 224, 289, 298, 363
  British 209–210, 212, 214, 221
culture
  dominant 209, 216–217, 219–220, 223
  emergent 216–217, 220
  residual 216, 224
  site of struggle 214–215
  whole way of life 212–215
curating (curator, curatorial) 47, 189–190, 236, 288

Dalcroze Eurhythmics 88
Damisch, Hubert 27
Dança Doente 197–198, 201
dance 1–9, 13–15, 17, 21, 23, 27, 29, 32–36, 38, 43–46, 48, 50, 56–57, 59, 63, 71, 86, 88–89, 92, 95, 97–98, 101, 103–104, 107–122, 127, 129, 143, 159, 188–189, 192, 195, 198, 202, 229, 236–241, 253, 258, 264, 277, 282, 312, 338, 340, 342, 346, 360, 362, 391, 394, 397, 408
  science 115–116
dance analysis 15, 17, 107–109, 111–116, 121–122, 127
Dance Studies Association (DSA) 10
data
  object-related 320
  person-related 320
  spatial-related 320
  time-related 320
data management 320–321
Davies, Siobhan 117–120, 122

Siobhan Davies RePlay 119
Davis, Tracy C. 2, 7–8, 11–12, 232, 248, 257–258
Debord, Guy 366–367
decoding 51, 145, 153–154, 200
decolonial 15, 122, 142, 234, 250, 307, 337, 354–356, 359, 362, 388, 413, 415, 417–419, 421
  pedagogy 337
decolonialism 7
decoloniality 354, 418–419, 432
decolonisation 162, 195, 251–252, 356, 418
Decroux, Étienne 28
DeFrantz, Thomas 7–8, 289
degenerate music (*Entartete Musik*) 159
de Langen, Marijn 28
Deleuze, Gilles 25, 31, 35, 48, 193, 196, 205, 390, 394, 401, 419
de Levita, Robin 155
Denzin, Norman Kent 307, 315, 332
dérive 367, 369, 374
Derrida, Jacques 251
Diaghilev, Serge 108
dis/ability 272, 287, 315
disability 62, 100, 257, 277, 282, 307, 369
discourse analysis 14–17, 29, 34, 155, 169–177, 179, 181–183, 190
discrimination 175, 271, 273–274, 278–279
discursive objects 190
dispositive 174
dissensus 214, 338, 350
distraction 139, 151, 344, 346–347
distribution of the sensible 198, 200, 214, 222
Dolaklak 237
dominant cultural order 145, 153
dominant-hegemonic code or position 154–156, 158, 160
Dorsen, Annie 82, 97
Doruff, Sher 355
drag artist 21

dramaturg 5, 36, 45, 47, 63, 189, 301, 393
dramaturgical 6, 15, 17, 29, 31–32, 36–37, 43–49, 51–53, 56–57, 60, 63, 81–82, 95, 128, 189–190, 194–195, 197, 211, 217–218, 221, 223, 284, 286, 288, 339, 343, 345–347, 350, 391, 404, 423
dramaturgical analysis 6, 15, 17, 29, 43–46, 48–49, 51–53, 56–57, 60, 190, 195, 211
dramaturgical strategy 195, 197
dramaturg-researcher 36
dramaturgy 1–2, 4, 8, 15, 32, 36, 43–50, 52–53, 63, 70, 78, 81, 127, 131, 140, 188, 221, 283, 285, 288, 337, 345–346, 349–350, 391, 393, 423. *See also* queer dramaturgy
 dance 48, 63
 major 53
 minor 53
 relational 43–45, 48, 53, 57, 195, 211
dynamics 37, 50, 85–86, 90–92, 100, 102, 113, 116, 118, 130, 189, 191, 198, 203, 233, 236, 271, 277–278, 305, 313, 322, 324, 326–327, 331, 395–396, 428

ear cleaning 151
ecology 2, 17, 85, 87, 90, 96, 197, 203–205, 392, 407, 413–416, 418–419, 421–424, 427–431, 433
effort analysis 85
Elisabethville 241–243
Ellis, Carolyn 296, 311–312, 314–318, 322, 324, 331
embodied fabulation 15–16, 247, 249–250, 256–259, 261–264
embodied knowledge 3–4, 112, 216, 321, 338
embodiment 3–4, 10, 15–16, 27, 33, 51, 67–69, 71, 82, 85, 96, 102–103, 109, 112, 114, 121, 135, 149, 215–216, 232, 244, 247–250, 253–254, 256–259, 261–264, 284, 286, 321, 326, 328, 337–341, 343, 351, 355–356, 359–363, 366,
376–377, 383, 389, 391, 393–397, 399–401, 403–404, 408, 416, 418, 420, 424, 426–427, 431, 433
Emergence 34, 398. *See also* McCormick, John and Hutchison, Steph
encoding 145, 153–154
Englishby, Paul 140
epistemology 9–10, 111, 171–172, 176–177, 251–253, 256–257, 277–278, 281, 314, 328, 360–362, 388, 390–391, 394, 413–414, 419, 432, 434
ervaringstheater 221
ethics 24, 82, 85, 93, 104, 189, 255, 295, 297, 300, 305, 307, 316, 322–323, 329, 338, 354, 398, 401, 404
 ethical awareness 322
ethnochoreology 113, 117–118
ethnographic film 236, 238, 240
eukinetics 110
eurocentrism 277–278, 419
Evans, Mark 88, 104
Evelin, Marcelo 187, 197
evenly hovering attention 151
event 1, 3–5, 7, 10, 27, 43–45, 50, 52–53, 55, 57, 67–70, 72–79, 81, 104, 133, 149, 152, 154, 157, 170, 176, 178, 187–188, 191–193, 195, 199, 231–233, 242–243, 248–249, 251, 272, 274, 288, 301, 304–305, 318–320, 330, 365, 367, 374, 378, 380–381, 393, 401–402, 420, 423
Every house has a door 388, 392–393, 399, 405–407. *See also* Broken Aquarium
exclusion 89, 175, 199, 234, 254, 271, 276, 278–280, 371
experience 2, 4–5, 13, 16–17, 24, 29–30, 32, 35, 44–45, 48, 51, 56, 63, 67–68, 70–72, 74–75, 79, 81–82, 87, 90, 95, 98, 102–103, 112–113, 115–117, 120, 130, 142, 146, 148, 152–153, 157–158, 161, 174, 182, 190, 192, 201, 215, 218–220, 243, 264, 273–274, 277, 279, 281–282,

284–286, 288, 293–299, 301, 304, 312–314, 319, 324, 327–328, 338, 341, 344, 351, 353–354, 359–363, 365–367, 369, 371, 374–378, 382, 392, 394, 398, 404–405, 414, 419–420, 427–428, 433
extended reality (XR) 97–98
extraction 111, 237, 430, 434
Farge, Arlette 249, 255–256
Felton-Dansky, Miriam 82

feminism 56, 94, 109, 250, 253–254, 271, 277–280, 288, 307, 313, 359, 362, 365, 403, 434. *See also* Black feminisms; Black feminists
Fensham, Rachel 9, 17, 82, 85, 89, 105
Fevered Sleep 399–400, 402, 405. *See also Sheep Pig Goat*
fictional soundscapes 151
field research 115, 188, 190–191, 193
Fludernik, Monika 152
Fluxus 369, 382
focalisation 28, 38, 70, 73–75, 77–79, 81–82
folk dance 111, 113
Forensic Architecture 342, 370–371
Foster, Susan 109
Foucault, Michel 3, 31, 171–177, 179, 182–183, 230, 232, 234, 255, 361–362
Freire, Paulo 340
Freitas, Marlene Monteiro 187, 197, 199
Freshwater, Helen 51, 82
Frith, Simon 157, 162
fugitive knowledge 337, 339
Fuhrmann, Andrew 17, 85
fungi 202–204

Garner, Stanton 104–105
gaze 239, 265, 283–284, 286, 429
gender 7, 30, 36, 56–57, 109, 113, 175–176, 179, 252, 257, 263, 272–274, 276–277, 282, 285, 287, 299, 305, 313, 315, 326–327, 380, 408, 418

genealogy 9, 229–235, 354, 374
of alternatives 234
Georgelou, Konstantina 16, 46–47, 198, 222, 337, 348, 350, 352–353
gesture 14, 38, 45, 85, 87–88, 90, 92–93, 100–104, 116, 138, 145–146, 181, 199, 223, 230, 232, 253, 258, 264, 276, 350, 361, 424
Ghosh, Amitav 234, 243, 274, 418, 434
Ghostcatching (1999) 34
Gibson, James J. 34, 147
Gibson/Martelli 34
Gielen, Pascal 192–193
Gilroy, Paul 210
Giurchescu, Anca 113
Gramsci, Antonio 153, 216
Green, Doris 111, 370
Greenotation 111
Grehan, Helena 82, 99–101, 214
Groot Nibbelink, Liesbeth 1–2, 16–17, 28, 43–44, 50, 54–55, 187, 197–198, 221, 223, 376
Grotowski, Jerzy 88
grounded theory 16, 361, 376–377
Guardian School 414, 416–417, 424, 432
Guattari, Félix 25, 48, 193, 196, 205, 338, 390, 401, 419
Gumbs, Alexis Pauline 406, 409

Haiven, Max 234, 244
Halberstam, Jack 234, 339
Hall, Stuart 145, 153–154, 210, 212
Hampton, Ant 359, 361, 370–375, 380
Haraway, Donna 56, 204, 362, 401, 419–420, 423, 430, 434
Harney, Stefano 337, 339, 355
Harriman, Tom 155, 159
Hartman, Saidiya 244, 255–256
Haseman, Brad 337, 340–341
Hatoum, Mona 235–236
Hay, Deborah 34
hegemony 145, 153–156, 158, 160, 182, 194, 197, 216–217, 224, 252, 280, 380

Heider, Karl 295–296, 314
Heitmann, Katja 264
Henley, Matthew 2–3, 122
Herbert, Ruth 152
Hernandez, Aline 29
heroism 138, 155–156, 158, 160, 200
heteronormativity 280, 324
Hewitt, Andrew 95
Hill Collins, Patricia 273–274, 277
Hirvanen, Maija 202–203
history 7, 21–22, 31, 34, 38, 46, 77, 81, 103, 114, 126, 131, 140, 142, 155–157, 159, 171, 176, 179, 182, 191, 200, 229–238, 240, 242, 244, 248–249, 252–253, 255–256, 258–259, 261–262, 265, 277–278, 283–284, 296, 328, 367, 374–375, 395, 399–400, 408, 434. *See also* performance histories of the present 229
Hoitink, Aniela 203
Holman Jones, Stacy 307, 311–312, 314–315, 317, 322, 331
Holzinger, Florentina 57–59
Ho, Rui An 187, 197, 200–201
Hutchison, Steph 34
hyphenated thinking 15–17, 413–423, 427–428, 431–434

identity 21, 28, 30, 32, 36, 85, 89, 112–113, 138, 149, 155, 158, 160, 162, 175, 203, 251, 271–274, 279–280, 284–285, 287, 293–294, 312–313, 324, 326–327, 354, 372, 388
  national 155, 158, 160
ideology 17, 87, 89, 93, 95, 145, 147, 149–151, 153–157, 159–162, 209–210, 220–221
imaginary, the 17, 21, 33–36, 76, 344
immersive theatre 213, 221
improvisation 63, 120, 339, 345–347, 351, 391, 396–397, 400, 403
inclusivity 279–280
Indonesia 156, 237–238, 240–241
inequality 274, 278, 282

insider 117, 294–296, 302, 314
installation 6–7, 24, 43–44, 55, 77, 180, 188, 195, 221–223, 235–236, 241–243, 263, 403
interdisciplinarity 7–8, 24, 114
International Federation of Theatre Research (IFTR) 10
interpellation 147–148, 156, 158
intersectionalism 7
intersectionality 15–16, 252, 271–282, 288–289, 409
interspecies 401–403, 409
intersubjective understanding 3, 26
intersubjectivity 24–25
interview 63, 81, 128, 131, 162, 196, 219, 260, 263, 281, 293–294, 299, 301, 304, 318–320, 329, 346, 377, 380
irony 52, 195, 218, 220
irreducibility 279–280, 284
Isenia, Wigbertson Julian 16, 293

Jang, Soyun 29
Jesus Christ Superstar 125, 128, 131–133, 138
Jetztzeit 232
Jordan, Stephanie 114, 122

Kaeppler, Adrienne 112
Karjalainen, Eedi 29
Karreman, Laura 1, 16–17, 21, 33–34, 36
Kathakali 89
Kerkhoven, Marianne van 48, 50, 52–53, 55
Kershaw, Baz 9
kinaesthetic imagination 97
kinesthetic spectatorship 104
kinetic empathy 264
kitchens 119
Kivy, Peter 152
Knipe, Sally 11
knowledge production 181, 230, 235, 237, 250, 257, 264, 276–277, 312, 362, 401, 414–416, 418–421, 423, 426, 429, 432–433

Köll, Nina 350, 353
Kress, Gunther 149–150
Kuhn, Thomas 26, 250
Kuppers, Petra 100, 369
Kuryel, Aylin 351

Labananalysis 110, 117
Labanotation 33, 110–111, 118
Laban, Rudolf 85, 91–92, 110, 112, 118, 122
Lacan, Jacques 35
La Didone 161
Lapadat, Judith 315–316, 323
Laruelle, François 390, 394
Latour, Bruno 191, 215, 419, 428
Law, John 10
Lecoq, Esteban 97. *See also* AΦE
Lefebvre, Henri 48, 85, 96
legal studies 271, 273, 276–277
legal system 271, 273
Lehmann, Hans-Thies 46, 213
leitmotif 129, 159
Lepecki, André 95, 198, 264
letter-writing 387, 403, 409
LILITH.AEON 97–98
Lindfors, Sonya 288
listener-spectator 152, 155
listening
  analytical 148
  background 151, 156, 160
  causal 148, 151
  cultures 161
  deep 151, 428
  distracted 151
  everyday 152
  habits 147
  hungry 161–162
  listening-in-readiness 151, 154
  listening-in-search 148, 151, 154
  modes of 146, 148–149, 151–154, 156, 161–162
    concert or recital 152, 154
  multimodal analysis of 15
  musical 152

  reduced 151
  secondary 157
  semantic 148, 151, 154, 156
Lloyd Webber, Andrew 128, 157
localisation 370
Lone Twin 368, 377
Lorde, Audre 274, 418, 434
Louppe, Laurence 88
Lowenhaupt Tsing, Anna 202, 204
Lubumbashi 241–242
Lury, Celia 9, 230

Maassen, Theo 209, 217–219, 221
Machin, David 149, 162
Mackenzie, Noella 11
Manning, Erin 93, 342, 355
mapping 33, 94, 189, 193, 196, 288, 359–360, 365, 367, 369, 377, 380, 383, 414, 416, 422, 426–427, 429, 431–433
  inefficient 380
  performative 359–360, 365, 369, 377
  sensory 413, 416, 429, 432–433
Marey, Étienne-Jules 35
marginalisation 212, 220, 234, 244, 247, 250, 256, 274, 278, 285, 312–313, 315, 330
Marschall, Anika 16, 271, 286–288
Martin, Jennifer 87
Marxism 210, 212, 214, 216, 224, 361
masculinity 282, 284–285, 287, 326
Mauss, Marcel 88
Maynard, Robyn 403, 409
Mayor, Adrienne 35
McAvinchey, Caoimhe 328
McCormick, John 34
McGregor, Wayne 102
McKenzie, Jon 169, 174, 183, 326
McKerrell, Simon 145, 149–150, 153
McKittrick, Katherine 244
McRobbie, Angela 210
Mead, Margaret 238–240
mechanistic-imperialist worldview 415, 418. *See also* Ghosh, Amitav

media archaeology 17, 34, 230–231, 233–234, 241
Melrose, Susan 337, 340–341
Menon, Dilip 232
Mepschen, Paul 350
Merx, Sigrid 17, 43–44, 50, 54–55, 223, 376
methodology 1, 6, 9, 11–13, 17, 22, 24–26, 28, 32, 38, 43, 45, 49, 87, 90, 145, 169–171, 174, 181–183, 224, 233, 235, 243, 250, 254, 256, 263–264, 271–272, 279–280, 293, 295, 299, 301, 311–316, 322, 328, 331–332, 338, 340, 342, 360, 389, 391, 394, 396–398, 404, 408
micro-actions 350–355
Mignolo, Walter 362, 418
migration 173, 204, 222, 279, 359, 361, 370–372
Mikołajczyk, Jacek 155–156
Miller, Jacques-Alain 35
mime 28
miniature theory 25, 30
minimalism 50, 218, 285–286
mixed methods approach 121, 232
Moments Contained 60, 62
more-than-human matter 17, 204, 419, 424, 427
Moreton-Robinson, Aileen 362
morphological analysis 118
Morton, Timothy 189
Moten, Fred 337, 339, 355
motherhood 325–327
Motion Bank 34
motion capture 17, 21, 32–36, 97, 102, 115–116, 236–240
movement analysis 13, 15, 17, 85, 87–88, 90, 98, 104, 109
movement ecology 90
multimodal critical discourse analysis (MCDA) 16, 145, 149, 153–155, 158–162
multimodality 14–17, 120, 145–146, 148–149, 153–156, 158, 160–161, 171, 338
musical

concept musical 132
integrated musical 130, 142
megamusical 142, 157
musical theatre 125–130, 132, 135, 137, 140, 142, 146, 148, 157, 161, 200
musical theatre analysis 15
musicology 114, 126–127, 395
music theatre 6, 14, 146, 160–161, 173
Muybridge, Eadweard 35, 118
mycelium 187, 202–205
mycelium thinking 187, 202–204
Mycoscores/Choreospores 203
myth 35, 81, 113, 156, 170, 173, 178
mythologising 155

Nakamura, Aoi 97. *See also* AΦE
NAO robots 37
narrativisation 147–148, 152, 155, 158, 161, 320
narratology 38, 70–71, 150
narrowcasting 161
Nash, Jennifer C. 277–278
Natural Contract Lab 413, 416, 422, 426
negotiated code or position 154, 160
Nelson, Lisa 347–348. *See also Tuning Scores*
Nelson, Robin 337–338, 340–341, 351, 356
Ness, Sally Ann 93
network 48, 93, 96, 187–193, 199, 202–204, 233, 236, 259, 363, 375, 423, 428, 433
new materialism 71, 231, 234, 236, 395, 418
Nicholson, Helen 9
Noh theatre 87
Noland, Carrie 93
nomadic theatre 28
notation 33–34, 108, 110–111

Oliveros, Paulina 151
Ono, Yoko 24, 369
OpenEndedGroup 34

opera 126, 128–130, 132, 136–137, 146, 161
oppositional code or position 154, 162
oppression 156, 234, 272, 277, 364
oppressive 220, 287
Orientalism 169, 181–183. *See also* Said, Edward
ORPHEUS 98
Ostendorf-Rodríguez, Yasmine 202–203
outsider 51, 133, 294, 296, 302

parenthood 313. *See also* queer parenting
Parikka, Jussi 231, 233
Parker, Andrew 313
patriotism 155, 157–158, 160, 162
Pavis, Patrice 36, 49, 51, 93
Paxton, Steve 86, 102
Pearson, Mike 48, 230, 234, 244
pedagogy 6, 21, 272, 277, 337, 340, 361, 403, 413, 418, 421, 424, 432–433
perception 57, 68, 70–71, 82, 118, 130, 136, 147, 151, 153, 187, 197–200, 289, 302, 329–330, 428
performance histories 31, 249
performance philosophy 15–16, 387–409
Performance Studies international (PSi) 10, 28
performative 3–5, 7, 12, 16, 27, 44–45, 87, 93, 115, 127, 153, 160, 175, 187–188, 195, 221–222, 247, 250, 253, 256, 260, 282, 284, 298, 301, 314, 321, 326–327, 332, 337, 340–342, 351, 359–360, 365, 369, 372, 377, 381, 387–388, 390, 393–394, 396, 398, 401, 403–404, 416–417, 421, 432
 research 337, 340–342, 393
performativity 10, 36–37, 311–313, 323–324, 326, 341, 343, 360, 388, 392–393, 395–396, 400, 408, 420
period movement score 87

perspective 9–11, 22, 26, 28, 34, 37–38, 43–44, 52, 57, 69, 73–77, 79, 81–82, 113, 128, 132, 135, 138, 150, 156, 175, 181, 191, 194, 197, 213, 215, 222–223, 233, 249, 294–296, 298–299, 302, 304, 307, 322, 326, 330–331, 340, 346, 349, 355, 361–362, 389, 398, 404, 415, 420, 433
Phelan, Peggy 252–254
phenomenological 33, 35, 51, 121, 149, 161, 286, 394
phenomenology 2, 7, 34, 71, 115, 121, 147, 394
Phillips Oland, Pamela 155
Phobiarama 55–56
Plato 24
plot 50, 75–76, 129, 137
politics of perception 57, 187, 197–200
politics of performance 209
Ponga Pandit 177
popular music 127, 148, 161–162
position 5–9, 13–14, 28, 44, 53–54, 56–57, 68, 72–76, 78–79, 88, 93–94, 136, 147–148, 150, 153–156, 158, 160, 162, 176, 178, 181, 183, 190, 192, 195, 200, 210, 241, 251, 261–263, 274, 278, 280, 282, 285–287, 293, 296, 302–303, 327, 330, 350, 356, 363, 391, 398, 433
positionality 21, 110, 257, 272–273, 286, 294, 299, 304, 316–317, 323, 330, 354, 362–363
postcolonialism 183, 229, 234, 237–239, 243, 254, 305
Postcolonial Spirits 229, 237–239
postdramatic theatre 46, 48
Postlewait, Thomas 191–193, 195
post-positivist methods 115
power 16, 26–27, 59–60, 85, 113, 142, 145–150, 170–172, 174, 176, 179, 181–182, 192, 209–210, 215–216, 231, 233–234, 236, 250–251, 253–256, 261, 271–272, 274, 276–279, 281–282, 287, 299, 303, 318, 322, 324–325, 344, 349, 360, 362–364, 369, 391, 395, 418, 429

practice as research (PaR) 337, 340, 356, 394–395
practice-led inquiry 15
practice-led research 3, 16, 337–343, 345, 349–350
presence 8, 21, 31–32, 36–37, 60, 72, 81, 98, 100, 108, 139, 203, 235, 239, 264, 277, 354, 380, 392, 426, 429
Price, Thomas J. 60–62
prison 171, 183, 328
privileged knowledge 4
Protopapa, Efrosini 47, 337, 339–340, 343, 345
PSi Lexicon 28
psychogeography 366, 372
public space 60–62, 72, 337–339, 351, 361, 369
pushbacks 370, 375

queer dramaturgy 32. *See also* dramaturgy
queer identity 203
queerness 282
queer parenting 16, 311–313, 323, 325–326
queer presence 21, 31–32
queer theory 7, 15, 31, 279
questionnaire 319

race 56, 155, 179, 252, 257, 271–274, 277, 282, 285–289, 299, 315, 380
racialised experience 339
Rae, Paul 2, 5, 8, 11, 232
Rancière, Jacques 198–201, 213–214, 224, 391
Raunig, Gerald 415, 418–419, 433–434
Ravn, Susanne 121
reception 51, 69, 89, 128, 155, 191–192, 211, 218, 239, 271, 273, 354
recital 152, 154
reconstruction 35, 68–69, 72–81, 232, 248
re-enactment 57
reflexivity 298–299, 312, 314–317, 363
relatability 322

relationality 43, 48–49, 53, 189, 354, 409, 413, 415
relational ontology 189–191
religion 179, 217, 272, 287, 315, 408
repertoire 244, 253, 284
representation 6, 60, 62, 70, 111, 136, 158, 172, 179, 181, 240, 262, 271, 296, 313, 323, 354, 401, 420, 424, 427
Revolution or Nothing 277
Reynolds, Dee 97
rhizome 193, 196
rhythmic milieu 85, 96–97, 101–103
Rice, Tim 128, 135
Robinson, Dylan 161–162, 362
robot design 37
Roelfzema, Erik Hazelhoff 155
Rotterdam's Independent Theatre (Onafhankelijk Toneel) 173, 184
Royal Shakespeare Company 125, 140
Rozendaal, Marco 36–37
Ruwe pit 218

Said, Edward 169, 181–183. *See also Orientalism*
SceneAround system 157, 160
Schaar, Annemijn van der 16, 311
Schaeffer, Pierre 152
Schafer, R. Murray 145, 148, 151
Schechner, Richard 5, 213, 282, 396
Schmidt, Theron 16, 222, 359
Schneider, Rebecca 248, 253–254
schooling 417, 431–432
science-art binary 316
score 16, 24, 34, 87, 107–110, 118–121, 127–128, 130–131, 134–135, 139–140, 157, 203, 346–347, 351, 369, 381–383, 396, 428
sculpture 60–63, 80, 188
searchlight theory 25
semiotic analysis 7, 70
semiotic, semiotics 2, 6–7, 49, 51, 70, 89, 112–113, 120, 147–150, 152, 155, 158, 161, 224
SenseLab 342

sexuality 171, 252, 272, 274, 277, 282, 284–285, 287, 293, 300, 305, 315
Shanks, Michael 48, 230, 234, 244
Sheep Pig Goat 400, 402, 405. *See also* Fevered Sleep
shimmer, the 21, 31–32
Simpson, Leanne Betasamosake 403, 409
simultaneity 273, 279, 284
site-specific 6, 16, 60, 62, 87, 180, 231, 234, 288
situated knowledge 3, 15, 56, 278, 359, 362, 365, 369, 400, 427
situatedness 7, 10, 16, 30, 32, 38, 43, 53–54, 56–57, 59, 61–62, 82, 273, 279, 354, 360, 366, 371, 375–376, 396
Situatie gewijzigd 218
Skwirblies, Lisa 16, 247, 249, 260, 286–287
slowness 285–286
small metal objects 85–87, 98–99, 101. *See also* Back to Back Theatre
social choreography 85, 90, 95, 102–104
Social Identity Wheel 281
social justice 251, 276, 279, 306, 408
social robotics 21, 37
Solar: A Meltdown 200–201
Soldaat van Oranje 155–157
somatic practices 115
sonic
  environment 161
  meditation 151
sonic or musical narrative 125, 146, 155, 160–161
Sophiensaele 282
sound groups 162
sources 11, 38, 52, 59, 103, 118–120, 126, 131, 149–150, 192, 212, 233, 244, 248–249, 252, 254, 256–258, 342, 378, 404, 416, 425–427, 434
Spatz, Ben 341, 355
spectator 5, 43–46, 49–57, 59, 61, 67–68, 70–72, 76–79, 81–82, 100–101, 105, 148–150, 152, 154–155, 157–158, 160–161, 179, 195, 213–214, 221, 223, 264, 272, 283–287, 371, 374, 376, 406, 433
spectatorship 15, 28, 43, 46, 53–55, 59, 61–62, 67–76, 78–79, 81–82, 104, 211, 221, 223, 289, 376
speculation 27, 173, 256
speculative fabulation 420–421
sports science 121
Stalpaert, Christel 16–17, 413–416, 424–426
standpoint theory 362
stand-up comedy 82, 218
statement 43, 53–57, 59, 61–63, 129, 181, 281, 287–288
state-of-the-nation play 155, 160
Steinbock, Eliza 31
STEM disciplines 9–10
Stengers, Isabelle 26, 419
Stewart, Kathleen 365–366, 373, 375, 383
STILL HERE – An Alliance of Care for the SZenne River (2023-) 413, 416–417, 420–424, 431–432
stillness 61, 63, 86–87, 101
Stoler, Ann Laura 234, 243, 254–256, 261
stories 34, 63, 200, 234, 242, 255–256, 276–277, 281, 294, 299, 318, 323, 331, 368, 371, 375, 379, 422, 428–429, 431, 433
story 57, 74–76, 98, 129–130, 132–133, 135, 155, 195, 201, 230, 255–256, 277–278, 281, 297–298, 322, 344, 374, 430
storying 414, 416, 422, 424, 429, 432
structural analysis 112, 119–120, 178–180
structure in dominance 153–154
structure of feeling 209, 215–217, 219, 222, 224
subjectivity 93, 115, 286, 294, 312, 314–316, 362
subversive affirmation 223

survey 11, 319
Szendy, Peter 152

tacit knowledge 4
Taylor, Diana 174, 216, 232, 244, 253–254, 264, 361–362
Taylor, Millie 17, 125, 130, 141, 210
Teatro Kadaken 293–294, 301, 303
technology 8–9, 17, 21, 24, 32–33, 47, 63, 97, 101–103, 134, 147–148, 174, 233, 236–241
Tempest, The 125, 140–141
Terrore Nello Spazio (*Planet of the Vampires*) 161
The Art of Touch (1995) 117–120
theatre archaeology 15
theatre collections 248, 252
theatre historiography 7–8, 191, 250
theatricality 28, 54, 71, 82, 137
Theodoridou, Danae 47, 339, 345
theoretical object 27–28, 34, 190
Tischkau, Joana 271, 282, 285
Tore Vagn Lid 67–68, 73
Toussaint, Lianne 202–203
tradition 6, 8, 12–13, 28, 57, 62, 71–72, 85, 88–89, 92, 95, 105, 115, 147, 155, 159, 162, 182, 210, 212, 218, 224, 238, 262, 281, 355, 394, 418–419
Trance and Dance in Bali 238
transdisciplinary 312, 391, 422, 432
transgression 175, 217–220
Transiteatret Bergen 67–68, 73
transposition 85, 90, 93–94, 101, 103
transversality 338–339, 343
trauma 155, 318, 371
Trouillot, Michel-Rolph 250–251
Truax, Barry 145, 148, 151
Tuning Scores 347–348. *See also* Nelson, Lisa
Turner, Cathy 44, 46, 48, 50
Turner, Victor 298

Ullman, Lisa 91
UrbanApa 287–288
Uytterhoeven, Lise 17, 85

van Beusekom, Josje 36
van der Tuin, Iris 28, 38, 205
van der Vegt, Chris 31
van Deursen, Frans 155
van Hove, Ivo 125, 128, 131, 136
Van Hove, Ivo 81, 131, 137–138
van Leeuwen, Theo 149–150
van Wijhe, Jeroen 138, 155–156
Vázquez, Rolando 337, 354, 356
Velour, Sasha 21, 31–32
Verhoeff, Nanna 28, 38
Verhoeven, Dries 55, 209, 221–223
Verhoeven, Paul 155
verisimilitude 322
Verstraete, Pieter 16–17, 82, 145, 148, 151, 161
violence 81, 140, 173, 276, 278–279, 342, 371, 415, 430
  and the archive 255–257, 259
  epistemic violence 162, 418
  police violence 276
  symbolic violence 276

walking-with 413, 416, 421, 423–425, 427–428, 431
Wan, Evelyn 16–17, 229
Way, Lyndon 145–146, 149–150, 153, 205
Wekker, Gloria 156, 289
Whatley, Sarah 17, 107, 117
White Chess Set (1966). *See also* Ono, Yoko
whiteness 251, 277–278, 280, 284–287, 299, 315, 356
  white fragility 282, 285
  white innocence 156
  white supremacy 155, 276, 278, 289
Wilhelmina, Queen 155–156, 159
Willett, John 93
Williams, Raymond 153, 209–217, 224, 273, 368
Wooster Group 161
Wrights & Sites 369, 372
writing styles 321–322

analytical-interpretative 321
  confessional-emotive 321
  critical-provocative 321
  descriptive-realistic 321
  filmic-intersubjective 321
  imaginative-creative 321
Wynants, Nele 233

Zeefuik, Simone 61–63
zéro 28
Zijp, Dick 16, 71, 82, 161, 209, 213, 217, 219–220
Zwinkels, Elle 30

About the Team

Alessandra Tosi was the managing editor for this book.

Lucy Barnes and Sophia Bursey proof-read this manuscript; Lucy compiled the index.

Jeevanjot Kaur Nagpal designed the cover. The cover was produced in InDesign using the Fontin font.

Annie Hine typeset the book in InDesign.

Jeremy Bowman produced the paperback and hardback editions and created the EPUB. The main text font is Tex Gyre Pagella and the heading font is Californian FB. Jeremy also produced the PDF edition.

The conversion to the HTML edition was performed with epublius, an open-source software which is freely available on our GitHub page at https://github.com/OpenBookPublishers

Hannah Shakespeare was in charge of marketing.

This book was peer-reviewed by Prof. Marvin Carlson, CUNY, Graduate Center, and an anonymous referee. Experts in their field, these readers give their time freely to help ensure the academic rigour of our books. We are grateful for their generous and invaluable contributions.

This book need not end here...

Share

All our books — including the one you have just read — are free to access online so that students, researchers and members of the public who can't afford a printed edition will have access to the same ideas. This title will be accessed online by hundreds of readers each month across the globe: why not share the link so that someone you know is one of them?

This book and additional content is available at
https://doi.org/10.11647/OBP.0469

Donate

Open Book Publishers is an award-winning, scholar-led, not-for-profit press making knowledge freely available one book at a time. We don't charge authors to publish with us: instead, our work is supported by our library members and by donations from people who believe that research shouldn't be locked behind paywalls.

Join the effort to free knowledge by supporting us at
https://www.openbookpublishers.com/support-us

We invite you to connect with us on our socials!

BLUESKY
@openbookpublish
.bsky.social

MASTODON
@OpenBookPublish
@hcommons.social

LINKEDIN
open-book-publishers

Read more at the Open Book Publishers Blog
https://blogs.openbookpublishers.com

You may also be interested in:

Gender-Based Violence in Arts and Culture
Perspectives on Education and Work
Edited by Marie Buscatto, Sari Karttunen and Mathilde Provansal
https://doi.org/10.11647/OBP.0436

Active Speech
Critical Perspectives on Teresa Deevy
Edited by Úna Kealy and Kate McCarthy
https://doi.org/10.11647/OBP.0432

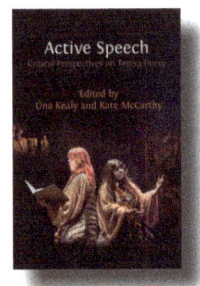

Teaching Music Performance in Higher Education
Exploring the Potential of Artistic Research
Edited by Helen Julia Minors, Stefan Östersjö, Gilvano Dalagna and Jorge Salgado Correia
https://doi.org/10.11647/OBP.0398

Rethinking Social Action through Music
The Search for Coexistence and Citizenship in Medellín's Music Schools
Geoffrey Baker
https://doi.org/10.11647/OBP.0243

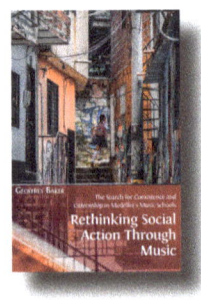

www.ingramcontent.com/pod-product-compliance
Lightning Source LLC
Chambersburg PA
CBHW062025290426
44108CB00025B/2778